As Wolves upon a Sheep Fold

As Wolves upon a Sheep Fold

The Civil War Letters of Ohio Surgeon
William S. Newton

Edited by Aaron D. Purcell

Voices of the Civil War
Michael P. Gray, Series Editor

The University of Tennessee Press / Knoxville

The Voices of the Civil War series makes available a variety of primary source materials that illuminate issues on the battlefield, the home front, and the western front, as well as other aspects of this historic era. The series contextualizes the personal accounts within the framework of the latest scholarship and expands established knowledge by offering new perspectives, new materials, and new voices.

Library of Congress Cataloging-in-Publication Data

Names: Newton, William S. (William Smith), 1823–1882, author. | Purcell, Aaron D., 1972- editor.
Title: As wolves upon a sheep fold : the civil war letters of Ohio surgeon William S. Newton / edited by Aaron D. Purcell.
Description: First edition. | Knoxville : University of Tennessee Press, [2022] | Series: Voices of the Civil War | Includes bibliographical references and index. | Summary: "William S. Newton (1823–1882) served the Union primarily as an assistant surgeon with the 91st Ohio Volunteer Infantry, but also spent a few months as acting surgeon with the 2nd Virginia Cavalry (US) and as surgeon for the 193rd Ohio Volunteer Infantry. Newton's units fought in the Appalachian Highlands, mostly in Virginia and West Virginia. He treated wounded soldiers after significant battles including Opequon, Cedar Creek, and the Battle of Cloyd's Mountain. Newton's letters cover his living quarters, race relations, transportation and communication, the comfort of a good meal, and the antics of his teenage son Ned."—Provided by publisher.
Identifiers: LCCN 2022009696 (print) | LCCN 2022009697 (ebook) | ISBN 9781621907206 (hardcover) | ISBN 9781621907213 (pdf) | ISBN 9781621907220 (kindle edition)
Subjects: LCSH: Newton, William S. (William Smith), 1823–1882—Correspondence. | United States. Army. Ohio Infantry Regiment, 91st (1862–1865)—Biography | United States—History—Civil War, 1861–1865—Medical care. | United States—History—Civil War, 1861–1865—Personal narratives. | Ohio—History—Civil War, 1861–1865—Personal narratives. | Libby Prison. | United States—History—Civil War, 1861–1865—Regimental histories. | Ohio—History—Civil War, 1861–1865—Regimental histories. | United States. Army—Surgeons—Correspondence. | Surgeons—Ohio—Correspondence.
Classification: LCC E525.5 91st .W55 2022 (print) | LCC E525.5 91st (ebook) | DDC 973.7/75—dc23/eng/20220225
LC record available at https://lccn.loc.gov/2022009696
LC ebook record available at https://lccn.loc.gov/2022009697

Contents

Illustrations

Figures

Map

Foreword

On May 13, 1864, captured Assistant Surgeon William S. Newton of the 91st Ohio Volunteers, along with other Union surgeons, was rushed off to the Guthrie House in Southwest Virginia to tend to an enemy general in the small hamlet of Dublin. The early morning journey was a couple of miles away and occurred after the convincing Yankee victory at Cloyd's Mountain; but the Ohio doctor and his medical colleagues caring for wounded on both sides, were taken prisoner in the process. Consequently, he and four other Union surgeons were quickly pressed into service to treat Confederates, including his new patient, General Albert Gallatin Jenkins, who was severely injured in the left shoulder and chest, requiring an arm amputation. John Hunt Morgan's Rangers had been lurking in the area, capturing supplies, equipment, and Yankees—Newton among them. Newton commented that Morgan's men were preying on their victims as "as wolves upon a sheep fold." Jenkins, too, was the 91st's nemesis as his "Border Rangers" plundered from western Virginia to Ohio, but now Newton and the other Union doctors had to save him as Morgan's army controlled the area. With surgical saw in hand and chloroform in place, the operation was about to be executed when it was interrupted by Morgan's medical director, who attempted to confiscate the instruments. After the Confederates realized the identity of the patient, they desisted, and the Union surgeons including Newton helped take the arm; but eventually, as often happened in field operations, Jenkins died. After a few weeks under guard and performing more medical services for the enemy, the Union surgeons were given an ultimatum: continue doctoring Confederates or be sent to an officer's prison in Richmond. Newton and his colleagues preferred captivity at Libby Prison, the inescapable confine for Union officers along the James River.

The Voices of the Civil War series' founding editor, Frank L. Byrne, wrote extensively about Libby Prison incarceration, correcting many fabrications about the so-called "Bastille of the Confederacy." Wartime propaganda and partial postwar sources tainted Libby Prison's image—for a time, it was regarded as synonymous with suffering, death, and impenetrable brick walls. But in reality, the Yankee-led Rose-Hamilton tunneling endeavor in 1864, the largest mass prison breakout during the conflict, began the process of tearing down the "Bastille's" reputation; it had further deteriorated a century later when serious study of Libby Prison by trained historians like Byrne, who compared contemporary letters and diaries to postwar accounts suggested a more agreeable experience could be had at Libby compared to other prisons. Indeed, Libby, as well as its Northern counterpart on Johnson's Island, in Sandusky Bay, Ohio, both had a death rate of less than 2 percent. Class mattered in Civil War captivity, and rank, more often than not, translated to better treatment. That point is accentuated in other publications in the Voices of the Civil War series, including *John Dooley's Civil War: An Irish American's Journey in the First Virginia Infantry Regiment*, edited by Robert Emmett Curran, under the general editorship of Peter S. Carmichael. Curran highlighted Dooley's capture after the Pickett-Pettigrew assault at Gettysburg. Dooley was sent to Fort McHenry, in Baltimore, then for a much longer stay at the island officer prison in Ohio. Dooley's elevation to the officer class only weeks prior made for a very fortunate imprisonment. While the Virginian was held in Ohio, he joined a theatrical club, the Johnson's Island Thespians, participating in various plays, as well as in other activities to ward off the boredom of his captivity. In a November 22, 1863, entry, Dooley wrote: "the Sandusky papers say that the Confederate authorities have received the provision sent by the Northern government for their Yankee prisoners at Libby Prison. Meeting of the Thespians at Block 11. Begin 'Descartes's Wife,' one of the Yankee books. Play 5 games of chess and am beaten 2 out of 5." In addition to Dooley's success at chess, his chances at surviving captivity rose dramatically since he was an officer. At the end of a chilly February 1865, a detachment of officer prisoners, including Dooley, were marched out of the prison gates and braced themselves to walk across the frozen bay for home; in the process, some Southerners slipped and fell since they had never been on ice before. This delighted some female ice skaters, who ridiculed them for their shaky passage, before they finally reached the safety of land and were transferred home.

The Voices of the Civil War series also offers another fine volume that complements *As Wolves upon a Sheep Fold*. Our readers can explore a Southern doctor's voice with Donald B. Koonce's *Doctor to the Front: The Recollections of Confederate Surgeon Thomas Fanning Wood, 1861–1865*. This volume has received high acclaim; noted Civil War historian Gary Gallagher wrote that it is "Filled with perceptive observations about military leaders, morale in the Confederacy, life in the Southern capital of Richmond, and a range of medical topics including the treatment of the wounded, . . . Confederate surgeon Thomas Fanning Wood's wartime letters and postwar reminiscences constitute a fine addition to the roster of published firsthand testimony about the Civil War." Indeed, Editor Koonce meticulously blended Wood's letters from the front with memoirs and newspaper accounts from his hometown. While in the 3rd North Carolina, Wood was promoted to assistant surgeon in just eight months. Just like Dr. Newton, he was promoted to full surgeon status as the war progressed. Between that time, Wood describes his impressions of city hospitals in Richmond and provides detailed battlefield observations. He chronicles surgeries, particularly amputations. He was at a number of prominent engagements, Chancellorsville, Gettysburg, and Spotsylvania among them. Wood memorably described the methodology of treating patients without painkillers. Besides the amputations that both Wood and Newton conducted, both men were in proximity at the same time and same area in the Shenandoah Valley during the same engagements. Wood was serving under Jubal Early, Newton under Phillip Sheridan. Acquiring both books provides an excellent comparative analysis of North and South.

Blacksburg, Virginia, some twenty miles from where the Battle of Cloyd's Mountain took place, is home to Virginia Tech. Besides the renowned Virginia Center for Civil War Studies, which was founded by Prof. James Robertson Jr., an icon in the field, the University Libraries' Special Collections and University Archives department houses significant Civil War primary source collections used by scholars from across the world. In 2017, Virginia Tech's Special Collections and University Archives won at auction Newton's collection of letters, which had previously been in private hands. With the recent processing of Newton's collection, they awaited a proper editor. Aaron D. Purcell, director of Special Collections and University Archives, took on the responsibility of resurrecting the "voice" of Newton, and his expertise as an archivist and historian shines through in this expertly annotated volume. He laboriously pieced together the collection of letters with newspaper accounts, pension files, scarce regimental histories, and microfilm records into an organized and coherent single volume. Newton's voice and perspective can now be heard.

As Wolves upon a Sheep Fold contains Newton's Civil War correspondence between himself and his wife, Frances. The letters delve into a vast variety of issues, including familial pressures of war on the home front and children, social issues of the day, and medical care in the war zone. Editor Purcell tracks Newton from April 1862, when he signed up with the 91st Ohio a year after the surrender of Fort Sumter. The regiment's aim was to help combat Jenkins and Morgan's partisans. Newton's imaginative pen captures aspects of camp life, lice wars, hospital foodstuffs, skirmishing and battling, and the subsequent care of the wounded. He writes about visits from his son Ned to camp, who fished throughout the region and avoided capture. The doctor documents the role of Black people as they escaped slavery. Charley Boreland, for example, absconded to the 91st to serve as a cook for Newton. Newton helped hatch a plan for Charley, who sought to free his wife and child, who were still held in slavery; if the scheme had worked, Charley and his family planned to stay with Newton and his family while working at their home in Gallipolis. However, when the ploy was put into motion, Charley disappeared. Another fugitive Newton noted was Mary Ann McDonald, who fled for Union lines in late summer 1863, and consequently, ended up in Newton's care. Newton again, under the paternalistic lens of the day, wanted Mary to pack up and serve as a domestic servant to his family in Gallipolis. He hoped his two boys, Ned and Mott, would teach her to read and write. This plan worked at first, but when Mary was falsely blamed for stealing from the family, she was let go.

Dr. Newton was eventually ordered to the 2nd Virginia Cavalry stationed in Charleston. While there, he wrote about the assassination of a hospital steward, who was having a sordid affair with the wife of a nearby apothecary. Newton also joked about being sent to Libby Prison, an ominous prediction. When he was really captured, he lacked food during his transfer and suffered pangs of hunger while at Libby since the full-time prisoners received rations rather than those like Newton, who were awaiting exchange. His transfer to Libby, his three-day stay, and his return to the Union ranks likely contributed to his poor health later in life. Purcell guides the reader through fighting in the Appalachian borderlands, highlighting Gen. Phillip Sheridan's Army of the Shenandoah versus Gen. Jubal Early's Army of the Valley. Newton chronicles a meeting between Ulysses Grant and Sheridan, and hospital experiences that include the aftermath of Berryville, Opequan (Third Winchester), and Cedar Creek, the last major showdown in the Shenandoah Valley. Newton became acting surgeon of the 2nd Virginia Cavalry in the fall of 1864, while official promotion to surgeon came in March of 1865, in the 193rd Ohio Volunteers, just as the war wound down.

After the conflict, Newton attended reunion events in Ohio. He became an advocate for his comrades who suffered in captivity, writing to the Ohio adjutant general on their behalf: ". . . we experienced enough to convince us, that the suffering and deprivation of our men and officers in the southern prisons has not half been told, nor can it be described on the page of history. To be realized, it must be experienced." In 1880, Newton applied for an invalid pension, arguing his capture, coupled with his short time in Libby and its "malarious atmosphere," the "insufficient covering," and the "insufficient and unwholesome food," brought on "dysentery, piles, and a torpid liver." Newton complained he never fully recuperated from the ailments, which in turn, adversely affected his medical practice in Ohio, rendering his "life miserable." The Pension Bureau agreed, and the claim was granted in early 1882. But near the end of fall 1882, Newton became incapacitated with stomach maladies, compounded by painful ulcers and liver issues. The doctor succumbed on November 18, 1882. Newton never made it to the reunions of Libby veterans. The prison had been moved from Richmond to Chicago later in the decade, taken brick by brick, and beam by beam, to create a tourist museum in Chicago as former Libbyans flocked there for reunions. Instead, Newton was buried at Pine Street Cemetery in Gallipolis; in the meantime, Frances received a widow's pension until 1896, when she passed away. She was buried next to her husband, side by side, at Pine Street Cemetery in Gallipolis.

Michael P. Gray
East Stroudsburg University

Preface

On October 8, 1867, Ohio native William S. Newton penned a letter to Ohio adjutant general Benjamin R. Cowen regarding the treatment of Union prisoners of war. During the Civil War, Newton served as an assistant surgeon for the 91st Ohio Volunteer Infantry and during the final months of the war as surgeon for the 193rd Ohio. He was captured by Confederate forces in May 1864 and briefly held at Libby Prison in Richmond. Newton's unpublished letter and narrative explained in detail the events that led to his capture and imprisonment. He explained to Cowen: "we experienced enough to convince us, that the suffering and deprivation of our men and officers in the southern prisons has not half been told, nor can it be described on the page of history. To be realized, it must be experienced."[1]

Like many Civil War surgeons who remained near battlefields after fighting had moved elsewhere, Newton performed his medical duties on both Union and Confederate wounded. In early May 1864, his regiment was part of the Battle of Cloyd's Mountain in southwest Virginia. It was a significant Union victory followed by the Battle of New River Bridge the next day, which severed railroad connections between Virginia and Tennessee. After the Battle of Cloyd's Mountain, Newton and his staff spent the next two and a half days attending to the wounded. On the afternoon of Thursday, May 12, 1864, a group of Confederates including a surgical team arrived and seized the small group of Union soldiers. The Confederates ordered Newton and his small staff to attend to their "many wounded scattered across the country."[2] They also pressed Newton to attend to Confederate general Albert G. Jenkins in nearby Dublin, Virginia. Newton did as he was told. He and other Union surgeons examined Jenkins and concluded that they needed to amputate to save the general's life. The Confederate officers advising Jenkins and the surgeons on site agreed with Newton, and they scheduled the operation for the next day.

On Friday, May 13, a messenger accompanied by a group of Confederate soldiers arrived in Newton's makeshift field hospital. They were there to escort Newton back to Dublin to perform the amputation on Jenkins. The soldiers, however, were new arrivals under the command of the infamous Confederate raider General John Hunt Morgan. According to Newton, all respect for life of the wounded disappeared when Morgan's troops arrived. They "preyed upon our hospital as wolves upon a sheep fold. Officers and men depriving our wounded and nurses of all clothing, blankets, etc. that they could possibly lay their hands to, and in some instances *dragging gum blankets from the stumps of recently amputated limbs* which had been placed under them." Newton was permitted to begin the procedure on Jenkins; however, he was unable to finish the task. He wrote: "Our surgical instruments too, were rudely taken from us, while in the very act of an operation upon General Jenkins, and his blood yet warm, wiped from them, placed in the case, and carried away."[3]

Newton and his hospital staff carried out the orders of the Confederate leadership for the next three weeks. Confederate soldiers disinterred the fresh graves of the Union dead to search for blankets, clothing, and other resources, while Newton was forced to prioritize the Confederate wounded. In late May the Confederate commanders offered Newton and his staff two options: assist patients in southern hospitals or report to Libby Prison. They chose prison. Their time in Richmond was short, only three days, but while in Libby Prison, Newton witnessed deplorable and inhumane conditions. He did not receive any rations while at Libby Prison, but Newton contracted malaria, dysentery, and piles as a result of his imprisonment. As a surgeon, Newton knew all too well the lasting effects of diseases and injuries.

Newton wrote frequently to his family during the war, beginning with his service in western Virginia (known after June 1863 as West Virginia) and throughout his service in Virginia and Maryland. Despite the significance of his capture and imprisonment in Libby Prison in early summer 1864, his correspondence with his wife did not mention what happened to him after the Battle of Cloyd's Mountain. Instead, his harrowing account was published in a local newspaper and was part of a postwar letter, both of which told different versions of the story. Upon release, he resumed his duties as assistant surgeon. In the summer and fall of 1864, he witnessed several battles during the Shenandoah Valley Campaign. Following the Second Battle of Kernstown, which resulted in Union retreat to Maryland, Newton was briefly dismissed for allegedly not staying with his regiment. The charges were quickly dropped, and in the following weeks Newton was part of the Battle of Opequan (Third Battle of Winchester) and the Battle of Cedar Creek. Throughout his letters, Newton waited patiently on a decision for a promotion to surgeon. In March 1865, just a few weeks before the end of the war, he finally received a promotion to surgeon for the 193rd Ohio Volunteer Infantry.

By the time he mustered out of the Union army in August 1865, Newton had suffered physically and mentally from the ravages of war. He returned to West Union, Ohio, to be a farmer but quickly relocated to Gallipolis. While there he served as postmaster and resumed his medical practice. There are a few references to his participation in postwar reunion activities, but mostly he became known as a community leader in Gallipolis. In 1880, at age fifty-seven, Newton secured an invalid pension. He died two years later in Gallipolis, Ohio, about fifty miles from Ironton, Ohio, where his Civil War service began.[4]

Throughout his Civil War service, April 1862–August 1865, Newton sent a steady stream of letters to his wife, sons, and other family members. In total, his family collected approximately 170 letters, official documents, and other materials documenting his service. His letters detailed the realities of war, such as the boredom of camp life, details of battles, and observations on human behavior during a very complex period in American history. Newton lived in two worlds—one just a few yards from an unclear front line of war, and, through letters with his wife, one back on the home front where perhaps he had even less control over his future.[5]

As a noncombatant, he observed life beyond the movement of troops and the brutality of war. Newton's detailed letters covered his living quarters, race relations, the extent of southern sentiment in occupied spaces during and after the war, transportation and communication, and the comfort of a good meal. Newton reported on his work as a surgeon and the details of several significant battles in West Virginia and Virginia. His letters expressed a deep interest in family affairs. In fact, two of his children visited him in camp. During the day, while he attended to the sick and wounded, his children would fish in nearby rivers and streams for their evening meal. His letters advised on family matters such as buying and selling property back in Ohio, naming his newborn child, urging his teenage son to live an upstanding life through better penmanship, prescribing medicines to remedy illnesses in the family, and preparing a new farm for when he could return home.

Newton's experience as a surgeon, observer, and noncombatant represents an important voice that is not well represented in the historical literature of the Civil War. While there are recent studies on Civil War medical history, only a handful of edited books based on firsthand accounts of Civil War surgeons exist.[6] Recent examples include: Donald B. Koonce, ed., *Doctor to the Front: The Recollections of Confederate Surgeon Thomas Fanning Wood, 1861–1865* (University of Tennessee Press, 2000); Michael B. Chesson,

ed., J. Franklin Dyer: *The Journal of a Civil War Surgeon* (University of Nebraska Press, 2003); James M. Greiner, Janet L. Coryell, and James R.
Smither, eds., *A Surgeon's Civil War: The Letters and Diary of Daniel M. Holt,
M.D.* (Kent State University Press, 1994); and Robert D. Hicks, ed., *Civil
War Medicine: A Surgeon's Diary* (Indiana University Press, 2019).[7] Newton's
letters offer more details of social history than medical matters, which is not
common in the published accounts of Civil War surgeons.

Newton's narrative expands our understanding of a lesser-known regiment, the 91st Ohio Volunteer Infantry. There were only three main sources
of information on this important Ohio regiment. The first was published
by the regiment's chaplain, A. H. Windsor, in 1865. Windsor's regimental
history is challenging to locate and is most often available only on diffi-
cult-to-read microfiche. In 1868, E. E. Ewing, a lieutenant from Company A
and K, published an epic poem about the 91st Ohio Volunteer Infantry. Then,
in 2005, Lois J. Lambert published a history of the 91st. The book, which is
also scarce, provides a general overview of the regiment's history and includes
a selection of edited letters from Lieutenant Colonel Benjamin Franklin
Coates. Newton discussed Coates frequently in his letters, and likewise
Newton is mentioned in the letters that Coates wrote to his wife during the
war. In terms of military contributions, a small number of historical works
discussed the 91st Ohio Volunteer Infantry. Most notably, Howard Rollins
McManus's *The Battle of Cloyds Mountain* (1989) and Patricia Givens Johnson's
The United States Army Invades the New River Valley, May 1864 (1986) in-
cluded some discussion of the 91st at the battle.[8]

As part of the Voices of the Civil War Series with the University of Tennessee Press, this book presents for the first time the entirety of William S.
Newton's Civil War letters to his wife and children. For many years, the pri-
vately held collection was only available to persistent researchers who knew
how to make contact or those willing to suffer through microfilm copies of
most of the letters at the Ohio Historical Society. A master's thesis from
1968 and a few recent Civil War military works make use of the collection,
but Newton's full Civil War experience has not been told.[9]

Greater access to the original letters occurred in 2017. That year, Special
Collections and University Archives at Virginia Tech acquired the Newton
Papers at auction.[10] Newton's description of the Battle of Cloyd's Mountain, which occurred approximately twenty miles from Blacksburg, where
Virginia Tech is located, was just one of the reasons why archivists at the
university pursued the collection. Virginia Tech is home to a growing number of collections of original sources on the Civil War in Virginia, repre-
senting Union and Confederate soldiers serving in the Commonwealth and
those from Virginia serving elsewhere.[11] The Newton Papers are a signifi-

cant recent addition that deserve a wider audience than just the researchers who visit the reading room on the first floor of the Carol M. Newman
Library.[12] This book, which contains Newton's Civil War correspondence
with his wife and children, provides new insights into the medical and social
history of the war, the war in western Virginia, local and regional history,
the perspective of a noncombatant, life on the home front, and the porous
lines between home and battlefront.

Acknowledgments

Since graduate school, I have always wanted to edit a book of Civil War letters, but other projects kept that from happening. Then, in 2017, the acquisition of a set of letters from a Union surgeon rekindled the possibility. The letters had been accessed and cited a few times before, but the full story of his Civil War experience remained untold. After reading through the letters from Ohio surgeon William S. Newton, I knew that I had to make time for the project.

Access is an important part of research and archival work. Researchers want to get to original sources, and archivists help researchers achieve that goal. As an archivist, I want researchers to use the collections for which I am responsible, but when accessible collections are not being used, there is an opportunity for archivists to bring greater attention to fantastic material. This project is such an example, and I hope that this book creates scholarly awareness for both firsthand accounts of the Civil War from noncombatants and for Civil War collections (diaries, letters, family papers, etc.) related to the Civil War in Virginia available at Special Collections and University Archives at Virginia Tech.

Completing the research for this project was analogous to turning over a big rock and then examining all of the inhabitants and new discoveries that lay underneath. Often one name, place, or regiment mentioned in the letters led to hours of searching through primary sources and published accounts for just a few words to add in a footnote. Other times, a new discovery had few leads and made it difficult to make a logical guess as to who, what, when, where, or why. Luckily a wealth of Civil War material such as regimental histories are available and full-text searchable through online projects such as HathiTrust, Internet Archive, and Google Books. Online databases such as Ancestry.com, Newspapers.com, Find A Grave, and the Civil War Soldiers and Sailors System Database hosted by the National Park Service provided unparalleled access to the people and places of the Civil War era. Plus there were many websites and message boards related to family history that gave me clues to the various people and places mentioned in the letters.

This book is a celebration of characters, stories, and supporters. First, I must thank the staff at the University of Tennessee Press. I shared the idea with several people there, including Tom Post, Thomas Wells, and then Scot Danforth, who jumped on the bandwagon. This is my fourth book with them, and I appreciate their enthusiasm and ongoing support. Archivists at Virginia Tech also coaxed me to bring Newton's letters to the reading public. I hope the extra hours I spent working on transcriptions did not detract from work obligations or keep my door closed more often than usual. In particular, John Jackson read the manuscript and his comments improved the finished work. He also helped me during the final stages of processing the collection.

Other archival colleagues also contributed to this project. Linda Showalter at the Marietta College Special Collections provided key information on Newton's family and pre–Civil War life. Further, Douglas Anderson, director of the library at Marietta College, waived all fees for using images of the 91st from their collection. Jack Dickinson at Marshall University alerted me to the fact that Newton published an account of his capture following the Battle of Cloyd's Mountain in the *Ironton Register*, which is included in this book. Mallory Fowler at the Cincinnati Museum Center and Gino Pasi at the University of Cincinnati provided scans of several important documents from the Medical College of Ohio. Lois Lambert's 2005 book on the 91st Ohio Volunteer Infantry led me to the Benjamin Franklin Coates Collection at the Rutherford B. Hayes Presidential Library and Museums in Fremont, Ohio. At the Hayes Library, Julie Mayle supplied me with copies of the Coates correspondence, much of which overlapped with the Newton letters, and copies of a difficult-to-find account of the Battle of Cloyd's Mountain. Larry Strayer, who has the largest private collection of Ohio Civil War material and a deep knowledge of the locations of other collections, assisted in tracking down details on several soldiers.

During the 2019 fall semester I had the good fortune of receiving assistance from the Virginia Tech history department in the form of a graduate assistant, Robert McLengian. Robert helped me verify transcriptions and search for historical details on Newton. I enjoyed our conversations each week and without his help I would have been much slower in organizing the book that follows. Dr. Paul Quigley in the history department read through the manuscript and alerted me to a number of important points and sources to include in this book. During 2020 and into the spring of 2021, as the COVID-19 quarantine forced me to work from home, I found free moments to work on this project. When the lack of information about the new super virus caused panic, I tried to imagine the confusion that doctors like William S. Newton faced when new and unexplained diseases took countless lives.

In 2020 I connected with Newton family descendants. Kristen (Kit) Lupsor and other members of the family helped track down details about the nineteenth century Newtons that I had been unable to locate or verify. Kit searched diligently for an image of William S. Newton. I thank her and her family for being so cooperative and for sharing an interest in telling the important story that their Ohio ancestors played during the Civil War.

My own family encouraged me to pursue this venture. When I shared my plan with them to create an edited book of Newton's letters, they agreed it was a worthwhile project. Caroline Marie Purcell, who was in the fourth grade virtually when the project started, enjoyed learning about Newton. She read aloud from the transcripts, especially when the content concerned the sometimes troubled teenager Ned Newton. She was my helper on this project from our map room, and I dedicate the book to her.

Editorial Policy and Practice

The purpose of this book is to make William S. Newton's Civil War correspondence accessible and readable for twenty-first century eyes without losing the author's voice, language choices, and overall intent. There were a number of guides to historical editing and examples from other books in the Voices of the Civil War Series that guided my work.[1] I chose readability over highlighting minute details. For readers interested in reviewing the fine details, the originals are available at Special Collections and University Archives at Virginia Tech. For external scholars, there are research fellowships that the Special Collections and University Archives co-sponsors with the Virginia Center for Civil War Studies based in the history department at Virginia Tech.

The William S. Newton letters arrived at Virginia Tech in 2017 after being in private hands for decades. The collection of original documents included printed transcripts of nearly all of the letters that Newton sent to his wife and children. The supplied transcripts contained plenty of inconsistencies, but were a good starting point to verify the content in the original letters. With help from graduate student Robert McLengian, I completed the transcription and verification of the content. Then I organized the content into chronological chapters of around fifteen to twenty letters each, based largely around consistent locations or activities that marked Newton's Civil War experience. To help keep the reader moving through Newton's experience, I created brief chapter introductions to help contextualize and summarize the letters that followed. The end of chapter 7 includes discussion of Newton's two differing accounts of the Battle of Cloyd's Mountain, his role in operating on Confederate General Albert G. Jenkins, and his subsequent imprisonment at Libby Prison. There is also a brief epilogue to present what is known about Newton's postwar life. Because Newton made multiple references to many of his family, friends, military acquaintances, and associates, I added an appendix of frequently occurring names and places.

Like those of other literate and educated Civil War noncombatants, William S. Newton's letters included many flowery words and phrases of the time. Thankfully, Newton followed his own advice to his son Ned on the importance of good penmanship. While there were some variations in characters and words, only a handful of words were undecipherable. He favored abbreviations to save page space, was inconsistent with spelling, used a variety of formatting, and drifted between giving complex descriptions and providing very basic facts. I preserved some of Newton's original spelling, punctuation, and errors, but I also wanted the text to be logical and readable. I inserted missing words in brackets, supplied concluding and other necessary punctuation, capitalized the first words of sentences, completed abbreviations when the word was unclear, and added footnotes when more information or references to other sources would be useful. Also, the spelling of surnames varied and parentheses indicate an alternate version. Finally, it is important to note that this book, as with other books in the Voices of the Civil War series, preserves the original words of the author, which include language that is offensive, racist, and unacceptable.

A handful of letters had missing portions, either from mouse chew or deteriorating paper. I included my best guesses for missing words or letters in brackets. A few of the dates were incorrect based on the context of the letter; the correct date is inserted in brackets and the letter is placed in the correct order in which it was written. An important chronological point to mention is that Newton's use of Virginia and West Virginia was uneven after the latter officially became its own state, separating from Virginia on June 20, 1863. Finally, rather than slow down the narrative with numerous and repetitive notes when names appear, I decided to include the appendix of frequently occurring names and places at the end of the book. Other less frequently appearing names or places are identified in accompanying notes.

Introduction

The biographical details of William S. Newton prior to joining the 91st Ohio Volunteer Infantry are sparse, but there is enough information available to chart his development as a Civil War surgeon. William Smith Newton was born on February 6, 1823, near the small town of Harmar, in Washington County, Ohio. The town, now part of Marietta, was located where the Muskingum River flows into the Ohio River, with Virginia (now West Virginia) located on the other side to the south. He was the son of Oren and Elizabeth Fuller Newton. His father, Oren, was an important figure in the community and was involved in farming and the grindstone industry. His grandparents were the early Marietta-area settlers Elias and Alice Stimson Newton. Elias was born in Norwich, Connecticut. He was a silversmith and served in the Revolutionary War. In 1801 he moved to the Warren Township and began farming. Elias was good friends with early Ohio explorer Ephraim Cutler, who was profiled in David McCullough's *The Pioneers* (2019). In late 1806, Cutler began building a home near the Ohio River in Warren Township, Washington County. During construction of the home that winter, Cutler and his family lodged with the Newton family.[1]

In 1839 sixteen-year-old William enrolled in Marietta College's Latin School, which was a preparatory school for younger students. The 1839–1840 catalog explained that the program lasted three years and was designed to prepare students for college, or in their words to "cultivate the power of the student." The school focused on "grammatical study," Latin, Greek, French, and "instruction in Written and Mental Arithmetic, in Geography, in English Grammar, in Chirography [penmanship], in Vocal Music, and in the German Language."[2] William completed two years in the Latin School.[3] In fall 1841 he advanced to the Marietta Academy, a preparatory school for the college.[4] The following fall, he enrolled as a freshman at Marietta College. The coursework was classical in nature with Latin, Greek, and English grammar as the focus. William completed his freshman year, 1842–1843, but he did not continue with courses or graduate from Marietta College.[5]

William demonstrated an interest in medicine and learned from his cousin Robert Safford Newton, who practiced medicine in Gallipolis. Cousin Robert began his study of medicine at the Medical College of Ohio in Cincinnati, the second medical school west of the Alleghenies. In 1839 he transferred to the Louisville Medical College and graduated in 1841. After graduation he moved to Gallipolis, married Mary M. Hoy, and opened a medical practice. His specialty was the pathology and treatment of cancer, which was a fledgling area of medicine in the mid-nineteenth century. Robert was later credited with inventing the circular incision for the removal of the breast. He taught and practiced medicine through a new type of approach known as eclectic medicine.[6]

Defined in the early nineteenth century, eclectic medicine focused on the use of botanicals and a closer interaction between the doctor and the patient to diagnose illness and prescribe treatment. Eclectic doctors relied heavily on herbal medicines, especially remedies from Indigenous peoples' traditions. They decried invasive procedures, mercurial remedies, bleeding patients, and the use of purgatives like calomel. Eclectic doctors believed in using a wide range of natural remedies, many of which were not commonly used in practice or discussed in traditional medical schools. In 1853 Robert and his brother O. E. Newton opened a clinic in Cincinnati to provide students with clinical instruction in eclectic medicine. William S. Newton observed his cousin treating patients with modern eclectic methods, which influenced his decision to enroll as a medical student at the Medical College of Ohio, also in Cincinnati. The school and many other medical colleges in the Midwest during this period taught eclectic approaches to medicine.[7]

In fall 1843 William S. Newton matriculated at the Medical College of Ohio in Cincinnati.[8] The school's curriculum of that period included preparatory courses, a series of weekly lectures, and clinical rotations in the school's hospital. Students were required to spend two days on the campus for lectures and two days in the hospital observing and assisting. In addition, the professor of surgery scheduled one evening each week for students to gain practical experience in minor surgery. To earn a degree at the Medical College of Ohio, students had to be twenty-one years old, have completed two full courses of classes (approximately twenty-six to thirty weeks) at the school, and record three years of medical experience with a respectable practitioner or preceptor. The practical experience of working with a preceptor was a very important part of the training. During the early part of the preceptorship, students would dissect a human cadaver, clean the skeleton, and keep it as the first item of equipment for a future medical office. Later, students would accompany their preceptor in the examination and treatment of male patients.[9]

The 1843–1844 catalog of officers and students included William S. Newton as one of the Medical College of Ohio's 185 students and listed R. S. Newton as his preceptor.[10] As a new student, Newton would have attended the school's opening lecture in fall 1843. The lecture by faculty member M. B. Wright focused on the field of medicine as a compilation of truths and its practitioners as exhibitors of integrity and moral courage. Wright encouraged the new matriculates "To mitigate the pain of body, to calm the troubled spirit, and to minister to the relief of the needy." He challenged the students to ask questions, anticipate opposition, and keep their minds open to new discoveries no matter how fanciful they might seem.[11]

Newton graduated in 1845 from the Medical College of Ohio and returned to Harmar.[12] Similar to an apprenticeship or residency, he began working alongside Seth Hart, a doctor in town.[13] By 1850 Newton had his own medical practice in Harmar. That year, he published a short description of his treatment of a serious injury in the *Western Lancet* medical journal. The brief article explained that William Childers, the twenty-three-year-old patient, had severely injured himself with a barrel saw while sawing staves. The wound, beneath the right ninth rib, was approximately six inches across and had cut through muscle and into the patient's liver. Newton attached the ten-inch long skin flap with sutures leaving openings for discharge, dressed the wound with lint, compress, and bandage, and gave the patient opiates for the pain. He visited the patient about three weeks later and reported that all cavities were closed and the patient was able to "resume his business." Newton shared the example with his medical colleagues to highlight the restorative power of nature to recover from such a severe injury.[14]

On October 28, 1845, William married Frances Ann Hayward of Gallipolis. They had seven children during their marriage. Three of their children, Oren Hayward (1846–1858), Lewis Garland (May–October 1848), and Fanny Lillian (1857–1858), died before reaching adulthood. When William enlisted in the Union Army, they had three children, Edward (Ned) Seymore (born 1850), Valentine Mott (born 1852), and Kate May (born 1860). Another child, John Beverly (born November 9, 1863), arrived during William's military service.[15]

In 1854 Newton and his family relocated to Ironton, Ohio, which is just north of Ashland, Kentucky, on the other side of the Ohio River. Newton was the eighth doctor in Ironton at that time.[16] The 1860 census listed Newton as a physician with real estate valued at $3,300 and personal wealth of $1,000.[17] He had an active medical practice in downtown Ironton and frequently advertised in local newspapers.[18] The announcement in the *Ironton Register* stated: "DR. W. S. NEWTON Physician and surgeon. Tenders his

Professional Cards.

DR. W. S. NEWTON,

PHYSICIAN AND SURGEON, TENDERS his professional services to the citizens of Ironton and vicinity. Office and residence, corner of Fourth and Centre Streets.

Dr. William S. Newton advertised his medical services in the *Ironton Register* beginning in the early 1860s until his military service began in fall 1862. *Ironton Register,* January 9, 1862.

professional services to the citizens of Ironton and vicinity. Office and residence on Buckhorn Street between Fourth and Fifth." The advertisement regularly appeared in the newspaper in the early 1860s, but ceased with the October 9, 1862, issue due to his enlistment the previous month.[19]

Newton's letters refer to a number of friends, extended family, and local residents of Ironton. They also contain many references to acquaintances from Harmar and other parts of southern Ohio. He also refers to his mother and maintained a separate correspondence with her. Further, Newton reported having an active correspondence with other family members, but none of those letters have been located. At the time of the Civil War, Newton had eight living siblings. His letters mention six of them who lived in the area, usually identifying them with the modifier Brother or Br. or Sister: Stephen, referred to as Steve; John, referred to as Brother John; Oren, referred to as Brother O.; Lucy L.; Mary Frances, referred to in several letters as Mary Frank; and Douglas E., referred to as Doug. His letters also refer to Will or Brother Will as a close contact in Gallipolis. Since William S. Newton did not have a brother with his same name, the references to Will or Brother Will would be his brother-in-law William Greenleaf Fuller (married to Newton's sister Lucy) or William C. Hayward (younger brother of Newton's wife). In most cases, Will or Brother Will would refer to William C. Hayward, who did not serve in the military and was in Gallipolis throughout the war, while William Greenleaf Fuller managed telegraph lines for the Union across the South and would have been less likely to be in Gallipolis on a regular basis. Newton also refers to his wife's parents—Solomon Hayward as "Father H."

and Catherine Haywood as "Mother H." Newton also refers frequently to Emily Hayward, noted as Em, his sister-in-law and sister to Frances Newton, who lived in Gallipolis. Surprisingly, few of his family members served in the military during the Civil War. One letter mentions his half-nephew Charles Humphreys Newton (born 1842, son of Stephen) who served as a lieutenant in the 2nd Ohio Heavy Artillery, but that reference was to Charles Newton's graduation from Marietta College. More details on his family and their backgrounds are included in the appendix.[20]

The volunteer soldiers in the 91st Ohio Volunteer Infantry came from Adams, Scioto, Lawrence, Gallia, Jackson, and Pike counties. As a local doctor who had kept a steady practice in Ironton, Newton knew the town's professionals, local farmers, and the younger generation, many of whom had been his patients. Likewise, a good number of Newton's medical colleagues from Ohio joined the Union Army as surgeons. In addition to discussing the lives of those connected to the 91st Ohio Volunteer Infantry, Newton was close with members of the 2nd Virginia Cavalry, which included soldiers from Ohio and western Virginia (West Virginia after 1863). His letters reflected a great interest in knowing more about local people, places, and events. The incoming correspondence from his wife has not been located or placed in an archives, but clearly she was communicating about a wide range of local details that claimed much of her husband's attention in the letters he mailed.

There are several obvious themes that cut across Newton's correspondence. First, Newton described the difficulties of fighting in Appalachian borderlands. As in other parts of the southern mountains, the lines of battle and occupation were very blurry.[21] Frequent changes to holding specific positions and geographic areas meant devastation to the physical landscape.

In August 1862, volunteers from the Ohio counties of Adams, Scioto, Lawrence, Gallia, Jackson, and Pike organized at Ironton into five companies of the 91st Ohio Volunteer Infantry. Regimental Colors of the 91st Ohio Volunteer Infantry, Ohio Department of the Adjutant General, Ohio Battle Flag Audiovisual Collection, Ohio History Connection.

Newton described the absurdity of attempting to hold a position when
the land had been stripped clean of all resources. The effects of wartime
resulted in environmental destruction, which in turn affected local econ-
omies.[22] In addition, Unionists in western Virginia demanded a separate
state and also wanted protection from Confederate attackers, which made
this borderland a priority for Union armies early in the war.

Second, Newton discussed race relations in several of his letters. He
was an educated white northerner, and many modern readers might expect
(and hope) that he was progressive on race. Instead, Newton was very much
writing from the context of his time, and he generally did not believe that
Black people were his equals in any way. He did not support slavery, but his

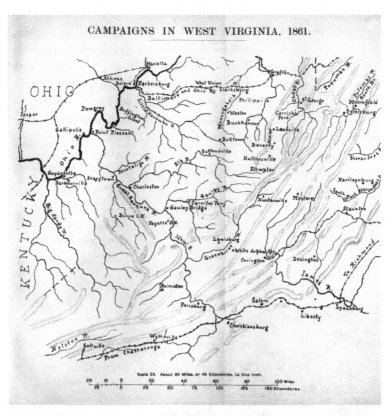

During the early years of the Civil War, Union regiments in the western portion
of Virginia (which became West Virginia in 1863) struggled with rugged terrain,
Confederate raiders, and a lack of supplies. Campaigns in West Virginia, 1861, in John
Formby, *The American Civil War: A Concise History of its Causes, History, and Results,
Maps* (New York: Scribners, 1910), map 10.

discussions about emancipated slaves focused on how Black people could be helpful and subservient to him and his family. Newton's views of race and his belief that Black people fit into only the fringes of postwar society mirrored the views and attitudes of many white northerners and southerners.[23]

Third, Newton focused on his family as a way to escape the visible horrors and monotony of war. As a surgeon, Newton was surrounded by largely uncontrollable disease and death. His methods and medical skills did save lives, but the scale of his work far exceeded the resources that were available. As a way to divert his attention from the realities of war, Newton focused a majority of his words on more personal matters, observations, and friends and family. Further, he discussed the importance of his horse, Old Tom, an ongoing inability to secure leave to visit home, and his attempts to quit tobacco.

His desire to focus his letters on his family leads into a final theme that Newton's letters described: his dreams of the postwar. Newton's military service was marked by an ever increasing closeness to the front lines and danger to his personal safety. He described some of what he knew of military matters, but his later letters were dominated by talk of buying property, farming, childrearing, and helping his family and friends find success in life. Newton discussed with his wife financial matters and the transfer or payment of large amounts of money. He indicated that the postwar and his return to Ohio were always on the near horizon, so he wanted to be prepared for peacetime.

There are, of course, other themes and details that readers will discover through the words of William S. Newton. This book contains edited transcriptions of the letters and documents that Newton created or sent to his family back in Ohio. In his correspondence from 1862–1865, Newton recorded an amazing journey through Ohio, West Virginia, Maryland, and Virginia. The collection documents the unique story of a surgeon, a soldier, a husband, and a father.

As Wolves upon a Sheep Fold

1

In the Cause of Humanity, April–December 1861

Ohioans contributed swiftly and generously to the needs of the Union throughout the Civil War. On April 12–13, 1861, Confederate forces bombarded and captured Fort Sumter in Charleston's harbor. Before the bombardment ended, twenty full companies of volunteer soldiers offered their immediate service to Ohio governor William Dennison. Three days later, on April 15, President Abraham Lincoln issued a proclamation calling for seventy-five thousand volunteers to help put down the insurrection. In response to Lincoln's proclamation, on April 16, the state legislature, with full support from Ohio governor William Dennison, "passed a bill appropriating one million dollars for placing the State upon a war-footing, and for assisting the General Government in meeting the shock of the rebellion." Volunteers from across the Buckeye State formed the first two Ohio regiments, which were officially organized in Columbus on April 18, 1861.[1]

Governor Dennison included a significant clause in the legislation that required that, before any Ohio regiment could "take the field," it must have a board-approved surgeon. He appointed a review board to examine all applicants as surgeons or assistant surgeons for Ohio regiments. Applicants were required to have some level of formal education, be practitioners in good standing for at least ten years (five years for assistant surgeons), and pass an examination conducted by the review board. This system of assessing and assigning medical officers lasted throughout the war, resulting in the appointment of 287 surgeons and 694 assistant surgeons for Ohio regiments. In addition, other physicians joined Ohio's war effort through the United States Volunteer Surgeons, often with official ranks such as major or first lieutenant.[2]

William S. Newton took immediate interest in serving the Union cause as a surgeon. The first document in his collection, dated April 12, 1862, on the one-year anniversary of the attack on Fort Sumter, is a legal certification of his qualification to serve as a volunteer surgeon. Throughout the summer, Confederate forces amassed in western Virginia, threatening Ohio. In August, volunteers from the counties of Adams, Scioto, Lawrence, Gallia, Jackson, and Pike organized at Ironton into five companies of the 91st Ohio Volunteer Infantry. Colonel John A. Turley from Scioto County commanded the regiment with Colonel Benjamin F. Coates second in command. The organization of the 91st occurred as Confederate "border rangers" led by General Albert G. Jenkins gained strength in western Virginia and moved closer to the Ohio border.[3]

In August, the Army appointed George H. Carpenter as surgeon and John B. Warwick as assistant surgeon for the 91st. Newton received his official appointment as assistant surgeon for the regiment a few weeks later on September 17, 1862. He joined the regiment, which prepared to engage Confederate forces led by Jenkins a mere six miles from Ironton. In the weeks that followed, Newton traveled to Point Pleasant, Ohio, east into western Virginia toward the Kanawha River, and eventually to Charleston.[4]

William S. Newton's first letters to his wife cover April until early December 1862. There is a great sense of urgency and expectation that Confederate forces, especially those led by raider John Hunt Morgan, were near and ready to strike.[5] The regiment saw no major battles during this time but were involved in a few skirmishes with rebel troops. During this time Newton reported on camp life, which included a lice outbreak, as well as numbers in the hospital and available food and supplies. He reported on the destruction of the landscape, which had been stripped of anything valuable, including the wooden boards from outhouses. Noteworthy is his description of the role of Black people in society, both as freed slaves and camp assistants. His letters conveyed a deep sense of loneliness, especially for his wife. Newton provided her with medical advice and instructions on which supplies to send him. News of a family Thanksgiving meal in Marietta indicates how much he missed the simple pleasures of life. He also told his wife that he was trying to collect Confederate artifacts for his sons. By late 1862 Newton had already grown weary of military life.

1

Auditor's Office, Lawrence County, Ohio,

Ironton, April 12th 1862

To all whom it may concern,

It is hereby certified that Docts. W. S. Newton & W. R. Earheart[6] are accredited by the Commissioners of said County as Volunteer Surgeons and any kindness extended to them will be in the cause of humanity and thankfully received.

G. W. Willard
Aud. Law. Co.

2

Ironton Ohio Sept. 8th/62

Dear Wife

This Monday eve, and as the mail goes through tomorrow I concluded to send you a few lines.

The Victor[7] was gone so long I began to think you were all captured. She has not made a trip since, and I think they are afraid to do so.

Jenkins with a regiment of cavalry occupied Guyan last evening and stationed his pickets some six miles down the river. The Catlettsburg folks sent all their valuables, papers, goods, etc., here this morning for safety.

All is excitement here, the Provost Marshall issued his proclamation to have all business houses closed at 9 o'clock every morning, that every able bodied man is to then meet for drill. The consequence is, instead of 20 or 30 men, we now have five companies, about 400, drilling, and getting ready for any emergency.

Two companies of the 91st were stationed at Coal Grove last night. And tonight about 200 of our citizens started by boat to go to Burlington and Proctorville, with two cannon, to guard the ford at those places.

I am still taking notes, and a little money, and if I do not leave soon, will have things in as good shape as possible for me to do, at the present time.

Have no assignment yet, and will not seal this till the mail comes, so if I get anything, will communicate it.

Write soon, kiss Kate, and tell the boys they must not forget what I said to them.

Yours truly,
Wm. S. Newton

3

Point Pleasant Oct. 29th/62 [Sept. 29, 1862]

Dear Wife

This is my fourth day in camp, and I think I shall like it pretty well. There has been about enough excitement to make it interesting. Mr. Ricker can tell you about it. My baggage has not come to hand yet I am going to Gallipolis tonight to look after it.

Am boarding with Mrs. Sisson[8] till my baggage comes. They are all well, and try to make it pleasant for me. I have no news, have got a small amount of money from the 2nd Va. Cavalry, and may get more. I will send a list for Roddarmour's[9] benefit.

I purchased cap, wreath & shoulder straps for fourteen dollars. Now, if I got the coat I am all right. Tell the children to be good.

> Your Husband
> Wm. S. Newton

4

Point Pleasant, Oct. 1st 1862

Dear Wife

Yours with baggage all came safely to hand this day, and I was very glad to get them, now if Mr. Jones has got the pants ready, I think you can send them by Nixon,[10] as he expects to come up again soon. At all events, he will know if anyone is coming. I shall stay at Mrs. Sissons until Saturday of this week, then I expect to go into camp regularly.

It is so dusty now that I shall spoil everything I have unless it rains, and I am almost glad I cannot get to camp sooner, hoping it will rain before that time.

As to taking Mrs. Gillen, you must do as you think best. If they will pay six dollars per week for both, I think you can afford to keep a girl, then you will not be all the time on your feet. I do not see how you could divide the house, so as to rent it to any advantage, you have not two Kitchens.

It will not be half so hard, if you can get a good girl, and when you cannot get exactly what you want, do with less, for I do not think they will be particular, so you give them plenty of bread & meat. You might try it, and if you cannot get along, no harm is done. If all should go on pleasantly, you might be able to get away from home by & by for Mrs. Gillen would see that all went on right and the boys could still go to school. While you and Kate might make a visit to G. [Gallipolis], or even Pt. Pleasant, if we should go into winter quarters here. Should the boats begin running regularly, Will has promised to send you some sweet potatoes & butter. It is almost impossible now to get butter, since all these regiments came, but they will probably be moved soon, somewhere.

At present, I have charge of the Hospital, while Warwick attends Surgeons Call in camp every morning. Carpenter is counseling physician, and takes charge of hospital supplies, makes out certificates for furloughs & discharges. We all have plenty to occupy our time, can hardly have time to get homesick, or know how time passes.

Our supplies have come, and we now have 18 in hospital, will lose two very soon. I prescribed for over thirty in camp yesterday. They are almost all threatened with flux,[11] some have it very bad. Ever since our forced marched to & from Buffalo, the fight there, has been the exciting cause, together with the dry weather, and if we do not get some rain, I fear it will be very much worse. I also have two cases, the wives of Geo. Miller [Millard] & Morgan[12] of the 2nd Va. Cavalry. They are here on a visit to their husbands. I shall make something extra by this, perhaps enough to keep me in tobacco. Tell Ned if he is a very good boy, and we stay here, I will send for him by & by so that he may know what camp life is.

Tell Mott I shall try to capture something for him on our next skirmish. Tell Kate that her Papa wants to see her very much. Tell wife that she must manage things to suit herself.

Yours truly,

Wm. S. Newton

Don't use those little white envelopes when you write, but get you some decent ones and write a letter to me every Sunday, mail it Monday, it will come through on Tuesday.

5

In Camp at Pt. Pleasant Oct. 5th

Dear Wife

Yours by Mr. Ricker came this eve. I am sorry to learn of Kate's illness, yet from what you say, of the color of the discharges, I do not think it is summer complaint, but cold working itself off.

Give her Act lead, prepared chalk, and diaphoretic powder[13] every 4 hours.

If she does not get better, get Dr. Wilson to see her.

Last evening I received orders from Headquarters, to accompany three companies of our Regt., with some cavalry of 2nd Va. on a scout. We started after dark, crossed the Kanawha on the pontoon bridge, marched eleven miles in to the enemy's country, arrived at 2 in the morning where we camped in some haystacks till daylight. We were just nine miles from Gallipolis. We scattered along among some farm houses, got our breakfast, then marched to the Ohio opposite Gallipolis and up the river to this place without seeing a rebel. Now this is the last time I am going on a scout at night, unless there is a better probability of a fight than we had last night. I told Col. Coates the same, and he agreed with me.

I am pretty badly used up, for the infantry march so slow we did not arrive at camp till noon today, and I was in the saddle the whole time.

Forces are rapidly concentrating at this point, and from present indications we will not remain at this place long.

Will was up to see me today, and took home my dirty shirt & drawers. Esther was also here with Mr. Vanden.[14] One Indiana, and one Ohio Regt. crossed the river today and pitched their tents here. Our new Brigadier Gen. Gillmore[15] is here, with his staff.

I should like very much to see Doug and tell him if he comes this way he must be sure to see me. Much love to the children, tell the boys to keep on doing well.

Your Husband

6

Point Pleasant Oct. 7th

Dear Wife

Having a few moments of leisure, I improve it to converse with you. Last eve I rode down to Gallipolis to get a good chance to wash my feet & etc., got a clean collar & socks. It is quite convenient to have a depot there, and Em has darned my socks, mended my old coat, and made herself generally useful.

Irene was quite unwell and came very near miscarrying, but was better this morning when I left. Our Regt. moved across the Kanawha yesterday. We are brigaded with the 34th Ohio (Zouaves) and the 4th Va. Col. Lightburn, two old regiments. We are now all encamped on the same field. The 4th on our left, the 34th on our right.

The staff officers are all in a row immediately on the bank of the Ohio. Myself & Warwick occupy the Assist Surgeons tent on the extreme left of our lines. We also have the use of the hospital tent at present, a luxury we will be deprived of when our sick are moved into our camp. We use this tent to eat in, for Surgeons Call, every morning at which time the Orderly of each company march all that complain, to receive med, or be sent to Hospital. The average number is about 40.

Dr. Carpenter left for home on leave of absence for one week, and I have been very busy attending hospital, signing passes, and certificates of disability on which to grant furloughs.

The latter is a very disagreeable business, for the men all think we can give them furloughs, when in truth our power is very limited, and we can only exercise it when we believe death or permanent disability would be the result if not granted. So when the men go to their captains, colonels or any other officers to beg for a furlough, they always send them to the Surgeon for a certificate, at the same time knowing how little we can do for them.

So you see we are in a tight place. I think your plan for getting apples the right one. Mr. R. will give you any assistance he is able to, and his judgement in the matter as to quality & price will be the very best.

Tell Ned I think we shall be able to capture the gun soon, and Mott that I found a sword, but it was not nice enough for him. We will make it all right in time.

Write soon and let me know how Kate is.

> Your Husband
> Wm. S. Newton

7

Camp near Red House Oct. 23rd

Dear Wife Yours of 9th & 19th came to hand this eve, this Thursday. On last Sunday we had another big review and while at it we received orders to start up Kanawha at 3 AM. Next morning Em & Eliza Neal[16] were up that day and took dinner with us, the most of which they brought along with them. Warwick & myself felt queer while preparing the same for ladies, they at the same time looking on.

We marched fifteen miles the first day, on Tuesday about 8, passing through Buffalo just before camping. On Wednesday we came ten miles, arriving here after dark, driving in the Rebel pickets. They tore up the bridge, so we had to move back a mile, to get room for our Brigade to camp. This morning we moved, having repaired the bridge during the night.

We marched today, only three miles, our cavalry skirmishing with a rebel cavalry seven hundred strong, driving them some five miles above Red House. We occupy their camp tonight using the same rails partly burned, they used this morning to get their breakfast. We should have moved on them faster today, but were compelled to wait for the Push Boats, which contained our supplies, and if we moved further, we could not get them, for the rebels had blockaded the river, and we were obliged to remove the obstructions as we advanced. Two steam boats arrived this eve, and we now have supplies. Three days rations were issued since dark to the men, and from the signs we shall move early tomorrow, and a fight will certainly be the result, for from the best information we can get, the *Rebs* have been reinforced and will dispute our advance at every available point, and they may be in force enough to thrash us. But our troops do not think so, and it will take a large force to stop us. This march has all been made without tents, the men not being allowed them. The Col. has one & myself & Warwick have our Sibley[17] with us. But this is the first night we have pitched it on the march, for the teams did not get up till almost morning. Some of the nights have been pretty cold, yet I have plenty of clothing. And sleep as warm as it is possible for us to do on the ground without tents. Two nights I only had one blanket, the others being behind in our wagon. Major Carpenter refused to march, and staid at the Point [Pleasant], wished me to excuse him to the Col., and say he was sick. All of which I did, but it was hard to convince the officers that he was very bad. He declares he will resign if they compel him to take the field this winter. He does not take to it kindly and the Col. says he must come, or quit.

There are many things I would like to write, but cannot do so for want of time as it is now late, and four of us are writing at this time, on the top of our mess chest. Mr. Kirker, Capt. Caldwell, Warwick & myself. Kirker is messing with us at present, Ricker having gone to Headquarters. Our men are tolerably well, we having sent those not able to march to General Hospital. We have no ambulance and are compelled to put our men in those belonging to other regiments, and they are very cross about it. I went to the Med. Director yesterday and had them straightened up, our men got to ride at all events. I tell you, it is hard for me to see the poor fellows marching with their knapsacks sick, and hardly able to crawl along, yet if I get off I can only relieve one of them at the time. We sometimes carry their loads, guns etc.

Am glad to learn Kate is better. Tell Mott I had an Orderly's Sword offered to me the other day, but it was not nice enough. If we get into a fight tomorrow I may be able to get a nice one for him. He must go to school every day and learn all he can, and perhaps he may one day carry a Generals sword. Tell Ned[,] Warwick captured an Enfield[18] at the Buffalo fight, and it will be my turn next. Gillen says he will get one for him yet. I left Mrs. G. almost well and I was glad of it, for she has been pretty sick.

I must bid you good night as the others are done and it is not prudent for us to keep a light burning longer. Write often and always remember to direct to 91st Regt. O.V.I.

						Your Husband
						Wm. S. Newton

8

Camp Pocatalico Oct. 25th/62

Dear Wife

I wrote you on the 23rd and as I predicted a battle of some kind on the next day. I thought a letter now might not be uninteresting. My letter was written from Red House. On the next morning our brigade started, the 4th Va. leading, 91st, 92nd & 34th following in the order written. The 2nd Va. Cavalry some three miles ahead, feeling of the enemy, trying to draw them out. As our Regt. came within about one mile, the Rebels opened on our advance with two pieces of artillery, and it was quite amusing at this time to see the effect on our men. While most all quickened their step, a few got weak in the knees, some sick, and the convalescents wanted passes to ride in the ambulances.

Our artillery, which had been at the rear, now came up on the double quick, and as they passed our Regt., I followed, determined if possible to get sight of a rebel. I had not gone far, till I met the Med. Director. He halted me and said I must send to the rear for instruments etc. and make every preparation for the wounded. This order was soon disposed of, and I again went on. I soon came up with our artillery, which had fired three or four shots. I took a position on the hillside above them, and tried to see what they were shooting at. They again moved forward 1/2 mile. I followed, and succeeded in seeing about 15 Reb Cavalry just passing over the hill, out of range of our guns. I dismounted & stood watching the movements, pretty soon two or three Rebs came back in sight, to, if possible, get a sight of our force. In this they did not succeed, for our cannon again opened upon them, and they soon passed out of sight without seeing more than two Regiments. We all now fell back a short distance, and in doing so, met the 2nd Brigade under Col. Keifer,[19] they having heard our cannon, came up if necessary to help us. We were then ordered to encamp which we did, on the ground occupied by the *Rebs* the previous night, and here we have been, all day expecting to move, but tonight we learn they are fortifying three miles above us. As a matter of course we expect to go into Charleston within a day or two, and the *Rebs* will go out. We may have a battle, & we may not. In all probability there is a force moving in from other quarters, and if we are not too fast we may get them in a tight place.

Can you tell me where Doug is. Is he coming this way with Morgan's[20] men. Write often as you can, for I like to hear from you often. You need not fret about me, I have plenty to keep me warm, and enough to eat as yet, and I relish it. My regards to Mr. K. and all enquiring friends.

Your Husband
Wm. S. Newton

9

Camp Pocatalico Oct 27th 1862

Dear Wife

Mr. Kirker just came in saying we could send a letter home by our Sutler. So having nothing better to occupy my time I thought I would write if only a few lines. I have written three letters in as many days, but as this will probably reach you before them, you may keep this till they come if you choose. In them I have tried to give you something of our march up this Valley. We have been in this camp now for two days & nights, within three or four miles of the rebels, and today (Monday) our teams were sent some two miles above for hay, and the Rebel pickets came down to dispute their right to it. Our Regt. was immediately ordered up for their protection. In a few minutes the word came that they were fighting. The 4th Va. were then ordered up, and firing is now going on. With what result we do not know, if we hear I may give you further word.

Warwick was ordered to go with them while I was at the Hospital, so I am compelled to remain in camp to care for the sick, and we have enough of them, for the snow & rain of yesterday was too much for men without tents. I went over the Poca Creek yesterday and established a Hospital in a large deserted house, the owner of which is a Rebel Major. I was not long till the 92nd had come there too. The 4th Va. also. I would not give much for the property when they get through with it, for the boys all know the whole history and they are not apt to be particular in their care for secesh property. Some four or five outhouses have literally been stripped of every board & shingle, and the frames of some have long ago warmed our boys by their heat. You or I had very little idea of the destruction of property in this war, the amount of provinder [provender] & provisions required to sustain a Regt. for one day is perfectly astonishing.

Word has just come from the fight which turns out to be only a skirmish. One of the 2nd Va. Cavalry wounded, but not seriously. The boat is about to start, so I must close.

My regards to all,
Your Husband
Wm. S. Newton

10

Camp Piatt 10 miles above Charleston Va.
Oct 31st 1862

Dear Wife From the above you see our present camp, whether we will remain here one hour, day, or week, no one knows except the Genl.

Yesterday morning we were two miles below Charleston, marched up to Elk River where the bridge had been burned by our retreating army a few weeks ago. We soon constructed a pontoon one, and while waiting, seven thousand of Morgan's Men of Ky. notoriety came up, composed principally of Tenn., Ky. & Va. troops.

Our Regt. here left in Gen. Hospital about thirty of our sick, which gives one time to write this letter to you. Carpenter has not yet joined the Regt. I received a letter from him since we marched, he was at Gen. Hospital at Gallipolis, assisting Dr. Davis.[21] Our men are most all sick with colds, the snow & rain of last Sabbath tells upon them. I think if our commanding officers were compelled to sleep out of doors a few such days & nights, they would see to it that our men had their tents, and wagons to transport them.

As we marched through Charleston & Malden yesterday, I tried to find a young darky who was willing to go with me, but their owners kept them scarce. The two we have are too old to do well, at least the cook is. His name is henry, and I have just sent him back a mile with my horse, to bring us a Sibley Stove.[22] Our other one, John Stinson,[23] lives at Malden, and we let him stop there last night as we passed, knowing how pleasant it would be for a man to see his wife after an absence of two months. Myself & Warwick can appreciate a matter of that kind at the present time. We do not think of going home, that is out of the question. And the probability is that we may go on to the Va. & Tennessee Rail Road.[24] Yet we cannot tell, we may be permitted to guard this part of Va. for a time, and if I should be detailed to Hospital duty, should like to send for Ned. Yet it would be still pleasanter to have wife & Kate come up, if the boys could be cared for at home.

I put on a clean collar this morning the first for ten days, as I resolved not to change until we reached Charleston. This resolve I kept.

My pants have not come yet, although I told our sutler to call on Will at Gallipolis for them. If Mr. Jones sends them to Will, he will have an opportunity to forward them to me.

Our tent is again crowded with officers and it is almost impossible to write, and if I should stop short you will know the reason.

Nig John has not yet come up, and I fear the Secesh have got him. We had promised to bring his brother in law along, yet we may never see him again. They will have to keep a sharp lookout if they keep him, for he is one sharp nigger, and chickens will have to roost high, if we do not have our share, he can beat the Zouaves in our brigade, and that is recommendation enough for anyone.

John has just arrived, brought us a can of peaches, says his brother will come up in time. They are issuing rations for three days, but have no sugar, coffee or meat. We have a little left, and I could not get along without sugar, for coffee & hardbread is my principal dependence. Our coffee is excellent, and the bread good, and when we come into camp late at night, as we did last night, all I want is a tin cup full of coffee & one hard cracker, then spread my oil cloth, saddle blanket, another double blanket, then the comfort, my saddle & overcoat for a pillow. I can sleep very well till about 4 o'clock. I then get cold in spite of blankets, and have to get up, stir up the fire.

The river has raised two or three feet, and I think there will be no trouble in supplying the army with provisions. If you can get opportunity, send the [Ironton] Register or [Cincinnati Daily] Commercial[25] occasionally, for we have not had a paper since we left Pt. Pleasant. I suppose they will arrange the mail soon. Write often & long.

Your Husband
Wm. S. Newton

Mssrs. Kirker, Rodgers,[26] Ricker etc. are all well and say through me, for their folks, write often, for they have not opportunity to do so at present.

II

Gauley Bridge Nov. 3rd 1862

Dear Wife This is Monday eve, and your letter of Sunday a week ago, has not yet been received, although Warwick got one from his wife yesterday, written on the same (26th) day, yours should have been. I presume this is no fault of yours, but the mail or Postmaster.

We marched from Huddleston, a camp named from the rebel captain who was killed at Guyandotte[27] at the time Dr. Morris was taken prisoner, a distance of seven miles. This place is one of the hardest looking places I have yet seen in Va. Nothing to eat for man or beast, except what we bring with us.

Last night I got one of my fidgety spells on me, caused by finding a young lizard quite too near my blankets, thinking a few more might hatch out, and crawl over me while asleep. I got up at midnight, struck a light, and wrote a letter to mother, the first since I came into the service. I found among Morgan's Artillery men today, some who were well acquainted with Doug. They spoke of him in the highest terms. They are veteran troops, and have seen hard service. We have two or three old brigades along with us, and their ranks are pretty well thinned out.

What we are going to do, go further, or stay here, is yet unknown to anyone, outside of Genl. Cox[28] & Staff. Unless the river should raise soon, Mr. Kirker will have his hands full in supplying us with food. Mr. Ricker too is in a tighter place, for he has the whole Brigade on his hands.

Should we stay here any time, I shall try to procure lumber enough to make a bunk, so that I may get off the ground away from the lizards. Lumber & nails will be hard to come at here for the rebels have destroyed almost everything.

I hope to get your letter in the morning, and will write again if I hear of any movement on the part of our Regt. We found among the ruins at Camp Piatt, Sibley stoves, which answer a fine purpose for warming our tent. Many of the Field and Staff officers availed themselves of the opportunity to supply this necessary article. It was said that several hundred were in the warehouse at the time it was burned. You can have no idea of the destruction of property in this valley on Lightburn's retreat. Tents, wagons, small arms of every description are among the ruins.

Tell Mott I could have gathered plenty of cavalry swords, gun barrels etc. but they were all bent up & rusted, in short, ruined. Yet the time will come someday that I can get one of each worth sending home. I hope the boys will be good, and improve their opportunities, for now is the time for them to be forming habits of manhood. If they are trifling in their mode of spending time now, they will be when they get to be men. I hope you will impress this thing upon them. I hope you do not sleep as cold as I have done for two or three nights. I tell you I think of home at such times.

Give my love to all enquiring friends. Kiss Kate for me. Write often.

> Your Husband
> Wm. S. Newton

12

If I knew, I would get them, I should like to have you send some Postage Stamps

> Camp Gauley Nov. 7th

Dear Wife

This Friday morning, and I have not had a letter for two weeks, probably some on the road yet. They may never reach this Providence *forsaken* country. I have seen hills and rough places in Wood Co., Va., but they are mole hills compared with these. The Village of Gauley is composed of four or five houses. One a brick occupied by Col. Lightburn & Staff. Other Headquarters fill up the balance of them. The 34th, 91st & 4th Va. were marched past the bridge and up on to this side hill, where grass will hardly grow, and here we are yet.

The 92nd being behind were fortunate enough to be left under the hill near headquarters although belonging to our brigade. You can from [form] no idea how fast time flies, a week is gone before we know it. I can account for it in no other way except our time is taken up with our duties.

As soon as breakfast is over, I go to the Hospital tent to prescribe for the sick. This done, I make out the morning report, and if I send it to Headquarters, I can get a little time. But if I go with it myself, dinner is ready by the time I get back. The afternoon is taken up in prescribing for those who have been on picket, and excusing those from duty or are sick, or lazy, and it is pretty hard to distinguish some of the time, for 3/4 of our Regt. are coughing, having been so long without tents.

The evening is taken up by examining the regulations, to know what our duties really are. Visitors are generally so plenty that we can hardly post ourselves.

Then comes the weekly & monthly report, besides the Statement of the Hospital fund. All these have to be made out according to regulations, and it takes a good amount of ruling, writing etc.

The mail has just been opened, and still no letter. You must have written, perhaps you did not direct right, you should direct to W.S.N. Asst. Surg. 91st Reg. OVG Gauley Bridge, Fayette Co., Va.

If you direct in this way, I will get the letter, and if we move, they will follow us. If I do not get a letter pretty soon, I shall try to get a leave of absence.

And this would only make a bad matter worse, for I should dislike to return very much, so I do not think of it, at present.

Our officers are generally well. Lt. Erwin[29] is in Hospital at Pt. Pleasant, where we left 62 men. We left 33 in Charleston, only a few have joined us. We lost not a man during the month of Oct., while regiments have lost 15 or 20. We may lose some before this month is out. I am satisfied that this march will tell upon our regiment before the winter is over.

We are in a hard place to get anything to eat. Chicken, pigs, etc. cannot be subsisted here, all is brought up the river in battens[30] and wagons, and there is not more than half rations issued to many Regts. While some have not had hard bread for two days, and flour has not been seen in camp for ten days.

Yet we cannot for the life of us, tell what we are kept here for, or what good will result from our guarding these poor hills & hollows, for the Rebels have long since skedaddled, and we are here for no purpose so it seems, to me.

You must write soon and often. Give my love to all. Kiss the babies etc.

Yours
Wm. S. Newton

13

Gauley Bridge Nov. 14th 1862

My Dear Wife

This is Friday evening, and as I have finished the duties of the day, I know no better employment than in this poor way of conversing with you, for I must say it affords but little satisfaction when I consider how long, *if ever*, in reaching you, this letter will be, I am almost discouraged about writing.

You will acknowledge that to a man who has been accustomed to sit by his own fireside, with his own wife & children, the comforts of home, then to be sit down on this barren side hill, no comforts except those afforded by a thin Sibley tent, filled with smoke and dirt, saddles, bridles, bread boxes, indeed all the traps belonging to four persons & one darkie. One darkie, John the Sutler, we paid, and discharged today. He got lazy and negligent. If I only had a young one, I could train him in such a way, that he would do our cooking & care for the horses too. Old Henry is a very faithful servant, always here, but so slow that it takes his whole time to cook & cut.

Kirker is also writing to his wife. We are both leaning on my bunk, and were it not that we are able to talk of home & converse of things past and gone, our situation would be almost intolerable.

Ricker, as you know, is Quartermaster, and messes with us. So you see we will always have something to eat if there is anything for the Regt. Newton Warwick, a brother of the doctor, is also with us, and we now have a very pleasant mess, and if we can have it thus all the time, it is all right. But on the march, tents were so scarce that we were compelled to take in more than we could well accommodate, even the niggers sometimes. And here this puts me in mind of an item. One night I felt something crawling. I struck a light and found in my drawers one of the rebel body lice. As soon as convenient, I stripped every dud, put on clean ones, and then commenced search. I found three or four more on my woolen shirt. After two or three hours spent thus, I wrapped the whole tight in a paper till morning, thinking if there were any eggs or little ones, Henry should scald the life out of them, all of which was duly executed. I told my experience in the morning, the others all being asleep during my search. I told them they were all lousy, and demanded a search. The next evening Newt found plenty of them. Sterneman[31] too had his share. But Kirker went to the woods when he made search. He denied finding any and I suppose we will have to take his word for it. I tell you we are on the watch for them, and make no bones of stripping for an examination at any time. I think we are pretty clear of them, and we do not intend to shelter the darkies again, for undoubtedly this is the manner we got them, as our boy John had worn cast off clothes, those worn by Toland's Zouaves, and they were lousy enough before we started from Pt. Pleasant. These lice are a curiosity. I had never seen one before. They are about the size of half a grain of coffee, with gray backs, and I do not think they stay on the body, but bore their heads into the clothes. As a matter of course, they must bite some time, but I never felt one. If you have any traps down there, it would be a good investment to come this way, for I am certain they could be sold in great numbers, if only effectual in destroying the vermin. I wrote a letter to the boys, although I had not received theirs. I hope they will read it attentively and profit by it. They are now old enough to reason and understand the necessity of the course I have advised. Hope you will impress it upon them.

General Crook, with two Brigades, has arrived from Summerville. They are fresh from the battlefields of the Potomac. They came down the Gauley, passed our camp, and stopped some five miles below us. Col. E. B. Andrews, Quartermaster Barber of the 36th are along. I rode down to see them yesterday afternoon, and spent a very pleasant hour with Col. Andrews. I met Barber on the way. He seemed very glad to see me, and promised to come up and see me.

My pants have not come yet. I have a regulation pair just like the soldiers, but they would not do on a Review very well. I still live in hope.

It is now eleven o'clock. The rest all in bed, and if I only had a woman to go to bed to, I do not believe it would be more than an hour till I too would be in bed. Oh, what a thought. I do not permit myself to think of such things very often, but old appreciations will sometimes crowd themselves upon us. Where we will go, or where winter is still shrouded in mystery.

Newton R. Warwick, was from Scioto County, Ohio, and younger brother of John B. Warwick. He rose to the rank of second lieutenant in the 91st Ohio Volunteer Infantry and was mentioned in several of William S. Newton's letters. 2nd Lt. N. R. Warwick, Eugene B. Willard Photograph Album, Special Collections, Marietta College, Marietta, Ohio.

Keep writing letters. They are worth something if they are old. Tell that I do not get the pie, but do have hard crackers, and occasionally a piece of cheese. This is a luxury to us.

Good night,
Your Husband.

14

Camp Gauley Nov. 23rd 1862

Dear Wife

This is Sabbath eve and I have received no letter today. This makes me lonesome, not that I have not company enough or plenty to do, for I have both, yet it is not exactly the right kind. Another thing, the Adjutant's wife came riding up in an ambulance this morning, took us all by surprise, and looked so much like a woman made us all think of home, and that there were other women in America.

So you see a mail arrived, but it turned out to be a *female*, enough for one man, but not enough for a thousand. I think if left to the popular vote, we would have elected the paper or letter mail, one for each officer & private.

Another important arrival, was three ambulances for our Regt., but am sorry to say the horses attached were all running at the nose, and we very much fear will give all the other horses the distemper. My horse I think is getting better of his lameness. At least, the symptoms are more favorable at present.

We are still on this hill, and may stay longer if they are able to feed us, and possibly may steer us further into starvation. We are hoping now that they will be compelled to send us nearer the source of supply. Our horses have corn but no hay. If we could see any use of this, or any good to be derived, it would be different. No Regt. or Co. of Rebels could subsist here for a single week, and for thirty miles down the river it is the same way. I don't know a better strategic movement than for us to move down and allow the Rebels to come in, for they would certainly starve here. We are short sighted and cannot perhaps see the wisdom of it. The Med. Inspector was around today giving directions, and caused me to issue an order for remodeling our camp. Cooking our beans etc., the rule is five hours. They make the doctors responsible for a great many things, one half of which if properly attended to would keep us entirely out of mischief. How is Mrs. Ricker getting on with little Aleck,[32] is he any better of his Hernia? How is Mr. Johnson, is he getting better of his lameness? How does the church prosper? Is Mr. Reeve[33] any notion of going to war, in short tell us all the news. Our Col. will probably take command of his Regt. tomorrow. The sentence of the Court

Martial has not been made public, but there is no doubt of his coming out in flying colours.

Write soon & often, give my regards to all enquiring friends. Your Husband

Wm. S. Newton

15

Camp Gauley Nov. 28th 1862

Dear Wife

Yours came to hand today, and I was pleased to learn you had left off boarding or rather that your boarders had left you. I hope you gave them to understand how much you appreciated their company. I received a letter from Sister Mary a day or two since, by Major Adney[34] of the 36 Regt., and by the way she writes, would not think strange if she enlisted in his company sometime. As a matter of course this is contraband and you must not say anything about it.

She gave me more information about affairs at Marietta than I have received for a long time before. And as she & Lucy expect to visit you, I need not detail any of it.

Our old cook Henry left us on Tuesday last. He wanted to see the old girl, as he left her at Pt. Pleasant to make her way to Albany, a town near Athens, Ohio. He was very anxious to learn her condition. He had been a faithful servant to us and I was sorry to see him go. We paid him 30 dollars for the two months. I have since got one at 10 per month that I like much better, is a good cook, and smart enough to saddle a horse, chop wood etc. His name is Charley Boreland. His master lives 12 miles below Charleston, has a splendid farm, but a rebel of the blackest kind.

Charley told me today that he wanted to go home with me when the war was over. I told him he might do so, if a good boy. The 2nd Va. Cavalry made quite a nice dash at the Rebels two days ago at Sinking Creek, in Greenbriar Co. some 40 miles from us.

They captured 112 Rebels, 120 horses, guns, tents, etc. In proportion, they passed our camp late this evening with the mounted prisoners, and two companies of the 91st have just been detailed to guard them. I learn that the infantry prisoners are just passing, but as it is dark, I will not go to see them. The Rebel Cavalry are a sorry looking set, with every possible colored blankets & clothes, old straw hats, ropes for bridles, and some were without rope halters even.

I think I shall visit them tomorrow, if I can get time, I may find some old acquaintances.

I suppose we are still destined for Fayetteville. Hard bread & coffee have been so slow coming up the river, or we would have moved before this. If it is so difficult to supply us here, I do not know what they will do twelve miles further on. I must stop tonight, and if I have an opportunity I will write more tomorrow. Give my regards to all, tell the boys to so conduct themselves that their father will always be proud of them.

Your Husband
Wm. S. Newton

16

Camp Gauley Nov. 29th

Dear Wife

I just received yours of the 25th with postage stamps. Am very much obliged for them, and went to the letter box and opened the one accompanying this. I also put a stamp on it. The box I learn, is at Camp Piatt some 30 miles below this, in care of some Chaplain. Whether he will bring it up with him is in question. The letter by Alvin Stimson,[35] also commission, all came right side up. Stimson is not well, is just the same, as before he went to Ironton.

The woolen socks I do not want yet, as I have not worn these I have with me. Should we go up into the mountains much further, I expect I will need them, for two soldiers froze to death up there & some of 2nd Va. Cavalry on the last scout were left in Hospital with their feet & hands frozen. The cold must be intense. I expect great pleasure upon the reception of your cherry turnovers. Much love to all, Your Husband

17

Camp Gauley Dec. 5th 1862

Dear Wife

Having an opportunity to send this by Mr. English,[36] a brother of whom is in Hospital here and belongs to our Regt.

Received a letter today, from Brother Steve and another from Doug. They had a fine dinner at Mothers on Thanksgiving day. All there except Jane, and from the letters, they think it is no joke. S. says it is the rye coffee that has done it all. He also says that they have been taking it clear at his house but it has done no good yet. Doug & Fuller are at home still, awaiting orders.

Your box has not made its appearance yet, but we are anxiously expecting it by our teams tomorrow, as they went to Camp Piatt two days ago. I shall give it up, if it does not come by them. Ricker will be on the look out for it.

My horse is yet lame, but think he will be able to carry me over to Fayetteville on Sunday or Monday next, as we have orders to move when our teams return. I learned we are to go about five miles beyond Fayetteville on widow Huddleston's[37] farm. Said to have two fine daughters.

I also received a letter from Em, and have answered it. Told Will to send me a barrel of corn meal. We have most got tired of Hard Bread. And as our boy Charley makes good cornbread I thought we would get a supply. By the way, we think Charley is one of the best darkies living. When old Henry left us, we thought we were broken up, but Charley is worth 4 of him.

He has a wife & boy baby at his old master's still and is quite uneasy about them. If I knew anyone who would take them for their work, I would send them to Ohio for his sake. Carpenter has been ordered to his Regt., and we have been looking for him daily.

But we today received notice that he had been granted a sick leave of absence for twenty days.

Unless he comes, I do not see how I am to get home. Unless I too get sick, in that case I might perhaps get off, but there would be no satisfaction in coming home sick. For when I go, I want to feel all right, not even a pain in my back.

Still direct your letters to 91st Regt. Gauley, for we can never tell what a day may bring forth in the army. They may take a notion that we can't be fed, and send us down the river. Providence grant that this may be [the] case. I would like to take a Christmas with you, but have no hope of such event at the present time. I sent Lieut. Neal home sick, and I fear he will be very sick. Should have sent some days sooner, but Red tape has prevented, I promised his mother to do so, when I left Gallipolis. His disease is Typhoid Pneumonia, and I would give anything if he was only safe at home now, and did not have to make the trip. Have got a good ambulance driver, and he will take all the care necessary.

Give my regards to Mr. R. & family. Take something a little more fervent for yourself & the babies. Your Husband.

2

The More Strange Faces You See the More Lonely You Are, December 1862–March 1863

William S. Newton spent most of the winter of 1862–1863 stationed at Fayetteville, West Virginia. The winter months were extremely cold, and snow was a constant through January. With some assistance, he built a small cabin that he shared with officers of the 91st. Little happened in the way of military encounters, but he did mention the more frequent interactions with local families who are southerners, or the "secesh." There was some sickness in the camp, including a mumps outbreak and a case of pneumonia, but there were few wounded for Newton to care for. Supply lines were steady, with Newton receiving letters and tasty food from home on a regular basis. Some of the homemade food arrived spoiled or not at all because of pilfering by Union soldiers during transit.

Much of Newton's food was prepared by Charley Boreland, a runaway slave who attached himself to the 91st the previous fall. Newton bragged on Charley's cooking, especially a surprise apple pie that all enjoyed to celebrate the new year. During this period, Charley asked for permission to return to his former owner's home near Charleston and free his wife and child, who were still in bondage. Newton agreed to Charley's plan and suggested that if successful, Charley's wife could stay with the Newton family in Ironton. In late February, Charley set out to free his wife and child, but he did not return.

In mid-February, Newton briefly visited his family. The letters gave few details of his visit, but the following November (covered in chapter 5), approximately nine months later, his wife gave birth to a son. Even with the short visit home, the combination of cold weather, static positioning, and lack of action contributed to Newton's homesickness. He wrote constantly about how lonely he was and suggested that one of his sons, preferably Ned, try to visit him. The letters also referred to Ned's growing behavior problems at home, which was likely the inspiration for having Ned join him in camp. He even admitted that he had difficulty remembering what his young daughter's face looked like. Newton suffered from rheumatism and responded to reports of poor family health. He provided a prescription for his wife, who had sore eyes and a cough. Newton discussed the death of his sister-in-law Jane (John Newton's third wife), most likely of complications from childbirth. Finally, in March, Newton and his wife began numbering letters, seemingly to keep track of when letters were received and to establish a chronology in the face of uncertain supply and mail lines.

18

Camp Turley Near Fayetteville Va. Dec. 9th/62

Dear Wife

Yours of 30th Nov. reached me today, I presume I should have got it sooner, had it not been for the move here.

We started on Sunday morning, leaving Camp Gauley at seven, marched 3 miles down to the falls of Kanawha, where we crossed over and commenced the ascent of Cotton Mountain. It was very cold, and I gave my horse to one of the Hospital boys and started on foot in the advance. We were very much hindered by the Post train teams, which had commenced the ascent about one hour before us. I marched on and on, thinking I certainly soon reach the top, having heard it was four miles up, and the same distance down. I asked a teamster how far it was yet, and when he told me about a mile, I was astonished, yet I trudged on, and at length made the top, marched along the top about a mile, and then could look off to my left, and see the camp we left in the morning. By this time noon had come, and the five mile walk made me hungry. My haversack was well supplied with crackers, cheese & billona from Kirker's meat shop in Ironton. But water there was none, plenty of snow covered the mountain but the more I ate, the more thirsty I became. The little drummer boy Gilbert[1] came along and told me he was going ahead, and if I would come on, he would have a cup of coffee ready for me. I accepted the invitation, thinking no more about it, but as I was passing the mouth of a coal bank, he hollered to me, that my coffee was ready for me. I could not get in, but he brought it out with the crackers all soaked good.

We now began the descent, and when I had almost accomplished it, became so fatigued, I sat down to wait for my horse. He soon came up, and I then rode on to camp, three miles from Fayette. We were halted to wait for our Regt. teams to come up. They came so late, we camped, for the night, in snow three inches deep, While the boys were pitching tents, I went to a house nearby, and engaged supper for two, Col. Turley & self. We found the ladies, secesh all over, yet very polite and agreeable. The husband of one, a prisoner taken by Capt. Hambleton a few days before, also in the house. He was good looking, but quite reserved at first. He finally told us his position, that he was a prisoner, and compelled to report himself once a week to the Genl. He talked freely of the war, and its cause, acknowledged that the South were mistaken in the sentiment of the North, that they supposed every man who voted the republican ticket was a hot headed abolitionist, etc. He was quite intelligent, asked grace at the table, made themselves as hospitable as rebels could, in short gave us a good supper, good biscuit, milk, etc. The Col. was called to prevent our men from running off with all the straw they had, to feed the cows. As we had been drinking the milk, of course the Col. must afford protection to the cows. I soon after left, giving the woman a dollar for our suppers. We slept cold and were glad to start at day break for Fayetteville, where we arrived before many of the officers belonging to the other Regt's were up. The 4th Va., 12th & 34th Ohio were all encamped in the town, and we were halted 1/2 mile out, and told to camp. Only one log stable near us, this I soon appropriated for my horse, and then went over to town to look for a house suitable for a Hospital. Med. Director gave me a choice of three, I chose one, now occupied by Zouaves. They promise to empty it tomorrow. Could you see the destruction of property here, you would not wish the war near you. Very few houses have any windows left, even the sash is gone, and nice ones with half the weather boards torn off.

We left 1/2 the Regt. at Gauley, as the teams could not transport us all. The teams left this morning for the left wing, and if they are not hindered will get over tomorrow eve. Warwick stayed back with the other half. Carpenter has not yet come to us, and sometimes I think will not, although he has been ordered to do so. Should he come I might get an opportunity to go home, yet I dare not think of it, for it makes me feel homesick. If I could just look in once more, and see how you all look, it would afford me much pleasure, yet when I think how short my stay would be, I almost dread the starting from home again.

On Saturday morning last, I received a dispatch from Fuller, announcing the death of sister Jane. As a matter of course, the Ironton relatives went up to the funeral, as they were to keep the remains for several days. I dispatched "that it was impossible for me to leave my Regt. at this time."

I had just the day before received a letter from Brother Steve joking no little at the prospect in store for them, the cause etc., and I had answered somewhat in the same tone, was very sorry after it had gone, but I presume he will not say anything about it or show John the letter. I do deeply sympathize with him, for he will hardly try again, at least I would not, for I should think the fates were against me. I have had no trouble lately about letters, the box has not come and I presume will not. Should you send anything again don't direct it to a Quartermaster, for they think they have a right to steal from them.

What did you send in the box that came to Mr. Kirker I could not tell, for only the plums had a label, and of course all others were considered public property. I brought the plums over with me, but they froze and bursted, and now I am afraid I cannot keep them till Christmas as I had intended. I am very glad the boys try to be good for I know they will succeed. My love to you all. Take care of your health. Your Husband

Wm. S. Newton

19

Camp Fayetteville Dec. 16th 1862

Dear Wife

Yours of 7th Ult came yesterday, having written on Friday Last. I did not answer immediately, but will try in part this eve. You must not sew at all if your eyes are weak, but get Mr. Wright[2] to give you Iodide Potass[ium] 3i Syr Sarsaparilla 3ii. Mix, then take a teaspoonful every six hours. Beside, take about a tea spoonful of Epsom Salts every morning, till they are better. I should think you might get some one to do your sewing by paying the money. I do not wish you to injure your health, or disfigure yourself to save a few dollars merely. For if the Paymaster ever comes, I shall have some, and I am trying to be very saving. Yet should feel very poorly paid for all my exposure & self denial. If when I came home, found you without *eyes*, or *even* with *sore ones*. I do not think there is any part of ones self, so important as the eyes.

We are still very busy building quarters, and quite a town has sprung up in a very few days. I have come to the conclusion that I will not do mine myself. If they build the quarters I will fix my cabin up as well as anyone. They have so changed the program, that mine will be so far from my stable, it will have to be moved or I will have to build another. So I am going to wait results. I can keep warm in my Sibley and here I will stay if they provide nothing better. I wish you to give Mr. Kimball a note which I will enclose in this, in reference to my taxes. I should like very much to be with you on Christmas, but as Carpenter has not yet joined us, I feel that the prospect is dull indeed. The health of the Regt. is about the same and I do not look for any improvement till they have more comfortable quarters. I had expected Lucy would be with you ere this, at least Mary's letter so indicated. But the death of Jane will perhaps prevent such a pleasure. My horse has almost recovered, and very proudly carried me through Fayetteville yesterday. If nothing happens him or me, will bring him home when the war is over.

Tell the boys if they were here, they could find bullets enough, for they are very plenty on the battleground as well as dead horses & soldiers graves. Write often if your eyes will let you, if not don't do it. Your Husband

Wm. S. Newton

20

Camp Fayetteville Dec. 21st

Dear Wife

I have only time to write a line by one of our Lieutenants who is summoned home to be with a wife in her last moments. His name is Wycoff[3] of Adams Co.

I looked for a letter from you last eve but did not get it. I suppose there is a screw loose somewhere.

We are having very cold weather at the present time. I manage to keep warm and sleep warm by piling on the blankets, coats etc. But I know of a *nest* that I would prefer to occupy to this, and if you were not very good at guessing, you might name the place. However, there are hundreds of men here that feel the same way.

Tell the boys they must be good, and Kate that her Papa will come home and see her some day. Write soon and often. If Mr. Kirker comes home, and you can get some good Canton flannel[4] you may send another pair of drawers. Make them a little larger, these seem flimsy and thin, and I have had to mend both pair. Still, I am not suffering, and if your eyes are sore don't you try to make them. If you can send a pair or two of socks that are good ones. I will not wear cotton till the weather moderates a little. I shall try to send by Kirker a pair of pants and boots that are no longer of use to me here. My regards to all.

Your Husband
Wm. S. Newton
Asst. Surg. 91st Regt. O.V.I

21

Camp Fayetteville Dec 25th

Dear Wife

Your last came on Wednesday last, a long time coming at least, I thought so, and as I had written before, did not answer immediately.

This is Christmas evening, and I feel very tired, for I have the men employed in building a chimney to my cabin, and you know I must have a hand in it. The fact is I can get but little done unless I am on the ground. I had calculated to take dinner in it today, and would have done so, had not Col. Turley employed all the teams yesterday in moving a building for his quarters. I am in no hurry about it now, and will not go in till the mud I have used for dabbing it gets a little dry. I have built 14 by 16 feet, with a good generous fireplace in one end, and will now be comfortable, for wood & water are convenient.

Charley will have his kitchen tent at one end and seems pleased with his future prospect of new quarters. My door and floor are yet to be made. I have a few boards in my tent, which will be applied in that way, the rest will be of puncheon.[5] Some of our Captains have made really fine quarters in this way. But oh fiddle, what is a cabin, or anything else without that necessary piece of furniture, *a wife Oh me miserum.*[6] Why entertain such thoughts or emotions.

You no doubt can appreciate somewhat that degree of loneliness which comes over one when they allow themselves to think of former associations and enjoyments, shut up here with a thousand men, very few of whom have any interest in the things that interest you, here to stay, the more strange faces you see the more lonely you are. Nor is our Regt. the only one, three others, a Battery, and part of 2nd Va. Cavalry, are all encamped so near that the bugle sound at Headquarters is distinctly heard by all. Yet so little interest is felt, that I have but once left camp to visit other Regts., except compelled by business. The fact is, I am content to stay at home, and attend strictly to my own affairs. After this, if I have any time, it is employed in writing to you, or reading when I have anything worth the reading which is not very often.

I have not yet received answers from my letters from Marietta & Harmar, indeed I have no particulars of the death of Jane, except what you gave me. I suspect her disease was not apoplexy but *Puerperal Convulsions,*[7] incident to her condition at the time, although not a very common occurrence yet enough so, to make it pretty certain.

I should really like to have Ned or Mott come up here awhile, and if it were not such a long and difficult road to travel, would do so. Mr. Kirker's leave of absence has not yet been approved. He has again made application, whether he will be successful this time remains yet to be seen. Give my love to all, and a Happy New Year to yourself.

Your Husband
Wm. S. Newton

22

Camp Fayetteville Dec. 28th

Dear Wife

Your last came through in four days, and was really refreshing. I hope they may all take the same route, and come with the same speed.

This is Sabbath, I have prescribed for 26 patients, taken a good wash, put on clean clothes, and now sit down to write you a short epistle. I moved in my cabin yesterday. Kirker & Newton Warwick are still with me, and the ample fire last eve cheered us not a little.

I made a table and window blinds for both windows after dark. With a few other improvements which I have in contemplation, we will be quite comfortable.

As to Albert Campbell, he is quite well now, and looks very fresh and hearty. But while we were at Gauley, he looked badly. Someone had stolen his blanket & I judge he must have suffered for the want of it. Kirker found it out and told me. I gave him the one you marked, and he has it yet, for there has been no opportunity to draw one.

He & Jonny Campbell[8] never complain, always ready for duty. In short, I am proud of the boys. If they don't make regulars there is no use in talking. Thomas Coles is also just as good. It would surprise you, to see them accommodate themselves to circumstances. Boys that have been raised as they have been are truly an example for all others. Our boys are now granted a few furloughs. It is about the only excitement we have in camp at present.

Lieut. Col. Coates leaves in the morning for home, and to attend the Ohio Senate of which he is a member. I will send this by him.

If I could only have the same prospect for home would not wait till tomorrow, but start tonight and keep a going. If I could just slip in the evening without anyone knowing it, I think I could spend 24 hours without going down street.

I am very sorry to hear that the boys quarrel & dispute. If brothers cannot agree, how will they get along when they go out into the world and associate with strangers. I fear they will not make for themselves many friends.

Tell them for me, that I hope another report of the same kind will never reach me.

Was called yesterday about a mile from camp to attend one U.S. teamsters at a secesh house where they had left him. The lady came for me herself and the Capt. & Lieutenants had quite a laugh, that a woman came to my cabin so soon after my occupation of it. But what troubled them most, she was quite good looking and quite lady like. I am to visit them again this eve on the same errand.

Don't forget to write often. My regards to all enquiring friends.

Your Husband
Wm. S. Newton

23

Camp Fayetteville Jany 1st 1863

Dear Wife

I am looking for your last tonight, as the one before came on Thursday, and I shall feel disappointed if it does not come.

This is New Year and we had a first rate pie for dinner made of apples. Charley brought it in just before we were done, and took us by surprise. Where the nigger got the apples we do not know, but we enjoyed it hugely. Capt. Caldwell presented me nice butter, so you see we did not starve this 1st Jany 1863.

I received a letter from Mary. She has about given up the idea of visiting you this winter, is afraid to start alone. They seem much cast down about Jane's death. It certainly was very sudden. Doug is pumping 40 barrels of oil per day, and selling it at ten dollars per barrel. He is getting rich very fast. I am afraid it will spoil him, are you not; Mr. Kirker I suppose will start for home tomorrow. If he does he will take this to you. It may come my time next.

We had quite a panic since I wrote you. Our Regt. was the first set on the list to get down to Tennessee. But by some hocus pocus we are here still, and are now brigaded with the 12th and 34th with Col. Toland as our commander, he being the oldest Col. in the Brigade. The 4th Va. started on three hours notice, and the 91st would have liked to bear them company. We have been together so long I could have cried when I bid goodbye to Dr. Philson[9] & Dr. Dayton[10] if it would accomplish anything. By the way, this is the same Major Dayton who followed and shot Major Phelps[11] for the intimacy with his sister, and we all felt, however much she has sinned in this matter, her brother is every inch a gentleman.

Indeed, the officers of the 4th were our warmest friends in this valley, an[d w]e were very sorry to part with them. The 9[2]nd have been ordered to take the place of the 47th on Tompkins Farm,[12] three miles above Gauley on the New River. Just in sight of our old camp in Gauley.

Have not seen Dr. Cotton[13] for a month, as they have been distant from us, some 5 to 15 miles all this time. His asst., Dr. Howell,[14] called on me today, and gave me all the news in reference to them. He is detailed to a battery now in our Brigade. Our force is now so small here, I should not wonder if the Rebs came in force, and made us skedaddle out of here. I suppose you would not care much, provided we get out with whole skins. It is not at all unlikely that we all move farther down the river to Camp Piatt & Charleston.

The roads over Cotton Mountain are terrible and subsisting an army on this side of it, a very difficult undertaking. I have not seen Kirker for some six weeks. He is below, busy in transporting provisions up the valley. I send some more men today, to Genl. Hospital at Pt. Pleasant.

I do not think there are so many sick in the Regt. of late. Carpenter has not yet joined us, and whether he is at home or where we do not know. I have my stable up and my horse in it. Now if we could only have some hay, he w[ould] be all right. We have had none for five or six weeks, and he shows it too.

I hope you are enjoying the holidays at Ironton, for there is not much here. Ask Kate if she is not most ready to come up and act as matron to our Hospital. By the way, I was so glad to see Clarke's letter in the [Ironton] Register in reference to the schools.[15] It was timely and to the point. How do the people feel now, have they not hurt themselves more than they have injured others? I think so.

Newt has been quite sick, but is now a good deal better. I do not like to have him sick, for he is a good fellow. When Kirker goes, he and I will be alone in our cabin. If I could only have my wife here, I would soon chase him off. No such *good luck* for me however.

This has been a busy week for us, our annual & monthly reports to make. The amount of Hospital stores & medicines all to be invoiced and sent to Surgeon Genl. in duplicate. The new supplies also came, and a report of their condition and quality sent back to the Med. Purveyor at Cincinnati.

So you see I am kept busy, not time to think or get homesick. I am glad it is so, for the time fairly flies while thus engaged.

Hope the boys will be good, with the beginning of the new year, for it is a good [tim]e to turn over a new leaf, and if I hear such a [re]port, I will remember them when the Paymaster comes, whether I am permitted to go home or not.

Have not heard one word from Gallipolis for a long time, think they might write occasionally. I expect the boy baby is all the matter they can attend to at present.

Remember me to all enquiring friends, especially to my dear wife & children. Kiss Kate for me, *twenty times.*

Your Husband
Wm. S. Newton

Friday morning. Your letter did not come on Christmas night. I got the last. Kirker starts this morning and oh if it was only me, it is now going on the fourth month since I saw home, a long time for me. Yet I will not despair. Much love to all.

24

Fayetteville Jany 3rd 1863

My Dear Wife

Yours of 28th Ultimo came last eve, and I think I have received all the others. You did right to direct yours to this place, and from present appearances, we will be here for some time to come.

I am very sorry to hear you have a cough, and you should take measures to get rid of it at once, the neglect of this would be almost criminal.

Take the following

Rx Fluid Ext. Senegou 3i

Spits Nitre Dulce 3i

Paregoric Elixir 3ii

Dose 30 to 40 drops every 6 hours. Mix

Mr. Wright will take a copy of it, and paste on the bottle, so that you can renew it if necessary. Now don't neglect it. Should the boys get Diphtheria, use Mur Tinct of Iron & Chlorate Potash, for a gurgle. But call Dr. Wilson and let him judge what is best, the case may be complicated with something else.

We have had beautiful weather for the past three days. Too pleasant to stay in if one had any place to go. But I presume it will not last long. Should like to use it in traveling toward home.

As you say it, it may not be this winter. I do not wish to go till the Paymaster comes, if it is not till next August. For when I come, I want to be able to straighten up all my business, pay all my debts etc. If Mr. Kirker wants to bring the boys let them come, for it will be an event they will never forget in the history of this country. Not that I have anything to busy Ned about, but I thought it would relieve you somewhat. Should he come, Mott will have to be very industrious, and help his Mother all he possibly can.

If Ned has good boots, hat, and warm clothes, it does not much matter how they look. Give him a coverlid,[16] comfort or something to wrap around him while riding up. Mr. Kirker can telegraph me at Charleston, on what would be better. From Gallipolis, and I can send an ambulance to Camp Piatt when the boats come. If Mr. Kirker does not bring Will, Ned had better not come, for unless they both come I do not think it best to take the trouble. Perhaps I may get an opportunity to come home, and then I will be able to see you all.

Newt Warwick says, "tell Ned he must bring all the books he can raise or pick up dime novels or anything else." He is a great reader, has now nothing but the dictionary, and he has been reading that for two evenings.

You can form no idea how many times a book will be read in camp if only permitted to go the rounds. I purchased three pounds of butter today at 30 cts. I wrote to Will to send some in a barrel of Corn Meal the first opportunity. I am getting very tired of hard bread, but today we had very good light bread issued to the Regt. Newt & I ate almost a whole loaf for supper. This is Saturday eve, and if I could only spend the morrow at my own home how different my feelings would be. Do the best you can, and what *you think* for the best in all things.

Your Husband
Wm. S. Newton

25

Camp Fayetteville Jan 8th/63

Dear Wife

I am again looking for a letter from you. I expect it will come tonight, and as many of our men are getting furloughs, it makes me anxious to go home. But the way to do it looks as dark as ever. Our Med. Director is an old bachelor, and cannot appreciate home and its endearments. I told him so last Sabbath, and hinted to him after pay day some of the Med Staff would want a leave of absence. Whether he will take the hint is a serious question. Mr. Kirker's leave of absence has not yet come, if you see him tell him, but don't say anything to anyone else, for he would not like to have it known and there is no doubt but it will come all right.

I saw a [Cincinnati Daily] Commercial of 3rd and it does me good to learn how Rosecrans[17] whipped them. Things begin to brighten and I hope it will not be long before this wicked rebellion is crushed. How many anxious souls are now waiting the arrival home of loved ones, and how many will be compelled to mourn the loss that can never be replaced in this world. How many are now lying cold in death.

This is not worse than the great number who now lie sick and emaciated in the many hospitals of our country. Our Regt. grows small, only 560 were reported fit for duty on dress parade the last time. 16 commissioned officers absent, just about half, the most of these on sick leave. So you see it is not those who fight only, whose ranks are thinned, but all suffer more or less. Could you see the anxiety of these men, when they cast lots to determine who shall have furloughs, you would, like some of the disappointed ones, drop a tear with them, in their almost despair.

Had I the power, I would give them furloughs much more liberally than it is now done.

Some of our commanders are very jealous of their power in this respect, and will not hear any advice on the subject.

My drawers are getting very thin, and if you cannot get a good piece of Canton Flannel, I would make them of drilling.[18]

My boy Charley is getting very uneasy about his wife and boy, and wants to move them out of Va. I try to quiet his fears, but he thinks if they were safe, he would come back contented. His wife is a good cook, washer & ironer. How would you like to take them in till we come home. If you would like it, I would give him a pass to Ironton, let him leave her there, and return to me again. I never saw her, this is his story, and if she is half as faithful as Charley, you can make her useful to you.

Let me hear from you on the subject. He will have to steal her away from her master, who is all-over secesh, lives fifteen miles below Charleston, is the owner of Charley also. I have tried to persuade him to leave her there till we move down but he is afraid we will be in too big a hurry for him to get his wife.

We are having a light fall of snow and when it clears up we may expect cold weather for a while. Write as often as you find time.

Your Husband

26

Fayetteville Va., Jany 11th 63

Dear Wife

Yours of the 4th did not come till last evening. Had almost given up, but it came at last and it was very welcome, although I did not know it was Saturday night, thinking all the time it was Friday, and as it rained all day I did not have my Sunday's wood prepared, consequently some had to be chopped today. Charley, being a hard shell Baptist, did not like to break the Sabbath, so I helped him so as to divide the responsibility.

Warren Hibbard[19] has been with us two days. He left again for Loup Creek this morning, where he is stationed at a receiving depot. Think he is having a good time with the Miss Huddlestons[20] with whom he is boarding, they are regular Secesh. Newt & Dr. Warwick got a very nice lot of things from home yesterday. In the eating line were canned peaches, blackberry jam, butter, light bread, short biscuit doughnuts, apples & apple butter. Dr. being at Hospital, they divided the spoils, so you see for a few days we will be all right. I never saw a better selection, and if they had only come in good time, would have been all that any epicure could wish. The pies were moldy, and the cakes in a very good state of preservation, considering that they were more than twenty days on the way. Will has not sent my corn meal yet, but I presume it is on the way. Perhaps at Piatt. Two or three teams will go and come from there this week. Mr. Kirker's papers have not yet come, and I do not know why. I enquired for them at Col's quarters last evening, thinking they might have sent them there.

We have no exciting news about our camp. A prisoner is occasionally captured at the out posts, and the 2nd Va. Cavalry do something in this way. They are out toward Lewisburg on a scout at this time. Their business is only known at the headquarters of Genl. Scammon. Sometimes I think it is doubtful, whether he knows. Col. Paxton generally accomplishes something when he goes however.

You asked about the pillow bed etc. On the march I carried the pillow & comfort. Carefully in the old trunk as you saw it start, but at Gauley I procured a good bunk and tick, filled the latter with hay that served as packing, in the Med. Stores & boxes. So with the blankets, comfort and pillow, I have quite a respectable bed, and many times when I lie down at night, bless the woman who had foresight enough to insist that I should bring it. For you will remember, I opposed the bringing of the pillow, but would not like now to part with it. Dr. Cowan of 34th Regt. gave me a pair of slips for it, also a pair of sheets. The latter I have never used, am waiting till I get a woman to sleep with, for it would be too great a luxury to be able to *strip off all* and get between sheets alone.

We are now quite comfortable in our log cabins, and if the Rebels do not disturb us, we shall not suffer from cold or storm. So long as they furnish rations, we will not complain, yet we would like to see our own firesides, furnished with that other piece of furniture which I think has before been mentioned.

Col. Turley told me last eve that he had a notion to send for his twelve year old boy to come to camp, whether he will is yet in doubt. If Mr. Kirker is willing to be troubled with the boys, let them come.

Have had quite a lot of weddings for Ironton. I should think it would almost make you grass widows[21.] willing to try it again. What say you?

It is getting late. Taps have sounded so good night.

Your Husband.
Wm.S.N.

27

Camp Fayetteville Jany 15th

Dear Wife

As one of our Hospital corps goes home on furlough, I thought would write you a few lines which he will leave at the Wharf Boat, unless the boat stops long enough. If so, he will probably call to you, his name is Wm Jones,[22] a first rate man, & one I can trust to any extent.

Am not at all well today. Have a slight attack of Rheumatism, my shoulder & breast are the seat of pain at this time, and I hold surgeons call this morning under many aches and pains, yet I hope it will be of short duration, for it reminds one of the comforts of home very distinctly. I have been so well all the time.

I have no news to communicate, and as I write with a good amount of suffering, shall not extend my letter to a great length.

Tell the children they must all be good.

Your Husband
Wm. S. Newton

28

Fayetteville Jany 18th 1863

Dear Wife

Yours of 11th came yesterday, and I was very glad to get it, yet was not pleased to hear of Ned's retrograde movement in the schools, and I cannot think he has been studying but spending his time idly and to no purpose.

I have written to him, hoping it will stir him up to better things hereafter. I am afraid he has lost all pride in such things, for if he cared anything about it, it seems to me he would work to maintain his position.

Our quarters for the first two days have been anything but pleasant, for the snow comes through in torrents and covers our faces and heads while sleeping. I have often thought what you would do under similar circumstances. I spent one whole day trying to stop the cracks, but the wind would send the snow under in spite of me.

Last night was one of the coldest I have experienced in this camp, yet I could, if all the surroundings had been right, keep very comfortable. I should want a bed in the *first place*, wide enough for two, then I should want the right one to occupy it with me. There is only one situation I can imagine, that would be preferable to the above. It would be to be snugly ensconced at home today with the wife & little ones all well. The money that government owes me, in my pocket, a leave of absence for ten days. Now, if you think of anything better, should like to hear of it.

I wrote you by Mr. Jones last Thursday, and when I wrote, I really imagined that I had gone up, for ninety days, for the rheumatism had taken hold of me in earnest, and only because I had so much to do, and no one else to do it, should have given up, but after attending surgeons call, about forty more came in upon me, and I had to keep hopping until noon. I then concluded to work it off, took my axe and chopped as hard as I was able, got to sweating freely, and felt better. At the same time, took as much cimicifuga[23] as I could stand, have followed it up, and today am about free from pain or stiffness. Some of the officers said I was trying for a sick leave, etc. I told them I did not wish any such thing, and I would not give a snap if I could not go home well. I would not go on any account whatever.

The time has passed which was indicated for the Paymaster to be here, and I feel, that there is no certainty now, that he will come soon. You must hold on to the little you have with tenacity till he comes, for my situation would indeed be deplorable if you were without money.

One Regt., the 12th, has not been paid for ten months, now is not that pretty hard when one considers that many families are dependent upon the pittance that is paid to privates.

Encourage Ned to better efforts and if he does not do better, I am afraid my visit at home will not be a pleasant one.

Mr. Kirker's papers have not yet come, let him know if he inquires, I cannot tell the reason. Have received no letters from Marietta or Gallipolis since those I told you of.

Write often, and give regards to all friends. Your Husband

Wm. S. Newton

29

Camp Fayetteville Jany 22nd/63

Dear Wife

This is Thursday eve, and Mr. Kirker just returned with boxes, teams, etc. all safe and sound, but has been detained. He says ever since he started, is not better if any, and I would not be at all surprised, if he resigned his position in the army.

I have been rather unwell for a week past, could not get anything to tempt my appetite but the sight of your cake, and tonight at supper 1/4 of a mince pie dispelled the loathing I before evinced for food. I tell you they will do me good, am afraid to spoil the cake by cutting for it looks so much like you & came so recently from your hands I expect it will almost spoil before I will consent to have it eaten. The apples too are a great treat.

Am afraid you took almost too much pains with my drawers, they look too fine for the country and the pants will never do to wear here, and I am almost sorry you did not keep them at home.

Lieut. Neal also came up, brought a letter from Em. They are all well, did not send the corn meal because Kirker had part of a barrel on the way, it will be best I suppose.

Finn looks very pale, and is not really able for active duty, although he has fleshed up wonderfully.

We hear the Paymaster is below paying off troops in the valley, but whether this is to be relied on is quite uncertain. Mr. K. did not see him on the way up. We still live in hope & confidently expect some of the greenbacks, that we may be able to send the *means* to the dear ones at home if not permitted to carry it home ourselves. A visit home for me, is yet a matter of doubt. If Carpenter was here, we could both get to go by and by. Warwick says he will go in March, and wants me to go in February, will do the whole, if it takes day and night to accomplish it. I could do the same for him, but the permission to go is the thing. This is one reason would like to be paid, for if they dismiss me for going, they might also deprive me of back pay. You will see the force of the reasoning. There will be a great pressure made for furloughs when the men receive their money. We still have a number sick, but mumps is the only prevailing disease. The men have had it since before we left Gauley, and not near all have had it. The men in different companies do not mix much but each keep in their own quarters, and when on drill, they are not mixed up, only with themselves.

Should I get an opportunity to go home, Charley thinks he will try to take his wife out of the valley at the same time. This you must keep dark, for he will have to steal her away, and it is not best to let every one know where she came from, or who belonged to, at least for the present, for they might implicate me in giving assistance to her escape. I can give Charley a pass to go to Ironton or any other place, but it would be a different thing about his wife.

He seems tickled with the idea of his wife going to Ironton. I read your letter to him, the whole of it, and he said you would have no trouble with her if you only told her what you wanted, she would not want any company, etc. I am glad Ned did not start up with Mr. K. for he would not have got here. Hope the boys will be good and that I may have a good report when I come home. Good night, Your Husband.

30

Fayetteville Feb. 1st 1863

Dear Wife

Your letter of the last Sabbath, and the one before the last, have not reached me yet, indeed I have not had one since the one Kirker brought me. That, I answered immediately, and hoped ere this, to have the pleasure of reading at least two from you, but in this was mistaken badly. I suppose the boats on the Kanawha, being used for moving troops, is the cause of my discomforture. We have had many rumors of the 91st moving down the Kanawha. Some say to Charleston, others to Coalsmouth below Charleston, yet we know of no order to this effect. You may be pretty certain if we are moved to either place, I will make a visit home shortly after we get there, for in that event, we will see steamboats, and the undertaking will not be a great one.

I had hoped to spend my 40th birthday with you, and am not certain but I would have accomplished it, but Warwick's eyes have been quite sore, and are not well, yet, and I cannot think of leaving him with the whole Regt. on his hands, and he disabled at the same time. Beside[s], if I go home, I will not try to get a permit from Headquarters, for this will take too long. But if the Col. will give his consent to my absence for a short time, it is all I want. I have heard nothing from Harmar, they probably think our Regt. has gone down the river with those that I left a week or two ago.

Col. Turley, indeed, all our officers who are married, express the most lively interest in affairs at home, and they have, most of them, left off the expression, "I want to see the children," but come out on the square, and say it is wife and she, *principally*, that they want to see as a matter of course, they all love their children, but wife is the great consideration.

I often find myself endeavoring to imagine how you all look, and then think perhaps I would recognize you, if the change has not been too great. What say you, do you think I could mistake you, and go, as Col. Paxton says, for some other woman. The boys faces seem familiar enough, but little Kate's is quite difficult to recall at times. Don't tell this to everyone, but it is a fact, and I cannot get rid of the feeling, and you don't know how unpleasantly it makes me feel. You must not let her forget me.

I really hope that the next letter will be dated at some point on the Kanawha, and I do not know but it would be wrong to wish to leave our present quarters before spring, for I am confident we will not have any more comfortable ones, let us go where we will. It is now raining hard, and the mud is very deep now. How we are to move, if the order comes, is a mystery. We have not half teams enough to move when the roads are good, and if we go now, they will be compelled to send a lot of the Post teams to our aid.

Hoping to hear from you soon, I remain yours truly,

Wm. S. Newton

31

Thursday Feb 26th 1863

Dear Wife

I am on board the Victor No. 2[24] bound for Loup Creek & if we get up on time, will cross Cotton Mountain this afternoon.We got to Gall[apolis] Tuesday morning to breakfast, found all pretty well. I shipped aboard this boat the same evening with Ricker's horse, but did not leave till 4 in the morning of Wednesday, got to Charleston about 4 P.M. and to Piatt about 7 in the eve, there I left Mr. R's horse, and took my own aboard, so you see my ride will not be a very hard one. The Capt. of our boat is quite sick, his wife is aboard and they have made me useful to them and they have been very kind to me.

My expenses up, will not be very heavy, as we are making a kind of exchange of civilities, both being in the service of the Government. Em got home all right, and they were glad to see her.

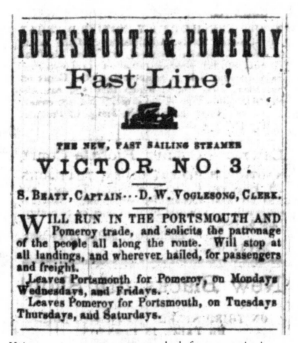

Union steamers were a common method of transportation in the western part of Virginia. William S. Newton depended on steamers for transportation, supplies, and the mail. Advertisement for the *Victor 3*, a Union steam transport boat, in the *Ironton Register*, May 14, 1863.

I got some paper collars at G.[allipolis] but cannot employ any darkie, so if Charley goes to Ironton you must send him on forthwith. My boxes will not be very far from camp. And I think I shall get them in good time. Had I known we could come this far by boat, would have brought Ned along. It is still uncertain about the boats coming this high.

You must take care of your health, and not neglect your medicine. Tell the boys to be good. Will let the boat take this back and mail it at Gallipolis. Write soon and often.

Your Husband
Wm. S. Newton

32

Fayetteville Feb 26th /63

Dear Wife

I am here once more in my cabin, safe over Cotton Mountain, rode 18 miles since dinner, got to Loup just at dinner, ate Dinner on the boat, and arrived at camp at 5 P.M. Pretty good traveling in mud so deep, but got back before they were looking for me, found all right, so far as my absence is concerned.

But no Charley here to get my supper, took tea with Capt. Crossley. Newt had a man from Co. D. messing and cooking for him, but he skedaddled soon after I came, and I am not sorry, for he is not one I would have chosen. What we will do for breakfast remains yet to be seen. I will go to the Sutlers if nothing better turns up.

I must have a cook of some kind and that shortly. Perhaps I can get a feminine to come, what say you. I tried to get a darkie I met in the road today, but he could only promise on condition.

Perhaps Charley may turn up yet. I could hear nothing from him on my way up. Found your last letter, and one from Mother. She is terribly afraid I will not take care of my health. Saw brother Doug at Gallipolis, only a few minutes, was on the S.B. Bostonia No. 2.[25] Says he is tired of making Oil, and will do something else or nothing. He may stop at Ironton on the way up.

I wrote you this morning on the boat, and as this will make two to day, and eleven o'clock has come, I will stop, that I may be up in time for Surgeons Call. Your Husband

W. S. Newton

33

Fayetteville March 4th 1863

Dear Wife

Dr. Warwick starts for his home this morning, and am about to send this with him.

I can imagine his feelings having had some experience in this matter recently.

I have felt very lonely for a day or two past, and almost feel sorry that I went home, for now I cannot have it in anticipation for a long time to come, and before I went, I could almost subsist on the idea of going. One other thing has made me sad, and were it not for the expectation that you might again work and fret over another box for me, would not tell you the story, but for this reason will relate. I brought the boxes up to Loup all safe, and thought there would be no difficulty in getting them here in good time and safely.

Mr. Gillens, I left at Piatt all right, the one to Tom Lewis[26] came all safe, the one with the hams ditto. But the one sent by you was broken open, and completely demolished. The cake, pies and pickles devoured, the piece of cheese came, a few of the poorest apples, the paper of tacks and the old newspapers was all it contained. I had told Tom Graham,[27] Mrs. Wright's[28] relative, what to expect, and not a thing she sent came. Also Sydney Brammer's socks met the same fate. The box sent by the Ladies has not yet come. I hope it has not yet started, and as our own teams went down today, hope they may bring it safe. If it started with the others, it too has gone up.

Could I have only surprised the thief while in the act, my revolver would have been in requisition.

I wrote yesterday to the Capt. Malbridge,[29] in whose care I left them, telling him the whole story. That he might know who to trust, and I think he will bring the offender to justice. I sold five out of the eight hams for enough to cover the whole expense, and could have disposed of twenty more.

As I shall have Regt., Hospital and everything else on my hands, & as there are a great many sick, you may not get another letter from me till Dr. Warwick comes back. But this not need hinder you from writing, for I want something to keep off the blues, and on this account I am really glad I have so much to do.

Tell Ned that April will soon come, and if it does, and we are in a position to send for him, and as I am entitled to two horses, will try to buy one for him to ride if we go on a march. He must be a very good boy in the mean time.

Will Falwell is messing with me, and cooks first rate. He likes it, and so do I. But they may not permit us long to do so. Have not heard from Charley. Give my regards to Mr R & family. Dr. is waiting and I will close.

Your Husband
Wm. S. Newton

34

No. 5
Fayetteville March 13th/63

My Dear Wife

Yours of 7th No. 2 is received, and I think I can appreciate your loneliness some what. If you don't think so just settle yourself among a thousand persons, with whom you have no particular feelings or interest, except what is common to all. No one with whom you can talk of home, or home affairs, then I think you will indeed be lonely. Were it not that I have so much to do, it would be at most insupportable. Major Blessing, I think, is better. Some of the Hospital boys are very sick, & Robt. Kirker has *lung fever* or Pneumonia. Is, I think, better today, is still in his quarte[rs] & prefers to stay there. I will k[eep] him there, unless he should get worse. You had better let his father know of it, and if he should get much worse I will telegraph to him at Portsmouth.

Tell the ladies their box arrived last evening in pretty good order, and if they could have seen the countenances of some of the boys when I told them I had received something for them, one poor fellow who had been at the point of death for a week past, brightened up and I hope is really better. I gave his Captain, the pillow which was sent, and told him to take it to Rider,[30] so that if he died, his head should at least rest on something better than a blanket or a knapsack.

I gave some of the fruit to our Ward Master, to be used as best he could, I retained some for the uses of the Ironton boys. Two or three of them need it now.

Surgeon Carpenter arrived today, took dinner with me, after which, I took him over and installed him in the Hospital. I introduced him to all, not forgetting the Matron. This is quite a relief to me at the present, & if he only stays, I am glad he has come. It has been very cold here for three nights past, and I hope will be favorable for the sick.

An order has been passed at Headquarters not allowing Surgeons to perform duty at Hospitals. Now if I could only be assigned to the Hospital at Gallipolis, I would willingly assent to be Asst. Surg.

Would not this be just the thing? I could let you come to see me then, suppose we petition for it?

I wish to write an acknowledgement to the ladies of Ironton for the box received. You may give it to Mr. Dumble,[31] and if he thinks best, may insert it in the [Ironton] Register.

Did you receive the letter with twenty dollars in it? As it is getting very late, I must stop or get no sleep.

So good night.

Your Husband
Wm. S. Newton

3

The Booming of Cannon
at Every Moment Strikes the Ear,
March–June 1863

During the spring and summer, William S. Newton witnessed much
more military action as the 91st Ohio and other Union regiments,
including the 2nd Virginia Cavalry, pushed deeper into western
Virginia. In the spring, Confederate general Albert G. Jenkins led a
number of small raids throughout the Kanawha River Valley.[1] By this
time, battle lines and territory were no longer clear as Union forces
attempted to hold strategic points and small towns.

In March, Newton and the 91st moved to Kanawha Falls, and
then he spent significant time in Summersville before eventually returning to Fayetteville. Newton described a series of skirmishes (one
lasting four days), encounters with bushwhackers, and incidents of
rebel forces seizing Union supplies. The increasing action resulted
in more soldiers and more patients in the hospital. Newton's medical services were in great demand for both soldiers and civilians. He
noted a growing number of deaths in camp and many others sick.

During this period the state of West Virginia was created from
parts of western Virginia. There had been an effort to form a separate Unionist state in 1861, but it took several conventions and the
involvement of President Abraham Lincoln in 1863 to make it possible.[2] Newton did not comment on the official formation of the new
state in June 1863, but he did mention the growing rift between Union
supporters and the local "secesh." In a May 5, 1863, letter, he describes
Colonel Benjamin F. Coates of the 91st conducting a rigid oath ceremony for civilians who had joined the Union lines. Newton noted the
many young women in the area, some who he believed were ladies and
others "real bad."[3]

Less security with the lines and frequent rebel raids did not deter
Newton from inviting his teenage son Ned to join him in camp. After
a lengthy passage from Ironton, Ned arrived in early May and spent
most of his time fishing in nearby rivers and streams. Ned accompanied his father on a few dangerous trips, but the letters back home
de-emphasized the possibility of capture or injury. Even with his son
nearby, Newton pined for his wife and wrote frequently. His horse,
Old Tom, is another regular companion who joined Newton on several expeditions. One significant topic is Newton's application for a
promotion following the unexpected May 1863 resignation of 91st surgeon George H. Carpenter. Newton and his fellow assistant surgeon
John B. Warwick both applied for the open spot and waited patiently.[4]

35

No. 6

Camp Falls of Kanawha March 16th /63

My Dear Wife

You perceive by the above, that we have moved once more. Yesterday,
Sunday at ten o'clock we received marching orders, and such on Sunday
I hope will not see soon again. Had just got through visiting my patients
when the order came. I went to Col. Turley to know if I should go with the
Regt. He said yes, but when I reminded him of Major Blessing & Robt.
Kirker who had been very sick he hesitated, but finally said the Major
should decide, that he was going to see him. I told him I wanted some time
to do my packing, so he took Capt. Caldwell along to bring backward. He
came at 12 M. Said I must go, Col. desired it, and Major was willing to resign
his claim on me for the good of the Regt. I can tell you I was very sorry to
leave the Major, but Bob Kirker was much better, and will get along if he is
only careful. Thus you see I was kept till noon, without making my preparation. When I got orders, the Regt. was drawn up ready to march, the teams
all loaded except mine. But I went to work with a will and just in one hour,
everything was packed, tents struck, and team started. I mounted Old Tom
and overtook the Regt. some two miles from camp. We marched 6 miles to
the foot of Cotton Mountain where the 89th had left quarters, since used
by the Post Teamsters as stables for their mules on passing to and from Fayetteville. A horrible place to camp you will say, and so it was, it rained heavy
during most of the night. Col. J, Quarter Master, Adjutant and myself, took
quarters at a neighboring house, got supper, lodging & breakfast. Rather

common, but better than the shanties or stables. We started this morning, as soon as it was light, and arrived at our camp by nine this morning. We are encamped at the foot of Cotton Mountain just below the Falls, in quarters built by the 23rd Ohio, which has gone to Charleston. The fire had not gone out in many of the houses when we arrived. I have pretty good quarters, but no accommodations as yet for the sick, and I do not know what we will do with them if they accumulate, unless we send them to Charleston.

Carpenter stayed at Fayette with the sick, and he will have something to do if he does his duty.

Our men feel as if they were out of prison almost, they were so glad to see the Kanawha again. We are just six miles above Loup, and the boats have been running to that point pretty regularly, and if we stay here, and you come to Gallipolis, I do not think there will be any trouble to get Ned up to camp. Indeed I feel as if *The Old Lady herself*, might come up see me. Col. Turley is sending for his wife and I presume if Carpenter gets here, he will have his wife here in short notice. Will could telegraph me when Ned could start, and I could meet him at Loup. He could put him charge of some one coming up or the officers of the boat would take charge of him without any hesitation, particularly those on the Victor No. 2 would do so.

The Rebels may be coming in on us by this time, but probably they have enough to attend to in other quarters. We were not able to bring all of our things, and the teams started back for them and will be here tomorrow. Should we move again I hope it will be down the river.

Tell Ned & Mott I shall expect to hear a good report of them, if they expect a visit at camp or Gallipolis. Indeed the visit must be a conditional one. If they are not good boys, they certainly cannot do any thing but stay at home.

Will Falwell is still with me, and we get along very well. He certainly is a very trustworthy young man. And very quiet with all.

Should like very much to look in upon you tonight, and would not object to staying all night with you. Have you any objections? How is your cough getting. Hope you will take care of yourself, and get well and fat before I see you again. I have been very well since my visit home. Have not heard a word from Will or Em except what I get through you, and the reason is, I have not written to them I suppose.

Have you heard or seen the letter I sent with the twenty dollars. Have not heard anything from you since the 7th, the one Mrs. Gillen brought.

As I have one or two other letters to write, must stop, or will not get to bed in time.

So good night.

Your Husband
Wm. S. Newton

36

No. 1
Camp Reynolds
Falls Kanawha March 23rd

Dear Wife

Yours of 15th Ultimo came to hand last eve and I have received all others up to this, as numbered. I had supposed when Carpenter came I would have comparatively easy times, but we were soon ordered to this place, leaving him behind with the Hospital, and since we came, he has sent all the old chronic cases here for me to care for. And this morning, we had 26 at Surgeons Call beside some in quarters not able to come.

McMullen's Battery, stationed at the Bridge, two miles above on the other side of the river, has no physician, and they come to me, & yesterday, today also, I visited some of the sick who were not able to report here. Two companies of the 1st va. Cavalry are also on duty near us, and they have no surgeon. They came for me to go down to Loup to day, but I declined, as I did not wish to take more on myself than I could do well.

There are a plenty of outsiders. They all call themselves Union now that they want favors. They come for medical advice. One today wanted me to go 16 miles to see his wife but finally took medicine.

I have some notion to hang up my shingle here after the war is over. There seems to be such a demand for doctors. Warwick has not yet come, but we look for him every day. When he comes, will be sent to Summerville to care for the two companies at that point. He will have easy times and report says, there are a plenty of the fair sex too. And from the invoice of medicines sent for to me, I should think the soldiers have had the worst of the fun.

I saw two or three ladies yesterday. Col. Turley was along, and we called on three at one house, one Union, one old maid, the other has a husband in the Rebel Army. The latter quite young and fair, but looks as though *she missed some things*. I did not ask her, but could not restrain the thought, for she has not seen him for some seven months. It is very possible she is like some *others*. No accounting for taste in this world. And I cannot see why one sex will risk everything to gratify certain feelings, while the other never *misses it*. Perhaps it is not so in every instance. This is a matter for meditation and speculation in my mind.

Mr. Brammer came here last evening on his way to Fayette. If he comes back tomorrow, will send this by him. If not will trust it to the mail.

Should John Dempsey[5] or any of the 2nd Va. Cavalry start to camp, you may send Ned up with them, if it is anybody you can trust. Tell him he had better have three or four fish lines, some twenty hooks of medium size, and a few little ones to catch minnows for bait.

Also a lump of Gum Asafoetida,[6] which he will find in the office on or near the top shelf in a jar. You can tell it by the odor. He must keep them all close, not show or tell anyone about them or anything else he has. If he does they will be stolen from him.

Should you prefer to keep him till you come to Gallipolis, and send him from that point, all right. Will can telegraph me, so I can meet him at Loup. Have heard or written nothing to Harmar yet.

Col. Turley's wife will come up with Warwick, also Lieut. Coles wife. An ambulance will meet them at Loup Creek. If I could realize that it would be any gratification on your part, would like to have you & Em visit the camp. But as it would only be to gratify *me alone*, I will not ask the sacrifice on my own account. Will try and forgo the pleasure. Major Blessing was better the last heard from, also Robt. Kirker. It is now late and I will therefore stop.

> Your Husband
> Wm. S. Newton

Should I send this by Brammer, will also send you money with which to buy fishing lines and hooks. But if by mail will not put it in. You need not send very much in this way for I do not think it will pay a large per centum on this investment. Let Ned have a decent hat and boots or shoes, if he comes up for I want him to appear decent and would like to have him act civilized. You can judge what is best for him.

37

March 25th 1863

This is Wednesday, and I have been waiting for Brammer to take the letter. I look for him today, so thought I would add a few lines. We received a telegram from Warwick at Gallipolis the women are with him, and will all arrive at 2 P.M. The Col. can hardly contain himself, is in excellent humor, and I would not be much afraid to ask for a furlough again. Just the idea of having two or three women in the camp is really refreshing.

Two more of our men died at Fayette Hospital yesterday. One a Gallia boy (Holcomb[7]), the other Rider[8] from Jackson Co. The one to whom I gave the pillow sent by the Ladies. Am very glad I gave to him.

We have been here now ten days and I am much pleased with our quarters. But two companies, B & K, are ordered to Gauley, our old camp-ground, that they may better guard the Gauley & New River roads. So I shall have more trouble in caring for the sick. Only six companies remain, yet I had 45 at Surgeons Call this morning.

I will send you a ring made by young Safford[9] of Co. B. It shows some skill in this line. Should Ned come before you go to Gallipolis, he must have his Uncle Will telegraph to me when he leaves Gallipolis, that I may meet him at Loup. Kiss Kate for me. Tell Mott to be a *man*.

Yours,

Wm. S. Newton

38

No. 9

Camp Reynolds Falls Kanawha

March 31st 1863

My Dear Wife

As we hear that Jenkins is in the Valley, near Pt. Pleasant, and has been firing on the Steam Boats, we can account for the non appearance of your letters. The last I received is No. 6. Mrs. Turley brought it up.

And I am now a little anxious, lest Ned is on the way here, for I am not certain but am expecting an order to go to Summerville. Two more of the companies, A & I, started for that place this morning. Warwick came on Saturday & left yesterday (Monday) for Fayette, to get his baggage. If Carpenter keeps him there, and comes over here himself, I will have to go [to] Summerville. Do not like the arrangement, for here I have comfortable quarters, have been to a good deal of trouble to fix them up, and now to start off again, and prepare others does not suit me. If Ned was only here would not care so much, for I could take him with me. It is about 30 miles, up the Gauley River.

Am still hoping that Warwick will return tonight, and go up there and leave me still in camp here.

Will let you know, as soon as the matter is settled. It will make no difference about your letters, for if they come here, will be forwarded to me by the first opportunity, so you need not suspend writing.

Tell Mr. Kirker that bob is much better. Newt Warwick saw him on Saturday last. He says Bob looks bad, was up and around.

As to his furlough, all I can do is write to Carpenter in his behalf, and this I have done.

If Carpenter will interest himself in the matter, I think his Captain would do his part.

Newt has just received a first rate box from home. It was opened, and some things of value taken, but he does not know to what extent. A razor &

strop[10] he has missed. He also found their tools, which they used to open it with. Think they must have got frightened before they were done. Dr was on the boat at the time.

Major Blessing was carried by our camp yesterday on a sled, his wife supporting his head on her lap. Poor fellow, he told me he did not expect ever to return. Carpenter, I understand, thinks he has cancer of the stomach. I hope not and hardly think the symptoms will warrant the conclusion. He is one of the best men in the Regt.

Col. Coates telegraphed us at Gallipolis a few days ago on his way to join us, but Jenkins has stopped the communication I judge, for it is now 4 or 5 days and he has not yet come.

This is the last day of March and I hope April will afford us better weather, then there will not be so much sickness among our men. I have prescribed for about fifty today & if the damp changeable weather continues, we shall have plenty of sickness.

Tell the boys the summer campaign is now about to open and I think there will be an opportunity to capture the long promised trophies. Tell them they must be very good for not their reputation alone, but ours depend on their actions.

Should I start to Summerville, will telegraph Brother Will, to keep Ned till they hear from me again.

Your Husband
Wm. S. Newton

I have no more stamps as they sell these for five cents. I hope you will send ten or fifteen the next time you write.

39

Summerville Nicholas County Va.
April 1st 1863

My Dear Wife

You will see that my predictions, in my last, are fulfilled. Last evening Carpenter came over from Fayette, leaving Warwick at the Hospital.

Col. Turley issued orders for me to report at Summerville forthwith, so this morning I mounted Old Tom at the Falls and at 5 P.M. arrived here, passing Co. A. & I. some six miles back. They started yesterday morning and arrived at 6 P.M. They are very much fatigued. We now have four companies, and as the Secesh are very close about us, we no doubt will see some fun very shortly. They are stealing horses some five or six miles of us, and Capt. Ramsey[11] of the bushwackers (Union) is now out watching for them at the ferry. No doubt some of them will bite the dust before 24 hours.

I shall have very nice quarters here, and also three or four rooms in the same house for Hospital purposes. Capt. Cadot is in command of the post. He will quarter with me. We'll also have the telegraph office in the same building. The house is large, and is a very good one. Carpenter can have my old quarters, in welcome. If Ned was only here I would not care, but how he is to get here is a question.

I told the telegraph operator this morning to send a telegram to Will at Gallipolis, just as soon as he could get one through. The Rebels have charge of the lines at Red House, and our supplies by the river are now cut off. We think they will not long hold it.

I do not know what to say about Ned coming at the present. There is now so much evidence of trouble, am afraid to have him come. We may be obliged to go down nearer to you very soon. If so, will send for him then. Tell him not to be discouraged, that the time will come soon. I feel as much disappointed as he does, for I had made great calculations on fishing, etc. when he came. It is now all knocked into fie.

There are women plenty, and the officers say some of them are real ladies, enough of bad ones too, as the men give evidence too plainly.

Must stop so good night.

Your Husband
Wm. S. Newton

40

Summerville April 5th 1863

My Dear Wife

This is Sabbath afternoon, and as I am now thirty miles further into rebeldom than ever before, I just thought I would like to communicate a few thoughts, not knowing whether they will reach you, for our mail facilities are very bad, not having had a mail since arriving here, we are however, expecting one tonight. We sent a man to Gauley yesterday morning, and look for him back if the Rebels don't catch him.

It was a very long and lonely ride for me, and one not calculated to inspire security. I kept a sharp lookout for bushwhackers, having no arms myself, had depended on the fleetness of Old Tom if they did not kill me at the first onset. Here everything is insecure, for the town is so situated, it cannot be defended with a small force, hence we depend upon a retreat into the entrenchments which surround the church holding our commissary stores. If driven from them, we may all expect a march to Richmond. If they will only let me ride my own horse, it will not be so bad. But I should not like the march on foot, someone else riding my horse. If we were left to guard Pt. Pleasant, instead of this wild country, it would have been some avail.

There are plenty of women in this region, some of them ladies, but quite a majority are common, and not a few real bad. Some of our *attaches* have girls outside the lines. They pay their board at a convenient place, for the accommodation of lodging two or three times a week, or as often as they can obtain a pass to stay outside the lines. As I being a Doctor, have a general pass, my opportunities are considered very great by those who are compelled to renew theirs daily.

I am quite certain that I was sent here so that others might have the accommodations they had prepared for themselves at Fayetteville. Perhaps it is all for the best, and if Ned had only been with me so that you could have gone your way visiting, I would not have very much cared, but I knew it would be a great disappointment to him.

Should think those in authority would sometime see the necessity of guarding towns where there is something, and not those so remote and so perfectly worthless.

Should we get a mail, and I hear from you, will perhaps add something more, before this leaves. Tell the boys to do right, that I have a gun, an Enfield, and may get one of the right kind.

Good by, Your Husband

Wm. S. Newton

41

Summerville April 9th 1863

My Dear Wife

Yours of March 29th (No. 8) came last evening. I think there is no doubt, from the tone of your letters, that you are low spirited. And whether the feeling is sympathetic or not, I had been unusually so for the past month, and the reception of your last, has contributed nothing to dispel the cloud, and I have been endeavoring to seek aid & comfort from a higher source. To say that I have succeeded would hardly be true. Yet there is a solace, and comfort, in the strict observance of duty, and if not made entirely happy, at least I am comforted by the exercise.

There is nothing calculated to make one feel his dependence more than to be situated as we now are. To me it seems that an arm of flesh is but feeble, when *so few* are so removed from help, and good running would hardly avail anything, when one has thirty miles to run before reaching any help. At the same time, there are two or three roads by which the *Rebs* might cut us off One, *Cross Lanes,* made famous by the capture of Col. Tyler's forces about 15 months ago,[12] is only six miles below us, and the very one they would take if they desired to get between us and Gauley.

We have news almost daily that they are proposing to make a descent upon us. The women often come in and report seeing squads three or four miles off. These only serve to make our pickets more watchful, for now in hearing, Company F are having a good time dancing in the old out building. They have a violin and call off in regular style, "Gents to the right" "Lady stand fast" "Swing partner" etc. Yet there are no ladies present. It really makes me feel solemn to think how soon they may be called to fight for their life. And some of them perhaps wounded, or dead. Poor fellows, I suppose they think, they may as well laugh as cry.

I received a letter from the Regt. last eve. The Hospital is moved from Fayette to Camp Reynolds, so Warwick & Carpenter are both there, with Miss Genny to cook for them. I suppose they have *fine* times. So far as the work is concerned, I am glad that I am alone, and if the Rebs will only let us alone will be satisfied. But this will certainly not long be the case, for we have now kept many of them from their homes & families for the last six months.

The Paymaster is in the Valley. I wrote to Capt. Caldwell to draw my pay, and send to Brother Will at Gallipolis, for I had as much with me as I cared to give the Rebs, thinking I would have no good opportunity to send it from this point. You will probably be there by the time it gets there. Have it loaned to someone, who will pay it back when called for.

The forces in this valley have not retreated but hold all the points they have ever held since I came here. My letters were delayed, no doubt, by the Rebel raid into Point Pleasant, and you probably have them before this. I have not failed to answer all yours. Hope you are alone by this time, and not bored by fortnight visitors. Good night.

Your Husband
Wm.S.N.

42

Summerville April 12th 1863

My Dear Wife

Yours of the 5th (No. 9) came this evening, and from what you write it would seem you had not got all my letters, for I have been here now twelve days, and I wrote you the same day I came and one from the Falls the previous day, neither of which you seem to know anything about. Now it is very dull to talk or write two weeks afterward, the interest is almost lost before the answer comes.

Now that Linc has come I suppose you will not be so lonely. I think you had better get a girl to do your work, and not kill yourself entirely.

I left directions at the Regt. if Ned comes there to have him forwarded immediately to Summerville.

We have exciting times here, and are expecting an attack almost nightly. They dare not attack with a small force, or we would have been troubled long ago. They are all around us in small squads, stealing horses, capturing Union men, etc. Some of our bushwhackers came in this evening, bringing four extra guns, which they said they found, but we strongly suspect they killed the men who had them. Their motto is "take but few prisoners" which I am inclined to think is the best plan after all. I board or mess with Capt. Culbertson. My clothes are all still at Camp Reynolds, except a change of underclothes which I brought with me.

They promised to forward them the first opportunity. Thus it is, when you have others to do business for you. I have pretty much made up my mind, to wait for transportation when ordered to move hereafter, and I think they cannot compel me to go, until they furnish it.

They also promised to send me an Ambulance. This too they have failed to do. I am endeavoring to take things easy, however, and *wait for the wagon*.

By the way, Lieut. Neal & myself, called on a Miss Eagle[13] (Secesh) the other night, who played the Southern Wagon[14] for us on the piano. It was rather flat, to see how ready they are to steal Northern music, by simply calling it another name. We can obtain butter & eggs in a small way at fair prices. The women in this country will trade anything they possess for coffee, rice or sugar.

Samuel Finley Neal was from Gallipolis and rose to the rank of major in the 91st Ohio Volunteer Infantry. William S. Newton referred to him as Finn, Captain Neal, or Lieutenant Neal. Major Neal, Eugene B. Willard Photograph Album, Special Collections, Marietta College, Marietta, Ohio.

I sent (Jones) my Hospital Steward out the other day to dicker and trade with them. In this way we can obtain supplies for the sick, and give them better rations than the Government supplies. All I am afraid of is that he and my horse will both be captured. I am uneasy all the time he is gone.

I presume this will be the last letter you will get at Ironton. I will direct the next to Gallipolis, thinking you will meet it there.

I understand Mr. Ricker is to be 1st Lieut. In Company H. to take Mr. Kirkers place. I have no more room so good night.

Your Husband
Wm. S. Newton

Will send Capt. Cadot Photograph. He is the commander of this Post at the present time. Put it away for future reference. Our Major[15] is dead and I would give five dollars to have a good one of him. He was one of the best man in the Regt.

43

Summerville Va., April 19th/63

My Dear Wife

Yours of the 12th (No 10) came today, and it is not necessary to say, I was also pleased to read one from Mother, which accompanied it. The stamps were all right too, they are worth five cents here and scarce. We have enough of sickness too, Co.s F & D which have occupied this place since the 15th of February suffer the most. I conclude it is on account of the severe guard duty they were compelled to perform before the other companies came, for A & I have very little sickness as yet. John Pool[16] of Co. F, a fifer, from Scioto County, died yesterday morning, his disease, *inflammation of the bowels*. They all feel the loss very much, as he was a general favorite. The drummer, Ira Crull,[17] of the same Co., is also very sick of Typhoid Fever. Two or three others have Pneumonia.

Co. D have more sick and disabled than Co. F, but not in immediate danger. You know it almost makes me sick, to lose a patient, and my dull & melancholy feelings, I attribute to this cause.

The weather has been very bad for a week or two. We have had two pleasant days now, and it tells on the men. Tonight a storm is brewing, and I fear very much, the result will be unfavorable to some of the sick ones. Carpenter sent a team with my trunk & boxes, also one box of medicines last week. He says if Ned comes to the Regt, he will take care of him, and forward him on the first good opportunity. This I feel quite certain he will do, so I think you had better let him come to the Regt. the first opportunity.

Will can put him on the boat, and if the boat does not go higher up than Piatt, he can go to Adjutant Gillen's quarters and stay, until an opportunity offers to get up to Loup or the Regt.

Tell Will to get him a pass from the Comr. Of the Post at G.[allipolis] to come to the Regt. Then Carpenter will attend to the balance. Tell Ned I hope he will conduct himself well. To be polite & respectful to all whom he may come into contact, that I may not be ashamed to own him as a son.

If he will do this, I think he will get along very smoothly. Teams will be coming up from the Regt., and perhaps an ambulance in which he could come very comfortably.

Yesterday morning we were reinforced by Col. Paxton, with about three hundred of his cavalry. They came in at 2 o'clock, and many of our men thought certain the Rebs had come. I was not frightened, for I had seen a telegram the evening before announcing their approach. Except for this, I would have been startled, for they made a huge rattling over the McAdam- ized[18] street in front of my quarters.

Col. P[axton]. went on a scout today with 100 men as far as Powell Mountain, (15 miles) and returned this evening without seeing a *Reb.* It had been reported that a Regt. of Rebs had left Lewisburg with the express in- tention of capturing our force here, hence the forced march of the Col., to our aid. They came from Piatt here (62 miles) without stopping. They were very much worn out. How long they will remain is not yet known, they may go home in the morning. They have had a hard chase in the valley after Jenkins, and captured over 90 of his men before coming here.

I do not believe there is any considerable force in striking distance of us, but the Regt. which left Lewisburg has probably gone toward Richmond.

No small squad will come in here, for they are too well posted as to our strength. Three or four thousand could take us easily, but I do not think they have them to spare from other places at present.

This is now 13 letters I have written to you in half as many weeks, and I do not feel that you have any *great big cause of complaint* on account of any negligence, and Mr. R. is now a man of leisure. As near as I can find out, he has not reported for duty at the Regt, and Lieut. Crossland is now the Q.M. of the 91st Regt. I think Ricker is holding off hoping something better will turn up, and if not, will probably take the position assigned him.

This letter I will direct to Gallipolis, expecting you will of course be there. I think after you have shipped Ned, you had better go up to Harmar and stay until Caroline gets her visit out at G[allipolis], then you will not have such a hurrah at your Fathers. I am afraid so many will soon wear your welcome out.

It is getting very late, and I must stop, so good night. Your Husband

Wm. S. Newton

Tell Will, he had better defer sending butter, or purchasing a horse for me. If nothing has been done, as it would be difficult transportation to this place

44

Summerville, April 22nd 1863

Dear Wife

Capt. Culbertson is going to Charleston, and I will send you a few lines to let you know that we are all yet able for our rations. I telegraphed to Will yesterday, to send Ned the first opportunity. Mr. Ricker was here and slept with me the night before. I have a good bunk, large enough for two, so Ned can sleep with me so long as we are able to stay in this place. We have 20 or thirty still in the sick list & they are from two companies. Those who came last are not sick much. Some ten or fifteen of the officers & men, of this detachment, go to Charleston, as witnesses on a Court Martial, Capt. Thomas[19] of our county is under arrest, as the guilty party. We are here alone again, Col. Paxton with his Cavalry, having gone back to Camp Piatt. Should you go to Harmar give my kindest regards to all the folks there. Mother has not yet written, but promises to do so, through Mary Frank's letter.

We still hold the post of honor, in the advance of all other troops. Give my love to all the Gallia folks. Kiss Kate just once for me, Good bye

Your Husband
Wm. S. Newton

45

Summerville April 26th 1863

Dear Wife

Your No. 11 came last evening, and as we send a messenger down to Gauley in the morning would improve the opportunity, as it is not presented every day. We have no regular messenger line, a convenience very much needed here. The only way is, to go out into the country, [im]press a horse from some of the Rebs, put one of the boys on, and start him to Gauley with our letters, and on the next eve we may expect him back with our mail.

Company F. lost another man with pneumonia, we buried him yesterday. Another will probably die very soon, the drummer, a son of Dr. Crull of Scioto Co. The Doctor came last evening, left Gallipolis Thursday morning. I telegraphed to have Ned come with him, answering a dispatch at the same time of the Drs. in reference to his son. I suppose you had some reason for not sending him, or answering my dispatch as I requested. Had got the arrangement complete, for his coming through with company all the way. Perhaps it is all for the best, as we are short sighted people and cannot tell what a day may bring forth, but I was really disappointed, thinking, the arrangement a good one.

I suppose Will has not purchased a horse, as he has not written anything about the chances there. Tell him I will make other arrangements, or do without one for the present. We were again startled, last eve, by the arrival of some 200 of the 2nd Va. Cavalry at this place. We had no notice of the march, and can hardly now tell why they came.

As near as I can tell, the Rebs have been fighting our forces at Beverly, Va., and all the posts occupied by our troops between that place & Summerville, have been evacuated, Little Birch, Bull Town & Sutton. Operators bade good bye to our Tele operator and skedaddled, so we being the outpost, Genl. Scammon sent the cavalry to strengthen this post. If we are in any immediate danger of an attack, we do not know it. Who do you think I found as Asst. Surgeon of the Cavalry? Why my old friend Dr. Nellis of Wood Co., Va. He is all goodness & grace combined. I went with him & Lieut. Neal, three miles into the country today, and got a good dinner. A Mr. Duffy,[20] strong for the Union, has two sons just from Missouri, who are merchants in that state, gave us the invitation. We had a real pleasant visit, three or four sons, as many daughters, comprise quite a household. They were very hospitable, & urged us to make our calls frequent. Finn says, he is going to do so, but I being a man of family, cannot expect the same inducements to influence me. I find very little enjoyment in a social way, and the nearer my duties are well performed, toward those I have under my charge, the better I feel.

And therefore I am found rarely absent from my post. Have rarely felt, the burden of my responsibility so much as the present. So many sick, and two deaths, others very low, makes me humble indeed.

Hope you will soon be in Harmar, a letter from Mary tells me, they too are expecting you. My love to all, so good night.

Your Husband

46

Summerville April 30th 1863

Dear Wife

This is Thursday evening and the third day out for Ned, and yet nothing definite except he started on Levi,[21] a boat never known to come up to Loup.

I wrote to Carpenter yesterday asking him to forward him in Ambulance. I got a telegram from Warwick last evening, saying he had sent an ambulance to Loup to meet Ned, and I need give myself no uneasiness concerning him. I received a letter from Newt this evening dated 28th saying he would go down to wait till boat arrived.

I suspect they have landed him at Piatt as far up as the Levi comes, and the main reason I had for his coming with Dr. Crull was that by the time you started him, the boats would not be able to run up, on account of low water. It may all turn out for the best, & I hope it will, but the expense on account of the delay must certainly be augmented, beside giving other people much trouble. Ira Crull, our drummer boy, is decidedly better, and just as soon as his typhoid symptoms abated, the mumps showed themselves, yet his father feels confident that he will be able to start home with him in a few days.

Most of the cases which have been really bad, are now on the mend. And to cap all I had quite an attack two days ago, but now feel much better. I thought of home very often in the past two days, took blue pill,[22] & Rhubarb enough to drive disease from me. In fact it is the first time I have taken a purgative or alterative since I came in the service, but I dare not risk a temporizing policy here, having seen the result too plainly to be mistaken.

They have cared for me well too, it is almost worthwhile to be sick, just to learn how much they hold one's life to be worth, whether they take a selfish view of the matter, or a disinterested one, is not so plain. Certain it is, Will Jones, my Hospital Steward, did not see me want for anything.

But even made toast, squirrel soup, cooked for my dinner today a pheasant, the breast of which I relished with the soup pretty well. In short this eve I had more of the soup & breast for my supper, and now I feel as though I would be well tomorrow, with the exception of a want of strength.

The fact is I have been kept on a heavy strain of mind, exceedingly anxious, concerning the termination of the cases, and did not falter till they began to convalesce. I hope the worst is over with our boys, and that sun, and warm weather will do much for them.

Should I hear nothing from Ned, will telegraph tomorrow to Adjutant Gillen, for I am confident they would telegraph his arrival at Camp Reynolds promptly. As I said before, will hope it is for the best, but regret my wish was not respected, for Dr. Crull came from G[allipolis]. to Summerville in two days, and would cheerfully have taken the charge.

The Sentinel has admonished me "Lights Out" and as there is not much to add, will soon comply with his challenge, though I do not generally respect it. The Hospital & Surgeons quarters are exempt, unless shot & shell are flying, in this case, we would willingly put out the lights.

Are you going to Harmar soon? Think you had better, till Linc gets her visit out, for you must be pretty thick now. Write often, Your Husband

47

Summerville May 3rd 1863

My Dear Wife

This is Sabbath eve, and the Messenger goes to Gauley in the morning, will therefore embrace the opportunity to get this off.

Neds arrival was opportune, for I was getting very nervous about him, not being well, expecting all the time, Carpenter would send me a telegram as soon as he left the Regt. I did not know of his arrival ten minutes before the ambulance came. Had dispatched to Piatt, to learn his whereabouts.

The Surgeons, Newt, and indeed every one had taken quite an interest in him, fitted him out with every thing necessary to make him comfortable. Newt insisted upon sending his overcoat, beside going to Sutler, and purchasing knickknacks for him.

He seems to have made friends, and enjoyed the trip very much. The Ambulance driver says that when they were obliged to stop for the night only 13 miles from his Pa, that he could not keep back the tears.

I was really glad to see him, and only regretted I had written such a doleful letter to you. The fact was my health was very bad at the time, and I only now feel that I have barely escaped an attack of fever, which came on me suddenly, and if I had not promptly met it, would not have yielded in less than three or four weeks. And as promptly as I began, it seems very slow to yield. I cannot get strength or appetite. Today I feel better and hope ere the week ends will enjoy my usual health and strength. Ned went fishing two miles off with Jones, Dr. Crull, and one other man. Ned caught fish enough for our breakfast. Today he saddled up Old Tom and rode to the Picket Posts, is much pleased with the horse Etc. I think he will get along very well. Has given me no trouble, and does not think of going without permission, any place.

In reference to seeing you at G.[allipolis], the only expectation I can have is that the Rebs will chase us down the Valley, and this is not likely to happen very soon. As I have just learned, the balance of the 91st is on the way here. If so, will arrive tomorrow.

There may be some advance movement on hand, in which we will all have to take a part. Anything is better than stopping in camp always. You will still direct your letters to this point, and give yourself no uneasiness about us, for we can now telegraph you any day.

If they can keep you, you had better remain & recruit your health, for

I have learned the past week, that good health is the great desideratum, if anything is to be enjoyed, without it. Friends, Relatives, money, all are as nothing.

Give my kind regards to all. Much love to yourself & little ones.

> Your Husband
> Wm. S. Newton

48

Summerville May 5th 1863

Dear Wife

This is Tuesday night now eleven O'clock, and I am sitting up because I cannot sleep all night, thought as I could not send my letter, would add a few lines. The whole 91st are now here, with the exception of a few sick, & Carpenter left at Gauley.

Whether they will let us remain here, is quite a doubtful question, for the Rebs are reported working the direction with a pretty large force.

It was said today, we were under marching orders for tomorrow, but I suspect a mere reconnaissance in force, toward Sutton, is all that is intended. Col. Coates has had all citizens w[ho are in] our lines marched before him today, to take [an] oath of allegiance, a very strong one, men, women [and] children. Ned watched the proceedings with [great] interest, thinks Col. Coates the best of gentlemen.

I feel a good deal better tonight, and feel I can rest a little if necessary. Warwick [is] willing to take the burden if I lay it down.

Lemuel Z. Cadot was from Scioto County, Ohio, and rose to the rank of lieutenant colonel in the 91st Ohio Volunteer Infantry. In spring 1863, William S. Newton reported that Cadot was the commander of the post in Summersville, West Virginia. Lieut. Col. Cadot, Eugene B. Willard Photograph Album, Special Collections, Marietta College, Marietta, Ohio.

If Carpenter will only join us, we shall have a good and pleasant time. I suspect he will not venture up here at present. Should the Pay Master come in any reasonable time, I think he (Carpenter) will resign his position. He has tried for a leave of absence, but not approved. His wife is very sick, and he is fretting over it very much.

Cannot the Gallian County folks, see that Capt. Cadot is made Major of our Regt. It of right belongs to him, he being Senior Captain. An effort is being made for Capt. Caldwell of Scioto Co. by some, I trust that Gov. Tod will do right.

It is getting very late, and I must stop. My regards to all.

Your Husband
Wm. S. Newton

49

Gauley Bridge May 14th/63

Dear Wife

Yours of May 10th just came, and I thought this was the best time to answer it. Ned is fishing in the Gauley River, he has been quite successful for a boy & he seems to enjoy eating them, and Jack Culbertson's black boy cooks them for him very well, he gave me one about six inches long for my breakfast, reserving three for himself. He got very tired on the march down here. By the way we feel very sad at the result of our move here, when we left Sommerville, we left quite a supply of forage, just as we arrived here Genl. Scammon ordered two wagon trains, in all 180 mules, back to bring the forage left behind. Our Quartermaster wanted to burn the forage, was not permitted to do so. Three of our companies were ordered back to guard the trains, and started, they were again halted, and 40 of the 2nd Va. Cavalry sent in their place. They went to Sommerville, loaded the teams, telling the Secesh the 91st were expected every moment, but when they drew in their pickets and started for Gauley, the Rebels came in, found how weak the guard was, they followed the trains, capturing everything. The Cavalry have now got all in, except eight. We only know of two being killed, the rest are in the hands of the enemy. One, Lieut. Ong,[23] of Co. F., is captured.

He took supper with me the evening before. We all feel, that if the 91st had been permitted to hold the post two days longer, this loss of 40,000$ to the Government would have been saved. Ned & I took supper Saturday eve at Owen Duffy's just in the place where the train was captured. In getting our supper, we were some three or four miles behind the Regt., but caught up with them before dark, and when we stopped we lay down on the floor of an old secesh, Ned slept well, but I could not accommodate myself to the place very well.

My health has much improved on the march, and here, you are mistaken about my habits, for if there is anyone one likes sympathy when they are sick, it is me. And you are as likely to hear of it as anyone I know. Carpenter has resigned and I suppose the resignation will be approved. Warwick is endeavoring to get the position. His commission is almost a month older than mine, he may succeed, but I do not believe it. I have written to Surg. Genl. Smith the circumstances in the case, and wait the result. They may appoint a new man, thinking we have not served long enough for promotion. I am content to do what is best, and try to do my duty to the men the best I know how. We still hold Gauley, our old camp of last fall, how long we will remain here is not known.

One of our pickets was shot this morning at 20 Mile Creek, five miles above our camp, yet we feel perfectly safe in our position here. There is no force, we think, can be spared to drive us from our position.

Should you go back to Harmar, give my kindest regards to all there.

We have no news of the Paymaster as yet, he may come soon or not. My regards to all,

Your Husband
Wm. S. Newton

50

Fayetteville Va. May 18th 1863

My Dear Wife

This is Monday evening, and I feel very tired, and will not promise to write very much, indeed would not write at all, if not wishing to let you know our whereabouts.

Yesterday *Sunday* as *usual*, we received marching orders. My team was down at Loup for rations, and I was not able to move, for more than an hour after the Regt. I got started at 4 P.M. went down to the ferry, crossed, and commenced once more to climb Cotton Mountain. Part way up, I took Ned from the ambulance, placed him behind me, and on we went, overtook the Regt. three miles from Fayette, they had stopped for a very late supper.

This over, we marched into this place at 10 O'clock P.M. of the same evening. The Rebs were threatening the outposts of Col. White of the 12th here.

We came to the rescue, and came purposely in the night, that they might catch a thrashing today if they made an attack. This morning our pickets were fired upon, four miles up the Rolla Road. Four Companies of the 12th were marched out with some of the 2nd Va. Cavalry. I was busy endeavoring to provide a place for the sick of our Regt. Carpenter stayed at Camp Reynolds with the Hospital. Warwick had accompanied a flag of truce to Summerville, with a view of bringing away two of the 2nd Va. Cavalry wounded in the late skirmish when the trains were captured.

Thus you see I am alone again, but this is not all, at 9 this morning, I received orders from Col. White, through Surg. Graham, to take two orderlies with the necessary instruments, bandages, & etc., and to report to Capt. Wilson, who was commanding the infantry & cavalry, sent out two hours before. I took Billy Falwell for my orderly, both of us well mounted, & started to find the skirmishers. We traveled some five miles on the Rolla Road, before we came up to the rear of the column, three miles further on, we left the infantry, and pushed on to where one of the Cavalry had, yesterday, in a skirmish, broken one of his legs. I stopped to adjust the fracture, the column moving on. As soon as this was done, we started to overtake the Cavalry, which we did, four miles further on. But they were retreating, having been fired upon, by Rebel infantry, just as we met them, the most of them dismounted, and deployed as skirmishers, hoping the Rebs would follow, and they have a chance to bushwhack them, but they were too sharp to be caught in the trap, so we waited about one hour, and then sent two squads over the mountain by another road, to if possible, learn their strength & character. They soon ran onto a hot place, and were compelled to fall back.

I am quite sure, one hundred shots were fired into our men, overshooting them, all the time. One horse came back without a rider, but we think was not killed, he may be a prisoner.

We all fell back to where the infantry were stationed. Some seven miles out, they will try to hold the position all night. Capt. Wilson then excused me from further duty, and accompanied by Billy, I soon came to camp, got there at dark. Ned much rejoiced at my return, and is now sleeping away, as quietly as if no Rebs were in a hundred miles of us.

And I too must seek the same rest or I will not be able for duty tomorrow.

I wish you would make for me, two woolen shirts, from something plaid, checked, or something that will not too soon show dirt.

May [make] them large sleeves, width, & length, for high water shirts I do not like, and we can by no others ready made. These I have are just about right for Ned. Have wore two linen shirts, both of which are dirty yet. You will probably have an opportunity to send them by some one coming up. I do not think we will remain here long, but most probably go back to Gauley, or down to Piatt, & few days will tell, and I will keep you posted.

Give my regards to all,

Your Husband
Wm. S. Newton

51

Fayetteville Va. May 20th/63

Dear Wife

We are here, and the enemy in front on the Rolla Road. They drove us in yesterday, and at 11 A.M. opened on us with three or four pieces of artillery. We replied with part of our guns. Our men occupy the breastworks, and have hardly returned their fire, saving our ammunition till it is needed.

This is now the fourth day since we commenced skirmishing. We have had but few casualties on our part today. Some yesterday however, it would be contraband to say what they are, for fear this does not get through. I have hard work to do. We all have a hospital in common now. The shell burst very near to us, yet we feel, we have as good position as yet can be obtained.

Ned is here with me, and enjoys the excitement very much.

They opened on us this morning at 4 A.M. and have kept it up almost constantly. We are hopeful and confident, of holding the place.

Give yourself no uneasiness for I shall take care of Ned and act prudent. As a matter of course I cannot write anything while the booming of cannon at every moment strikes the ear.

My regards to all the friends, much love to Mott & Kittie.

Tell them, I have often thought of them, during the last three days. In haste your husband.

Wm. S. Newton

52

Gauley Bridge June 27th 1863

Dear Wife

Yours by Lieut. Medlicott[24] came in due time, was very glad of your description of folks at Harmar, for I have known very little about them for a year past, nothing of how they looked, talked, or acted, matters of no small interest to me, who had always known so much of them, and now to know comparatively nothing.

My commission it seems, is still born. It has not come. And if sent, I suppose was intercepted by Col. Turley' s order, I remain at my post, do my duty, the best I know, say as little as possible, and wait for the troubling of the waters, whether someone will always step in first, remains to be seen. I have not had a fair chance, being separated from the Regt.

They have had every opportunity, I none. The Gallia Co. officers here, were ready and willing to afford me any assistance necessary. Companies D & H from my own county, would have helped me. So would Company A officers, but they were all at Fayette, and I dare not leave my post to go there, the Col. would not have permitted it.

So I have been obliged to content myself with writing a letter to Capt. Looker,[25] Aid De Camp to Gov. Tod, asking him to make my statement to the Gov. If I could only have had an opportunity, to have obtained the signatures of those officers at Fayette, it might have availed some good. But the Cols particularly, and activities in the case, will probably overrule my feeble effort, and I fear Neal has grown lukewarm since he found opposition, lest his own popularity should suffer, although Ricker says, he told Neal exactly how the matter stood, and how much more the men would give, to have me promoted, especially our own county & town boys. It may all work out for the best. I shall try to think so at least. Am entirely ignorant what kind of tactics they used, but I know that a great amount of telegraphing was done, and they are not done yet.

Last evening, Col. Coates got uneasy about the safety of the Wharf Boat at Loop Creek, & telegraphed Col. White. He ordered Coates to send a Co. of men to guard it. Coates replied, "he could not spare a whole Co." as so much of our force was then out on a scout. But that he would send Lieut. Crawford with 20 men, which he did. Afterward, Col. White telegraphed Gen Scammon, the Genl. sent Companies I & B Va. Cavalry (Capt. Hambleton) up on the other side of the river.

They arrived at 3 AM. this morning, and camped just opposite the boat, put their pickets and went to sleep. Just before day, they were surrounded by Rebel cavalry, and all made prisoners, this was better than the Rebs could have hoped, for their intention was to burn the boat with our Com[pan]y Stores, expecting to find no force there. Daylight coming on, our Lieut. with his 20 men, could discern what was going on. He saw them all disarmed, and mounted, ready to move with their prisoners. He ordered his men to fire on them across the river, which they done with such aim as to empty several saddles, and repeated it so often, as to throw them into confusion, at the same time called to the boys to dismount and take cover under the bank, which most of them did, and escaped. Crawford kept up such incessant fire, the Rebs were obliged to run, and leave the most of their prisoners. The horses too, many of them escaped in the confusion. Robert Kirker is a prisoner, I wrote his father this evening. Dick escaped by swimming the river. Capt. Charley Hambleton also escaped in the confusion of the firing. He feels very bad, and is quite unfortunate for him at this time as he is expecting to be promoted to Major. It was a most unfortunate affair. Lieut. Crawford could have aroused the camp, had he only known who it was, that was opposite to him. He heard the firing on the pickets, but kept very still, lest they were all Rebels. But when daylight came, his timely aid, rendered the affair much less disastrous, than it otherwise would have been. A party of Rebs, on a scout, also this morning, halted one of our trains at Mrs. Tompkins farm, and took from it fifteen mules, with which they made tracks. They are unusually active, all around us, and are showing any amount of daring.

We may be surprised here, but great care and vigilance is used to prevent it. Capt. Ricker, with his own, and one other company of cavalry, are on Picket at Loop tonight. We also have a Co. B, Capt. Niday, down there, which leaves our force here very small. Hope you will get well & fleshy while at H[armar] for I don't like to think of you so poor as you was while here. Ned is busy fishing etc., does not seem to tire of soldiering. We still board with Miller, and have made almost enough outside to pay it so far.

Are any new Regts. forming at Marietta, if so would like to get the Surgeoncy of one of them if they keep me out of my rights here. Have not yet heard from Will, but learned that Mrs. Blazer[26] arrived safe with the 200 I sent by her. Write soon and often. Give love to all. Kiss Kate for me several times.

> Your Husband
> Wm. S. Newton

4

Still Rumors of a Fight,
July–October 1863

William S. Newton spent the majority of the summer and early fall
of 1863 stationed at a hospital near Fayetteville, West Virginia. Many
companies of the 91st Ohio Volunteer Infantry pursued Confederate
raider John Hunt Morgan in Ohio during July, but Newton did not join
them.[1] Elsewhere, Union forces in the Western Theatre led by Major
General William Rosecrans were moving through Tennessee and inch-
ing toward Georgia. Newton was optimistic about the war ending soon,
perhaps within six months if Union victories continued. While tending
patients, Newton observed the daily realities of war. He became emo-
tional after seeing the body of Colonel John T. Toland, the beloved colonel of the 34th Ohio Volunteer Infantry who was killed at the raid of
Wytheville in July. Newton reported on some skirmishing in the area
but explained that diseases such as typhoid fever were killing soldiers
instead of enemy fire. Others in his family were also sick, including
Newton's wife, who was visiting family in Harmar and Gallipolis.

His application for a new commission remained unanswered.
He learned that his friend Assistant Surgeon John B. Warwick had
received the commission as surgeon of the 91st Ohio Volunteer Regiment. Still, Newton held out hope that his experience and time served
as an assistant surgeon would result in a commission as a surgeon of
another nearby regiment. He used his military and family connections
to inquire in Columbus and elsewhere on the status of his commission
application, but as with his other experiences in military life, he continued to "hurry up and wait." In the meantime, Newton reported on
the contentious election for Ohio's governor, which featured Harmar's
own John Brough and the exiled Clement Laird Vallandigham.[2]

The status of emancipated slaves in society was another element
in Newton's correspondence of late summer 1863. In August he introduced Mary Ann McDonald, a former slave who was emancipated

by the Union army following the raid of Wytheville. It is likely that Mary was sent to the hospital for examination and Newton claimed responsibility for her wellbeing. He decided to send Mary to Ironton to assist his wife and family. As part of the plan, Ned and Mott met her in Charleston and took her back to Ironton. He was concerned that "negro traders" in Charleston might "steal her away from the boys before they get a boat," but she safely made it to Ironton.[3] Newton explained to his wife that Mary "belongs to you, that your interests are hers." He suggested that "the boys teach her to read" and possibly write, but Newton made clear that Mary did not have any level of independence. In an August 23 letter he told his wife: "You can make, or mold her into anything you desire."[4] The addition of Mary to the Newton household was not an easy adjustment. The letters were unclear on the details, but rumors about Mary's trustworthiness circulated through Ironton and found their way to Newton. The breaking point was the accusation that Mary had stolen personal items from the family. Some of the lost articles were later discovered and had simply been misplaced instead of stolen. Newton's inquiries confirmed that all accusations against Mary were unfounded. Nonetheless, by October Newton's wife had lost all trust in Mary and discharged her from service. She was no longer mentioned in their correspondence and there are no existing records to trace what happened to Mary Ann McDonald in the decades that followed.

Family was the main topic of Newton's letters during this period. During July and early August, Ned was staying in camp, and fishing took up most of his time. In one letter, Newton explained that Ned caught a fish of ten pounds and had to use a boat oar to subdue it. Ned returned to Ironton sometime in August. Newton also wrote a letter to his other son Mott with a similar invitation to join him on the front lines at some point. He encouraged Mott to be a good role model for his younger sister Kate and to help his mother when needed. By this point in the war, Newton decided that he did not want to practice medicine in Ironton once his service was complete. He discussed selling his house to Colonel Benjamin F. Coates, also a doctor who was planning for a return to medicine at the end of the war. The transaction did not occur, but Newton was clearly planning for the postwar and returning to his family. Newton applied for a leave of absence so he could spend some time with his family in Ironton in November. He advised his wife to keep that information private until it became official.

53

Gauley Bridge July 5th 1863

My Dear Wife

Yours of 1st ultimo is at hand, came today, and I need not tell you, that coming from the old stomping ground, gave it additional relish, then to think that you are there to see Charley[5] graduate, a pleasure you had not thought of. Tell Br. S. I suppose he thinks he is getting old, now that his *baby* has taken in the degree of & all.

Well, time flies, and we are all fast passing away, for it only seems a short time since you and I first visited Br. S. Charley then was a very small boy, yet when I consult the figures and think, that 1845 is almost 18 years ago, am not surprised that boys can grow & graduate even in that space of time. Many events have transpired, many recollections, the memory of which, is very pleasant, others, we could wish buried in oblivion. Experience is sometimes a harsh, but a very faithful and instructional teacher. Shall we not so live, that the experience of the past, may be a safe guarantee for the future. And our efforts to be useful, be crowned with better success.

My commission never reached me. Have incidentally learned, that it went to Head Quarters at Fayette, was there sent back. Have not heard a word on the subject from there, nor have I deigned an inquiry, thinking the least said the soonest mended. Am quite certain there is something hanging at Columbus, for Warwick has not been commissioned as yet.

Have written to Surg. Genl. Smith, telling him the circumstances, "that my position in the Regt." would be attended with embarrassments, that my usefulness would be limited very considerably, and very respectfully asking,

Charles Humphrey Newton was the son of Stephen Newton and the half-nephew of William S. Newton. Charles graduated from Marietta College in 1863. After graduating, he served as a first lieutenant in Company D of the 2nd Ohio Heavy Artillery. In a July 5, 1863, letter, William S. Newton referred to Charley and his graduation from Marietta College. Chas. H. Newton, Class '63, Eugene B. Willard Photograph Album, Special Collections, Marietta College, Marietta, Ohio.

that I be assigned to other duty. I submitted my letter to Col. Coates. He volunteered to write also, which he did, by the same mail, and gave me the letter to read & mail. I have kept a copy. One that I shall be proud of, whether I am promoted or not.

If he had dared to give me this letter at the time, Gov. Tod would have never recalled my Com[mi]s[sio]n, for Coates influence at Columbus would be worth all the Turleys in America. But he dare not interfere, lest his inferior rank would get him into trouble. He does not hesitate, to say to Surg. Genl. "that I am a good, efficient, Army Surg., 'eminently fitted for the position' and deserving a better position than I now occupy."

He said all, and more, than I could have asked. He a physician, and Senator, will have an influence in the right place, and now that Col. Turley has so plainly shown his partiality, I think my position even as Surg. with him, would be very unpleasant. Hope I shall not long be kept in doubt. I yesterday, with Capt. Waller & newt, took dinner at Munsey's[6] over Gauley River, had good cherry pie & etc.

Ned hardly has time to accompany me. He is very busy fishing, spends the day catching the little ones for bait, then at night puts out his trot, with 30 or 40 hooks. He wants me to tell you that he caught one on Friday morning weighing ten lbs. The soldiers had a good laugh, for he used one of the boat oars as a club, with which he pound the fish over the head, because it did not hold still. The only wonder is, that he did not knock it loose from the hook. He was alone at the time, and captured five in all.

Have six in Hospital, none very bad. Hope you will write often. Tell Mother her letter is behind yet, and I am afraid it will be.

Give my love to all, and kiss my little daughter.

Your Husband

Wm. S. Newton

54

Gauley Bridge Sunday July 12th 1863

Dear Wife

Yours of 8th came today, and we had almost concluded, you were spending the time so pleasantly, you had forgotten the Dixie correspondence or thought it of secondary importance. We are here just as you left us, except a change of Capt. Millers [Millard] Cav. Co., for Capt. Waller. Not so with other commands however, for Genl. Scammon & staff passed up to Fayette yesterday. The 9th & 13th Va. Regts had gone before, the 23rd Ohio has since crossed Cotton Mountain, and report says, the 34th Ohio & 2nd Va. Cavalry have gone, but taken another route.

The good news from other points has excited the Genl. to move on toward Bolton, while our little command are to hold the Gormley & New River Roads. Col. Coates has sent fatigue parties to blockade the roads, in such a way, that they will not be able to dash in upon us without some notice of their approach. The Genl it is said, is determined to do something, and I presume he can get a fight by traveling to Rolla, whereas from best information, four regts are now watching our movements. Should present indications of success attend our arms, two or three months certainly will find us at home again. God speed the time.

Neal writes to know if I will sell my house, saying the Nail Mill will go into operation this summer, and houses will be in demand.

You will have to answer the question, when you go home, have thought for a few days past I would like to read my newspaper in the back yard, listening for the fall, of a *Bracken*[7] or *Summer Sweet*,[8] interspersed occasionally with interruptions by Kate May, and perhaps *some other body*. Reflections like these, are not meant for a soldier, however, I will therefore "dry up" as the boys say.

Have heard nothing from Columbus, or anywhere, to indicate any change of position etc.

Hope I may be assigned to other duties, before we shall again join our esteemed Col. I have not made any inquiries, nor has he ever intimated to me the fate of my commission. But for this, am satisfied he would have ordered me to Fayette before this, to go with the advancing column, for I have always been the pioneer, in every movement yet, and when comfortable quarters were established, hospital located, and things working all right, then Warwick or Carpenter would follow on, and if another move was made, I was the one to go, whether alone or otherwise, and I am getting almost tired of it. I presume they would like very much now, to have me at Fayette, that they might send me with the moving column, while others stayed behind, but I am now in a separate command, have the Hospital, sick in quarters, all to myself, and they cannot very well change the programme. All of which I am thankful for at the present, though this may be the hottest place, and we may have to do some hard fighting, or good running. I am content, not to be on the march these warm days.

I told Ned, if we were ordered to advance with the rest, I should be compelled to send him to the rear, but he demurred very strongly, as he is quite anxious to see more of soldiering.

He has almost worn out his pants. I patched those you made while here, and the others need it, but I have nothing like them.

Should John [Turley] hear anything from Gov. Tod, let me know of it. I presume I should hear from Surg. Genl. this week, and perhaps not.

Give my kindest regards to all, and tell them to write to me. Good night.

> Your Husband
> Wm. S. Newton

55

Fayetteville Aug 4th 1863

My Dear Wife

Have been waiting several days for a letter from you, not having received one for two weeks or more.

I suppose you are at G.[allipolis] and will therefore direct this to that place. Hope if Linc & Stephenson are there still, you will make your visit short for Mother H. was almost crazy when I was there, and if you & children remain long Father will be. I don't think he more than half liked it when I went there the last time. They were just agoing to heal, and I fancied the welcome was not very cordial. It may have been a mistake, but I thought so. I did not stay all night, but got up when the papers came in and went to the boat. I took breakfast next morning with Andrews, perhaps it is all right.

Warwick has just come in bringing your letter of the 1st. So I feel much better and the content is indeed refreshing. I don't refer to your crying about your absence from G[allipolis]. but the papers you alluded to, if that matter was off my hands I would feel like another man. I think your visit there has not been devoid of interest and perhaps profit.

Major Cowen our Paymaster is expected tomorrow. If he comes will try to send a remittance by the Pay Agent of the State, will send the receipt to you.

You had better draw it and place it in bank with the balance. Warwick has received his commission and been mustered as Surgeon two days ago. I had hoped I would hear from Columbus before this event. Neal writes however, that Capt. Looker has promised to give me the promotion, and appoint me to the first vacancy. If you think best, and Neal gets an opportunity, let him sell the house, for I do not think I shall want to practice Med. in Ironton after the war is over. If I could realize 2500. in money would prefer to sell it, although it should bring 3000., it cost me 3450. I think there are several places I would prefer to practice, places where I might get my pay for the services rendered.

I have just returned from Gauley Bridge. Miss Jenny Hill & Mrs. Tyree,[9] are both sick, the latter very sick. Not expected to live. They sent for me last Friday but Col. T[urley] would not consent to let me go. They sent again, yesterday Warwick went to see the Col. & he obtained permission & a pass. Lieut. Glassie was determined to have me, although both the Surgeons of

5th Va. were there and attending the case. But poor woman I fear she will not recover. You will probably hear from me again soon but in the meantime write. My love to the boys & Kate, tell them they must be good.

Your Husband
Wm.S.N.

56

Fayetteville Va., Aug 7th 1863

My Dear Wife

I today sent by Lieut. Atkinson 200.$ to brother Will, with the request that he send it to you by the first opportunity. You had better place it in bank with the other.

I will also send to H. S. Neal the recommendations of the officers of our Regt. for my promotion. I hope it will not be long before an opportunity offers, for my transfer from the reg. Those most active to procure Warwick's promotion seem now very willing to do all they can to work amends. I am sure that they feel that they have deprived me of my right in this matter. But I hope it will all end for the best.

I also send in this fifty five dollars which I collected for W. W. Kirker, you will just pay this amount to him.

Lieut. Crossland will take this, did not know he was going when I sent the 200. to Brother Will. Will try to have Crossland take it down to you if it can be found in Gallipolis. Tell the boys they must be good.

Your Husband
Wm. S. Newton

John B. Warwick was a doctor from Scioto County, Ohio, and the older brother of Newton R. Warwick. He was appointed assistant surgeon of the 91st Ohio Volunteer Infantry. In May 1863, George H. Carpenter resigned as surgeon of the 91st and both Newton and Warwick applied for the position. Warwick was promoted to the rank of surgeon for the 91st on May 23, 1863. Newton made frequent references to Warwick in his correspondence. Major Warwick, Surgeon, Eugene B. Willard Photograph Album, Special Collections, Marietta College, Marietta, Ohio.

57

Fayetteville Va Aug. 8th 1863

My Dear Son [Mott],

Have long owed you a letter, and will now try to pay up my honest debts. You have no doubt learned before this, that in your absence I was in Ironton, but not at home, for I could not get into the house, was in the back yard and sat for some time on the porch.

But it did not seem like home, for Mother, Ned, Mott, not even little Kate was to be seen. It made me sick of home very soon, and the back yard had grown up to weeds & bushes. I hope you & Ned will do all you can to put things in order, and not leave everything for Ma to do. You must help her all you can, and remember as you make yourselves useful, in that way will also make yourselves happy, for true happiness consists in being usefully employed and thereby rendering happiness to others. You must keep a watchful eye over little Kate, try to amuse her. Never make her peevish and fretful. Teach her those things which you will be proud to have her know, when you & she have grown older. Never learn her bad things, or talk before her anything you would not wish me to hear, or that you think I would not approve.

You have no idea how much you can contribute to your Mothers aid & happiness, and how proud I would be of you, if you strive to act and do just right. Neddie was a good boy while with me, and I heard good accounts of you, so I hope you will both be good at home.

Don't let the neighbors have it to say, that your Mother has a hard time to manage her boys. How much better it would be, if they could say, "How much help the boys are to their mother." You must always let her be the judge of what is best. She is much older than you, and can always judge best for you.

Don't tease her to let you do things when she has decided that it is not best.

She don't like to be teased, it makes her so unhappy. She don't like to refuse you anything that is proper & right, and the best way therefore is to be satisfied when she has made her decision. You will never make soldiers, unless you are willing to be governed.

I am hoping ere long, that I will be able to see you all. And if everything works right I will be able to let you go soldiering with me. That if you are good boys, you will both have an opportunity. Boys who do well at home, can be welcomed when they go abroad. I shall not fear to take you, nor be ashamed of you among strangers.

I expect to send this, by Orderly Sargt. Charley Hall, [10] Co. I, who goes home to carry money for the boys in his Company. He gets this furlough, for meritorious conduct, not having missed roll call, or been absent from duty for almost a whole year. Don't you think he deserves it?

Quite a number of our boys went home on what they call a *French*,[11] while we were in Ohio. Consequently a number of them who did not report promptly, are now in the guard house.

I suppose Ned took his saddle home with him, and I hope by the time I am permitted to come, the horses back will be well, and if I bring Old Tom along, you can both ride out.

Tell Mother she must get a good girl to do her work, and take care of herself. I have written to her twice this week, and hope she got both letters, for they were valuable.

Hope you will remember all I have written in this, and will try to write again soon.

> Your Father,
> Wm. S. Newton

58

> Fayetteville Va. Aug. 11th 1863

My Dear Wife

I had not intended to write you another letter till I received one.

But circumstances alter cases. Today happening in the 9th Va. Hospital, I there found a colored girl aged 20, who came from Wytheville with the 34th Ohio. As she is desirous of going to Ohio, have concluded to send her to you. She is a good cook, washer, etc., has been used to doing house work, and if you manage her right will answer your purpose much better than one who had a house near by. Yours will be the only home she will have, and if you are pretty sharp, she will make but few acquaintances. Her name is Mary Ann McDonald.[12] Be firm, but kind to her as she seeks an asylum in a free country.

The Provost Marshall Capt. Hilt[13] has promised to give me the necessary papers, and I expect to send her, with Lieut. Henry Duncan,[14] of the 9th Va., who lives in Ironton, and goes home to take money for the Ironton boys of his Reg.

Have not heard a word from Columbus. Our mails are very irregular, at present, and perhaps this is the reason I have not heard from you more frequently. And I presume you have enough to do, to get things straightened up. I hope, if this girl there once, you will impress upon her mind, that *there is her home*, and that I have been at a good amount of *trouble & expense* to get her there, and that I shall expect strict obedience, and close attention to her duties, if she expects a good & permanent home.

It may be a day or two before I can get her started, and then may add something more to this.

Your Husband W. S.

Newton

[added to above letter, mailed together]

Wednesday eve Aug 12th

Will start Mary Ann early tomorrow morning, with a Mr. Krible,[15] & Beller,[16] our Hospital cook, they both go home on furlough. They may leave her in Gallipolis with Brother Will to ship to you. Will write to Will and he may do as he thinks best. Am anxiously waiting a reply to my letter, containing the money. You will therefore let me know as soon as convenient. I have been to a considerable trouble to procure these papers, and if you get the girl, and she can be useful, and save you, I shall be well paid for the trouble & expense.

We have nothing new or strange here, everything goes on in the regular order. I am still waiting patiently for promotion & transfer, it may come soon & it may not come for some time. Give my regards to Mr. Kingsbury & family.[17] Much love to you all, write often.

Your Husband

Wm. S. Newton

59

Fayetteville Va. Aug 14th 1863

Dear Wife

Am still looking for a letter from you, our mail has failed now three days. I suppose on account of boats, and I am afraid will lose all I have invested in the colored girl sent you. The Negro traders about Charleston will steal her away from the boys before they get a boat.

I feel quite anxious about it, and shall till I hear from you. I want you to write all about everything, for it seems an age since I got a letter from you. Have only received one from you since you left Marietta.

If the mail comes through, I expect to get at least three or four.

Next Sabbath our Reg. expects to go to the front, some ten miles out. I will stay here in charge of the Hospital, in all probability, as I now have charge, & Warwick has the Surgeons call to hold every morning. We have quite a large number, considering we left all the sick behind at Gallipolis. The weather is so warm, and our men have had so much guard and fatigue duty to perform, it is to be wondered at.

Have you heard from Harmar yet? I wrote to Mother, but have not yet heard an answer.

Am still in hope I will be assigned to other duty, and am confident that it will be done.

If so, think I will get an opportunity to make you a flying visit. Would like very much to stop with you a few days. Think I would be content to sit quietly down in your sitting room and never see another face except those who belong there. Mott & Kate, I can't remember how they look. I sometimes try to call up their features but they are so indistinct, it affords no pleasure.

Has Neal had any offer for the house? I want you to write everything. How you found the house, the yard, etc. Got someone to clean your house, you need not try it. You will live just as long and have just as much, if you don't kill yourself working.

My shirts you made, are all the same color now. They fade so much, and look very plain now. Did you get your money, & that of the Kirkers?

Give my regards to all enquiring friends and much love for you all.

Your Husband
Wm. S. Newton

60

Fayetteville Aug. 17th 1863

Dear Wife

This is Monday morning, and as Matthew Stafford[18] of 2 Va. Cavalry goes home on furlough will send a few lines, while breakfast is being got ready, as I shall have no time after, before he starts.

Your letter of 9th came yesterday, the only one for two weeks, and it was not half long enough. I wanted two or three. Col. Coates offered me two thousand dollars for my house, and pay the cash all down.[19] Don't say anything about this except to Neal. If he purchases, he expects to live in it and practice Med., and by buying my house, of course expects, I will hunt another location in which to practice. He does not offer enough & I think he will pay more. He made this offer, and told me to write to Neal, and see if he can get a better offer. I told him he might have it for 2600. You may tell Neal but let him know that I think it is not enough.

And see if he cannot do better with it.

Tell Ned I hope he has not forgotten the admonition I gave him before parting. He must not do so, for it will not be well with him, when I come home. And other privileges he might enjoy will certainly be curtailed. He is old enough now, to seek the right kind of company, to act & do as he thinks I will approve. Never to do anything without first counseling with his mother.

I want him to follow this course strictly, and if he does not respect your authority, as I said before, there will be a day of reckoning.

It is very unpleasant to be compelled to write thus, and I hope he will not give occasion to have it repeated.

> My love to you all, in haste,
> Your Husband
> Wm. S. Newton

61

Fayetteville West Va., Aug. 23rd, 1863

My Dear Wife

Yours of 16th came yesterday. And I was very glad to learn that Mary Ann had arrived safely, for I began to think all I had invested in her, had been lost.

Should have been pleased to know the particulars. If they gave her any trouble at Charleston, if the boys treated her kindly, etc.

But as our Cook[20] will return this week, will get the particulars from him, with all the variations & comments. You must let Mary feel and understand, that she belongs to you, that your interests are hers, and never talk as if you expected, she would have any other home but with you. Let the boys teach her to read, and if she makes progress, and desires it, teach her to write. In this, she will feel that you take an interest in her, it will give her employment of mind, and at the same time contentment.

Tell her, I shall be glad to hear of her acquirements, and if she does well, I will do well by her, give her clothing as you think she needs them, but don't make her proud, for if I am not mistaken, in the shape of her head. You can make, or mold her into anything you desire. Col. Coates thinks, it is a great shame, he did not know of her, for his wife needs one very much. He considers that I have made a point in advance of him.

Col. Coates has written for his wife & boy to come up. He wanted me to send for you at the same time. I told him you had just got home, and would hardly be willing to start so soon again. He never suspected the real cause. How do you think you would enjoy a trip up the valley now?

We still have plenty of sickness. I have some ten fever cases in Hospital, and beside some ague in quarters, we have not room for them in Hospital. One man, George Theobald,[21] Corporal in Company G, died yesterday of typhoid fever. We will bury him today, and so few of our men are here, except the sick, it will be a difficult performance. They have the grave prepared, and I am only waiting for Lieut. White to come in and take charge of the funeral.

We expect the whole Reg. to come in on Tuesday next, and then the 9th Va., will go out and take their place, for ten days. The 12th Ohio go next.

Thus you see they diversify their duties. Our men will again go on the fortifications and by the way, if this war ever ends, this place will be visited for years to come, as a place noted for its defenses. You, or any one, not acquainted with the fact, would be surprised at the extent of the works here. They will stand as a lasting monument of this wicked rebellion, whether they will be noted for any serious engagements, or long sieges, is a matter of some doubt in my mind. We can, it is estimated, resist an attack of ten or twelve thousand, and do it successfully.

This place, is where Col. Jack Toland showed his fighting qualities, about a year ago. Had two horses shot under him, and then on foot, led his men in the thickest of the fight.

And the other day, when they carried his dead body past my Hospital, I could hardly restrain the tears, for I remembered his virtues, and forgot his vices. Poor old Jack, he was not prepared to die. But I cannot refrain from saying, I believe him to be the best military man in the valley.

I spent a very pleasant evening with Col. White, commanding this Brigade, at his invitation. Am resolved it should not be the last. He too was a doctor before the war began. Is one of the most candid men I ever met. So different from some other Colonels I could mention. The men almost worship him.

Our Reg. this morning received a full set of instruments for a brass band. The money to purchase them was mostly contributed by the officers of the Reg. They cost over eleven hundred dollars.

Most of the officers paid 25$ apiece. I did not go in, and Col. Coates told me I did right under the circumstances. They taxed the sutler some 200. which I suppose he will not be long in getting it back. Am still in the dark about a transfer, hope I shall not always be kept thus.

Tell Mrs. Kingsbury if she will get both the Pres.[cription] filled, and keep Mattie at the medicine, it will not be long till she will see an improvement. Remember me kindly to them all.

Tell Mr. K. I think he might write to me. There is certainly enough of interest transpiring each week in Ironton, out of which to get items for one letter. I suppose you were not sorry to learn that the schools were to be under his supervision.

I received a letter from Mother, and answered it. Write soon and often.

Your Husband
Wm. S. Newton

62

Fayetteville Aug 27th 1863

My Dear Wife

Yours of 23rd came to hand this eve, and was *as ever welcome.*

As you say it makes me feel quite sad, when I think of selling my home, but I have been convinced sometime, if I can dispose of my property there at a fair price, I will seek another location for the practice of Medicine. Still I think the least said about the matter at present, the better.

I had no idea of taking up with Col. Coates offer, and told him so. But he was quite anxious that I should let Neal know of it, and see if he could get a better offer.

I told Coates he might have it for 2600. and I would wait on him for one thousand of the money, one, or two, years, provided he paid interest on the same. He is now at Gauley Bridge on a Court Martial,[22] and I will write and let him know how the matter stands. Am not certain but think he wishes to settle there soon, whether the war is over or not.

Am sorry to learn your girl is sick, for you must have your hands full. You had better get another, for we have got our foot in it, and must do the best we can.

I received a letter from Em today, of the same date of yours. Caroline & children were still there. She says my horse is doing very well at last accounts.

The Med. Inspector of U.S.A. was here last night, inspecting our Hospitals. He was the rank of Lieut. Col. In him I found an old acquaintance. W. H. Mussey of Cini.[Cincinnati], is the man, and his position is a nice one.

The work on our fortifications still goes on, and so does the sickness of our men increase. I have fifteen cases of fever, and some of the typhoid cases are very bad. Yet upon the whole, I think they are getting along as well as we could expect. Dr. Mussey thinks we are too crowded, but did not suggest any way to remedy the difficulty. Warwick & I have rigged up a shanty outside in which we eat sleep etc. Some of the cold nights recently have made us think of more comfortable quarters, but we shall have them to build if we get them.

Nothing from Columbus, as there are no new Reg's forming. I shall have to wait a vacancy, I suppose. You know my feelings on this subject. Suppose you write to John about selling the house, find what he thinks.

My routine of business here is becoming quite irksome, and I cannot feel the same toward some of the officers that I did sometime since. But try to act as if nothing had happened, how well I succeed I do not know. Am convinced that my time is usefully employed and while I can do good, and know that my services are appreciated by the men, and that I am earning my money honestly, will be content.

Tell Kate her Pa would like very much to see her, and she must not forget me.

Your Husband

Wm. S. Newton

63

HEAD QUARTERS,

Hospital 91st Reg. Ohio Volunteer Infantry

Camp Fayetteville Aug 31, 1863

Dear Wife

I have only time to say a few words, by one of the boys going home.

This is Monday morning, am in my usual good health, but still waiting for the troubling of the waters.

Have heard nothing from Coates, what have you done with the house. If Neal can get the 2800. with a good advance, and good security with interest on deferred payment, let him sell. It will also be necessary to have the relinquishment of mortgages from Brother John in order to make the title satisfactory. If the sale is likely to go on, you had best write to John, and if still willing to do as he intimated to you, have better have it done.

I had a long talk with Col. White, and he is strong in his expressions, says I must have a transfer, or resign my position, that he would not stay a moment unless it was to write for a transfer.

They are about establishing a Hospital in Charleston Va. again. Dr. Graham of the 12th went down this morning, and said, if it was done, he should recommend me for the place. If you were in a condition to come and stay with me, this would just suit me. He also says that a vacancy is likely to occur at the Pt. Pleasant Hospital, if so should prefer that. All these matters should be kept quiet, say not a word, the best may turn up yet for me.

Hope by this time the girl Mary is much better, and you are all well, and in good spirits. Write often, for your letters are very scarce. When the school begins you will I hope be rid of some of your anxiety.

Tell Ned he had better brighten up on his studies a little, that he may take an advanced position in his classes. He has been soldiering so long, am afraid he is rusty.

My love to all, Children must be good to mother.

Yours Truly,

Wm. S. Newton

64

Fayetteville Va., Sept. 4th 1863

My Dear Wife

How little we know how to manage affairs in this world. I thought I was doing you a great service sending Mary, that you would not always be troubled with a girl running home & seeking company abroad. That if she proved to be worth anything you would be almost independent, but such is life. We know not what a day may bring forth.

I hope you will not kill yourself in trying to save the girl, and now I heartily wish, I had left the whole matter to someone else, and you would not now be encumbered, and beside since sending her, have heard some stories, not altogether to her credit. They may all be lies, for no one escapes suspicion here, and the story came through the darkies, and looks very unlikely to me.

If she behaves all right, and stays at home very well, if not, it will give you a good opportunity to tell her, how easy it is to have bad stories raised on her.

We have a new Asst. Surg.,[23] just appointed. He comes from Barnesville, Belmont Co. Ohio, and I think will do very well. It may be the step first taken, to make the way clear for my transfer. He is a 1st Asst., and this in itself looks that way. I still have charge of the Hospital, and things go on very much as I wish, enough to do, and my time employed.

Warwick & Wellons attend the quarters, and have pretty easy times, but I prefer to run the Hospital all alone. I wish you would tell Dr. Wilson, that I have called the attention of our Col. to his claim, but with no results as yet. Col. Coates says there is no way by which he can get his pay, for they would not pay for Dr. Corson's[24] bill, who attended the Reg. almost a whole month during its organization. Gov. Tod claimed that he appointed Surgeons in time, that if they had reported in time, no others need have been employed. Dr. Carpenter is the one who should pay Dr. Wilson. He received over 1000. dollars and was not on duty a whole month. Tell him to make out a bill & send to Lieut. Crossland, our Quarter Master, and this will bring the matter before the Col. properly.

Saw Ricker two days ago, he is expecting his wife home soon. Remember me to them when they come. How do the boys get along now. I hope they are good. Much love to you all.

Your Husband
Wm. S. Newton

65

HEAD QUARTERS,
Hospital 91st Reg. Ohio Volunteer Infantry
Camp Fayetteville
Sept. 12th 1863

My Dear Wife

Have received two letters from you, since I wrote, which was on the 8th, a circumstance which has not occurred before during the war. Am glad you have had time to write, for I have been very much afraid you would get down sick.

I hope the worst is over, and Mary may prove herself worthy of the care & expense we have incurred on her account.

Things go on here, much after the old style. Col. Turley has gone home on a leave of absence for 15 days. Col. Coates is in command. The Regt. went to the front this morning. Dr. Wellons went with them. Warwick attends those left sick in quarters.

I still run the Hospital, and have had ten, to twelve, very sick all the time. We number 22 in all, sick & convalescents. We lost two this week, from typhoid fever.[25] Most of the remaining cases promise fair to recover.

Have you received yet the last 200. dollars from Will. Think I will send it direct hereafter, and then I will not be kept so long in suspense. Have written to learn how my horse is getting along, but get no reply.

Think Will is absorbed in business or something else, as he very rarely answers my inquires, or acknowledges the receipt of money when sent to his care.

I received a letter from Mary Frank. She says brother S. has sold his house for 6000 dollars. Half in money, the balance in town lots, a pretty good sale. Stephen has also purchased the house next to Br. John, the one Mr. Dunn[26] built. Thus you see changes take place. Should I sell, where I may land after the war is over, is uncertain.

From present appearances, the war will not long continue.

Scouts report 8 or ten Regiments of Rebs at Princeton, if so, no doubt a movement against us, a year since the retreat from this valley and no doubt there are many of the troops raised in the valley below us, that would like very much to come in, if for no other purpose, than seeing their families. I know very well, that I would fight in such a cause, if for no other.

The pickets over at Gauley were fired on, & driven in last eve. The report is, they are advancing on us, through Lewisburg & Raleigh both, we are incredulous, but may have a fight.

Ask Ned if he ever expects to be a man; and if so, if he is trying to make himself of any use. He is old enough to know that now is the time for preparation, and if he neglects his opportunities the time will soon be past. Nothing gives me more concern than his seeming indolence, and want of self respect. Goodbye,

Your Husband
Wm. S. Newton

66

HEAD QUARTERS,
Hospital 91st Reg. Ohio Volunteer Infantry
Camp Fayetteville West Va. Sept. 14th 1863

My Dear Wife

I feel very lonely this evening, and feel inclined to converse with you for a short time.

But this is only the shadow for which, we try to grab the substance. A poor substitute for the reality.

Have been trying to think today, how little Kate looks and talks, but cannot arrive at anything satisfactory. It has now been seven months, since I saw you all at home, a longer time than I had calculated, and very much longer than the time will be before I see you all again, if my health is spared. I spent the evening with Col. White, and told him I must go home in Nov. if the war ended or not. He will do all he can, to give me a leave of absence. I do not feel contented in my present position, and hence cannot enjoy the few pleasures allotted to soldiers, in the way I was accustomed to do.

Tell Ned, I went to gather chinkapins[27] to day, a business I think he would enjoy. They grow within 100 yards of the Hospital, and will be fine, when we have a good frost or two. Henry Bowman[28] has gone back to his company. Geo. Kirker[29] has returned, and drives the ambulance. John Stewart[30] & Stevens[31] drive the others.

Mrs. Coates is down at Mrs. Huddlestons,[32] Coates went down last eve to see her there, fearing to have her come this side of Cotton mountain, till things get more quiet.

Still rumors of a fight, but the Rebs don't come. The messenger between here & Gauley, with the mail, was halted just outside our pickets last night. Instead of halting, he put spurs to his horse & escaped. They did not fire on him, for they were too close to the pickets to escape themselves if they made so much noise. This only convinced us that the woods abound with bushwackers.

I purchased two more shirts of 9th Va. Sutler for which I paid $8, but they are high water, otherwise, they are quite fancy made.

I suppose you have enough of politics, judging from the papers. Am heartily glad I am not there to join in the excitement. There is only one side here, hence no chance for differing. We all vote for Brough[33] when the time comes.

I do not know but one butternut[34] in the Reg., and he is down sick in the Hospital. Do you think he will get up in time for the election?

Tell the boys it will not be very long till I shall be at home, and I want a good account of them, so that my visit will be a pleasant one. I don't want to feel, as if I ought to be engaged in correcting their misconduct, but would prefer that we all have a happy and pleasant time together. My regards to all. Much love to yourself,

Wm. S. Newton

67

HEAD QUARTERS,
Hospital 91st Reg. Ohio Volunteer Infantry
Camp, Fayetteville Sept. 19th 1863

My Dear Wife

Yours of 13th came last evening while I was absent attending a Mrs. Jones who had a miscarriage. She lives something over a mile from camp.

An exception to the gen. rule her husband is with her, and was very much frightened, not without cause, for she flooded to such an extent that no pulse could be felt for more than one hour. I was really refreshed, and relieved by your letter. To know that you were all on your feet and able for rations, was a satisfaction fully appreciated. And now Dr. Warwick is in a fix. His wife & two little girls are all sick with some kind of fever. So we go, first up, then prostrated again, enough to show us our dependence upon a higher power, were it not for this we would soon forget ourselves.

I also received a letter from Em. She has not been very well and excused herself from writing, on account of helping Linc clothe her little ones, which was probably a valid excuse. She says my horse is doing well and improving in flesh. This is all I care for, I will make my money out of her in due time.

We have not lost a man in Hospital this week, but fear we will next. One a deserter is very sick with Typhoid fever, and was brought here in a very feeble condition from Gauley Bridge.

Most of the other cases are doing very well. Our Reg. is still out to the front, but will come in on Tuesday next. Col. Turley will probably return next week.

I told Col. White last evening if he would only get me detailed to the

Hospital at Charleston, or Pt. Pleasant, I would be very gratified. He is going to Charleston the first of the week, and said he would see the Med. Director, and he was full in the faith that the arrangement could be affected. He is fully posted in reference to my feeling toward the Col., and does not think much of him either.

Dr. Wellons is still in front with the Reg., and has had two or three pretty good rain storms to try the beauties of soldiering in tents. He has much to learn yet, but this winter will accustom him to camp life.

We have 20 or thirty chickens running loose about the Hospital. The hens lay a few eggs, and we the Surgeons occasionally get a few for breakfast. I sent two men this morning for a cow & calf, for the use of the Hospital.

Col. White gave me the privilege and says the Secesh must contribute this much to the cause of the Union. Write soon and often as the mail privileges are very deficient on account of low water.

Your Husband
Wm. S. Newton

68

HEAD QUARTERS,
Hospital 91st Reg. Ohio Volunteer Infantry
Camp Fayetteville Sept. 24th 1863

My Dear Wife

Your last letter was dated Sept 13th now eleven days. Rather too long a time for one very much interested.

Yet the content of it was so much better than usual, that I have rested quite easy.

But really I begin to want a letter very much and like to hear from home at least once a week. Col. White tells me that he got a letter from his wife every other day, and writes as often to her. You can hardly imagine how long the time seems while waiting for a transfer, and I have pretty nearly given it up. Yet may get a Hospital at one of the places before mentioned.

Col. White is now at Charleston, and promised to talk with Med. Director Kellogg in reference to the matter.

I have drawn up an application for leave of absence, and Col. Coates has approved it. Col. White agreed to the same. It will have to go to War Department at Washington. It will take effect Nov. 6th. If this goes through all right, as a matter of course I will be at home when you get in limbo. Keep shady in this subject for it is not best to say all we expect in the world.

Tell Kate I will send her some Chinkapins if I meet with an opportunity.

They are so pretty I think they will make her eyes shine. Was out yesterday a short time, and got a pocketful.

Tell Neal I am glad he is again to be Senator. The Lawrence & Gallia boys in the Reg. are all right, and I will take particular pains to know, that they have an opportunity to express their preferences.

The Poll Books were here, all ready to take the vote, but no tickets. I suppose they will be supplied. We are still quite anxious about the result of Rosecran's fight.[35] If whipped the war will last six months.

Verge Gates[36] is here teaching our Brass band. Major Cadot knocked a pistol down, which was discharged, and entered his heel, making a very painful wound, and a considerable disagreement among the Doctors whether the ball should be taken out, and how it shall be done.

If he had been a soldier in our Reg., the thing would have been done yesterday. But Dr. Buck[37] of the 12th is a cousin of Gates, hence, the diversity of interests in the case.

Tell the boys they must improve the time while in school, for they will soon have to be *somebody* or *nobody*. My regards to Mrs. Ricker & Johnson. Your Husband

Wm. S. Newton

69

HEAD QUARTERS,
Hospital 91st Reg. Ohio Volunteer Infantry
Camp Fayetteville Va., Sept. 25th 1863

My Dear Wife

Yours of 17th & 20th both came this eve, and as I have the fidgets am up in the night, and as unable to trouble you in any other way, will write.

Your Sabbath which was cold, was the same here and we kept up good fires all the time. It is a consolation to know you have good quarters and plenty of coal, while we are dependent on the wood, and quarters that you would consider quite airish,[38] it even seems so to us who are accustomed to it. Most of the boys are doing well in hospital, but as fast as I got some well others take their place, but I do not think the cases are so bad that come in now. We have quite a respectable boarding house. In numbers at least, Nurses, sick etc., make over 30 all the time.

The hardest thing of all, is the allowancing of food, for the convalescents, some of them have good appetites, and want much more than is good for them. I have let thre[e] make themselves sick, eating, jus[t] to show them that I am not sti[ngy] and the experiment has paid [off], for they are all willing that I may direct now. Will send three or four home in a day or two, as they will not be able for duty, for some time yet, poor fellows they are very glad to go, and it . . . to give them the cer. . . .

I am very much pr[oud to] hear of the boys promotion, and I hope they will show themselves worthy of it. If they could only realize the importance of improving the good chance they now have of making something of themselves, it certainly would be a real comfort.

Ned in particular should try to learn penmanship, an accomplishment which he will only acquire by great pains taking.

If they will only learn to write well I will make them a nice [p]resent, as soon as they observe it, and beside they are the ones most benefited.

Tell my little daughter Kate that her Pa will come home soon, and I want her to be a very [good litt]le girl. Tell Mary I am glad to hear a good account of her, and if she only does right, will see that she has a good home, and good friends.

Mrs. Coates is still here and seems to enjoy staying, they have a nice boy, and are proud of him.

The ball has been taken from Gates's heel, and he is doing well.

I send you the photographs of Dr. Miller 34th Ohio, & Lt. Joel Hull of the 91st. Have had them so long, they are faded some.

You will hear from me as often as I have anything of interest to communicate. My regards to all enquiring friends.

> Your Husband
> Wm. S. Newton

70

HEAD QUARTERS,
Hospital 91st Reg. Ohio Volunteer Infantry
Camp Fayetteville Va., Sept. 30th 1863

My Dear Wife

Yours of recent date giving, yours ups & downs with Mary came yesterday. Am very sorry, and feel if I could be there, it would be different. I think I could control her if at home.

You will do as you think best in the matter.

We have nothing new here except the Paymaster. I suppose we will be paid off in a day or two, think I will send you a receipt, if the pay Sgt. is here. Am almost out of money, but will try to send you part of the two months pay. We get along very much after the old style.

I still run the Hospital, and feel best while engaged in steady business and know what I have to do, and no one to interfere.

I hope you will receive the 200. sent to Will. I had no idea that he would use the money, but asked him to put it at interest or send it to you. I do not understand it, unless his finances are getting low.

May I bring Mott with me in Nov., if so you must have him ready. Have not time to write more this morning, Your Husband

Wm. S. Newton

[added to above letter, mailed together]

Thursday Oct. 1st 1863

Will enclose Receipt on the Treasurer of County for 150. which you had better have placed to your Cr[edit] at Iron Bank.[39]

I hope to come home before we are paid again. I therefore keep enough for traveling expense.

Hope you may receive the other which will make your bank acc[ount] look rather respectable

Yours truly
Wm.S.N.

71

Fayetteville West Va. Oct 2/63

My Dear Wife

Yours of 29th Ultimo is received Sun. I hope you are well satisfied in your own mind about Mary, for I have taken the trouble to enquire about her deportment while at the 9th Va. Hospital, and find that the suspicions raised concerning her were wholly unfounded. The fact that you found part of the missing articles would leave room for doubt concerning her guilt in the matter, and I feel that you have thrown her adrift now & no one knows what will become of her.

It may be all for the best, but I can but regret it, and hope that you have not acted hastily, and find room for regret hereafter. I mailed a letter yesterday with a receipt on County Treasurer for One hundred & fifty (150) dollars, which you will have placed to your credit in the Iron Bank. I think you had better write to Will to send you the 200. which he has now held something over two months.

I got a note from Em today per Charley Vanden,[40] saying she had sent me a jelly cake, some grapes, etc. which Charley says I will receive today with some he is getting.

Will be quite a treat, but some sick boys I have will get the grapes, for they seem to relish such things, with great benefit.

I also received a letter from Med. Director Kellogg, saying that as soon as Warwick returned from his leave of absence, which he supposed would be granted him, he would take measures to relieve me. In which I suppose he means to give me a Hospital at Charleston. This at present would not suit me, if it will interfere with my going home.

But of this say nothing, for it is not best to talk about it, till it comes to a certainty. Hoping you will find plenty of apples, potatoes etc. and lay in a good supply of coal. I remain yours truly,

Wm. S. Newton

72

Fayetteville West Va. Oct 8th 1863

My Dear Wife

Our mails are very irregular, have not received a letter from you since announcing the discharge of Mary.

So I conclude you are busy doing the work, or the mails don't bring them, I will therefore write, and perhaps one will come for me by & by. I received a letter from Mother, Doug & Mary. Delamater[41] was there on his

UNION MASS MEETING!

AT IRONTON, OHIO,

On Tuesday, September 29th.

Hon. BENJAMIN F. WADE,
Col. CHARLES ANDERSON,
Gen. JOSEPH H. GEIGER,

Have accepted invitations, and will address us upon the all-important issues presented in the present canvass for State Officers.

Come out, everybody. Hear, ponder, and decide for yourselves. All we need, to arrive at correct conclusions, is investigation. The issues presented are so plain, that he who runs may read.

Dinner will be provided for all that may come.

By order of Executive Com.
W. H. SPICER, Chairman.
B. F. Cory, Secretary.

In an October 8, 1863, letter William S. Newton referred to a large Union meeting held in Ironton in late September. The meeting was to stir support for pro-Union War Democrat John Brough who successfully ran for governor against exiled anti-war Democrat Clement Laird Vallandigham that fall.

way to join his Reg., to which he had been appointed Chaplain, his wife had gone home to her Mother.

Doug enquired when I would be at home, saying he intended to visit Ironton this fall or winter. I have written to him the probabilities in the case, and should not wonder if we should meet there.

Warwick started for home yesterday on a 20 day leave, and promised to be back on time that I might go. He is very kind and obliging, and is disposed to please me, so far as he is able. The Col., I think, is not so much at ease, for in the narrowness of his heart, is not able to comprehend how we can be such good friends. Sometimes I think he is quite jealous of our intimacy.

I see from the [Ironton] Register, you had a grand Union meeting.[42] Traitors must have kept in their holes that day. We are preparing to take the vote of the Reg. On the 13th, we will have some five hundred voters. So many are under age, and cannot vote. Don't think we will have over ten for Vallandigham in the whole.

As the time approaches, the month yet to pass, looks longer than six, before I expected a leave of absence. I can hardly wait, if I could only sleep the time off, would not care, but I do not sleep more than 4 hours any night, and have left off sleeping in the day that I may better sleep at night. I do not know I care, whether the house is sold or not. I like to feel that I have a house to go to.

Hope the boys are doing well at school, especially they must learn to write well.

Shall I bring my horse home, perhaps I can make him useful in collecting while there. Must not speculate too much, for I may not be able to come. My regards to all friends.

Your Husband
Wm. S. Newton

5

The Formation of Character,
Is Perhaps the Most Important,
October–December 1863

The last three months of 1863 were busy for William S. Newton. On October 8 he was ordered to Charleston as acting surgeon for the 2nd Virginia Cavalry. He was placed in this position because Dr. Matthew McEwen, the previous surgeon for the regiment, had been dismissed from the military. Upon arrival to the new post, Newton first learned of McEwen's departure, but his letters did not elaborate on the details of why. The responsibilities of acting surgeon were significant, and Newton made frequent comments about the complexities of the position, especially the amount of "red tape" to overcome. Newton demonstrated his ability to be a regimental surgeon, but by the end of the year he expected that the appointment was indeed temporary, and that he would return to the 91st.

Newton spent most of his time working in the hospital and interacting with the local secesh. He had quarters in the one of the nicest homes in town. John C. Ruby, owner of the home, was a Charleston grocer originally from Gallia County, Ohio, who joined the 22nd Virginia Volunteer Infantry (CSA) and served as the assistant commissary of supply.[1] Despite his animosity toward the rebels, Newton explained that he would not abuse any part of his accommodations. While Newton attended to the sick and wounded, several companies of the 2nd Virginia Cavalry, 34th Ohio Volunteer Infantry, and 91st Ohio Volunteer Infantry launched a successful raid to Lewisburg in November. Newton explained that "They drove the Rebs out of Lewisburg, captured their train, burned their stores, and brought away over one hundred head of cattle." The raid also brought fifteen prisoners and many refugees (likely emancipated slaves) back to the camp in Charleston.[2]

The success of that expedition led to a second raid in early December. Newton was part of the entourage most likely because the officers expected more intense fighting with Confederates. However, the regiment did not encounter the enemy and after reaching Lewisburg decided to return to Charleston. The second raid, which according to Newton took twelve days, was more remembered for the difficult journey. The regimental history of the 91st explained that the second raid was "one of the severest and most unpleasant marches the regiment ever made."[3]

Many of Newton's letters during this period were much shorter and more to the point than the preceding letters to his wife. In fact, the increased workload resulted in the rejection of his application for a brief leave of absence. In late November, he returned home to visit his new son who was born earlier that month. When Newton returned, he brought his son Mott back with him. Similar to Ned's experience as a guest, Mott enjoyed being in the camp and spent more time with other people than his father.

Newton celebrated Thanksgiving and Christmas in Charleston apart from his family. The end of 1863 marked his first full year of war and some major milestones in his life. During the last three months of the year, Newton's wife gave birth to a new son who remained unnamed at that point. His November 13 letter mentioned the momentous event, saying: "I am heartily glad it is now over, and you out of danger."[4] There also seems to have been trouble at home related to Ned. Newton sent a letter to Ned emphasizing honesty and the importance of proper penmanship. These family changes and challenges wore on Newton, who remarked that he had forgotten what his daughter Kate's face looked like. Newton advised his wife to settle accounts and prepare their home to be sold. At the end of December he made a quick trip to Gallipolis and brought Mott with him. Because of the suddenness he did not have time to arrange to meet with any of his family and left Mott to continue back to Ironton.

73

HEAD QUARTERS,
Hospital 2nd Va. Cavalry
Camp, Charleston West Va. Oct 10, 1863

My Dear Wife

You will no doubt be surprised at the heading of this, and so am I. On the 8th an order came, for me to report to Med. Director Kellogg immediately.

So yesterday I packed up & started for Charleston, stayed all night with Mrs. Tompkins, and today arrived here, reported, & Kellogg assigned me to duty in the 2nd Va. Cavalry. The Surgeon having been dismissed [from] the service.

Kellogg told me that my position would be that of acting Surgeon, but of this say nothing till the position is fixed. I would have waited until I know all about it, but I wanted to apprise you of the changes the first opportunity.

When I received the order I supposed I was to be in charge of the Post Hospital about to be established. I knew nothing of the dismissal of McEwen until I came here.

Our Hospital is in one of the finest houses of the town, and I am quartered in the parlor with a nice bed, cane bottom chairs & sofas, all belonging to some rebel, but I will take good care of them, and see they are not abused. What will grow of this I cannot tell, but will inform you as opportunity offers.

You will direct my letters to

Hospital 2nd Va. Cavalry,
Charleston Va.

By doing this they will not go to Fayetteville.

Mrs. Tompkins & daughters send their love, and wished to be remembered kind[ly] [et]c. They treat me very well, and will not have anything for meals & lodging. I slept there, with a Dentist, who has just returned from two years service in the Rebel army, was at Guyandotte, when Dr. Morris was taken prisoner.

It seemed strange to go to bed with one, so lately our enemy, & says he has repented etc., came on to Charleston with me.

Hope you will get on well with Ann Quinn,[5] take care of No. 1.

Your Husband
Wm. S. Newton

74

Hospital 2nd Va. Cavalry
Charleston West Va. Oct. 12th/63

My Dear Wife

Have now been here two days, and have had a most intolerable skin disease similar to hives, it has kept me from sleeping for two nights.

I hope the worst is now over, have taken Sulphur and sodas enough to drive the disease from the system.

Am now acting Surg. of this Reg., and if I could be the Surg. I would not care. It has been my province most of the time, and someone else gets the extra pay.

Last evening on examining the portraits hanging around the parlor, I discovered one that looked like John Ruby. On going to the book case, I found two or three with John C. Ruby[6] written in full.

I then enquired and found that not only his, but that of wife sister-in-law, Mother-inlaw, & Father-in-law, all in very large gilt frames, was this not a discovery.

Mattie & Mrs. Gillen have both been here & can tell you all the particulars. John Ruby is Quartermaster in 22nd Va. Reb Reg., and I am here living in his house & using his furniture. So the world moves, and such is war. Mrs. G. will tell you how near I came being Court Martialed today.

How glad I would be to spend this nice weather at home, but such cannot be, but I still live in hope of seeing you all next month. Mr. Ricker was sent to Gallipolis yesterday to inspect some horses. I only saw him a few minutes.

We have only a few very sick here, and only one, that is seriously sick. You must direct your letters to this place, in the following manner.

> Wm. S. Newton
> Acting Surg., 2nd Va. Cav.
> Charleston, West Va.

Tell Mott if I stay here, and he is a good boy to learn, gets his lessons well. That I want him to come up and stay with me awhile. Can you get him ready.

Tell Ned I hope he has not forgotten the admonitions I gave him. Tell Miss Kittie, "her Pa will come by and by."

> Your Husband
> Wm. S. Newton

75

> Hospital 2nd Va. Cavalry
> Charleston West Va. Oct. 20th 1863

My Dear Wife

Yours of the 11th came this morning, had been to Fayette & back again. Have not yet got a letter direct from Ohio, although I have now been in Charleston almost two weeks. You have seen Mrs. Gillen ere this, and know all about the situation here.

Gillen is in hospital still, and I have written a certificate of disability that he may get a leave of absence for 20 days. If mine only comes, and his are approved, we will try to come home together.

I am not entirely satisfied with my position here. Although I am in charge and acting Surgeon, cannot help but feel that the position is only temporary. Still I am so comfortably fixed as to quarters, I should not complain. I heard that John Ruby with all his folks are in Dixie, that he was pretty nearly run ashore as to property, had spent pretty much all his wife's portion before the war began. Ed Ruby, also in Dixie, is a worthless, dispirited young man.

Mr. Ricker does not expect his wife since the recent order of the General concerning Officer's wives.

You would be surprised to see how many Rebs, and how much society there is in Charleston. Some of the officers seem to enjoy themselves hugely. I have no acquaintances outside the military, and I presume this is best as it gives me time to attend to my own business, and to some considerable reading. I wrote to Will to ship my other horse, as I now am entitled to feed for two, being assigned to Cavalry service. Besides, I will have an opportunity to sell one here, and save the expense of pasture.

Should I come home next month, will have a good time I expect. You may be certain am looking forward with considerable anxiety to the time, how dreary the winter would seem if I am not to see wife and children, Mott & Kate, it has been so long since, I hardly know how they look. How is Mattie Kingsbury, and that, if she goes to Burlington, I will write to Doug not to come, though he might find someone else, with whom to spend his evenings. Give my regards to all friends, and much love to Children.

> Your Husband
> Wm. S. Newton
> Acting Surg.
> 2nd Va. Cav.

76

> Hospital 2nd Va. Cavalry
> Charleston Oct 24th 1863

Dear Ned,

Your letter with Mothers came yesterday, and I was very much pleased to learn of your progress at school, and hope the report is a true expose of the facts in the case. I am like poor Vallandigham "over the border" watching the progress of events, and I think quite as much interested, if not more than he, especially in what is taking place at my own home.

And as you are among the number and likely to act a conspicuous part in that home, it is useless to say I am very much interested in the way and manner in which you perform your part.

In this, I do not wish to be understood, to mean, simply your attainments at school, for this would be a very narrow view of things.

Your education is a very important interest, but there are other considerations of great moment. One, the *formation* of *character*, is perhaps the most important. And as the armies of U.S. are now manufacturing history, so you, every day are forming character, either *good*, or *evil*. Now, how very necessary it is, that you should consider, that you will be estimated in after life by the actions of each day.

I have often heard the remark, of this, or that man, "Well, he was a very mean boy," or ["]a very good boy." And almost always the character of the boy, foreshadowed that of the man. So if you wish to be, a good & useful man, you must also be a good boy, and bear this reputation, among your companions & schoolfellows now.

Our Reg. & 34th Ohio, under command of Genl. Duffie, have just returned from a scout in Wyoming County. I am quite sure you would have been pleased with the sight, for the column was half an hour in passing our hospital. Two Reg's mounted, make a much longer string than infantry would do. Old Tom is the same as when you last saw him, ready for any service, he has a good stable and plenty of forage. I sent for the roan mare last week, but I got a letter from Will saying that she & Mr. Andrews horse were both missing, and perhaps stolen. Is not this too bad. I think if I had been there, they probably would be hunted up. They may have found them by this, if they have, I will hear of it soon.

Have had enough to do while the Regt. was on the scout. The sick in camp & hospital were all under my care.

I go out to the camp in an ambulance carrying the Pannier[7] Etc., the sick come up to the ambulance for the rations.

Ask Mattie Gillen, if Genl. Duffie is not a very nice man, & graceful in horsemanship.

The Genl. and Brigade Surgeon came to inspect my hospital one day, and the sick boys are not yet done talking of his oddities, in language, etc.

Tell Mott & Kate that Papa wishes to see them very much. You have been with me enough to know whether there are any others whom I would like to see. You will therefore know what to tell them, and whom to tell it; say to them, they will probably hear from me again in a few days. Tell Arthur & Ned Ricker their Pa has gone to Clarksburg, Va., for what, or how long Genl. Duffie only knows. *Be good.* Your Father,

Wm. S. Newton

77

Hospital 2nd Va. Cavalry
Charleston Oct. 26th 1863

My Dear Wife

Yours of the 22nd came this morning, and as Dick Kirker goes home in the morning will write a few lines. I wrote to Ned yesterday, and I presume you will get this, as soon as that.

I have nothing new, we were doing duty every day, just the same, not very many sick. Gillen is still here, and not improving very fast, a leave of absence is necessary to make him all right. We are both anxiously awaiting the result of our papers.

Dr. Warwick will be up tomorrow on his way to the Reg. I know he will miss me when he gets there. He does not like Wellons a particle, and will fret, and foam, when he is compelled to do duty with him alone. We are to-day making up the invalid roll, of such men as are not able for active service, or duty, I feel, is full of responsibility. Many wish to go who are not worthy, others who should go, are not willing.

I should like very much to go home with Dick & Capt. Hambleton, but will have to write, am afraid my chances to get home here are not so good as they would have been at Fayette, for if my leave of absence had not come, I think Col. White would have ordered me home.

I still live in hope, for papers always come back in some shape.

Good bye. Your Husband
Wm.S.N.

78

Hospital 2nd Va. Cavalry
Charleston Oct 31st 1863

My Dear Wife

Your last of the 25th came two days ago, but as I had sent one the same day, have deferred writing until now. Did not think of writing until tomorrow, but today I received the blanks for my monthly report, and knowing my time would be occupied with them, I have concluded to write a few lines now. I find plenty to do, although we have not very many sick, but when we are in close contact with two Brigadier Genls, there is always so much red tape it keeps me busy. To attend to all the orders issued, write papers for the Hosp. Attendants, sign reports and provision returns. All of which must be signed by the Surg. in charge.

Dr. Ayres, our Brigade Surgeon, called on me today. I told him that I wanted to go home soon, was expecting a leave of absence, and if it did not come, I wanted his help. He said he would help me. If I should go in that way, would have to make my visit as near the time as possible, and my stay must be consequently very brief. I still hope for the coming of my papers. Mr. Ricker will be back from Clarksburg today.

Gillen is still with me, and very patiently looking for his papers to get home. We have no news. Every thing seems to move along in the old way. Except Genl. Kell[e]y, our Division Commander is now in the valley, reviewing the troops. We had a grand review on Wednesday last. I tried to slip out, but about the time, Major Hoffman[8] sent me an order to appear in my proper place & position. I mounted Old Tom and joined the column without sash or sword, trembling all the time, lest Genl. Duffie should discover the omission and order me from the field.

I thought then, I would very much like to have sash & sword, but now that it is over, am again careless of their possession. Still, if I have a good opportunity, must purchase the articles. Tell Ned I have left off reading *light literature*, and as he has already perused a large amount of the poor trash, I think he had better follow my example.

Give my best wishes to all friends, and much love to the little ones.

> Your Husband
> Wm. S. Newton

79

> Hospital 2nd Va. Cav.
> Charleston West Va. Nov. 3rd/63

My Dear Wife

Am not in such good spirits about getting home as when I last wrote, for our Brigade have gone into Dixey for a scout of ten days, or two weeks, taking all the Surgeons & Asst. Surg's with them, leaving me in charge of all the sick. This morning I received orders to take charge of the 34th Zouave Hospital, in addition to my own, beside holding sick call, for both Reg's and Battery in camp, thus you see, without some special interposition, I am elected until return of the Brigade, which I still hope will be in time for me to reach home before some other coming events.

Should my leave of absence in the mean time come, will try to have Kellogg relieve me from duty sooner. Adjutant Gillen & Col. Dove are still boarders with me. Adjutant hoping for papers. Col. Dove is in command of this camp with his lame foot.

I scarcely hear from Fayette. A letter from Coates, & one from Hospital

Steward, and Old Tagg,[9] is all I have had. In Fact I am not very solicitous for news in that quarter.

Major McEwen has been back again, was in Washington City, and came back for more proofs of his innocence. He may succeed in gaining his position. If energy will accomplish it, he certainly will succeed. My love to all.

Your Husband
Wm. S. Newton

80

Hospital 2nd Va. Cav.
Charleston Va. Nov. 9th/63

My Dear Wife

As Adjutant Gillen goes home in the morning, I will take the opportunity to send you a few lines although your letters seem very scarce of late. I send the photograph of my present Hospital Steward and will send my own if they are finished in time, they must have time to print them, and promised to have them done tomorrow. I thought if I was not able to come, I would send my shadow, the next best thing to be done. I am not proud of the picture, for I am getting too old to make a fine picture one. You must not understand by this that I have given up the idea of getting home, for I still have hope that my papers will come. As the 91st is also on the scout toward Lewisburg & Dixie, any papers may be at their HdQuarters. If not, and our Brigade returns, will in all probability get an order from Surg. Ayres to go. This is now my best chance.

I know how disappointed you will be if I do not get there, and I think of it every night when I lie down.

Col. Mussey, Med. Inspector of this Dept., is now here, and is looking very sharply after Dr. McEwen, former Surgeon, and if I am any judge should think McEwen's chances for restoration rather limited.

Adjutant thinks I should make efforts to get the position, but the time is not yet come. So keep quiet. In fact, I rather think it would be best to stay close to the Reg. At present but will lay aside interest if I am able to get home safely will most assuredly do so.

There are some very pleasant ladies near the Hospital. The Misses Ruffners[10] have sent me two nice bouquets, and will bring or send one for the Adjutant this eve, which he intends to take to Ohio. Hope he will show to you as a specimen.

Much love to you all, write often

Your Husband
Wm. S. Newton

81

Hospital 2nd Va. Cav.
Charleston Nov. 13th 1863

My Dear Wife

Yours of the 8th and Post script by Mrs. R. came this morning. I was not surprised, for I had been expecting such a result, and have been suffering from anxiety, much more than if I had been at home for I know how you would feel in relation to the affair. I am heartily glad it is now over, and you out of danger. You know how to take care of yourself, and hope will do it. What does Kate think?

Our Brigade came in today, fatigued and worn out, with some fifteen prisoners, a lot of refugees. They drove the Rebs out of Lewisburg, captured their train, burned their stores, and brought away over one hundred head of cattle.

They captured two Reb flags, one of which they trailed in the dust, while marching into town.

It looked real provoking, and I suppose many of the secesh were mad enough to bite.

I went to Head Quarters to see Dr. Ayres, he was sick, and could not go to see the Genl., so I went to Kellogg to see if he would not order me to Gallipolis, that I might get home, told him I had sent my papers on etc. He said he would telegraph concerning them, and just this moment, his orderly called with a letter saying my papers had been disapproved, and of course he dare not in the face of this, give me permission. How little they consider the wishes or feelings of officers at the War Department is distinctly shown in this affair. You don't know how disappointed I am, for I had thought to surprise you by making my appearance in your bedroom on Sunday sometime. But here I am, and so much red tape to overcome, I am really discouraged.

There is another movement in contemplation, if this does not come off, I still have a prospect that Duffie will give me an order to go. With all the bad there is some good, the Pay Master is here, and if I can get an opportunity, will send you something to buy bread for the boy, for I suspect he must have teeth and will therefore need something to keep him growing. Col. Dove stays with me. He was mustered as Lt. Col. And is now in command of the Regt. He is still very lame, and I dress his foot morning & evening. He says, anything he can do shall be done, to make me Surgeon, but this keep still, for there are many wishing the position, and trying to obtain it. I don't want it, unless the officers desire it.

Will send you my Photographs if they are sent in time. Do not think they are very good or pretty either, although they may be true to life. Hope you will take the best of care, for I want to see you after the war is over. Ask Kate if she will sell her little brother. If I don't get home, let Mott come with Mr. Gillen.

Your Husband
Wm. S. Newton

82

Hospital 2nd Va. Cav.
Charleston Va. Nov 24th/63

My Dear Wife

You will see from the above that we are again safe at Head Quarters. We got on the Bostonia[11] at 10 O'clock, found Mary, Doug, Miss Barber, Ann Reppert[12] & Mrs. Capt. Brown[13] all in great glee. We sat up till one or two in the morning, was called up at 4 A.M. to visit Miss Barber who had taken quite sick with vomiting & purging. So I did not get much sleep.

We arrived at Gallipolis at 9 in the morning, found Will at the wharf with his wagon, Father N. was much better, thought the pills had done him good service.

They had got along very well, and all seemed glad and willing that Em should stay longer.

A young Mr. Waddle came in saying they had heard from my horse, and that it was at Buckeye Furnace. I employed him to go for him, and if he is successful, Brother Will will send him up to me the first opportunity. We were at Nina's to ten, had a very pleasant time.

We slept at Father H. in the same old bed, where I first slept with a woman. And I could not help thinking of Moore's lines, "Be an angel my love in the morning, but oh, *be a woman at night*."[14]

This will not seem strange to you when you remember all the circumstances, but accidents will happen in the best of families. And we are told that men & women who live & love together, are pretty sure to have children. We at least have one evidence of affection, among the many *changes* that are taking place.

I have thought of this often since I left home, and endeavor to place the best construction possible upon it. Perhaps all is right.

We left G.[allipolis] this morning at 3 A.M., arrived here at 2 P.M., a very quick trip. At Red House, I telegraphed for an ambulance to meet me at the landing as it was raining.

The ambulance was there waiting, and we got up in good style, the mud is very deep here, and transportation quite difficult.

Everything seems to have gone on very well during my absence, quite an additional number sick in Hospital. Take good care of our boy. Much love to all.

> Your Husband
> Wm.S.N

83

> Head Quarters 2nd Va. Cav.
> Camp Toland Nov. 27/1863

Dear ~~William~~ Wife

Will not lose this piece of paper because some one had scribbled on it, but will appropriate a part, and so make it answer my purpose. One of my patients, a Mr. Anderson,[15] has a furlough, and is going to Ironton, will send this by him.

Yesterday was Thanksgiving day, and as I had declined a very pressing invitation to be present at home on the occasion, had expected it would be no more than any other day, after I entered this valley. But not so for about 10 yesterday I received a pressing invitation to dine at Head Quarters at 3 P.M. Dr. Ayres, Capt. Ricker, Adjutant Clark[16] compose the Mess, Col. Dove, Dr. Cowan of 34th & self were the guests. Not a woman except the two Col. Ladies who got up the dinner, were present. We had a turkey served in good style, with all the other nice things. Wine by pitcher full, was also served, and I need not tell you, that in a crowd of six, as good judges as we considered ourselves, that some of it was drunk, and that the dinner lasted long after dark, none being permitted to leave, until all the ceremonies were gone through with. Mott is well contented, sleeps with the steward, and tags him wherever he goes. They both rode to Piatt & back, 20 miles, the next day after our arrival.

I have pretty hard work to keep him clean, it is so muddy, and he wants to go so often.

Shall have to come down on him a little in this particular.

Mrs. Ricker called on me, and went through the Hospital. I think she intends to start home on Monday next.

How long do you suppose it will be, before you can come up & visit us.

Some of our neighbors were quite sure you were here, when they knew Mott was about. Did not think it possible, so small a boy could leave his mother. Anderson is waiting, so good bye.

> Your Husband
> Wm.S.N.

84

Hospital 2nd Va. Cavalry
Charleston Va. Dec 1st 1863

My Dear Wife

It is now one week since I arrived here, and not one word have I heard from home. I can scarcely believe that you really thought, that I was not an interested party, concerning home affairs. *Sickness* would be the only *reasonable* excuse for this silence. And I really hope this cannot be of a serious nature.

I am well aware, you could not control the *state* of *things* while I was at home. Nor could I then, any more than now, keep regretting that the circumstances existed. I think I made the same provision for the wants of those dependent upon me, that an interested party would have done. I do not wish to claim any credit in the matter, but I am certain, *very few*, in the service, receiving the same pay, have appropriated more to the use of their families. And in this I do not claim that I have done any more than was my duty to do, but still hold to my first conviction, that in justice, I should hear from home once in ten days. If unable to write, someone certainly could be found who would write a short letter.

Mrs. Ricker expects to start home tomorrow morning, if so will send this by her. The weather has been such that she has not went out much. She & Mr. R. were here one evening.

Col. Coates is here on Court Martial, and I learn Col. Turley is about to be placed under arrest for gambling, etc., *but of this say nothing.*

Mott is very well contented, goes up to see the Misses Ruffners, when the cook goes for milk, etc. They give him cider & apples, and fret him not a little. He is not so averse to the Secesh Ladies, as when he first came.

Coates wants me to go to Gallipolis with him and others on Saturday, but I cannot do this, as I have enough to do here at present.

If you have not written, I hope you will when you receive this. My love to all,

Your Husband
Wm. S. Newton

85

Hospital 2nd Va. Cav. Dec. 3rd/63

My Dear Wife

Yours of last Sabbath came today, and I feel much relieved for I was getting very impatient, to know how you were getting along. Two weeks is a good long time when one is anxious.

I have at least received the stray horse, only twenty six dollars charges, for advertising, keeping etc. Mr. Lasley[17] of Buckeye Furnace, charged fifteen dollars for two weeks keeping & advertising. I think he intended to keep her out and out. He certainly is patriotic, at least Will thinks so.

Mott is having pretty good times. He yesterday rode to Malden (5 miles) and back. Cannot ride as well as Ned. Am very sorry, however, that Ned is not willing to do all your errands. Cannot understand in what manner he expects to get through the world, if he expects to be anybody, will have to change the programme materially.

Tell Em she must write to me, when she gets home, for Will never writes a word, unless it is on special business.

If Mrs. McNeal can pay you 8 dollars more, you may receipt the whole bill, & if she thinks this too much do as you please.

Did not say any thing to Doug about the pump. You had better get Mr. Lanton[18] to order one, put it in and pay him for it.

Lieut. McNally[19] will take this to you, he goes home under orders.

You must keep the little one from taking cold, Keep Kitty out of the wind.

No more time, write often

Your Husband

Wm. S. Newton

86

Hospital 2nd Va. Cavalry

Charleston Dec. 19th 1863

My Dear Wife

This is Saturday evening. Have just returned from a twelve days raid 100 miles into Dixie. We have had a very fatiguing march, the weather was very fine until we reached Lewisburg. There, after chasing the Rebels out, we stayed two days. Then we fell back slowly at first, waiting till the Infantry brigade, had got almost to Gormley and Fayette. The 12th & 9lst Ohio, 5th Va. & 23rd Ohio, comprised the Infantry. The 34th Ohio, 2nd Va., & part of 3rd Va., the mounted brigade. McMullins Battery & part of Simmon[d]s,[20] were also along. These necessarily retarded our progress, especially on the return, when the roads were bad, the weather worse, and the horses almost rundown.

In crossing big & little Lowell mountains[21] we suffered from rain & cold. The trees were almost broken by the rain frozen to every twig. It was a grand & beautiful sight, the trees all covered with ice, and needed only the sunshine to make the scenery magnificent. Would the weather been as cold as yesterday & today, we must have perished with the cold. I suffered very much today, the cold was intense, and we came from Mrs. Hudleston's 32 miles since daylight, the ground frozen very solid, some horses barefooted, all combined to make our march tedious.

We arrived at 4 P.M., found Mott visiting at Mr. Ruffners, he seemed quite glad to see me, but made quite as much fuss over Dick and the others. I found three letters from you all of which had been broken open by Mott.

In relation to selling the house, I feel as if I was not very particular, and when I consider that one or two hundred dollars should be expended in repairs very soon, and that the interest in the price of the house, would more than pay your rent, as a matter of economy, I am sure it would be best. But again, when I consider, that I will have no home if this is sold, my heart almost fails me. If the war should continue, my three years out, I feel it would be better if you were with your folks. Circumstances must control these matters somewhat.

Dr. Nellis is expected soon, has written that he will be here. If Col. Powell was here, I think I could get a better position. The other Officers have pledged themselves to make no move in the matter, till McEwen's fate is definitely settled, and I fear by that time, I shall have been ordered to join my Reg. Will take no step in the matter. If the Officers do so all right. I shall not ask them to do so. Col. Dove was married on Thursday eve, while we were all gone. Mott & Steward Higgins[22] went to the wedding.

Enclosed find a letter, which some Rebel Lady had written to her Husband this among other things I captured at Lewisburg.

Am very tired, and will stop, good night

> Your Husband
> Wm. S. Newton

87

> Hospital 2nd Va. Cavalry
> Camp Toland Dec. 22nd 1863

Dear Neddie,

Having just returned from a long scout, will give you something of my experience & thoughts on the way. We were compelled most of the time to step out of doors, because the Genl. & his staff would fill the few buildings at each place of encampment.

Now to be a staff officer is very nice at such times, and worth working for. I notice that all staff officers are good penmen. Is this not a sufficient inducement to attain this accomplishment. There are many others, one *especially*, that of *strict integrity*. Now a General would not have a man, upon whose word he could not have implicit confidence. He depends upon his staff officers for information, if they deceive him, how long do you suppose they would hold their position. They must also be strictly honest. If he found them appropriating money or property not their own, he certainly would be afraid to have them do business for him, and would dismiss them forthwith.

So it is in all professions and business transactions through life I want you to think of this.

The boy moulds his capacity for business when he becomes a man. If he is educated, and has these other accomplishments, *integrity* and *honesty*. He can always procure positions and places of trust, if he has always been honest while a boy, his reputation as an honest man has already been formed.

But on the contrary, if he has done dishonest acts while a boy, he will hardly obtain position, or get an opportunity to redeem himself, for who would trust the man, who while a boy, was looked upon with suspicion. We may do wrong and repent of it, but we cannot continue to do so, without being found out. We may hide it from parents & friends for a reason, but that *all seeing eye* will soon bring it to light, when shame & confusion will surely follow, not only ourselves, but parents & friends all, suffer, when those near & dear, do dishonest acts.

Rumors of wrong doing have frequently excited some doubts in reference to you, I have refrained, heretofore, from making any allusion to this subject, for it is very painful for a father to distrust his son, or have suspicion in any way concerning him aroused. If you have done anything to arouse suspicion, *for goodness sake, so guard your actions*, that you may outlive, and do away with such impressions, now while you are young.

For I would much prefer when dying, to know I had left an *upright honest boy*, than to know he possessed all the wealth of Girard.[23]

These are some of the thoughts that occupied my mind, while on the scout in an enemy's country. When we lie down to sleep at such times, we are very apt to think of home, and what would be the condition of those we love, if we were not permitted to see them again. As you are the eldest of my boys, I thought, with what confidence, could your mother look to you for help, if I should be taken away. Did you ever think of this; Are you now so conducting yourself, if deprived of a Father, your Mother would look to you for assistance, in taking care of and providing for, your brothers & sister.

How much happiness you would give your mother, if you were always a good boy, and how much more confidently she could look forward to a happy old age if she could rely implicitly on your obedience & good conduct.

And then, you should set an example before the other little ones, that you will be proud of when you become a man, how much responsibility rests upon you. I want you to write me a long letter, and tell me, how you feel about this matter, whether I can depend upon your assistance to mother, if I should not be spared to get home. I wish to know also whether you have any thoughts of fitting yourself for usefulness, for it is only a few years, till this question must be answered.

I brought home a gun captured in the camp of the 22nd Reg.[24] It would make an excellent shot gun with a little alteration, and I should be very glad to send it home, if I could have confidence, it would only be used when mother approved, and only taken out, when she gave permission. The little Roan Mare is coming out finely. Dick takes excellent care of her & old Tom. I rode Tom on the scout, he performed the journey very well, and only for his mischievousness would have gotten home all right.

He tried, just for fun, to kick another horse, and kicked the fence, and thereby hurt his own foot, which harmed him. He however came through very well, but is still suffering from his indiscretions. You must write, and let me know, what your resolutions are, in relation to the matters of which I have written. Give my love to mother, Kittie & *little one*.

Your Father
Wm. S. Newton

88

Hospital 2nd Va. Cavalry
Charleston West Va Dec 27 1863

My Dear Wife

Yours by someone, after stopping at Reg, four or five days came yesterday.

Am sorry to learn you have so much trouble with the boy, perhaps he is crying for a name[25] and yet I am unable to suggest one, for fear it would not be the right one, or acceptable to all concerned.

Mrs. McClain[26] has shown herself, where, and what, does she propose to do. In fact, I did not know she had married the second time till Ricker told me.

Dr. Nellis came last evening. I presume I shall be ordered somewhere soon, perhaps to the 34th Ohio. As Dr. Cowan has been promoted to Surg. in the 1st Ohio Vol. Cavalry. That Reg. is now at Chattanooga, a long way from home.

If I should be assigned to duty here or go to my own Reg., I think I shall send Mott home, as I shall not be in charge and cannot of course always have my own way. He would like to stay longer, but as his school is going on next week, he had better go with it.

Christmas has been observed here by dinner parties, dances, etc. I went at 10 evening, looked on awhile, and then stayed longer to take care of some of my med friends. Colonels & Majors outranked all others, the Genl. not being present.

Henry, I suppose, will be on his way to Columbus, if he desired I think could make a change in the rank of some persons, whether he will do so, remains for the future to tell.

Mrs. Davidson[27] is expected, and if she does not stay too long will send Mott with her. I must stop, for will not have my interests attended to at Head Quarters, if I do not look after it myself. Are you getting any flesh or strength. I want you to fat up and renew your strength, for I think I am getting younger.

Hope Ned will read my letter to him very carefully, and practice accordingly.

Your Husband W. S. Newton

Direct your letters as usual till you hear from me.

89

Gallipolis Dec 30th 1863

Dear wife

This is Wednesday eve. Myself, Mott & Mr. Ricker came this afternoon. If I could only get one more day would see you if only for a few hours. But Kellogg will be back tomorrow and I must be there when the order is issued.

Am very glad I came, for I saw Henry and had a long talk with him, and I am quite certain he will attend to my interests at Columbus. Some effort is being made in 2nd Va. for me but I have no hand in it, but I do not much care whether the effort succeeds. I prefer Ohio service and will be better pleased with something in that direction.

I gave Em some money with which she purchased a dress for you, & looks so much like one of old, you would almost affirm that I had chosen it. She paid 37 1/2 cts per yard for it.

You will send the account of Jas Craig.[28] I want the status when the business was done. I think it is made out, if not copy it from the book, the amount I think is 16$. The gun I send, you will take it into your possession. If Ned is not satisfied, put it into the hands of Mr. Lanton[29] till I get home. Much love to you all.

Your Husband
Wm. S. Newton

6

Shipwreck of Your Own Hopes, January–February 1864

During the first two months of 1864, William S. Newton spent most of his time managing the hospital in Fayetteville, West Virginia. There were only a handful of patients and he reported that his quarters were very pleasant. Like other regiments in the region, the 91st Ohio Volunteer Infantry was in winter quarters and saw little action. The weather was severe at this time, with ice on the Kanawha River preventing steamboats from travel.[1]

During this period, Newton continued in his role as acting surgeon for the 2nd Virginia Cavalry and frequently had surgical command of several other regiments. He learned in late January that Matthew McEwen was restored to the position of surgeon for the 2nd Virginia Cavalry. Thereafter, Newton returned as Assistant Surgeon for the 91st Ohio Volunteer Infantry with the specific assignment to the hospital in Summersville, West Virginia, under the control of Captain James McMullen's 1st Ohio Independent Battery. He interacted frequently with officers of several nearby regiments, often joining them and their wives for dinners. Newton also mentioned the increasing frequency of rebels arriving in the camp wanting to pledge their oath to the Union and separate themselves from the Confederacy.

With fewer military matters to discuss, Newton spent these months focused on family. His teenage son Ned had a series of behavioral setbacks during this period, such as taking out the gun that his father had sent home, and Newton was very concerned. He told his wife that Ned needed discipline and good penmanship. Alternatively, Newton suggested that Ned would benefit from reform school or a "farm managed by the authorities of the state."[2] He wrote two letters directly to Ned to stress the importance of character, respect for elders, and, once again, penmanship. Newton referred to an incident where Ned insulted his mother in public. Such behavior, Newton believed, was intolerable and a horrible example for Ned to set for his siblings. On that topic, after several months of waiting, Newton suggested naming their newborn child John Beverly, after his brother John Newton and the middle name Beverly in honor of his medical colleague Dr. John Beverly Warwick. Also during this period, Newton discovered that his daughter Kate was learning to read.

The letters during these early months of 1864 cover the more personal and mundane. Newton continued to try and sell his house in Ironton and mentioned several investment opportunities. But there are hints that Newton and the 91st Ohio Volunteer Infantry were preparing for significant military maneuvers. In mid-February General George Crook became the new division commander, under orders from General Ulysses S. Grant to push into Southwest Virginia. As part of a multipronged offensive, Crook and others began planning spring operations for the Kanawha Division.

90

Hospital 2nd Va. Cav.
Charleston West Va. Jany 3rd 1864

My Dear Wife

It seems almost an age since I saw you or received a letter. I returned home this morning after spending three days at Gallipolis, on account of no boat to come up the river. I almost run the risk of going home, but now feel thankful I did not, for it would be impossible to get up the river. Six Steam Boats now in mouth of Kanawha ice bound, and we came very near being cut down last night by the ice. Have not been so frightened by Rebels or anything else.

Your Ma & Em were very much afraid I could be drowned on the way up, and gave many admonitions to be careful. Had a nice time & plenty to eat while there. Dined, or supped with all round, and began to think would have to stay there.

Kellogg has not yet returned. When he does, and orders me to other duty, will let you know what it is. I feel gratified, that Mott went home when he did, for now I should be afraid to send him.

Hope you will admonish Ned at the right time, to be very careful of his reputation as a scholar, an honest boy etc. For nothing gives me more solicitude at the present time.

Adjutant Gillen is here, and but little improved. Col Coates says the charges against Col T.[3] have been smothered, so say nothing.

We still have very cold weather, but indications of a change are now evident.

I presume you keep pretty close to the fire, and *poke it occasionally.* Tell Ricker I was at Head Quarters this morning, & everything seemed all right. Kiss the baby & Kate for me, tell the boys to improve well their time.

Much love to yourself

> Your Husband
> Wm. S. Newton

91

> Hospital 2nd Va. Cav.
> Charleston Jany 8th 1864

My Dear Wife

Tomorrow morning I start for Fayetteville. It is very cold and I dread the trip very much. I presume I shall again experience the inconvenience of being on the front. It has now been two weeks since I received a letter from you, and indications are that it will be two weeks more, before I receive another. Navigation is closed on the Kanawha, and if it should keep so, two weeks more, we shall be obliged to get out of this, or starve. Provisions can hardly be supplied by trains. Director Kellogg told me today I was to have an independent command at Fayette, Viz,[4] McMullens Battery & one Company of cavalry, and report directly to him.

Should this be the case, will have things all my own way, and I think it will be pleasant. Kellogg I think wants to have Ayres join his own Reg., and break up the Brigade Med. Department. This accounts for his willingness to assign me to the 34 Ohio, although the application was made by Surg. Ayres & approved by Genl. Duffie.

Perhaps it will all be for the best in the end. I saw Neal & Senator Curtis[5] of Marietta, and they will speak a word for me at Columbus at the right time. McEwen is not yet definitely heard from, and no action is had in reference to Surg. in 2nd Va.

Gillen is here still, with but little improvement. Think he will probably get his resignation papers through the department.

How does Mott act since he got home? He created quite a sensation here, and behaved himself manfully. Hope he will continue to do so. Some of the young ladies make special inquiry concerning him.

Tell Kate she must learn to read and spell with her blocks, and keep them nice & clean so little bubbie can have them to play with when he gets old enough.

Tell Mr. Kingsbury if anyone will pay 3000. for the house to sell it for me, possession given the 1st of April. Write often now, for they may be a long time on the way.

> Your Husband
> Wm. S. Newton

92

> Hospital 91st Reg. O.V.I.
> Fayetteville W. Va. Jan 12th/64

My Dear Wife

I arrived here on the evening of the 10th, found things pretty much as I left them, Wellons running the Med. Dept. in camp. Warwick & I are both in quarters near the Hospital. Our quarters however, are quite different from those I left in Charleston. Yet we are able to keep warm, have not very much to call us abroad, and so stay pretty close.

We went to camp yesterday and I was very much surprised at the hearty welcome from the Colonel, down to the privates. They all seemed very glad at my return, and greeted me with many words & handshaking.

The Col. invited me to his quarters, to see Mrs. Turley & the baby. In short, I was almost overcome by the deference manifested on all sides.

Dick is with me. Capt. Pinckard, Chief Q.M. sent my baggage, & Dick, in an ambulance. I rode Old Tom. By the way, my little mare died three days before I left Charleston. She & all the horses had lung fever. And while I was at Gallipolis, on New Years Day, Dr. Gilliam[6] rode the mare ten miles into the country at the same time she was quite sick. Dick told him she was not able to go, but he would take her, and spurred the poor thing all the way, as I have since learned. Adjutant Gillen and all the others say, that he killed her, and should be made to pay.

He did not say one word, or go near her, while she was sick.

Neither did I mention the subject to him, lest I should *say, and do, too much.*

I have not had a letter from you, since the one dated on Christmas day, almost three weeks.

Warwick says, "These women get very independent" "They know very well we won't leave them" "So draw themselves up in their shell, and make no demonstration till they want something." I suppose Mott could tell you everything, and I begin to wish for some evidence that you all exist.

The 91st have a very nice & comfortable Camp about 1/2 mile outside of the town. They have built the houses much better, and do not have so many men crowded into them. Instead of 4 houses, to each company, they now have 8. The companies are getting smaller too. The Col., Capt. Caldwell, Major Cadot, Adjutant Hull, all have their wifes with them in camp, quite a number of the men also have their women with them.

The poor Doctors are all wifeless, and I supposed are doomed to be for sometime to come. I still hope for something to turn up that will eventually take me out of this command. Perhaps the new Governor will give me a better position. I see from the papers, that we also have a new Surg. genl.,[7] which may also make some difference. Hope you have plenty of coal to keep you warm. We burn wood and have much difficulty in keeping warm.

Write often. Your Husband
Wm. S. Newton

Have just received yours of the 3rd. You may call the boy John Beverly. Am pleased with the idea of naming for Br. John, and as I think Beverly is pretty, would like it for the middle one. I shall certainly devise some plan to give Ned employment, if I put him to some trade.

93

Hospital 91st Reg O.V.I.
Fayetteville January 17th 1864

My Dear Wife

This is Rebel paper on which I now write, captured at Lewisburg. I have other, but I thought to be curious, and take a banter given by Warwick. We have both agreed to use this, in writing to our wives today.

Have not received a letter since the one acknowledged in my last, they come very rarely. And were it not for the full faith and confidence I have in you I would at times almost despond. Yet when I reflect how many the cares & duties you have to perform, and how well you like to sleep, and how often your rest must be disturbed, by that great boy *John Beverly*, I cannot find it in my heart to attach any blame to you. Oh how I wish Ned would be a better boy, & give you aid & comfort, instead of being a cause of solicitude.

Sometimes I feel as if I must try to get out of the service, if for no other purpose than to look after the boys, then again I think they certainly will do better. Ned has good sense, and certainly will see the propriety of maintaining a good name. It would be a very hard story, should his father be compelled to quit the service on his account. And then how much happier we all should be, if we could only think, each was doing his duty and using his best endeavor for the peace and happiness of all concerned.

I received an order yesterday to take charge of the battery & Cavalry, about 225 men. I also made application for the building formerly occupied by Col. Turley, for a Hospital. If I get it, will be very comfortably fixed. It is now occupied by two lieutenants of the 12th. They both have their families. If I could only know the Rebs would not come, would like very much to have you all come and stay with me.

Should you conclude to give the boy the name, you should write to Br. John and tell him of it. He may object.

Give my regards to all enquiring friends.

Your Husband
Wm. S. Newton

94

Hospital 91st Reg Friday evening
Fayetteville W. Va Jany 22nd 1864

My Dear Wife

Yours of 18th Ult came today and as you expected filled me with many misgivings. Not that I expect any evil result from the circumstance, related by Mrs. Wright. And I hope you will not allow such reports to trouble you, don't listen to them, or enough of persons will there be to keep you worried all the time. Nor would I talk of these things before the children. If you talk to Ned, take him alone, not before others. Such matters spoken of frequently, get to be common and cease to make the impression. I still have faith, if you take Ned by himself, and talk to him in the right spirit, he certainly will listen, not only listen but remember.

If he cannot act in such a way, as to shield himself from the penalty of the law, let the law have its course. Perhaps it is for the best, and if the law will not take hold of him, I trust that I will be able to devise some means to dispose of him, if not exactly in accordance with his feelings and my own, still duty will prompt me in the matter. There is such an institution as a reform school. Also a farm managed by the authorities of the state, on which boys, who get too large to mind their mothers, are taken & learned to work. A trade of some kind is very useful, and may be of immense value to him in after life. I am determined that something of the kind shall be done. I will not have the peace and quiet of home disturbed by one heedless & disobedient boy. He shall be turned out into the world, and learn how to appreciate the comforts of home. I don't say this because it is pleasant, far from it. But while I am striving to make a home comfortable, *no one boy* shall, by his *pure ugliness*, destroy all the pleasure that might be enjoyed. I really think Ned possesses too much good sense, if this matter is properly presented to him. When he has tried the realities of the world, outside of home, I think he will appreciate a fathers & mothers care & kindness.

How sad the thought, that after so many years of toil & anxiety, so many hours & days of work in teaching our little ones, and so much care in clothing them, that we should get such a return as this. I will not complete the picture.

Your Husband
Wm. S. Newton

95

January 22nd 1864

My Son Edward,

Some time ago, I wrote you a letter giving you as I thought good advice, it was the advice of a *parent to his child*. One whom I trust you will acknowledge, has at all times shown & manifested an interest in you. And you in return wrote an answer to my letter which greatly encouraged me. Little did I think that so soon your delinquencies would be complained of, or that I should again be compelled to admonish you in reference to your conduct. Where are those resolutions that you were to write down and read every day? Is your word of no avail? If your word is worth nothing now, is there a prospect that when you become a man it will be any better?

Is this the reputation you desire to make for yourself? For reputation is what you are making every day. How sad it is for a father thus to write his son, and that son but 13 years of age. An age which, more than any other, if of the right disposition and habits, would contribute to the happiness of the parents, for at this age children *can do very much* to lessen the cares & duties of those parents. Has it ever occurred to you, that you have something to do, that you have duties to perform? As I have told you before, you are the eldest of our living children, and the others look to you for an example, now are you pursuing the course you would like to have Mott & Kittie follow.

Your brothers and sister have died, died younger than you are. Did it ever occur to you that you might sicken & die? If such should be the case, are you living in such a way, that your memory would be cherished by us. If you are not doing so, is not this sufficient to prompt you to do better? There is still a higher, a more weighty object, which should induce you. Of this I will not speak, your own good sense will teach you what that object is, and I trust will consider it.

Now Ned, do you wish to make shipwreck of your own hopes, and blast the hopes of your parents, simply to gratify a depraved appetite or taste for pleasure that are *not pleasures,* for "there is no lasting pleasure in doing wrong." You have seen enough & read enough to know what is right, and when you are contributing to the happiness of others. You also know when you are making yourself & others miserable. Now choose which you will do. If you choose one course, all right. We shall be very thankful & grateful too.

But if you choose the other, I know you will not be happy, and will render the whole family sorrowful, besides put me to the trouble and inconvenience of a trip home, beside the necessary steps to procure a new home for you.

I want you to write immediately on the reception of this, and decide definitely whether you are willing to give strict obedience to your mother. I don't want any deception in the matter, but straight open truth, that I may act accordingly.

> Your Father,
> Wm. S. Newton

96

> Hospital 91 Reg. O.V.I.
> Fayetteville West Va. Jany 25th 1864

My Dear Wife

Tomorrow evening I go into my own quarters, and in addition to battery & Cav., will also have charge of 9th Va. Hospital during the absence of Dr. Morris, who has a leave of 20 days.

All seem to get home but poor me. They go on Surg. Certificate, and as yet I cannot find a complaint to suit any case. Perhaps it is best to be thankful, that I have good health and to be content therewith.

There are many things to regret, and I am trying to resolve to make the best of my condition. At the same time endeavor to do the duties incumbent upon me to the best of my ability, asking aid & strength from above.

There are many drawbacks to a strict performance of duty in the army, and in the whirl and excitement of camp life one forgets almost his accountability. I am resolved to overcome, as much as possible, these impediments, and hope I shall be kept humble, that I may resist temptation & live nearer in the discharge of duty to God & man. I also hope you may be able, to so manage our boys, that they will be a help & comfort to us, as they grow up.

Capt. Caldwell goes home tomorrow. His wife & Mrs. Findley accom-

pany him. Will send this by them. Mrs. Cadet & Hull are still here, also
Mrs. Crossland. Took dinner with the latter last Sabbath. You would almost be surprised at such a good meal at this place. Roasted chicken and
stuffed venison, good apple & cherry pies, with cake, etc. "How much we
suffer for our bleeding country."

Major McEwen is restored I understand to his position, I presume it is
all right.

Hope the time will not be too far distant when we all, will be restored
to our homes & families. But much seemingly remains to be accomplished,
before this can be done.

Rumor says we are to be paid in a week or two. This certainly will be
acceptable, for most all the officers are short of money.

Counsel the boys to be good, and learn & live for a purpose, to have
some usefulness in prospect.

My love to them all,

> Your Husband
> Wm. S. Newton

97

> Hospital 1st Indept Battery
> Fayetteville West Va. Jany 29th

My Dear Wife

Yours of the 21st came last eve, and I will answer by 1st mail, as the transportation is so very tardy. As you see I am running a hospital on my own
hook, have a very comfortable room for myself, only a few reporting sick.
And were it not for the care of 9th Va. Hosp., would feel as if I was not earning US very much.

I am indeed glad to learn that Ned is doing better. If he knew what a
relief it is to mind, he certainly would try to do the best he could. For I feel
as if no privileges could be granted him, I could not trust him to go away
from home, lest he bring us all into trouble.

I had hoped to have attained a better position, and then if he improved
in his writing, I could make him of use to me in the service. Am very much
pleased to see the improvement in penmanship as shown by the specimen
sent, and still hope he will surpass my own. Should really be proud of it. I
showed the specimen to Col. Turley, and he said it was doing well for Ned.
He looked at it a long time, said if he kept on, would make a Sergeant Major
in any Reg.

So I want him to look around and see the profit there is in it.

James G. D. Findley was a farmer from
Delaware County, Ohio. He made numerous advancements in the 91st Ohio
Volunteer Infantry—he enlisted as a
private, was appointed sergeant major,
was promoted to first lieutenant, and
later appointed adjutant. In a January
29, 1864, letter to his wife, William S.
Newton mentioned that Findley's good
penmanship helped secure promotions.
Adjutant Findley, Eugene B. Willard
Photograph Album, Special Collections,
Marietta College, Marietta, Ohio.

Sargt. Findley has now got to be a 1st Lieut. He started in as a private,
but his good penmanship recommended him for promotion.

Dr. Warwick's middle name is Beverly, and when I told him of your wish
to call the boy John, he said "if I would put the Beverly to it, he would buy
him the best suit of clothes that could be got." So liking the name, that if
you did not object, would like it very much. You must write to John and let
him know he has a namesake.

Got a letter from Mother. She says, "she has not heard a word from you
since I was at home."

So think you had better let them hear from you. We have had such
pleasant weather for a few days. It has made me quite homesick. I feel as if
I would like to be among the trees in the back yard, pruning the grape vines
etc.

I see by the paper that Amanda Furnace[8] is to be sold soon. I have a note
or bill of acceptance on Child & Walker.[9] You had better enquire of Geo. W.
Willard[10] whether anything can be done in the matter, if he thinks he can
save it. You may say to him I will give him a good per cent on the collection.

The amount is 100. dollars with two or three years interest. You will find
it among the notes.

Am invited to tea this evening at Adjutant Hulls. Warwick is invited
also. His wife I find, is almost an old acquaintance. I once traveled with her
on board a steamboat. She then lived at Delaware, O. I suppose this is the
key to the acquaintance. Good bye,

Your Husband
Wm. S. Newton

Will send Photograph which you will recognize. Had corn & beans for dinner. Both had been dried but were very good

98

Hospital McMullens Arty
Fayetteville West Va.

Feb. 1st 1863[4]

My Dear Wife

Yours of the 25th came through in four days. The mails & boats on Kanawha have been very irregular lately, which I think in a great measure accounts for the delay.

It gives me great pleasure to learn of the improvement in conduct, and penmanship, which your letters & enclosure, exhibit in reference to Ned. I do so wish he would have some ambition to do right. We could always feel proud of Oren[11], and I felt I could trust him, was sure he would not do a dishonorable act. You have no idea what a consolation it would be, if the other boys would copy him. If they would only feel that they were laying the foundation now, for usefulness, they certainly would give up some of their spirits & habits, and try to be somebody.

How much pleasure it would be to take them with me, and how much they would see & learn to fit them for business. But I fear they only think of the present, and not what the future will bring.

It might be that I could make a Hospital Steward of Ned, a very honorable & responsible position. Besides, he would be proud of the pay, and it would be a very nice business beginning. A good penman & a boy of steady habits could fill the place very well, and it would be very pleasant to have him along in that capacity if only qualified.

I have no Steward at present, he is at home very sick, and may never return. He lives at Moscow, Ohio, some 15 miles above New Richmond, is the son of Dr. Johnson,[12] & I learn a good boy. Warwick invited me to dinner yesterday. We had a turkey etc., all very nice, for this country.

Think if you would feed your boy Diaphoretic powders[13] they would quiet him, and not hurt him either. Kate was very fond of them, and has taken many from me, dry, from the spatula. I don't think the camphor[14] in them would choke him, and would help throw off the wind from the stomach. There is very little opium in them, and then the gum tartar counteracts the effect of it, so that his bowels would not be bound. Try it if you have trouble.

Have Mr. Wright get you a gallon of ale, & try the virtue of it. You have used it with a good result. Direct your letters as before, only say In Charge McMullens Art. Good night, love to all.

Your Husband
Thus W.S. Newton Asst
Surg. 91st O.V.I.
In Charge McMullens Art.
Fayetteville, West Va.

99

Hospital McMullens Arty
Fayetteville West Va Feb 4th 1864

My Dear Wife

I should have received a letter from you last mail, but as it did not come will write to you. Most of the officers wife's and those who made great preparations to keep them all winter have either become tired, or consider it not a very appropriate place for women. Mrs. Coates was not here more than ten days, Coates having received an order to go to Columbus. They spent some weeks in Charleston, paying 13$ per week for board. This counts up pretty fast. On this account, I prefer to be here, it cost me more while there three months than six on the front.

The expense of capturing my horse, then the loss of it, was no small item to me.

The Pay Master is here, and we will be paid for two months in a day or two, finishing up the year 1863. Shall probably send home 150$ by the first opportunity. Was never nearer out of money.

A dispatch came last evening saying that Genl. Scammon, Capt. Pinckard & others were captured at Red House, on board the S.B. Levi. The boat was burned.[15] Don't you think the Genl. had an unpleasant march last night! It was very cold, and I presume the Rebs double quicked him, for fear of being overtaken.

The Rebs also captured 8 horses from two wagons, some six men the guard, the two teamsters etc. All taken from 12th Ohio, on their late scout to Raleigh.

If the 91st had met with the mishap, it would have been attributed to their green discipline etc. As it was the 12th I presume it is all right.

Would like very much to see you all, but I presume it will be some time, unless fortune favors me in some way. Some 8 new recruits for the 91st, 10 or 12 for the 12th Ohio, & five for the artillery arrived here today. As you see our ranks are filling up, getting ready for spring operations. At which time, I presume our out posts will extend further into Va.

Hope the boys will do all they can to lessen your duties & troubles. In this way, they can gladden my heart & make themselves happy.

Give my love to them all. Tell Kate I am glad she is learning to read.

Your Husband

Wm. S. Newton

100

Hospital Feb. 6th 1864

Dear Wife

I have only time to enclose 150$ before Capt. Culbertson leaves for Ohio. Deposit it in bank and acknowledge the receipt as soon as possible.

Received yours of the 1st last evening. Will write again soon. No news.

Your Husband

Wm. S. Newton

101

Hospital McMullens Arty
Fayetteville W. Va. Feb. 9th 1864

My Dear Wife

In the hasty note by Capt. Culbertson, containing 150$ dated Feb. 6th, I forgot to say I was forty one years old, indeed had not had time to say it, or hardly anything else, nor do I write now. Because I have anything particular to write, but more because it is a pleasure thus to spend an hour.

You might say, in this I am selfish, but were it not, that I expected to give pleasure to others, would not so frequently engage in the pastime. Hope you will get the money safe, and deposit it in *Bank*.

I have not been more pleasantly situated during my term of service.

At present I have enough to do, and leisure, for reading, writing etc. And till now, have not had a room all to myself, could not always do just as I wanted, without interfering with someone, and what is more important, could not engage in those *duties without which*, I never feel contented. Now I have no one to avoid, can turn the button on my door, and be all alone when bedtime comes. You can hardly realize what a luxury it is, and I trust the hour is profitably employed. The little *Red Testament* so long idle, is now employed, morning and night, the consciousness of having tried to perform my duty, affords me much consolation, and enables me better to say no when temptation presents itself in its various forms.

Have one cook detached from the battery. He & Dick do all the cooking, washing, & care for the horse.

Have but one sick man, and he is able to be about & take his rations. If we had more it would be better on account of expense, for I have rations to buy, besides the butter, potatoes & turnips, which we get at the Picket Post. If we had four or five, their rations would keep all, with the vegetables we are able to purchase. Still I am not spending six dollars per week as some do for board alone. Yesterday, Dick lost our Le[a]ther bucket in the well, I bent a nail for a hook, and with it, & a horse shoe tied to a rope, he fished it out. I told him to try for another one, or we would have one to buy, as we had not enough for use. So over he went, and was not long in fishing up a very nice tin one. I was watching, and as soon as he got it to the top, he run home with it. I asked why he was in such a hurry. He said he was afraid someone would come along and claim it. It was rusted somewhat, he scoured it up, & brought it into my room, saying he would take mine to pick water. He was very proud of the bucket, and said as soon as it got warm, he would go and find two or three more, as there was a dozen or so, down there.

He asked when I received your last letter, why you did not say something about Mott. He thinks Mott might send him some word.

He seems as much pleased, when I get a letter from home, as if he had always lived there. He is learning to read & spell very fast, and likes to have me read aloud to him.

Give my regards to all, & love to the little ones.

Your Husband

Wm. S. Newton

I send Capt. Davidson's[16] photograph as I have no good place to keep it.
P.S.
Mix Sulphur with molasses, two teaspoons of Sulphur, to two teaspoons of Molasses. Then a dose will be, a teaspoonful every morning, this will keep the children from having the itch.

It will not taste bad, give it three mornings in succession, then stop there.

Wm.S.N.

102

Hospital McMullens Battery
Fayetteville West Va. Feb 10th 1864

Dear Wife

I have this day written to Brother John, to draw on you, for five hundred, in shape of draft or some way, which he will indicate to you. As he had not said anything to me, I can only offer to pay. And whatever instructions he may give you in the matter, follow out. If he wants a draft on Cincinnati, go to the bank, give your check for it & send to him, or get the bank to forward it for you.

Keep this wholly to yourself, as the children's happiness will not be lessened by ignorance of the fact. Have told him the probable amount you would have to your Cr. in bank.

Got yours & Neds letter last evening. He must not evade the question. I wish to know from his own hand what he intends to do. I desire to preserve the evidence in his own handwriting. You will therefore tell him.

Your Husband
Wm. S. Newton

103

Hospital McMullens Battery
Fayetteville W. Va. Feb 15th 1864

My Dear Wife

Yours of 10th is at hand, about Ned joining Sons Temp.[17] I do not know what to say. Do boys of his age join now? They were not allowed in former times, and I very much fear the being out at night will over balance the good. If he could go at just the right time, and return immediately after, I should not have any objection. Boys congregated together after night are always looked upon with suspicion and the reason is parents do not allow good boys to run about at night. If they did, the boys would soon be suspected of something wrong, whether they really were so or not. Then there are most always some bad boys who give the others a bad name from the very fact they are found in company. Hope Willard will take the note on Child & Walker, and if possible, save it. Will pay a good commission for collection.

I have made out my papers again for a leave of absence, and as they do not go to the War Dept., but to Genl. Kell[e]y's Hd. Quarters at Cumberland, Md., have some reasonable expectation they will be approved. But don't say one word about it, for I do not care to have it known that I made the application.

If they are approved, will prob. see you sometime in the latter part of March, between 20th & 30th. Col. White approved here, but as we now have a new Div. Commander in the person of Genl Geo. Crook, it is hard to say what he will do in such matters. All who know him are pleased with the change of Genls. The whole valley are also pleased with the return of Col. Powell. Crook & Powell, they all say, will accomplish something. Am glad you are able to get out with the boy, & when spring comes, hope you will not be so confined with him.

In mid-February 1864, Ohio native
George Crook took command of the
Third Division of the Department of
West Virginia. Under orders from
General Ulysses S. Grant, Crook
planned to push Union forces into
Southwest Virginia. Maj. Gen. Geo.
Crook, Eugene B. Willard Photograph
Album, Special Collections, Marietta
College, Marietta, Ohio.

Got a letter from Doug. He says John [Newton] & Col. Mills[18] have sold
their interest in Bucket Factory.

Let me know if you get any communication from John.

Also if you have received the money by Capt. Culbertson.

Good Bye.

Wm. S. Newton

104

Hospital McMullens Battery

Feb 21st 1864

My Dear Wife

Have been waiting for a letter several days, and should have received
yours of last Sabbath on Friday. This is now Sunday eve, and I always feel
like thinking or talking with you, even in this poor way. It affords some
satisfaction, although I must acknowledge it is a poor substitute for one
hungry for the associations of home and family.

There is not much to disturb the monotony of our camp, yet the same-
ness is to be disturbed by the sending out of a hundred men, in three different directions. The 100 belonging to 91st is under command of Capt. Niday,
crosses New River and goes toward Lewisburg. The object is to [im]press,
or capture, horses. These to be used in mounting scouts for the spring campaign. Almost every day, rebel deserters and refugees come into our lines
anxious to take the oath, and be sent where they can obtain the necessities
of life.

They rarely enlist, but are very anxious to put as wide a space between themselves and the Rebel conscription officers as possible.

They are a sorry looking lot, both men & women of the white or yellow hair gentry. I wish you could see a few specimens. Would not give my boy Dick for a large squad of them.

I wrote to Judge Johnson[19] to act as Agt. for me there, & if an opportunity presented, to sell my house. I received an answer from him, saying he would do the best he could, that 3000. was probably the best that could be realized.

If he should come with anyone, play the agreeable as much as circumstances will admit.

The small lot seems to be the great objection, let them understand that the Cour[t] House Yard serves as a substitute for ground in raising the little ones, and that it is quite as pleasant to have them there, beside saving our own fruit.

Have not heard anything from John, but suppose you will very soon. Nor have I yet heard that you received the money by Capt. Culbertson. We have not had a mail for three days, expect one tomorrow. Much love to you all.

Your Husband
Wm. S. Newton

105

Hospital [Mc]Mullens Battery
Fayetteville W. Va. Feb. 24th 1864

My Dear Edward,

Your letter with one from Mother & Mott all came today. But what feelings they produced in my mind. I will not now undertake to describe or portray, and I have waited six hours that I might sit down and write, without any excitement, that we may reason together, concerning the future, for *we all have a future*, which depends very much on the manner of spending the present. Now let us ask, how are you spending the days & weeks allowed you, to fit & prepare you, for usefulness. Are your best endeavors used, in the first place, to render all about you happy, and prosperous. Are you teaching your little brothers & sister lessons that will contribute to their happiness, and help them to form habits that will make them good and agreeable companions & associates. These are duties you owe to them, *as an older brother.* They look up to you for an example. Is your example a good one, and one that you can look back upon when you have grown to be a man, with satisfaction. If it is not, had you not better pause & consider, for I as your father tell you that this will have a great bearing on your good name & conduct in after years. And this is not all, what an influence it will have, on your brothers & sister. You too will be held responsible for the influence you exert toward them.

What would be your feelings, *if a man*, should you see *another man, a stranger*, impose upon your mother; would you not risk your life in resenting the *imposition*, or *insult*! *If not*, you are not of my *blood* or *kindred*. Then how much more *despicable* is he, that would abuse, or offer an insult to his own mother! Just stop and think of this thing. In all my boyhood, and in that of my brothers, none of us ever dared or thought of such a thing, as resist our mother, and I can hardly keep cool now, while waiting to think I have a boy, who would do such a thing.

You certainly are not demented, or crazy, yet how could I suppose a boy almost 14 years of age, could commit such indiscretion. I truly hope no one knows of it. I hope the neighbors will not hear of it, for what would they say of you, and what would they say of your training, and teachings heretofore, I can hardly contemplate the picture, or the detestation in which a boy would be held, raised as you have been. If your temper leads you to do such things now, unless curbed, how soon may we expect you will suffer *public disgrace* from some crime, committed by giving a loose rein to such rashness. I shudder at the thought, and am so grieved, cannot look on a visit home with any pleasure.

Should I obtain a leave of absence, how much happiness can I promise myself, with such actions going on at home. Do you ever think, that others must suffer for your misdeeds also, that as a family we are all alike responsible for the deeds of the rest.

Did you think it would afford me any happiness, to know that you were taking the gun out, contrary to my express command, and have you reflected that if, some accident should take place, how much misery you might cause to your parents & others.

I do wish you would think of these things, consider them well, for a change must be effected. The manner I shall not now undertake to prescribe. I hope you will not compel me to give up my position, to restore order at home. I do not think you have improved in penmanship since the specimen you sent me, and which I was proud enough to show others.

I would be ashamed to say you wrote *this*, *last*, after exhibiting the other.

Character is said to be exhibited in the penmanship. If yours is the true exhibit of character, how uneven & unbalanced it must be. I fear your energy & resolutions are short lived, and to little purpose. Can you not do better! Will you not try! And before I see you, let me see some specimens of improvement, both in penmanship & character. Your happiness as well as mine depends upon it.

Let me hear from you soon. I wish to know of your prospects and resolves.

So that I may shape my course accordingly. I am now forty one years old, and had not expected to write thus, to a son of mine. Did you ever think that I, or your mother, might not be spurred to furnish you with home, or the comforts of life. If so, what are your prospects? Who would be willing to take you, and for what purpose are you making that reputation, that will ensure your welcome, if we are taken from you! Think of this.

Your Father
Wm. S. Newton

7

To Be Realized, It Must Be Experienced, March–June 1864

After several months of limited activity in winter quarters, William S. Newton and the 91st Ohio Volunteer Infantry embarked on the most challenging campaigns of their military service. Under the leadership of Union brigadier general George Crook, the 91st along with other Ohio and Virginia regiments pushed into Southwest Virginia and then into the Shenandoah Valley. In May, Crook's Kanawha Division routed Confederate forces led by General Albert G. Jenkins at the Battle of Cloyd's Mountain near Dublin, Virginia. Although the battle was brief, the fighting was extreme. The diary of John Holliday, a sergeant in Company C of the 91st Ohio Volunteer Infantry, described the scene as a "terrible Storm of lead."[1] The 91st Ohio Volunteer Infantry suffered casualties but, according to Newton, fought bravely. After successfully destroying the New River Bridge near Radford, the Kanawha Division saw action near Lynchburg.[2]

As in his previous letters, Newton was still trying to plan for his postwar life. He bought a farm from Colonel Coates in early April and attempted to sell his home to the publisher of the *Ironton Register*. Newton's letters during this period included more details of military matters. The 91st was on the move that spring and thus he was no longer confined to a hospital located in an actual structure. Newton discussed dramatic activities in camp, such as the shooting of a hospital steward who was having an affair with the wife of a local druggist. Ironically, in Newton's April 30 letter to his wife, he jokes about being sent to Libby Prison, only to be sent there a few weeks later.

After sending that late April letter, Newton did not correspond with his wife until July 11. During this gap of time, Newton experienced the most significant events of his military service. A few days after the Battle of Cloyd's Mountain, he was captured by Confederate forces, participated in the effort to save the life of Confederate General Albert G. Jenkins, spent several days in Libby Prison, and upon release returned to the 91st. Newton's Civil War correspondence with his wife did not discuss any of these details. Instead, Newton provided two slightly different accounts of his experiences. In June 1864 Newton's firsthand account of the Battle of Cloyd's Mountain and subsequent capture by Confederates appeared in a lengthy article in the *Ironton Register*. Newton provided a second and slightly different account of the same events in an 1867 letter to Ohio adjutant general Benjamin R. Cowen regarding the treatment of Union prisoners of war. Together the postwar letter and newspaper account add important details to the few published accounts from soldiers engaged in the Battle of Cloyd's Mountain. This chapter concludes with a reprinting of the newspaper account, a transcript of his 1867 letter (which is part of the Newton Papers), and a brief analysis of the events he described.

106

Cumberland Md. March 3rd/64

My Dear Wife

Yours of 26th received, and answered, but I have today entered into an agreement with Col. Coates for his farm and have delivered to him my horse Tom, valued at 200, in part pay. I also agree to pay on 1st of April twelve hundred dollars, and execute two notes, due in one & two years for eight hundred each, with interest at 6 per cent.

I got possession on 1st of April, and I want you to go to Gallipolis, get ready to move by the 1st of April, and take possession of that property. You can get Will to superintend the packing of the goods you have taken out of the boxes, and have them delivered on the Wharf Boat. We can also make an arrangement with some boat for their delivery at Manchester. I wrote you in reference to the money to be paid by Davidson, you had better entrust the matter to G. W. Jackson.[3] He can compute the interest, receive the amount, and place to your credit. And if it is right to pay the tax, he will be able to judge of that, and if right allow it.

I also want you to send me, from his bank, a certificate of deposit for twelve hundred dollars, with which to finish the first payment. You will advise with him, the best way to send it, whether by mail, or express. This will leave you some four hundred dollars, or more, of ready money, with which to make a start at living in your new home. Settle up all accounts at Gallipolis, leaving at present, the borrowed money, as Will is not now probably in a condition to pay the 1000, and it is also drawing interest. Col. Coates had made some arrangement with Mr. Baldridge,[4] the former owner of the farm, to cut the present wheat crop, also to sow some ten acres in oats, on which, he will also sow clover & Timothy seed. In fact, I have written, or requested Col. to write, to Mr. Baldridge, to have a general supervision of the fencing, and look after things, a little advising with you in all important matters. He has great confidence in the honesty of Baldridge, says he is very close however in his business transactions.

You need make no provision for eatables etc., for I am informed you can purchase the necessities of life much cheaper at West Union than other places. For instance, butter is 25 cts. & other things in proportion. Flour is also to be had there without the expense of shipping etc.

The boys will have enough to do, to look after the outside fencing, keeping it up so that the farm will not run over with stock. They can pasture some of the town cows, always receiving the amount per month in advance, so in this way they will create no bad debts.

I will write to Ned, telling him how much depends on his faithfulness, and good management to make a good start in farming.

Am in hopes something will turn up, so that I may get home in time to see you transferred, but you must make arrangements just as if I was not coming, for it may be impossible with me. Warwick has sent in his resignation on the plea of bad health in his family, his wife having valvular disease of the heart etc. Coates thinks the paper will be approved and if so, will probably stay with Reg. until their time is out, which will be some time in August. Hope you will think I have done right in this matter. I have thought of it, day & night, in fact am almost sick of fretting and worrying over it. Hope it will all turn out for the best for all concerned.

Perhaps Br. John can give you good advice how to proceed in matters, but your time will be all taken up, as you will have very little time to fix for moving. Still take things as they come. Em will help you out some.

You will be able in some way to accomplish it all. Give my love to all.

Your Husband
Wm. S. Newton

107

Charleston West Va April 4th 1864

My Dear Wife

Am here again, arrived at 4 P.M. last Saturday. Stayed one day in Gallipolis, found Mother H. much improved. Took tea with Will & Rene, found all things as usual, had a pair pants made for me thinking it would be some time before I would get an opportunity again.

Dr. Miller came yesterday, whether I will remain in 34th remains yet to be seen. I understand the 91st are clamoring for my return to them, have heard nothing from my papers lately sent to the Capitol.

Sickness in this command about the same. They lost 4 in hospital during my absence, one the same night I returned. Dr. Ayres was glad to see me. Mr. Ricker started for Ohio next morning. Nothing new, my love to all the little ones, tell them to be good.

Your Husband
Wm. S. Newton

108

Hospital 34th Reg
Charleston West Va April 10th

Dear Wife

Yours of the 8th by Mr. Ricker has come to hand, the first since I left home.

Am sorry to hear of Mrs. Johnson's illness, was afraid from the symptoms detailed by Sherman[5] that she would have a run of fever.

Hope they will keep her stimulated and not give her much medicine. Turpentine emulsion, Whiskey & Quinine[6] will generally meet all indications.

Our men here recover on this treatment surely and speedily. You must get 4 or 5 grains of *Morphios Sulphur*[7] of Mr. Wright, and make up some powders for John Beverly. You saw me make those for him all you have to observe is not to get too much, and if you do not get enough in each you can add more according to effect. Try and get him along until May, at which time I think the symptoms will change, so you can do without them altogether.

I suppose I shall lose Dick. They offer two or three hundred dollars bounty, and he proposes to send his money to you, to have it put in bank and taken care of for him. He has no one with whom to make the deposit, and I am to furnish him with your address so that when he gets his bounty he can send to you, and you are to take charge of his bank account.

I shall also owe him 20$ which will be the beginning of his account.

Am very much pleased and gratified to learn of the good conduct of the boys. I do not see anything to hinder us being very happy, if we only do right, and there are much better prospects for continued happy days & weeks, for if the boys do right, my plans for their future employment will be very much modified. They should try to gain a reputation for business integrity, which will be more for them as capital, than all I can defer them with dollars & cents.

If they can establish this kind of capital, it would be a pleasure to enter into some kind of business which would give them pleasure and profit, a little start in business is much better than a life of drudgery, and if they show themselves capable, there is no trouble in getting this opportunity. Will send the boys some berries of the Holly, two apiece. Let them plant them, and if they succeed in raising trees, will give them 50 cents apiece for them when they are large enough to set out in the yard. Good Bye, Your Husband

Wm. S. Newton

Tell Mott to ask Mr. Oviatte[8] if he has sent my gold pen. It has not yet come to hand.

109

Charleston W. Va. April 16th
Saturday evening

My Dear Wife

I wrote yesterday, but quite a tragedy having occurred here last night, will try to give it.[9]

A Mr. Nelson, a young man, and Hospital Steward to Med. Dir. Kellogg, was shot and almost instantly killed by Mr. Dinges, a druggist of this place. It seems Dinges had suspected Nelson of too much intimacy with his (Dinges) wife so Dinges pretended to start for Cincinnati two or three days before last night. He returned in the middle of the night, finding Nelson in bed with his own wife neither of whom had a particle of clothing on. Dinges tried to shoot him in bed, but the revolver snapped twice when Nelson jumped out of bed, and tried to wrench the weapon from Dinges, Nelson grabbing his own pants and Mrs. Dinge's drawers, started to run down the stairway. Dinges then shot him in the left side and back. Nelson ran on down two stairways and jumped out of the back door, looking toward the river, ran along the bank & up the landing to the street, where he first fell in very deep mud. He then dragged himself to the office door and called for help. The other clerk heard, and hurried to his assistance, got him into the office, but he only lived five or ten minutes. He still held *his pants & Mrs. drawers* in his hand, both covered with mud, himself naked & muddy, presented a very unsightly appearance. I was there this morning, while he was being dressed. It was a sad sight, one for serious reflection. Dinges was arrested this morning, handed over to the civil authorities, they examined and acquitted him, and he is now at large. The wife is to be sent away, leaving a child only eighteen months old.[10]

What do you suppose her reflections be now, and with all her beauty &
charms her meditations must be horrible.

You may think I have taken great pains to give particulars, *but the affair
has created so much excitement* here that nothing else is hardly talked of.

I sent the Photo of Col. Dove. Mott will want to claim it. But you must
take care of it. Dove always asks about *Montague*, as he used to call him.

When at Gallipolis, Father H. dug some horseradish, and gave 1/2 doz.
nice roots to me. I came away forgetting them. Yesterday, Mrs. Nowline[11]
sent, by a little darkie, a bottle full, grated, and nicely prepared. Said it was
sent from Gallipolis. I presume it was the same I left.

The Hosp. boys all think it is the very ticket, for cold meat.

We are still threatened with a forward movement, the mud only pre-
vents. Kiss all the children for me. Tell them to be good.

Your Husband

Wm. S. Newton

110

Charleston W. Va.

April 19th 1864

Dear Wife

Have just received an order to report to my Reg. at Fayetteville.

I suppose you will be glad of it, & I am not sorry, except I am so much
further from home and letters will be so long in coming. You must write the
oftener, and so will I, in this way, will try to keep posted. I suppose this order
has grown out of the Warwick & Wellons fight. Think Coates had it done,
for he said he would, does not like Wellons and will dispose of him in some
way. Has preferred charges against him, and if he followed them up would
dismiss him.

Col. Turley is here before an examining board, which has already retired
ten or twelve officers. Whether he will be dismissed remains to be seen.
Two or three from Ironton are among those dismissed. I shall start this
evening or tomorrow for Fayette, so direct your letters to me at that place.
91st Reg. O.V.I.

Tell the boys that I would like to think of them always with pride &
satisfaction, and it is in their power to have it so.

Your Husband

Wm. S. Newton

I send you Photograph of Capt. Hedden,[12] on Gen. Duffie's Staff.

III

Fayetteville West Va.
April 21st 1864

My Dear Wife

Am once more in camp of 91st Reg. O.V.I. and from the many welcomes & congratulations from officers & men, am inclined to think I am appreciated, and a man of some importance to the Reg., it now being over six months since I done duty here. Warwick says "He & Col. Coates begged of Kellogg for mercy's sake, *and the good of the service*, to send me back, & detail Wellons for duty at Charleston.["] He wrote to Kellogg that the men had all lost confidence in Wellons, and would not call on him for treatment, making the duties on Warwick very arduous, having all the work to do. Coates came to me at Charleston and asked if I would be willing to come back, if they could get the exchange made. I told yes certainly, and it was accordingly done, and here I am. An ambulance was in waiting at Loup Creek this morning for my baggage.

Col. Turley & Capt. Glassie accompanied me up, part of a train (eleven mules) were captured last evening just 1 mile above Mrs. Tompkins. We passed an hour after, & saw the wagons yet standing in the road, met one of the men captured, who had made his escape after going with them five miles. We stayed all night only three miles above, and were not a little solicitous about our own horses during the night.

I am occupying Wellons quarters, which are quite comfortable, with a cook house close by, a man to cook for me. Think I shall like the arrangement very well, and hope my expenses will be less than at Charleston.

Heard of Rose's death before leaving Charleston. Can hardly realize it. Saw Warren this morning, and he was feeling darkly.

Oh, what feelings Sherman must have, and how thankful he should now be that there are no little ones to be orphans.

I shudder at the idea, and think how destitute would be my situation if you were gone.

Take care of your own health. Be careful of doing anything which will in any way change your ordinary way of living.

My letter to your Pa was answered by Em, saying they had received the holly trees and were very much pleased. Your mother is much better. Mrs McCormick & old Mrs. Shephard both dead.

Tell the boys I want them both to write a letter every week. *Good long ones* if I remain here. If we start for Richmond will let you know if possible. That a forward movement will be made soon is quite evident. Three Reg. have already arrived in the valley, others are expected. Much love to you all, kiss the little ones for me, get fat & healthy yourself and we will all hope for a speedy reunion.

Your Husband

112

Fayetteville W. Va

April 23rd 1864

My Dear Wife

Yours of 18th is at hand, detailing the suffering & death of Mrs. Johnson. It is sad indeed, and my heart bleeds for Sherman, for I know he loved his wife dearly.

And Mrs. Ricker, I hope she is not seriously ill, for what would they do without the mother, now that the father is in the service. Was Mr. Ricker at the funeral. Warren could not go, and I hope he was able to get there. Tell Ned I shall not be able to send more seed, unless I find them in the woods. The birds are fond of the berries, and they take all that are worth anything. Tell my little Kate she must be more of a lady, than to be romping around, and getting crippled & scarred all up. Got a letter from Mary Frank, all well at Harmar, Doug still on Bostonia.

Will send you the Photographs of Col. Powell, preserve these pictures, for they will someday be of value & interest.

You say my letters are scarce. Now I think I have written three times to your one, ever since I have been in the service. So you know the remedy.

Your Husband

Wm. S. Newton

113

Fayetteville W. Va

April 27th 1864

My Dear Wife

Having a photo of Col. Turley, a present this afternoon, thought I would send it home by letter.

The Col. has been very sick since he & I returned from Charleston together.

And what is strange, he has taken quite a notion to me, and is not willing that Warwick shall attend him, but sends for me three or four times every day.

Yesterday Warwick went in to see him before I had finished visiting the sick in quarters, prescribed for him, and made up the powders.

But Col. swore he would not take them, till I came and approved. Warwick is somewhat nettled at the turn of affairs, and I only look at it as a whim of the super anointed man.

New Regiments, or rather old ones, but new to this locality are coming into the valley, & from the force accumulating something certainly is intended to be done.

We have so many sick, it looks like a hard chance for our Reg. to move, 102 at sick call expected this morning. Many others who have just recovered from measles are not in a fit condition to march, how the matter will be arranged is yet to be developed.

Dr. Miller, before I left Charleston, would have me leave my negative for a photograph. He sent me one for my autograph, and it is so much better than those I had taken, I have ordered a Doz. to distribute among my friends. As you are one of the number, will send you one when I get them.

Keep a stiff upper lip, don't mind anything you hear about renting house, am not likely to give a lease of my house without you knowing all about it.

> My love to you all.
> Your Husband
> Wm. S. Newton

114

> Fayetteville West Va
> April 30th 1864

Dear Wife

Yours of 25th came this evening. Have been a long time without one and I suppose the time will soon come, when a letter will be still more valuable.

I learn today the 23rd & 13th Va. are already on their winding way, and we will probably get orders tomorrow. If so, the next letter you receive will probably be written on a cracker box under some tree. We shall have about 200 sick and disabled here. Dr. Kay[13] of the 12th will be left with the sick. Warwick & I both go. Col. Turley is yet sick, and will hardly be able to march with us. He still holds his partiality for me.

I sent my lock box to Gallipolis with my surplus clothing, in order to have as little to lose as possible. I only retain one change, 1 pair blankets, so if I should see Libby Prison, you will know where to find them. Hope the boys will render you every assistance possible, and make as little work, and take care of little brother when not at school. Received a letter from John X. Davidson[14] today, wishing to purchase house. If for sale at some price. You can do as you please. If he wishes to pay 1,000 down, and will pay interest on deferred payments, give security that will satisfy Henry Neal,[15] and you wish to leave, all right.

I am not particular at the present time, I may never need it more. He wished an answer, you will let him know, or get Henry to do it for you. We march with a big force, and something certainly will be done, and I presume someone will be hurt, perhaps killed before we return. I sent photo, Dr. Miller sent me three by letter today. Col. gets one, Finn Neal another, and you the third.

Miller got six, but gave away three in Charleston, two went to the ladies, one to my old orderly of the 34th.

Will probably get more if we do not leave too soon.

Did Oviatte get my gold pen? If so, tell him not to send it but you keep it, till you hear from me.

> Good Night
> Your Husband
> Wm. S. Newton
> Give the within to J. X.
> Davidson

115

The *Ironton Register*, June 9, 1864

LETTER FROM DR. W. S. NEWTON

—

Battle of Cloyd Mountain—The Part Taken by Lawrence County Boys— The Great Victory—Death of General Albert Gallatin Jenkins—The Respective Losses, &c, &c

Ironton, June 7th, 1864.

Having been requested to furnish some items and incidents of the battle of 9th May, at Cloyd's Farm, Pulaski county, Va., between the Union forces commanded by General Crook, and the Rebel forces commanded by Brig. Gen. A. G. Jenkins, I will try to comply, but briefly. On the 3d of May we took up our line of March from Fayette, which had been our outpost for almost a year and a half. Our force consisted of three brigades of infantry. The cavalry having taken a different road, did not join us until about the 12th ult. On Sunday, 8th of May, we reached a point near Dublin depot, 120 miles from our starting point. Next morning, 9th, were marched about three miles, at which place our advance was fired upon, and rebels said to be in force in an advantageous position. Gen. Crook's intention seemed to be to flank their position, for at this point the 2d and 3d brigades (Field and Staff all dismounted) were led a circuitous route of six miles over high mountains, not getting into position till near 12 M. Skirmishing had been going on all the morning. Two rebel pieces were engaged, shelling the road and woods, and firing at short intervals. Our artillery could not be placed in position, and was therefore used but little.

The impression seems to be among us that only a small force was in front, and would retreat as soon as we closed in upon them, but in this we were mistaken, for we were soon made to know that their position was not only well taken and fortified, but they also had the force to hold it, unless outflanked and outnumbered.

When our brigade (2d) was ordered to advance, we were on the rebel left, 12th Ohio in the advance, supported by the 91st Ohio. On the right of the 12th, the 14th Virginia was in the advance, supported by the 9th Virginia. Our boys all went into the fight with a good will, and behaved gallantly. Did not see a Lawrence county boy fall out of his place unless killed or wounded; all this was the universal testimony of all after the battle, which lasted about one hour.

The rebels were completely routed, and pursued closely. Their loss was not as heavy as ours. They were behind breast-works making it necessary for our men to expose themselves and charge upon the works.

We buried 84 officers and men. We also buried 80 rebels on the battle-field. About 70 rebel wounded fell into our hands. These, with the severely wounded of our side, were taken to the residences of James and Joseph Cloyd,[16] they having fled their homes during the battle. We appropriated their fine houses to the use of our wounded.

Five Surgeons were detailed by Medical Director Kellogg to stay with our men, Gen. Crook not halting his force until he had punished the enemy severely, and burned the bridge, a fine structure, which will hardly be replaced for two months.

Our stay at Cloyd's Farm was nearly three weeks. Three days after the battle we were surrounded by John H. Morgan's cavalry, which had the day before fought Averill at Wytheville. They informed us that we were all prisoners of war, and not likely to be exchanged. Our men were badly used, having their clothing, blankets, hats and shoes, and in many instances, their money taken from them. Two of the Surgeons lost their watches, one his boots, &c, and another his horse. The other having sent their horses on with the command, did not sustain this loss unless captured afterwards. On Thursday evening, May 12th Rebel Surgeon Watkins[17] came for us to visit Gen. A. G. Jenkins, who was wounded in the left shoulder and breast. On our visit we counseled amputation at shoulder as the only chance for life. He was carried from the battle-field to the house of Mr. Guthrie,[18] some two miles distant from our Hospital. On the morning of the 13th we were again requested to visit and amputate Gen. Jenkins' arm. Morgan's men, in the meantime, having surrounded us, we were kept till afternoon. When ready to go, our instruments were taken from us by order of Morgan's Medical Director. On learning our errand, they very graciously allowed us to proceed, and were careful to accompany us, and secure the case immediately after the operation, which they witnessed with some interest. The operation was successfully accomplished under the influence of chloroform. The General expressed much gratitude for the service, and assure us of every assistance in his power in getting through the lines.

On the morning of the 9th day after the operation, secondary hemorrhage took place. We were sent for at 2 A.M., arrived at 3, but Gen. A. G. Jenkins was dead, having died only a few minutes before. We were indeed sorry. This feeling was not induced by professional pride merely, for the General was a true gentleman, and had treated us with great kindness.[19] Indeed his whole command seemed willing to make our stay comfortable, and we were well pleased when this force acted as our guard, and John Morgan had been relieved.

On the 24th of May we started for Richmond, most of our wounded having been removed to Emory and Henry Hospital,[20] situated some fifty miles below, on the Virginia and Tennessee Railroad.[21]

We left some thirty or forty men in care of rebel surgeons, Pride[22] and McFarland.[23] In doing this, we felt great confidence that these surgeons would

Albert Gallatin Jenkins was a U.S. representative from the western part of Virginia. With the outbreak of the Civil War he joined the Confederacy and rose to the rank of general. In May 1864, George Crook's Kanawha Division routed Jenkins and his Confederate forces at the Battle of Cloyd's Mountain near Dublin, Virginia. Jenkins was severely wounded during the battle. To save his life, Union surgeons, including William S. Newton, successfully amputated his arm. However, an attendant accidently knocked loose the ligature on a main artery and Jenkins died. In his accounts of the amputation, Newton spoke highly of Jenkins. Albert G. Jenkins, Representative from Virginia by Julian Vannerson, [1859], Library of Congress Prints and Photographs Division, Washington, D.C.

do their whole-duty toward our men. We arrived at Richmond May 26th, marched to Provost Marshal's office, then to Libby Prison, where we staid two days on very short rations. May 28th, we were taken from Libby in ambulances, a distance of twelve miles, to Aikens' Landing, at which place the Flag of Truce Boat, New York, was in waiting.

It is quite useless to say that this was a grand sight to us, as well as the fleet of gun boats and iron-clads, which stood picket just below on James River.

It is impossible to give the exact loss of each regiment, as the slightly wounded were all sent forward in ambulances. The relative loss may be judged from the number of severely wounded left in our hands, which list was taken from our Hospital record:

No. of Regiment	Severely Wounded
2d Va. Cavalry	7
9th Va. Infantry	60
11th Va. "	2
14th " "	35
15th " "	1
12th Ohio Infantry	37
23d " "	41
34th " "	7
36th " "	3
91st " "	8
3d Penn. Reserves	13
4th " "	9
Teamsters,	3
	———
Total	336 [226]

Of this number, 33 had died.

Very respectfully,
W. S. Newton,
Surgeon 91st O.V.I.

116

Letter to B R Cowen Adjt Genl of Ohio

Gallipolis Ohio Oct 8th 1867

Hon B R Cowen

Adjt Genl Ohio

Sir, Your circular requesting information concerning the treatment of Prisoners of War held by Confederate authority during the late rebellion was just received, and I will endeavor to follow the program as laid down.

1st my name. W. S. Newton

Gallipolis Ohio

2nd Rank. When mustered out of service was Surgeon 193rd O.V.I. commanded by Eugene Powell, formerly of 66th O.V.I.

My most active service, however, was while Asst Surg of 91st Ohio, 2nd Brigade, 2nd Division, Army West Va., commanded by Genl. Geo Crook.

In 1861, the Confederate government opened Libby Prison in Richmond as a central prison for Union officers. Libby Prison was overcrowded, rife with sickness, unsanitary, and food was in short supply. In late May 1864, William S. Newton and his fellow Union surgeons spent three days in Libby Prison before being released. Despite not having rations while a prisoner, Newton contracted dysentery and developed other health problems because of his brief imprisonment. "The Libby Prison," by George O. Ennis, Richmond: Selden and Co., ca. 1861–1865, Library of Congress Prints and Photographs Division, Washington, D.C.

Our Brigade was commanded by Col. C. B. White, until expiration of service, and then by Genl. I. H. Duval, both brave, prudent and gallant officers possessing the full confidence of their men & officers.

My own imprisonment though brief was long enough to show the utter want of feeling in most of the Confederate Officers toward Union men or officers. Some noble exceptions to this rule I can call to mind, Genl. Albert G. Jenkins, who died while under our treatment after the loss of an arm. He made every effort to restore to us our surgical instruments of which we had been deprived by the command of Genl. John Morgan, long before we had finished operating upon the wounded, who had fallen at the battle of Cloyd Mountain.

Here my history as a prisoner begins, on the 9th of May 1864, the hard fought battle and defeat of the Rebels took place after the rout. Genl Crook pursued the enemy and burned New River Bridge on the morning of the 10th of May. By his command, Surg. N. F. Graham of 12th Ohio, Surg. Welch[24] of 15th W. Va. Asst's Surg's Johnson,[25] Thatcher,[26] of 14th W. Va. and myself were detailed to remain with and care for our wounded (some 400 in No) and about 100 Rebels left in our hands, these on both sides were severely wounded as the slightly wounded were taken along in ambulances. Tuesday 10th of May we worked hard amputating & dressing the wounded of both sides. Wednesday ditto, and part of Thursday ditto. On afternoon of Thursday (12th) Confed Surgeons made their appearance, two of whom had been taken by Genl Crook, and ordered to report to us for duty, which they did, at the same time informing us that they had many wounded scattered throughout the country, demanding their whole attention. They also asked us to visit some two miles distant, Genl Jenkins with a view to amputation. This visit resulted in the contemplated amputation next day, provided the Genl and his counselors agreed.

Friday 13th a messenger came for us to visit and operate on Gen J. But with him came a portion of Genl. John Morgans command, which preyed upon our hospital as wolves upon a sheep fold. Officers and men depriving our wounded & nurses of all clothing, blankets, etc. that they could possibly lay their hands to, and in some instances *dragging gum blankets from the stumps of recently amputated limbs* which had been placed under them for the protection of carpets bedding etc. I have seen them remove these blankets and at once habit themselves with the blood stained trophy, receive commendation for this heroic deed from their companions in arms, who had been guilty of like atrocities. I also heard this conduct represented by a Rebel surgeon who happened to be more humane, to his Genl, and ask if he countenanced such treatment. The Genl replied yes, and with an oath said he approved it all, and more he hoped few of the D—d Yankees there wounded would ever live to see their homes again. We were also deprived of the hospital stores, so far as they could be carried away, and made useful to the Confederate wounded at other points.

This caused us to defer our operation until the afternoon of 13th ult, hoping thereby, in some means are to protect our men from the wholesale robbery practiced upon them our presence was of little value, for our surgical instruments too, were rudely taken from us, while in the very act of an operation upon Genl Jenkins, and his blood yet warm, wiped from them, placed in the case, and carried away. Although very grateful for our services, yet his rank was ignored, and his efforts vain in his attempt to restore them again. Our dead too were not allowed to rest undisturbed, for very many of them were disinterred, with the pretext that they were looking for friends, and if we can rely on more testimony, all blankets & clothing of value were appropriated to Confederate use.

We were allowed to remain at Cloyd Hospital some three weeks, and under Confederate rule to care for our wounded, until the most of them were removed or died. At this time, they gave us the alternative of going further south, to labor in Rebel Hospitals, or to Richmond & to prison. We chose the latter, and were in this time landed in Libby Prison, where we met many who had been on low diet so long, that our own case seemed as nothing, and during our three days stay, rations of no kind were issued to us. On the first we were told that our names did not yet appear on the rolls. On the second, we were marched to the office with the expectation of being released, which for that day proved to be a failure. We were told, however, that our rations had been issued to the other hungry officers. On the third day, just at ration time, we were again marched to the office, and this time on to Akins Landing, where our flag of truce boat was in waiting. To us who had only been deprived of the sight some three weeks, how glorious the old flag appeared, and we could only contrast our condition with those who had been confined for months, and were still left behind, and be thankful to those who had interfered in our behalf, and so soon restored us to our old flag, yet I repeat, we experienced enough to convince us, that the suffering & deprivation of our men & officers in the southern prisons has not half been told, nor can it be described on the page of history. To be realized, it must be experienced.

Very Respectfully

[Wm. S. Newton]

The Battle of Cloyd's Mountain has been covered in only a handful of sources. Besides the battle reports in the *Official Records*, there were a few firsthand published accounts of the battle mostly focused on the military details.[27] The most detailed account of the Battle of Cloyd's Mountain and the days that followed came from E. C. Arthur, who served as regimental historian for the 23rd Ohio Volunteer Infantry (which included colonels William S. Rosecrans and Rutherford B. Hayes).[28] Listed as Alfred Arthur in the official roster, he served as a private and musician for the 23rd. Between January and April 1889, Arthur published a lengthy eight-part essay called "The Dublin Raid, Campaigning with Gen. Geo. Crook in 1864," in the *Ohio Soldier*, a biweekly newspaper "devoted to the interests of the surviving soldiers of the war for the Union." Arthur's essay became the basis for many later secondary sources on the Battle of Cloyd's Mountain.[29]

In the February 16, 1889, installment of "The Dublin Raid," E. C. Arthur focused on the medical care that surgeons administered following the Battle of Cloyd's Mountain. Arthur's reporting and Newton's two accounts provide clarity on what happened after the Battle of Cloyd's Mountain, especially the details of the how Union surgeons attended to wounded Confederate general Albert G. Jenkins. Arthur explained that the arrival of John Hunt Morgan's cavalry resulted in pillaging of Union medical supplies, wounded, and even the dead. Arthur described the successful amputation of Jenkins's arm by Union surgeons. He wrote: "Dr. Graham, assisted by Drs. Newton and Smith performed a most skillful operation, in the presence of confederate surgeons, taking the left arm off at the socket." Arthur continued saying that General Jenkins commended the Union surgeons for their service. In fact, Jenkins wrote a letter to John A. Seddon, secretary of war for the Confederacy, asking that all the captured Union surgeons be allowed to safely return to their lines. Arthur's article reprinted the letter from Jenkins. Arthur explained that Jenkins prepared to report to Union officials in Charleston, West Virginia, but in the early morning hours of May 21, an attendant accidently knocked loose the ligature on a main artery. The Union surgeons were summoned, but Jenkins suffered a hemorrhage and died before they arrived. Arthur's essay continued with other medical details of the Battle of Cloyd's Mountain, but he did not discuss the imprisonment of Newton and the other Union surgeons after the death of Jenkins.[30]

Arthur's essay named Newton as being one of the Union surgeons involved in the amputation procedure and thus part of the overall chaos that continued after the Battle of Cloyd's Mountain. There were great similarities between the accounts from Arthur and Newton. Arthur described John Hunt Morgan's forces as "grizzly Kentucky ruffians," which matched Newton's descriptions of uncivilized raiders with little respect for the living, the dying, and the dead. Another common thread in their account was the sense of reciprocal respect between Jenkins and the Union surgeons. The accounts seem to indicate that, had Jenkins survived, Newton and his fellow surgeons would have been safely returned to their Union regiments. Finally, the accounts confirm that the Union surgeons did all that they could to care for the Confederate wounded, especially Jenkins, despite being held as prisoners.

Unlike Arthur, Newton was a direct participant in the Jenkins operation. Newton's two accounts, one published in the *Ironton Register* and the other a postwar letter related to his prisoner of war experiences, add new details to what happened to the Union surgeons after the Battle of Cloyd's Mountain. Newton's newspaper account of being captured, tending to Confederate general Albert G. Jenkins, and then being detained at Libby Prison was repeated in the 1867 letter, but there are discrepancies in the two sources. As one difference, the savagery of the Confederates was much more pronounced in the postwar letter than in the newspaper article. In Newton's newspaper description, he explained that the amputation procedure was tense because of the Confederate presence but that the operation was a complete success. Newton's postwar account, however, explained that Confederates seized their medical instruments during the middle of the operation, which indicated that the operation was not completed nor successful. This version almost implicates soldiers under the command of John Hunt Morgan as sabotaging the operation. The purpose of the postwar letter, to shed light on rebel atrocities, and the passage of time likely affected Newton's memory of the amputation procedure.

Newton's imprisonment at Libby Prison was another important part of his military experience, which was described in both accounts. In 1861 the Confederate government transformed a three-story food warehouse located on the bank of a canal beside the James River in Richmond into a prison and hospital. Named Libby Prison after the family who had last leased the warehouse, it served as a central prison for Union officers. Conditions in the prison were grim. Libby Prison was overcrowded, rife with sickness, and unsanitary, and food was in short supply. There were several documented prison breaks and uprisings by inmates.[31] Libby Prison was often used to briefly house prisoners of war who would be exchanged or transferred to other Confederate prisons. By 1864 it had become a transfer point for prisoners on their way to another location. Still, Libby Prison housed an enormous number of Union officers. A newspaper article in the Richmond *Examiner* on May 28, 1864, the day that Newton was released, claimed that, from the First Battle of Bull Run in July 1861 until the previous day, over 97,000 prisoners had been registered at Libby Prison. Even more specific to the time period when Newton was imprisoned at Libby Prison, from May 1 to September 1, 1864, 16,086 Union prisoners registered and passed through the building.[32]

Newton described his brief tenure at Libby Prison in both accounts. Newton's newspaper account established that, on May 24, three days after Jenkins died, he and his fellow Union surgeons began the march to Richmond. This group of Union surgeons included Newton (91st Ohio), N. F. Graham (12th Ohio), Walter F. Welch (15th Virginia), James J. Johnson (15th Virginia), and Charles H. Thatcher (14th Virginia). Newton's postwar letter suggested that they were given the choice to assist in southern hospitals or go to Libby Prison and that they made the dramatic choice of prison. The newspaper account explained that they arrived at Libby Prison on May 26. A list of Union prisoners, held by the National Archives and Records Administration, confirmed that on May 26 Newton and his fellow Union surgeons arrived in Richmond and were booked as prisoners at Libby Prison.[33] A newspaper article in the Richmond *Examiner* from May 23, 1864, confirmed that when Newton arrived there were four surgeons in Libby Prison assigned to the hospital. It is likely that Newton and the other new surgeons were not needed for medical duty. Further, by this time Confederate government officials would have received the letter from the recently departed General Albert G. Jenkins ordering the return of the Union surgeons to their lines.[34]

During his brief stay at Libby Prison, Newton explained that he was given little if anything to eat, most likely because prison administrators expected to return him and his fellow surgeons to Union forces as quickly as possible. Both accounts mentioned the lack of rations, which indicates that food was scarce and reserved for prisoners who were long-term residents at Libby. Apart from discussing the lack of food, Newton's accounts did not provide significant details about the living conditions inside Libby Prison. It is likely that

Newton and his fellow surgeons were held in a specific part of the prison designated for short-term or transfer prisoners, rather than interacting with other Union detainees who would have shared war and prison stories. The three days at Libby Prison took a significant toll on Newton's health. Later medical examinations, explained in the epilogue, confirmed that Newton contracted dysentery, most likely from contaminated water or from any food that he might have had during his brief stay at Libby Prison. He also developed piles (hemorrhoids) and a "torpid liver," which in nineteenth-century medical terms referred to a number of gastrointestinal maladies. Newton's later correspondence did not mention the effects or how long he was sick, but he later explained that he never fully recovered.[35]

On May 28, 1864, Newton and his fellow surgeons were released from Libby Prison and delivered to Union forces at Aiken's Landing. Newton's two accounts described the process and the great feeling of joy at being released after three harrowing weeks of being prisoners of the Confederacy. His postwar letter, which was focused on prison conditions, referred to the poor conditions of southern prisons and the inhumane treatment of Union soldiers. The only known announcement of his release appeared in the July issue of the medical journal the *Cincinnati Lancet and Observer*. The article included a list of officers who had been unconditionally released by rebel authorities and were on their way to rejoin their respective commands. The names included:

> Surgeon N. F. Graham, 12th Ohio Vols., Assistant-
> Surgeon W. S. Newton, 91st Ohio Vols., Surgeon N. D.
> Furguson, 8th New York Cavalry,[36] Assistant-Surgeon
> D. W. Richards, 145th Pennsylvania Vols.,[37] Surgeon
> W. S. Welsh, 15th West Virginia Vols., Assistant-Surgeon
> J. T. Johnson, same regiment, Surgeon C. H. Thatcher,
> 14th West Virginia Vols., and Chaplain John L. Irwin,[38]
> same regiment.[39]

Newton, Graham, Welch, Johnson, and Thatcher were all captured after the Battle of Cloyd's Mountain and subsequently imprisoned at Libby Prison. Also, Chaplain John L. Irwin of the 14th West Virginia Infantry was captured after the Battle of Cloyd's Mountain, briefly held at Libby Prison, and then released with the Union surgeons on May 28, 1864. The other two surgeons, Richards and

Furguson, were captured near Spotsylvania Court House and Mechanicsville, respectively, and detained at Libby Prison before being
released on May 28.

Newton's first letter back home was on July 11, so the details of
what he did after his release in late May were not clear. He may have
spent time in a hospital to recover and then returned home for a brief
leave, before starting back to the 91st Ohio Volunteer Infantry. By July
the 91st Ohio had advanced up the Shenandoah Valley near Winchester, Virginia. Fresh from a brief period of recovery and travel, in
July Newton was stationed near Martinsburg, West Virginia. In the
weeks that followed, Newton witnessed some of the most brutal fighting of his Civil War service.

8

In Line of Battle All Day, and I Am Very Tired, July–August 1864

William S. Newton continued to be in harm's way during the summer of 1864. In July he returned for duty as assistant surgeon of the 91st Ohio. The regiment had advanced up the Shenandoah Valley near Winchester, Virginia, and would be part of Union general Philip Sheridan's summer campaign. Sheridan's Army of the Shenandoah combined a number of regiments, including many from Ohio and West Virginia, to pursue Confederate general Jubal Early's Army of the Valley.[1]

Newton was first stationed near Martinsburg, West Virginia. In a letter from July 21, 1864, he recounted heavy fighting the day before during the Battle of Rutherford's Farm (July 20), also known as the Battle at Stephenson's Depot or the Battle of Carter's Farm, just north of Winchester. Newton explained that the 91st and other Union regiments engaged with twelve regiments led by Confederate general Jubal Early. The 14th Virginia Infantry broke through enemy lines and routed the Confederates. But the fates of the Union army changed a few days later at the Second Battle of Kernstown (July 24). Newton reported that the 91st Ohio "lost 68 in killed or wounded" and counted "25 or 30 amputations, half at least are Rebels." In this pivotal battle, the Confederates pushed Union forces back across the Potomac River and into Maryland. In the process, many Union regiments were uprooted and scattered across the region. Early then led the Confederacy's last significant raid into Union territory, which included the burning of Chambersburg, Pennsylvania, on July 30.[2]

Newton and the 91st Ohio engaged with Confederates near the Maryland and Virginia border for the rest of July and into August. He was impressed with Maryland. In an August 2, 1864, letter, Newton said: "This State of Maryland is rich in the products of the soil & women. Union sentiment here is pretty strong, & manifests itself at every little town." In the same letter, Newton mentioned that, after the routing of Union troops at the Second Battle of Kernstown in late July, Dr. Wellons headed to Cumberland, Maryland, but was still reported absent without leave.[3] Alexander Neil, an assistant surgeon of the 12th Virginia Infantry, recorded a great deal of confusion after the Union's loss at the Second Battle of Kernstown. He explained that after the battle ". . . we arrived in Martinsville all in confusion, our troops scattered to the four winds & no organized command."[4]

Following the Second Battle of Kernstown, Newton and many others stayed behind in Winchester to tend to the wounded while their regiments retreated to safety in Maryland. Newton rejoined his regiment in Maryland a few days later. In an August 3 letter, Newton explained that he and twenty-two other officers (including Wellons) were dismissed from military service for allegedly straggling behind after the battle and circulating exaggerated reports of losses. Colonel Coates went to work to resolve the charges against Newton, which were quickly dropped. In an August 4 letter, Newton wrote that he had been restored to his "command, with appropriate apologies & compliments." On August 8, Newton sent his wife a packet of documents related to the dismissal. The documents included an endorsement letter signed by the officers and surgeons of the 91st Ohio pleading for Newton's reinstatement and return to the regiment. Newton was quite taken with this show of appreciation and respect from his fellow officers. He emphasized the importance of the papers and told his wife: "Look at them all, and *preserve them*. They may be of use in after life."[5]

During this period of intense fighting, Newton mentioned a few family details. In a July 17 letter he inquired about Ned and Mott, who were working in a store in Ironton to get business experience. In the same letter he asked about his daughter Kate. Such discussions were excellent distractions for Newton. Only a few weeks prior, he had been captured and imprisoned. Further, during this period he witnessed significant fighting and human suffering. Newton summed up his return to the front in a July 23 letter that said: "I am heartsick with the horrors of war, and long for the time when we will all get home, in peace & quiet.[6]

117

Hamden July 11th 1864

My Dear Wife

Having some three hours, which hang heavily, will write you a few lines, and also send the photograph of Lt. Ewing which he presented today. We traveled hard all night, and day was dawning before we reached Portland, where we breakfasted and took cars at 9:15, arrived here at 11:45 and will not get away till 3:15. The day is very warm, and I very much fear I will be troubled with heat on my back & breast.

Finn, Lts. White,[7] Ewing & Kendall[8] joined me in a real picknick dinner here today. We took our grub and went to the shade of a large tree. There we ate, smoked, and tried to sleep, but was too warm.

Will try to make it up tonight. Hope you are in the cool, drinking ice water.

Think we shall be at Parkersburg several days, as the scare is almost over.

My love to all,

Your Husband
Wm. S. Newton

118

Martinsburg July 15th 1864

My Dear Wife

We did not move on last evening, as my letter indicated. The order was changed, the 3rd Brigade instead of ours, were to move last night. Col. Duval commanding our Brigade (the 2nd) is in command of the forces here, Major Cadot of our Reg is in command of the Post. This is only temporary and we may not be here one day. Our horses have just come up, have been in the cars two days & nights without food or water, and look very bad. They lost my halter & bridle on the way up so I am just as bad off as before.

News are very conflicting. Some say Lee has left Richmond, & Grant has possession, and is following him. Others say "Lee is marching on Baltimore & Washington with almost his entire army."

Our position here is a precarious one, for this is their direct route, and if we attempt to hold it will in all probability be out numbered & overpowered.

Still we hope for the best, and if they come to attack the 2nd Brigade, somebody will get hurt if not killed.

Our Reg has not been paid, while all the Va Regs have, & our boys are getting very much dissatisfied. Gov. Brough, if he knew the situation, would make an effort in our favor. Much love to you all.

Your Husband

Wm. S. Newton

119

Martinsburg July 17th 1864

My Dear Wife

This is Sabbath day, and we are still here, fortunately so remains to be learned. Both the other brigades have gone on, and ours alone is left to defend the town. If a large force comes we will have to get out, if one of reasonable size some one will get hurt before we give up our position, for Col. Duval is a fighter.

Yesterday we moved through town, and took a position on Shepardstown Pike. Our Reg is in line of battle, behind a stone wall, which commands the road. We have but little shade to protect us from the hot sun.

Warwick & myself have a good room, with a family by the name of Robinson. Our tent pitched near, with Pixley & Old Tagg to run it. We eat & hold Surgeons call at the tent, can then retire to our room, read & write, as I am now doing. There are four young ladies under the same roof, all secesh and very passable in personal attractions. Their father died, while member of the Rebel Legislature.[9] They all dress in black, but I think mourning day is almost over, judging from the gaiety last night on the piazza. It looks now as if we would remain here some time, but cannot tell. You can write and direct to this place, the letters will follow us. I wrote yesterday to John A. Turley, wishing to comfort him, in his now afflicted condition, and I really hope, before we get into another fight, we may have him with us. He is brave & energetic.

Quartermaster, Chaplain & Adjutant Findley all have rooms in this house, which is a very large one. Coates took a room, but does not sleep in it, lest an alarm should occur, and he not found in camp, although his tent is not more than 4 rods from the house.

How do the boys get along tending store. If they will only engage in business, stick to it well, and show themselves worthy of confidence, how easy for them to become useful, and how easy you would feel, in reference to support, should I be taken away. I feel the necessity of pressing this matter upon them, and insisting that they should not idle all their time away.

Tell Little Kate her Pa thinks of her every day, and hopes she will learn to be a *real little lady*, not to romp & run the streets, but sit down & learn to read & write, also to sew nicely.

My impression is, we shall move to the Kanawha, when we move from here, yet we cannot tell what a day may bring forth. If you can get something for shirts, half cotton & wool, that will look well, I do not believe they will draw up like the flannel, get two made, and if we come your way I can get them, these will not be large enough in a very short time. My love to all.

Your Husband
Wm. S. Newton

120

Martinsburg West Va.
Thursday July 21st 1864

My Dear Wife

I write you on the excitement of another severe battle, fought yesterday afternoon, by a few cavalry & 2nd Brigade, commanded by Genl. Averill. We were on the way to Winchester, and had reached within three miles of the place, When Genl. Early's whole Corps engaged us, consisting of twelve Regts, and so certain were they that they would whip us, they had neglected to support their artillery.

We drove them & captured 9 pieces of artillery, 200 prisoners etc. But the 91st suffered badly, Capt. Crossley, Lt. Ed Wilson,[10] Eugene Williard[11] & Brady Steece[12] are all wounded, but not seriously. I have just got here with 60 wounded in my charge, the above among the number. Have traveled all night long, after a hard days work, and much excitement. Capt. Finn is all right. I sent him to the rear yesterday, quite unwell, and how glad I am, for he certainly would have been killed or wounded, for he is very brave. Co. A did not suffer like F & K. Only 18 of K are left fit for duty.

Albert Campbell is the only Sargt. left, not killed or wounded.

The Rebels shelled us most unmercifully, and there was no hill or good place to establish a field Hosp. We all had to take it alike. Old Tom had not got over the excitement yet, although I rode him all day yesterday, and nineteen miles during the night.

Will probably remain here a day or two, and then if the Reg does not come back, will try the front again. Gallipolis boys are all right so far as I know.

In haste

Your Husband
Wm. S. Newton

121

Winchester W. Va.

July 23rd 1864

My Dear Wife.

Two days ago I wrote you from Martinsburg where I had taken 60 of our wounded, lest they should fall into the hands of the enemy.

I traveled 19 miles, in charge of ambulance train, without a guard, and returned yesterday the same way. Capt. Neal came back with me, when arrived at the battlefield, found our men had gone on and taken possession of this place. I got in here at 11 P.M. having worked very hard, and lost two nights sleep, and traveled 50 miles.

This morning at daylight, we were marched out in line of battle. The other division of Crooks command having come in from Harpers Ferry, were then cannonading the enemy. We have been in line of battle all day, and I am very tired. The enemy have retreated, and we hope for a days rest. The men poor fellows need it very much, braver men never went into a fight.

Our Reg lost 68 in killed and wounded, 34th Ohio 30. 9th Va. about the same. Did not learn the loss in the 14th Va. but not heavy.

Am trying to get the Ironton wounded home as far as possible.

Genl Crook is made a Major Genl, and in command, & Col. Duval commands a division, & Col. Johnson[13] is now our commander of Brigade.

The Rebel loss in killed is 90, their wounded 150 that fell into our hands, the number carried off is said to be very large.

I am heartsick with the horrors of war, and long for the time when we will all get home, in peace & quiet.

We have had 25 or 30 amputations, half at least are Rebels.

Am too tired to write, and you must not get anxious if you do not hear from me. Have not heard one word from home, since I saw you.

My love to all

Your Husband

Wm. S. Newton

122

Sandy Hook Maryland

Thursday July 28th 1864

My Dear Wife

I last wrote you at Winchester Va., three days after we had punished the enemy badly, yet at great loss to us. On Sunday evening last, after I had written to you, we were marched out to the support of two brigades which were being pressed back. We went, but had hardly gotten into line, when the wounded & stragglers by the fifties & hundreds, were passing to the rear.

The enemy had been largely reinforced, and were driving ours back. Our brigade held their line but were slowly & strongly pressed back. It soon became evident that all should be routed.

The Cavalry behaved badly & rushed through our retreating columns, breaking the lines, & everyone seemingly must take care of himself. Old Tom served me well in this retreat of 22 miles, was never prouder of him in my life. We had the ambulances loaded with wounded, some dying, and I dare not give you anything like a description of the retreat. Our brigade by keeping to the woods came into Martinsburg pretty well organized. I stopped at Bunker Hill with ambulance train. Here, Col. Shaw[14] 34th Ohio, died from his wounds, & here I learned that Lt. Ewing had been badly wounded, and in the hands of the enemy. He was the only officer from our Reg. lost. We had not much more than reached Martinsburg, and were unloading the wounded, when the Rebs commenced shelling the town. We again loaded the wounded, and sent to the depot to send them to Cumberland. But the cars did not stay for them, and we were obliged to send them to Wmspt, Md. Our forces still held Martinsburg till evening, which gave us time to cross the Potomac with the whole train. We passed through Wmspt, Hagerstown, Sharpsburg and are now at Sandy Hook.

Our Cavalry hold the fords at all the places mentioned, also the ford at Harpers Ferry. We will probably remain here a few days to rest, write and let me hear from you.

Have been quite well all the time, but am heartily tired of moving.

Give my love to all

Your Husband
Wm. S. Newton

123

Camp 4 miles from Harpers Ferry

July 29th 1864

Dear Wife

I wrote you yesterday, and then I thought we should remain at Sandy Hook a few days to recruit our men who are worn out with marching.

But last evening we were again marched across the Potomac at Harpers Ferry and 4 miles on the Harpers Ferry Road. Report says we are again to march up the Shenandoah Valley, which will be strongly resisted by the Rebs.

You will hear from me as opportunity offers. My love to all.

Your Husband
Wm. S. Newton

124

Gap of the 4 Roads, 6 miles from
Middletown Aug 2nd 1864

My Dear Wife

This is Tuesday morning, we have only marched two miles in the past 24 hours, but on Sunday we marched 20 miles, the day was already hot, the men dropped by the way, stricken down in a few moments. Report says 15 died. We had two were obliged to leave yesterday in very critical condition. If we chase after the Rebs much longer, our command will be very small.

Still, it is much pleasanter than being chased, for when this is the case, there is no resting place, while Old Tom keeps his legs, I am all right. Am very tired of marching & fighting, will be very glad when my time is up, little more than a year will let me out. Dr. Wellons, run away to Cumberland, from Martinsburg, and is now reported absent without leave. You can form very little idea of the scenes I have passed through on the past three weeks. This State of Maryland is rich in the products of the soil & women. Union sentiment here is pretty strong, & manifests itself at every little town.

We are pretty well worn out, officers & men, and will be content to stay here and watch the return of the Rebel Cavalry.

Have not yet heard one word from you. If you direct your letters to 91st Reg 2nd Brigade, Genl Crooks command, I will get it all right.

Give my love to all.

Your Husband
Wm. S. Newton

125

Three miles from Frederick City, Md.
Aug 3rd 1864

My Dear Wife

I wrote you yesterday from Wolfsville, afterwards I received a special order from Maj. Genl. Hunter, dismissing me, with 22 other officers, from the service of U.S., alleging as a reason, that we had straggled after the battle of Winchester, and circulated exaggerated reports of our loss, etc.

As a matter of course, I and all others, connected with our Reg were astonished.

Coates[15] & others have gone to work to have the order countermanded. The officers & surgeons of the Brigade have certified to my innocence in the whole matter.

Shall have to go by the way of Washington if I get out, and may show some of the papers furnished me there. We are all ordered outside the Dept. to await the decision of the President and I know no better place to wait than at home, so if you should see me some time soon, don't be alarmed.

They may issue an order keeping me here as Brigade & Division Head Quarters have taken an interest in the affair. Don't report me as coming for I may not come.

My love to all

Your Husband
Wm. S. Newton

P.S. Col. Coates has ordered me to remain for the present, to keep quiet & say nothing.

Wm.S.N.

126

Three miles from Frederick City
On the Monocacy Aug. 4th 1864

My Dear Wife

Have just received advices, that our Division Commander, had visited the Hd Qts of Gen. Hunter. That Genl. H. had ordered his Adjut. Genl. to issue an order, restoring me to my command, with appropriate apologies & compliments.

So, I suppose, this ends my expected visit & stay at home, don't know whether to be glad or sorry, certain it is, I was rather pleased with the prospect of getting home, still I did not like to go, when it would be necessary to explain my appearance, with a dismissal from any Maj. Genl. Hope all will be for the best. I still try to do my duty in all things.

My love to all, Your Husband

Wm. S. Newton

P.S. It is now three o'clock P.M. The order has not yet come. Still I am assured by officials that it is made out & passing through the various commands.

Oh what is war, and how much longer, have we to submit to the many hardships. You would scarcely know the men, with whom you are well acquainted, so changed are they with the hardships called to endure.

We are expecting a move in about 24 hours, toward Harpers Ferry again. The Rebs are said to be numerous in the neighborhood. Tell the boys I hope they are very good, and give very little trouble, but make themselves useful.

Wm.S.N.

127

[included with 128 and 129]

Sandy Hook Near
Harpers Ferry Aug. 8th 1864

My Dear Wife

I send you this, with *some papers* which I wish you to *read carefully* and you will see how easy it is, for a man to get out of the service, and then how quick they will yoke him again, if he happens to be worth anything.

The other papers, signed by officers of the Reg & Surgeons of Brigade, were gotten up for me, without the asking. Look at them all, and *preserve them.* They may be of use in after life. The Genl. Order 53 & 59, which dismisses & restores me, keep also. You will see Wellons is dismissed in the same order restoring me. I do not think he was fairly dealt with, nor will the officers here, make any effort to redress his wrongs.

I think we have the largest army now extant operating here. Something big will be done in this neighborhood. Have not yet heard from you. Tell Em to write. If yours do not reach me, perhaps one from *her will.* Direct to 91st Reg, 2nd Brigade, 2nd Division, Army of Kanawha. If sent in this way, there will be no difficulty in getting all letters written. Tell the boys to do just right, *do as they would* if I was there to look after them.

Hope you will write soon and often. Give my regards to all. Much love to *yourself* & little ones.

Your Husband
Wm. S. Newton

128

[included with 127 and 129]

Head Quarters of 91st Regt. O.V.I.
In the field August 2, 1864

Sir:

I have the honor most respectfully to request that the dismissal of Asst.

Surg. Dr. S. Newton of the regiment as per G.O. No. 53 Hd Quar Dept of Va July 29, 1864 be marked for the following reasons: the same asst surg Newton did not leave Winchester, Va. until the army fell back from that place and did not leave the hospital at Martinsburg where he was attending to the wounded, until after the infantry had passed through that place and only escaped by a hasty retreat through an alley to the East of the Williamsport Road.

When he reached the road not knowing that the Regt. had marched back into the town and hearing that it had gone to Hagerstown he went to that place and rejoined the Regt. the next day on his march to Sharpsburg. Asst. Surg. Newton is a very efficient and faithful officer and his removal will be a great loss for the Regt. and his place cannot be as well filled.

> I am sir
> Very respectfully
> Your Able Servant
> B. F. Coates Lt. Col.
> Commd. Reg.
> Thayer Melvin
> A.A.G.D.W.Va

129

[included with 127 and 128]

Wolfsville, Maryland August 4th/64

We the undersigned officers of the 91st O.V.I. have read with deep regret the order dismissing Asst. Surg. W. S. Newton of this Regt. We believe him innocent of the charges therein contained and bear cheerful testimony to his high qualifications as a medical officer. His cheerful and inviting devotions to duty while he was with us and the noble traits of character displayed during his intercourse with us. Stamping him as a true gentleman in every sense of the term.

We consider his unfortunate removal as an injury to the service as well as a great and irreparable to our Regt. And in leaving he takes with him our kindest regards and well wishes for his future success.

B. F. Coates Lt Col.	A. R. Warwick R O.V.M.
Commd Reg	J. B. Warwick Surgeon
L. Z. Cadot Major	K. R. Culbertson Capt 91
A. H. Windsor Chaplain	S. F. Neal Capt "
James G. D. Findley Adjt	J. L. Williams 1st Lt.

Jas. M. White 1st Lt.
Thomas K. Coles 2nd Lt.
Charles N. Hall 2nd Lt.
L. K. Stroup Lt.
John Kaps Capt.
Lewis A. Atkinson Capt
John A. Hamilton 2nd Lieut
Jas Crawford Capt
Thomas W. Rose 1st Lieut
W. D. Burbage " "
A. D. Crossland AAQM 2 Brig 2 Div Army Kan
Joel Hull Lt. AA ALS 2 Brig 3 Div Army Kan
Samuel P. Baldridge 2nd Lieut

The above are the signatures of all the officers present with the Regiment together with two on detached service.

James G. D. Findley
Adjt 91 Ohio Infantry

J. S. P. Carroll Capt. Co B 9th V.V.I.
C. McConley 2nd Lieut Co B 9 Va
H. C. Duncan 2nd Lieut Co. D 9th Va Vols
Oliver Phelps Capt Co E 9 W Va Vol Inft
J. W. Johnson 1st Lt Co H 9th V.V.I.
O. W. Karr 2nd Lt Co H 9th V.V.I.
Robt Laughlin 2nd Lt Co G 9 Va

9

We Are Now in Face of the Enemy, August–November 1864

Throughout the late summer and into the fall of 1864, William S. Newton was involved in a series of significant military engagements. Beginning in mid-August, the 91st Ohio Volunteer Infantry and other regiments in General Philip Sheridan's Army of the Shenandoah pushed back into Virginia to engage the Confederates led by General Jubal Early. Newton reported on a number of skirmishes with Confederates and his effort to establish field hospitals to treat the many wounded. In early September he witnessed the Battle of Berryville (September 3–4). Newton wrote to his wife that "Our Brigade (2nd) stopped the Jonnies, fought & whipped them, bringing in 80 prisoners. . . . The firing did not cease till ten o'clock & then we who were in the rear did not know which side had whipped till morning. These are the times which try the patriotism of men."[1]

On September 18, Newton reported that General Ulysses S. Grant visited with Sheridan at their camp near Summit Point, West Virginia. He told his wife that "We are evidently on the eve of some important movement."[2] The next day, on September 19, Union forces led by Sheridan attacked Early's forces at Opequan Creek, just outside of Winchester. The Battle of Opequan (Third Battle of Winchester) was one of the most important battles in the Shenandoah Valley. Union forces prevailed, but losses on both sides were high, with approximately 5,000 casualties for the Union and 4,500 for the Confederates.[3]

Newton and other medical staff spent the rest of the month managing a field hospital to care for the many wounded and dying. A few days after the Battle of Opequan (Third Battle of Winchester), he explained the scale of his work, saying: "[I] have been so busy with the wounded, since our great battle of the 19th, have not slept, ate, or rested."[4] The work was further complicated as wounded soldiers returning from smaller subsequent battles, such as the Battle of Fisher's Hill (September 21–22) referred to in a September 24 letter, flooded the field hospitals. Still, Newton had the same optimism of many of the soldiers under his care. He explained to his wife: "The wounded men, even those who have lost a leg or arm, have time to cheer and say it is worth all it has cost them."[5]

On the morning of October 19, General Jubal Early's Confederate troops launched a surprise attack on Union forces at Cedar Creek, near Strasburg. Newton later recounted that the Jonnies had "unceremoniously routed" him from his position.[6] The Confederates drove the Union troops back nearly three miles, before General Philip Sheridan, on his way back from Washington, DC, led a successful counterattack that afternoon that crippled Early's forces. Losses on both sides were heavy, 5,500 Union casualties and 3,000 Confederate casualties, but Sheridan's forces captured nearly all of the Confederate artillery. The Battle of Cedar Creek, which Newton described in an October 23 letter to his wife, marked the last major battle in the Shenandoah Valley campaign. After this battle, General Early's Confederate forces would not lead another serious offensive against the Union.[7]

Newton's letters in this period have significant details about working in a very active field hospital and the progress of the Union army. Many of the letters were written in haste because of his increased responsibility for the large volume of sick and wounded soldiers. He mentioned other onsite doctors and the complexity of their task. In a November 14 letter to his wife, he used a piece of paper that on the reverse side included an early draft of a death notice for a Pennsylvania soldier who had been under his care. It is likely Newton wrote countless letters of that type during this period to officially record the death of a soldier. The letters to his wife noted the lack of supplies, numerous amputations, details on soldiers who were near death or already expired, and the scourge of lice throughout the camps and hospital. But there were also moments of hope and triumph. In October, Newton mentioned the arrival of Dorothea Dix and a large amount of rations and supplies for the hospitals outside of Winchester. He commented on the successes of Union commanders George Crook, Philip Sheridan, William T. Sherman, and Ulysses S. Grant against the Confederate forces led by Jubal Early and James Longstreet. Further, during this period he makes several references to the danger of being captured by raiders led by cavalry commander John S. Mosby.[8] Despite the threat of being captured again, Newton held out hope that the end of the war was near.

The severity of the battles did not dampen Newton's plans for reuniting with his family. At this point his family were staying in Gallipolis and he visited them there in July. He was so lonely that in September he wrote, "Don't you almost wish I was wounded? I would take a slight one, if only to get home."[9] Instead, he took the more prudent path and put in an official request for leave. In an October 28 letter, he marked his 19th wedding anniversary and pondered the past and the future. The intense fighting also drew on Newton's religious beliefs. In an August 16 letter, he explained that Union soldiers were committed to winning the war at all costs but believed that their prayers to *"An overruling Providence"* would result in the end of the war.[10] Praying for an end to war was directly connected to the common belief on both sides that God favored their cause.

Newton's letters also described the randomness and suddenness of death. In an August 27 letter, he explained that an unsubstantiated report had circulated announcing "that a shell struck & killed me last evening." Newton told his wife that: "There were at least a hundred men ready to say I was killed, but how the report started I cannot tell. All I know is there were enough shell[s] to kill a doz surgeons dropped in close proximity, but nary one touched me."[11] About two months later, Newton explained to his wife that Dr. Thomas J. Shannon, also an assistant surgeon from Ohio in charge of a division hospital, had been killed during a routine mission. Newton reflected that the same fate could befall him.

During this period, Newton referred to the presidential election of 1864. His previous letters that mentioned Ohio elections were very clear on his picks (usually pro-Union Democrats), but Newton offered no indications of his choice for president. Instead, he held hope that whoever was elected would help accelerate the cause of the Union. By late November, Newton made clear that finishing the war was the only way to have real peace. The Union cause came at a high price of life and destruction, but he and countless others believed the sacrifices were necessary.

130

Cedar Creek Va Near
Strasburg Aug 14th/64

Dear Wife

Here seems to be an opportunity to send a line and I embrace it.

We are now in face of the enemy. They are also in our rear, captured a part of our supply three miles in our rear. We know nothing of expected movements, as in all large armies. I have kept perfectly well, and now that the green corn is plenty, I have plenty to eat. I often think of home, especially I would like to sit down to a dish of corn & beans of your cooking. I think it would be better than corn seasoned with a short allowance of salt. I knew nothing of soldiering, until this summer, and will *not tell* or *try* to *give you* a *description* of things as we find them here.

Dr. Thatcher[12] was again captured by the Rebs at Martinsburg, was taken to Winchester, and then our men drove them out so quick they had no time to take him along, so he joined us again yesterday. He still carries the revolver in his boots.

We have been hoping, and have had some assurances as soon as we have whipped out the Rebs from the Shenandoah Valley, for the 6th, 9th, 13th & 19th Army Corps, Crooks Command, will be allowed to go back to West Va., of which Dept. he now has the entire command. Whether this boon will be allowed us, remains yet to be seen. That we are anxious for it is not a question.

Had quite a spirited fight last eve, but they are getting so common we take no account of it, unless we lose a hundred or two. Hope you will get this, as I have not yet got one letter, nor heard from home.

Give my love to all, but keep writing. Have only a pencil and that is not ½ inches long, so cannot write very well.

Your Husband
Wm. S. Newton

131

Cedar Creek near Strasburg Va. Aug 16th 1864

My Dear Wife

Our Chaplain starts today for Winchester, where Lieut. Ewing is found to be wounded, and not killed, as reported. The chaplain has permission to go home with him, he is wounded through the left lung.

The Rebel force hold a strong position, only three miles from us. The pickets & skirmishers drive each other every day, and a constant firing is kept up, and toward evening, two or three Regs are sent to their support to gain a good position for the night. In these engagements, three or four men are killed, 8 or 10 wounded, so a constant excitement is kept up. Whether a general engagement is brought about is uncertain.

Our rations are very scarce, all the green corn now in reach is used up, so that it is not safe or profitable to forage beyond our lines.

I have hoped that something would turn up to send us back to the Dept. of W. Va., of which Genl. Crook now has the exclusive command. Genl. Hunter & staff have been relieved, & report now says they are now absent on leave of 20 days. Our Reg. will not now number more than 400 men, the killed, wounded & sick have so reduced us. Other Reg in brigade are even more reduced than ours. We all still hope for the end of this war, and would be killed, maimed or anything else, to end it. *An overruling Providence, I believe* will bring it about at the proper time.

Give my kindest regards to all

Your Husband
Wm. S. Newton

132

Hall Town Near Harpers Ferry
Aug 26th 1864

Dear Wife

I wrote you on the 24th. Just as I finished, our Reg was ordered out with our Brigade to make a reconnaissance in force. We went to the point designated, but got into a hot place, the loss in wounded of the Brigade 30. Our Reg lost 13 of the number. One has since died. One, we performed exsection of the arm, taking 4 inches of the bone below the shoulder joint. In this way saving the arm with a false joint. It is better than an empty coat sleeve.

This morning indications are that we shall move soon. On our right, heavy fighting was going on all the afternoon.

We learn this evening that the enemy attempted to cross the river in force, but our men drove them back, with loss to them, and ours was three or four hundred.

Dr. Wellons is making every effort to be restored, Coates wrote him that he was willing to help him, "but to be *candid*, he was not wanted in this Reg."

I am still without a letter from you. Have just learned Capt. Crossley's arm was amputated at Cumberland. I regret this very much, and did not think it would be necessary when I took the ball from the wound.

My regards to all,

Your Husband
Wm. S. Newton

133

Saturday Aug. 27th Camp Hall Town
Near Harpers Ferry

My Dear Wife

I wrote yesterday and would not have written today, except for a very current report, that a shell struck & killed me last evening. After 3 P.M. our whole Division were ordered again to look into the enemy's camp. Both the 9th Va surgeons being sick, I was ordered to care for that Reg. They formed a part of the advancing column, and in the front line, as a matter of course were where the thickest of the fight raged. I tried to keep well in the rear, but other columns coming up, was compelled to follow very close. Our Reg 91st was a support to the 9th & 14 Va. Regs. We soon found Longstreet's Rebel Infantry. They were waiting for us, and gave us a warm reception from behind rail piles & breast works. Still we drove them from their cover, killing & wounding a large number. Our loss too was heavy, 23 of the 9th Va. fell, while only 4 of the 91st were wounded. The 14th loss about the same, as the 9th this is all owing to position. Solid shot & shell from the artillery however, are not particular where they fall, as apt to drop or burst in the rear as any other place. There were at least a hundred men ready to say I was killed, but how the report started I cannot tell. All I know is there were enough shell[s] to kill a doz surgeons dropped in close proximity, but nary one touched me. No letter yet. Your Husband

Wm. S. Newton

134

Charlestown 8 miles from
Harpers Ferry Aug 31st 1864

Dear Wife

Another month has passed and no letter from you since leaving home. Something must be wrong. You do not direct the letters right. If you send as before, to 91st Reg—2nd Brigade, 2nd Division at Harpers Ferry, there can be no mistake.

The long looked for Paymaster came yesterday, but paid for only 4 months, so the others are just even with me, and I, of course, got none except the money loaned to others, which will be sufficient to run me to the 20th of Sept, at which time they promise 4 months more, bringing it up to this date. Our boys all have smiling faces this morning, they have been so long without money & tobacco. I am really glad to see the change, poor fellows, they have marched long, and fought many battles. Quite a large number have given up their lives to their country's cause, and still a larger number are now suffering from wounds received in the same effort to put down this wicked rebellion. God grant that the end may soon come. Give my best regards to all, and much love to you & little ones.

Seems to me, you might get one letter through to me. As ever,

Your Husband
Wm. S. Newton

135

Charleston Va Sept. 1st 1864

My Dear Wife

Young Vance[13] goes home today, and kindly offered to take a letter I had written yesterday, but mail did not go. One came, but as usual, no letter for me. Warwick says, "you have thrown off on me." My faith is still strong however, that there are a whole batch of letters for me somewhere. We still hold our position here, & think the largest part of the Reb army has gone toward Richmond. Although a large cavalry force of ours was driven back two days ago, Col. Charley Kingsbury[14] says, they followed them to our infantry picket line, which is not more than three miles from our ambulance.

I do not think it is Genl. Sheridans intention to bring on a battle, but merely to hold this large force, while Grant does a bigger thing elsewhere. But to do this, it is necessary to constantly send out Cav, or a brigade of infantry to find them, and thus we have fighting every day, and run into the hottest places, have the sharpest engagements of the war. We got on to them so close, there is no chance to retreat, but must take the rail piles or breast works before halting, for if we turn our backs at such times, the slaughter would be double, 100 men in killed & wounded is a common occurrence.

Tell Mott I have purchased another horse for my orderly, *Jas Turner*, which I think will suit *him* very well when I get home. I know Ned wanted Old Tom, and he is just as good as ever. I found an orderly was of no benefit on the march, or in our present mode of battle, unless he was mounted. We are obliged to subsist most of the time by foraging, and if they go, they must ride in order to bring anything. Jim Turner just came in, with a large bundle of hay on each side of his horse, a sack of green corn before him, and this is the every day, but they have to keep a close lookout for Mosby & his gang of guerillas.

Sometimes they all start out, with a guard of 20 to 30 men, then there is not much danger, for the Rebs go in small squads dressed in our uniform, and if they can catch two or three of our men, outside of camp unarmed, they are pretty certain to gobble them up. The Rebs are generally armed with revolvers, in this way they can get close up to our men without exciting suspicion, till they cry halt, then there is nothing to do but go with them. Our men are becoming sharp, and do not allow them to get too close, without a close scrutiny.

A few days ago, five officers from the 6th Corps were captured in an ambulance in the streets of Charlestown, and driven off to the woods, ambulance and all, none of our forces being near enough to notice what was going on. This alone has a good effect on our straggling officers & men, there is very little visiting the ladies, outside of our lines.

Hope you will keep trying to get a letter to me, for I am very hungry for one.

Wm.S.N.

136

Head Qts Division Hospital
Summit Point 16 miles from
Harpers Ferry Sept. 9th 1864

My Dear Wife

Just received two letters from you Aug 7th & 16th, the latter mailed at Charleston W.Va. I begin to think your postmaster sends your letters the wrong direction for Cadot has not gotten any from his wife except one by private conveyance.

We are in the Army of the Potomac, and with the 8th & 19th Corps are with Gen. Crooks command, thus you see all mail matter comes by Baltimore & Harpers Ferry. I think Mr. Nadine has shown the cloven foot, and if I were Father H, would ask for his lease of house. How he can claim to rent a house for a given time, and have no lease I can't see. Hope you received the large envelope containing orders and recommendations, as I very much wished to preserve them. Not that I cared so much for the dismissal, for I have wished a dozen times since, that the restoration had not taken place.

On last Saturday eve just as we had got snugly encamped at Berryville, the Rebs attacked and drove in our pickets. The order to move out was given quick. Our Reg was guarding the train, and we marched within 300 yards of the Reb line, yet they did not fire on us, though we were scarcely out of range before the battle began. With our division, we could see stragglers from the First Brigade falling back in confusion. The shells began to fall thick & fast on the pike where the train was moving. Still we moved on in good order. Our Brigade (2nd) stopped the Jonnies, fought & whipped them, bringing in 80 prisoners. Rain began to fall, dark came on, we could not march, but stand in the rain. I got to a fence, my orderly held the horses & there we sat in the rain & dark all night. The firing did not cease till ten o'clock & then we who were in the rear did not know which side had whipped till morning. These are the times which try the patriotism of men.

But you don't know how glad we are when we whip, it takes away all the aches & ails. In short, we forget the fatigues, loss of sleep etc.

My position now, with the Division Hospl, will keep me in the rear, and if we do not get too far, so that old Mosby catches us, our place is a comparatively safe one. Am much pleased to know that Ned is trying to make himself useful. I hope to be very proud of his business qualifications when I get home.

Take good care of yourself & the little ones.

In haste,
Your Husband
Wm. S. Newton

137

Field Hospital 2nd Infantry Div.
Near Summit Point Va. Sept. 9th 1864

My Dear Wife

Have written one letter today but an opportunity offering of sending, will write a few lines more inasmuch as I have received two today, feel more inclined to answer. Am busy getting sick list ready, to send to Genl. Hospital. This is quite a responsible position, for I have to decide for the whole Division, being in charge of Div. Hospital. Think the Surgeons of the various Regs should take the responsibility. I send 16 in the morning, and they will not be with the command again for months. We send a strong guard along to prevent capture. Our facilities for writing are very poor, and as there are several standing waiting for an opportunity to write will give them an opportunity. So good night, and I will go to bed in the ambulance. My love to all. Your Husband

Wm. S. Newton

138

Head Quarters 2nd Div. Hospital
Summit Point Va. Sept. 15th/64

My Dear Wife

Yours of the 6th came yesterday just, after I had dispatched one by Lieut. N. R. Warwick who goes to Kanawha Valley for Co. property left there.

We have nothing new except the capture yesterday of a South Carolina Reg. on our left flank, we heard the cannonading, but our Division was not in the fight.

Our Hospital is running smoothly, and as fast as we return to duty & send to Genl. Hospital, others sicken, and take their places.

Thus you see our number is kept up, yet I feel that I am in position to do the most good for the Gov. The most annoying feature I now have to contend with is the vermin with which the sick are covered. Poor fellows they have been kept so long on the alert constantly under arms scarcely ever camping where water more than enough for coffee could be obtained. In this way, they have no opportunity to wash & dry clothing, having only one suit, they dare not run the risk of leaving them. I have now a man detailed to wash for them. The Sanitary agent camps & messes with me, he furnished clean underclothes while the others are being washed & dried. In this way, we hope to keep our tents & blankets free from the detestable scourge of the soldier. Some of the men feel quite irritable on being stripped & washed on their first appearance, but as we serve all alike, they readily comply.

Am very much pleased to know Neddie is trying to make himself useful to Uncle Will. But sorry to hear that you are all sick. Hope it will only be temporary. I cannot see how law is administered in G.[allipolis] if Father H. cannot by giving proper notice, obtain possession of his property. It is a strange construction of law, and the rights of owners.

Mother was very anxious to have you visit them this fall, if you cannot get a house, think you had better spend a month with her. Em will look after Kittie & Ned. Mott & John B. can go with you. Am certain you could have a very nice time.

Doug I suppose is at Hartford City enjoying the smiles of Miss Jennie.[15] Should anything occur there, would like very much to see and enjoy the solemn occasion. This would carry us back 20 years in our history. How much of our life is embraced in those twenty years, joy, sorrow & regrets have been interspersed. Yet we cannot say that the Great Ruler of events has not dealt justly with us.

Some of those events I would gladly recall. Others are still a pleasant source of reflection. Our experiences I trust will not be lost to us, but by it, shape our course for the future struggles with the world. Hope you will not be discouraged, but write often.

Your Husband
Wm. S. Newton

139

Summit Point Va. 18 miles from Harpers Ferry
Sunday morning Sept. 18th 1864

My Dear Wife

Your letter of 6th Ult done me more good than all communications yet received, for it came fresh, the other two were a month old. Am now anxiously waiting for another, the train came from Harpers Ferry this morning & I presume a mail also came. *Lieut [Gen.] U. S. Grant* came up from Harpers Ferry yesterday, to Head Qtrs. Of Genl. Sheridan. Every one was on the *qui vive*.[16] We all wanted to see the Genl., who outranks all others, and I would have gone over, a distance of two miles, but thought certainly he would visit my Hospital. In the evening we learned that a telegram from Washington had called him back in great haste. He did not stay at Genl. Sheridan's two hours.

We are evidently on the eve of some important movement. Time will only show what it is. Will also send some more of my bad cases to Sandy Hook today. Will still have a goodly number on hand, and if we move, the ambulances will have something to do.

In the summer and early fall of 1864, Union General Philip Sheridan led an aggressive summer campaign against the Confederates. Sheridan's Army of the Shenandoah combined a number of regiments, including many from Ohio and West Virginia, to pursue Confederate General Jubal Early's Army of the Valley. The battles of Opequan (Third Battle of Winchester) and Cedar Creek resulted in significant casualties for both sides. Maj. Gen. P. H. Sheridan, Eugene B. Willard Photograph Album, Special Collections, Marietta College, Marietta, Ohio.

My horses are getting to look very well under the care of orderly Turner, the new one is the fattest and by some would be thought the best, but to my eye, Old Tom outranks all others. We got a doz. loaves of soft bread from the Ferry yesterday, also some butter, have done without the latter so long I hardly know how to use it. Med. Dir. Robinson & myself are doing very well now, in the way of good quarters living etc. He is a young man, but been in the service from the first, has a wife at Cincini. She was here at Harpers Ferry and lost their only child a few weeks since.

Wood, & fence rails, are getting scarce, and a move is almost desirable on this account.

This is the best part of Va., the country is very level, Cavalry can operate finally, and saves our infantry many long marches.

I do not know how long I may be in charge of Div. Hospital, or whether it will be desirable in winter. One thing I have not forgotten, the promise of Med. Director Blaney that I should have a 30 days leave, as soon as the campaign was over. This he promised us, on account of our reporting so promptly after being released from Libby Prison. He said he would approve an application as soon as active operations were over. So I think I have a sure thing of it. Perhaps I will be there yet to help you set up housekeeping. Should you go at it, get some one to do the work for you, and not make yourself sick, because you can do it a little better. Take time, as the boys say, *"run slow."* Tell the boys to do as I have often counseled them, then they will please me, and be much happier. They are now old enough to have some dignity & judgement, hope they will exercise it. My love to all
Your Husband

> Wm. S. Newton Asst Surg.
> 91st Reg O.V.I.
> In Charge 2nd Div. Hospital

140

Winchester Va Sept. 22nd/64

My Dear Wife

This is Thursday eve & the first moment I have had since our hard fought battle of Monday (19) to write, read or rest. Having charge of Div Hosp, everything seemed to fall on me, and while the battle was going on, I marched 8 miles with my train, put up my tents, got ready for the wounded by 2 p.m., and from that time on, all night even, the wounded came in as fast as I could get places for them. After filling my tents & flies,[17] took a large brick house and filled 4 rooms as thick as they could lie on the floors. Our brave boys went in nobly, and were very anxious to wipe out the odium of our retreat from this place on the 24th of July. All who were not sick pressed on eagerly, and in the after part of the day, when they began to bring the *Jonnies* to the rear by hundreds, could hardly restrain the sick from going to the front. The papers will tell you more than I can write, we whipped them soundly, and captured 3 to five thousand prisoners. The command pressed on to Strasburg, driving & capturing many more.

A messenger just came in from the front, says a hard fought battle was had today, all ambulances are again ordered out. There will be many more wounded, and I don't know what will be done with them, for all Winchester is now a hospital. I got here at 8 o'clock this morning, have been engaged every moment operating & dressing. This is now the 4th day, and many are not properly cared for. Our Reg suffered heavily, do not know the number, Co B & I suffered most. Orderly Morton[18] was killed. Lieut. Hamilton[19] is wounded, others from Gallia, but have not heard definitely. Capt. Atkinson is badly but not fatally wounded.

Our Division will not lose less than eight hundred in killed & wounded. The 8th & 19th Corps will still lose more heavily, for they were much longer engaged, going into the fight early in the morning. But when the breast works were to be carried, the Army of the Kanawha were the boys to do it. They have made their mark as usual, carrying all before them, many have given up their lives in the struggle, many are maimed for life. I had thought our men had fought enough for one campaign, but seems they are still called on, and I never saw them obey more willingly. Your letter of 6th is the last I have received. Am very impatient for something later.

Surgeons from Washington arrived this evening, and I think will render sufficient aid, judging from the one, who has been assisting me this afternoon. Have not seen the Reg since the fight, only the wounded, and a small part of them, as they are so scattered around town. Will try to look them up tomorrow. Give my love to all.

Your Husband
Wm. S. Newton

141

Winchester Va. Sept. 24th 1864

My Dear Wife
I wrote you from this place on the eve of 22nd, and have been so busy with the wounded, since our great battle of the 19th, have not slept, ate, or rested, till tonight, when I told our Med Director I would stop long enough to write a letter to my wife. He granted the request, said I would be fully justified in so doing. The fact is, I came here with my Div. Hosp., three

days ago, to find everything in a state of *Chaos*. Dr. Hysel[20] of 9th Va. had been detailed in charge of sick here, but had no system or order, till some Washington City surgeons came on, who took charge of things by order of the Surg. Genl. U.S. They had not even a table on which to operate, for our Dept. I had one fixed up, and when I tell you that every case belonging to our Division, necessary to be examined, under the influence of chloroform, or operated upon, has been sent to my table. You will know that I have had enough to do in the way of surgery. I have not done all, but have been held responsible by the *Med Dir* and have had to decide on whom operations should be performed, and how it should be done. In fact, I believe I have operated in all except *four cases*, and in these, I assisted. I feel tonight very much fatigued, but hope we are through with all the bad cases, but every day these wounds are to be dressed, and tonight 100 more are just in from Strasburg, from the fight of yesterday.

Our troops are still pressing on, capturing & scattering Genl. Early's Rebel army. The news from the front is most cheering, the particulars you will best gather from the papers.

An order came tonight, for Med Dir Robinson, Dr. Smith[21] in charge of 1st Div, & Dr. Newton in charge of 2nd Div Hospital, to report to the front. Med Dir Robinson is as yet, undecided whether to obey it. As he is ordered by Dr. Brinton,[22] who is a superior officer, to Dr. Leete,[23] Med Dir of Dept, to remain in charge of sick & wounded here. I presume if a suitable escort can be furnished, we will go, but this will make no difference in your letters reaching me, for they will be sent on to the command. Have not had one since the 6th. Suppose if there are any, they have gone onto the Reg, so you must still direct as before.

Hope you are all getting on well, for we feel in fine spirits after the great victory. The wounded men, even those who have lost a leg or arm, have time to cheer and say it is worth all it has cost them.

Have procured leave of absence for most of the wounded officers of our Reg, and some are on their way home. Don't you almost wish I was wounded? I would take a slight one, if only to get home. Must stop. So good night, my love to all.

Your Husband
Wm. S. Newton

142

Winchester Va Sept. 28th/64

My Dear Wife

This is Wednesday eve, and I am still in charge of Div. Hospital, or as it is called here, South Church Hospital. I had expected we would be relieved before this, some of the surgeons have been, and gone after their commands. I presume we will be, as soon as arrangements can be perfected. The duties are very hard here, and do not seem to grow less, for wounded are being sent to the front almost every day, and tonight a train from Harpers Ferry is passing through town, going to the front, said to be 800 wagons. Some 10,000 troops are along.

They have been passing for the last three hours, and still they come. Hope they will be done by bedtime, for they make a very great noise on the paved streets. If they trouble me, how must the wounded suffer, who cannot turn, or change their position.

The women here, are very attentive to the sick & wounded soldiers. They not only visit the hospitals, but bring delicacies & substantial food. They bake & wash, cook anything for the nurses, if they only say it is for the sick or wounded.

Yesterday I met a farmer & his daughter, inquiring where supplies were needed. I directed them to my Hospital, and when they drove up, I was there, to show them a place to put them, and play the agreeable to Miss. She gave every wounded man 1/2 of a *turnover* with her own hand. 107 were thus furnished with a piece of good apple pie, besides sending as many more to Dr. Kemp[24] & Johnson's[25] Hospitals. When they unloaded the spring wagon, we found besides the pies, a sack of apples, a whole mutton, 15 chickens, 1/2 doz. loafs of bread & a small cheese.

All these, were brought 5 miles, and cooked by a few ladies, who delegated this pretty miss to give them to our boys.

She was very particular to inquire whether they were all Union, as she desires they, and not rebel soldiers to have them. There is also quite a rush of *Secesh ladies* to the York Hospital,[26] where most of the rebel wounded are cared for. They too, I understand, are quite partial to this class of wounded. A Reb doctor, by the name of Love,[27] is very popular with them, hardly giving him time to attend his patients.

The Court House, & yard, is thronged with Reb prisoners. Still, the most of them having been sent off.

No letter since the 6th from you, expect they go on to the Reg. & I don't know where our Brigade is now. Can hardly write with this ink, and am so sleepy will stop short off.

My love to all

> Your Husband
> Wm. S. Newton

143

Winchester Oct. 8th 1864

Dear Wife

Your letter of 18th gave me much information, that you were fixed, if not keeping house. There is some pleasure in knowing that you have a place and can pay for the accommodation.

My hospital is getting thinned out somewhat, sent fifteen to Martins-burg yesterday, have one or two die each day. Some are getting able for duty. Our number, exclusive of cooks, nurses, etc., is 70. Other hospitals of our Corps number less, as they have been able to send to Genl. Hospital a greater number, on account of the wounds being slight. My eyes have been much affected by dressing so many wounds. So much so that for two days, I have avoided them as much as possible. Then Dr. Morris and Monahan[28] are here assisting, and they have taken the most of such work off my hands.

There are many scenes transacted here, which show the horrors of this Rebellion. Such as parents looking for sons, brother seeking brother, and wife in search of husband. Those who have braved the dangers of being cap-tured by guerillas come here, to find their friends or relatives, perhaps dead & buried. Others search whole days on other Hospls and at last find the dear one, in the last agonies of death. All are anxious to take their friends home, whether living or dead, and this makes much confusion & trouble, for they think, doctors can accomplish anything if they only use their influ-ence, hence we are importuned.

My eyes will not let me write more. My love to all friends, and kiss to the little ones.

Your Husband
Wm. S. Newton

144

Headquarters South Church Hosp.
Winchester Va. Oct. 13th 1864

My Dear Wife

Yours of Sept. 30th came back from the front today, almost a month had lapsed since hearing from you. I went out the wagon train last night with three doctors, and we looked over a large mail. We found letters for some of the wounded under our care, but nary one for us, got one [for] Dr. Morris. He was busy at my room, making out tally sheets, for as you must know, we held an election for our boys. We did not expect to take the vote of any, except our own, but they came in on us, from other hospitals & detachments, till the number ran up to 156, and from this number 40 counties were represented. Thus you see a big job on hand for each county must be furnished with a copy as well as the auditor of state. Have just got the vote of Ohio Regs in Crooks comd, and send it to the editor if he wishes it for the public.

I am really sorry you have taken Ned from the store, to send him to school, especially if he was doing well there, I feel a year or two of *experience in business* would be worth more to him than any school. He has been kept at it so closely, I would much prefer that he would learn to apply his knowledge, and by this means, learn the value of an education.

If Brother Will can use him, and will train him to business, he will soon be able to make himself useful, and think something of himself. If boys ever learn to esteem themselves, it is when they are usefully employed, and can feel that they can accomplish something.

When they feel they can be trusted and are responsible then it is they see the importance of being something.

Tell Ned that if Uncle Will trusts him to the business for him, I hope he will not *betray his trust*, but faithfully perform all given him to do, whether in the store or out. Anything given him should be *well* done, for this is the only way to succeed in any undertaking.

Our men are doing well, and getting less, every day almost, we send a few on to Genl. Hosp. I know nothing of the movements of our Div., except that they were at Cedar Creek, two miles this side of Strasburg, where they held their election. Hope you all continue to write, for Dr. Morris gets letters from his wife every two or three days. I expect she writes oftener than you, tell Will & Em they might write once in a while. Give my kind regards to all. Love to yourself & kisses to little ones,

> Your Husband
> Wm. S. Newton

145

> Winchester Va. Oct 17th 1864

My Dear Wife

Had not expected to write from this place again, for two days ago I was ordered to the front, but Med Dir Robinson was not ready when the escort went, and perhaps it was for the best, for they were attacked and some eight or ten wounded, most all officers, and I might have been of the number.

Today I expected again to go, but no orders were given, and while waiting two letters were brought from the front, one of Sept. 5th from you, and one from Col. Turley of old date. It seems Mr. Ricker was the bearer of my letter, have not seen him, but hope to if I get to the front in the morning.

Got a letter from John yesterday. He informs me Doug is to be married tomorrow, that they were going to see it done etc. Also that much gossip was indulged in at his expense, in and about Marietta, and some ladies had rendered themselves quite silly.

John had been east on a pleasure or health tour and expressed great satisfaction at results. Had gained 20 lbs. Good meat, and thought it solid.

The Sanitary Commission have been very active and have distributed a large supply of everything for the comfort of the sick & wounded soldiers. We in the Kanawha Valley never know anything of the resources & advantages of this institution. Miss Dix[29] & all the notables connected with it have been here.

I hope the time is not far distant when I shall see you all again, for Med Dir Blaney promised to approve a leave of absence, as soon as the active campaign should be over. If he does not forget his words, I shall have a clear sailing for a thirty day leave.

You would be satisfied to see how many stragglers & hangers on there are at present in and about Winchester. Quartermasters, sutlers, and all their clerks are conjugated here, waiting to be ordered forward as soon as the dangers shall have passed by. Then the guards & detachments, teamsters, etc. make up a large force, who would all run if we should be attacked. I am quite tired of seeing it, and hope soon to be with the fighting portion of the army. Hope you have got coal, clothing, etc. to make you all comfortable. Give my love to all, and tell them to write, for they will turn up some time. You will hear from me again soon.

Your Husband
Wm. S. Newton

146

Hospital 2nd Div Army West Va.
Near Cedar Creek Va Oct. 23rd 1864

My Dear Wife

This is Sabbath evening, and once more I am back to my old place & position from which the Jonnies so unceremoniously routed me on the morning of Wednesday 19th. As I wrote you, we were compelled to light out, & fall back.

I had arrived the evening before, had changed my under clothes, and left them, the dirty ones for the Rebs. We saved almost every thing, had we stayed to save all, would now no doubt be well on toward Richmond, for the people living near by, say we had not left three minutes before they were on the same spot, picking up the spoils we had left. If the little I lost, saved me from falling into their hands, they are welcome.

Five Hosp. Tents, 17 sick men, boxes, blankets, etc. were loaded in the shortest conceivable time, one of my wagons was at the ambulance train, and had to be sent up. If this had been in its proper place, we would have secured all, but in the hurry we could not think of everything.

After starting ambulances & wagons, I mounted Old Tom with much difficulty, for the noise & hubbub made by moving out the train, and the firing of guns on the left, and on the Pike in our rear, had well nigh crazed him. He would not be still a moment. I succeeded, however, and kept to the left of the pike and of the town, where the firing was pretty brisk. Col. Thoburn,[30] commander of a division, Dr. Shannon,[31] who like me, was in charge of Div. Hospt. and others, rode into the town, and were killed. My curiosity was not great enough to lead me in, I was satisfied with hearing the guns that Rebs must be there, and that they were firing on the train. I kept on till I had passed it, got my ambulances & wagons as near as possible together, told them to keep so if possible, drive on slow, but steadily, in this way protected by darkness & fog. We pushed on till out of danger. We met Genl. Sheridan with a strong Cavalry force going to the front. He seemed to infuse courage & security to all, men who were going to the rear with their arms fleeing to a safe position. As soon as he passed, they stopped, and many went to work making coffee. I pushed on the loaded ambulances, took my sick to Winchester, delivered them at the Sheridan Hospital then started the empty ambulances all to the front.

I followed them up with no company except orderly Turner, he was well armed with Two six shooters, and we kept a sharp lookout for Mosby's men, that is the time for them, when small parties are going without an escort. We reached New Town, 8 miles from Winchester, just in time to establish a field hospital, where the 6th & 19th Corps were in the act of establishing theirs. Had my tents put up, straw & rails hauled, all ready for the arrival of the wounded, then followed for three days, dressing amputations, & sections, etc. Our own men were in the main, first attended to, for Sheridan not only whipped them, on the same evening, but drove them on to Woodstock, 6 miles beyond the point of attack in the morning, capturing 46 pieces of artillery, and recapturing 15 pieces which they had taken from us in the morning, making more than 60 in all. We also captured trains, Med. Supplies, horses, cattle, & many prisoners. After our own wounded were cared for and sent off to Winchester. They sent to my hospital 66 Reb wounded, we went to work on them, and when finished, we packed them in ambulances & waggons.

Started them off also for Winchester. Now if you think I have had nothing to do since the fight, you are very much mistaken.

We still stay here at Cedar Creek, how long the command will be here no one knows. Hope we shall get back somewhere for good winter quarters, before the cold weather sets in.

Your letter of the 12th came yesterday, was very glad to get it. Genl. Powell is here, or was this morning. Col. Kingsbury is here, his hands full of business. He is very pleasant, and put me in the way of getting a field operating case of instruments, captured from the Rebs. It is one they had captured from us, at some time previous. Hope the war will soon be over, if Genl. Grant does as well, as Sheridan & Sherman have done, it seems as if there was not much more to do. Have built a furnace under my tent today, and hope to sleep warmer than last night.

My eyes are still sore, and I must not tax them more. Give my love to all

Your Husband
Wm. S. Newton

147

Hd Quarters 2nd Div Hosp
Cedar Creek Va Oct 28th 1864

My Dear Wife

This is the anniversary of our wedding day, nineteen years ago we started in life as it is termed by many. We had but little, and in this respect considering our responsibilities, our position is not much changed.

But how changed & varied are the circumstances, friends, and we ourselves as you will see by looking at our photograph taken when we were more youthful than now. The physical though much changed, I trust the mind & heart, think and pulsate just as they were wont to do.

And when my mind goes back to the early associations of our married life they are the most pleasing of all others, and I could almost wish to live them over again. I think with our past experience, we would make more of life. But I feel that age is creeping upon us, and we have much to live for yet.

The little ones dependent upon us, is enough to occupy our whole time & talents. My time here is now much occupied, and I am glad it is so, for then time flies on, and I am conscious of being useful. The paymaster is here, and I hope to send you by Dr. Morris some money. He pays four months, two are still due at the end of this month.

Will send you the interest bearing notes, so that you may deposit them in a safe place, and they will draw interest all the time. If you spend eight dollars per week for board, you must economize in other things, lest we run behind. I should feel sorry to bear the exposure & anxiety now endured and not get something ahead.

The wind is very high, and it is almost impossible to keep our tents up, the candle will hardly burn so I must stop.

If you have not sent my overcoat, you need not do so, for I took one of ours, from a Jonny this week, which will answer my purpose very well.

Give my love to all
Your Husband
Wm. S. Newton

148

Hd Quarters 2nd Div Hospital
Cedar Creek Va Oct 31st 1864

My Dear Wife

With this I send you 400 dollars, comp interest bearing notes, which I think you can deposit with Geo Jackson, and he will be willing simply to take care of them for you. They will be quite as good as the note of any one man, and have this advantage, viz. we can always put our hand upon them if needed.

I was paid for four months only, and may yet get pay on my order, for two months more, if things remain quiet.

I presume we will hold this position until after the Presidential Election, if able. After that, will probably fall back to a place more convenient to hold, and less difficult to supply with forage, stores, etc.

Let me hear from you, as soon as you get this. Dr. Morris expects to go to Gall[ipolis] and will deliver the same notes I send, you will see they have been bearing interest since July, and are now of some value, over six dollars already in interest. Shall make an effort to get home as soon as we fall back. I hope then to find every thing all well & right.

Give my love to all friends,
Your Husband
Wm. S. Newton

149

Hospl 2nd Div Army W. Va.
Cedar Creek Nov 6th 1864

My Dear Wife

It is now almost a month since a letter from you has reached me, one was sent from Winchester on the 18th of last month but it was rather old, and it seems almost impossible to get a letter anymore, until all others have theirs. Today they all received letters, even Orderly Turner got two from his wife but none for me. My mess think that I write a large number of letters, compared with the no. received, and I get real vexed once in a while and I think I will just stop writing, till parties become interested enough to answer a part at least of those sent. I am quite certain you must get two or three a week, while I dont get one in three weeks. Nothing of interest has occurred since the skedaddle & victory of the same day, and if you watch the papers, in reference to the operations of Genl. Sheridan in the Shenandoah Valley you will keep posted better than I can tell you.

Genl. W. H. Powell commanding a Div of Cavalry near Front Royal, called on me last eve, and stayed to supper, his star does not make a fool of him, he is just the same, but declares that Ricker is not going to be mustered out, as he (Ricker) thinks, for he, Powell, needs him for inspector on his staff. I met Powell at Kingsbury H. Quarters, and we had an old fashioned time, talking over the events of the past. Powell is to send me a cow, for the use of Hospital this week. The cost is small here.

I suppose ere this you have the 400.$ sent by Dr. Morris, if Mosby did not catch him. Mosby's men are a perfect pest, for no train of wagons, or small squad of men escape him. He keeps the men & officers close in camp, and this is the only real good he effects. If others were as closely employed, and stayed as closely at home as I, there would be but little use for him in this particular.

The *Grey Backs* infest our camp, and two nights ago was up all night fighting them. The sanitary Agt. Messes with me, and furnished a change of under clothes. I had every fellow up looking, made them turn out, at 12 o'clock. Think you would have laughed to see all the grimaces etc. in finding a good supply of the *critters*.

We hope we are now clear of them. Are in morning, to be ready to move, on a moments notice, just as soon as we vote, we think we shall move back to a place on the Rail Road. Then I am going to try for a leave of absence. My love to all friends.

Your Husband
Wm. S. Newton

150

Field Hospital 2nd Inf Div
Army West Va Nov 14th 1864

My Dear Wife

Yours of 8th came today, the latest I have received for a long time. Cannot imagine what has come over you all. I am afraid proper care is not taken to preserve health, or you would not so many get sick.

We are now only three miles from Winchester, came here next day after election. The Rebs thought we had passed Winchester and they would come down and have a good time, so when they came and found us out here, did not like to go back without learning who was here, so attacked Genl Powell on our left, he pitched into them, and gave a *regular Army W. Va. whaling,* captured *two guns,* the only artillery they had, 170 enlisted men and 17 commissioned officers. This was a pretty good haul for the new Brigadier. Saw him today, and if the army will only fall back, will get an opportunity to go home with him. He expects to go in three or four days. Genl Crook said I might do so, as soon as we fall back. Am afraid Powell will get off before the Rebs leave our front, in that case I will be left behind.

If I could only feel that I was going home to stay, there would be some satisfaction, but as long as the rebellion lasts, who can be satisfied at home or abroad? Those at home are not easy by any means, and those who have soldiered two or three years cannot go home now and feel that they have nothing to do in the matter.

Would like to save all the money I can conveniently, so that when I do come home to stay, I can go or stay where the best opportunity offers, and will have too a little capital to work with, have often felt the need of something to do with, and have made many sacrifices to pay debts that are contracted to keep up appearances.

I hope this day is now passed, and with the experience we have, shall be able to pilot our boat through in safety. I say I hope for this, and if health is spared us, have as fair a prospect as we have ever had, to accomplish this end. Had not heard before of Mothers sore throat, how long has it troubled her, and is it likely to be anything serious, would like to have you get them all cured up once, would like to get one more *hearty cheerful letter from home.* I get them so rarely that I get clear out of patience, then when they come, I have the *blues* the balance of the time. Then I think how miserable it is to look on the dark side of things all the time, and will not allow myself to do it.

I think Em might take care of Jonny while you write, at least twice a week, or once in a while write herself. I thought after you had moved to

G.[allipolis] I would get letters often, but instead they are much less frequent. You all get together and talk so much, you think of no one else, and *one* away out here in *the cold* is forgotten.

My eyes do not perform their part well, and I have to be very careful of them, I do not believe, it is because of old age, for Dr. Robinson who is a young man is troubled in the same manner. Hope you may all have one grand *thanksgiving* and that fortune may so smile that I may be there to see.

Your Husband
Wm. S. Newton

Rough Draft of Letter on Reverse

Field Hospital 2nd Inf Div Army of W. Va.
Near Kearnstown Va Nov 14, 1864

I hereby certify that Andrew Ward,[32] Private Co. E 54 Reg Pennsylvania Vols was wounded in Left Thigh at the Battle of Winchester Va Sept 19th 1864 from which he died on Oct 11th 1864.

Asst Surg 91st Ohio Vols.

151

Hospital 2nd Inf Div A W Va.
Kernstown, Va Nov 22nd 1864

My Dear Wife

Have been waiting a number of days in expectation of a letter from you. But none coming will try to write one more. We still occupy the same spot as when I last wrote, and I cannot find that we are to fall back, as has been constantly affirmed. Genl Crook has gone on an inspecting tour through his Dept., & when he returns something may turn up.

I can hardly ask for a leave while in the immediate front, with an expectation that it will be successful.

It may be Christmas before I get there, but be assured the first opportunity will be embraced by me, for I am nearly out of clothes of every description, had expected the shirts & socks some time ago, but Newt Warwick has not yet arrived. If he does not bring them, I shall feel disappointed, but will try to squeeze along the best I can.

Clothing of all kinds is very much needed among the troops, tents are not furnished even, and the men are suffering from sickness on this account.

Hope you are all better than when you last wrote. Received a letter Br. John yesterday, he speaks in the highest terms of Doug's new *wife & family*. Thinks D. has done just the right thing.

Now I wish we were all to go home to remain there, no more war, but peace, happiness & plenty. My warm regards to all friends, a kiss for the little ones.

Your Husband
Wm. S. Newton

10

The War by All Is Now Considered Over, January–August 1865

William S. Newton's 1865 letters to his wife and family were focused on the final months of the war and his military service. The wartime letters recorded life in winter quarters, a series of promotions for officers, and news from the front. Newton recounted the capture of Union generals Crook and Kelley in February, but his interactions with rebels were limited. Instead, he focused on tending to the wounded in his hospital near Winchester. He was also asked to care for local residents, some secesh, and willingly supplied his medical services. Newton's April 24 letter explained: "I can hardly wait for the time, as the war to us all seems over, for the muster out of the reg."[1]

The concentration of so many Union regiments in the area put Newton in contact with notable commanders, including Colonel Rutherford B. Hayes, also from Ohio. The early months of 1865 brought promotions and new commissions for many Union soldiers. Newton discussed his promotion to surgeon as early as 1863 and served as acting surgeon of the 2nd Virginia Cavalry that fall. But the official promotion to surgeon came only a few weeks before the end of the war. On March 18, 1865, he became surgeon of the 193rd Ohio Volunteer Infantry and kept that post until he mustered out with the regiment on August 9, 1865.[2]

In early 1865, Newton had more freedom to take leave and visit family. His letters mentioned visiting Harmar and Gallipolis. His postwar dreams of moving to a farm came true in March when he completed the purchase of a farm in West Union, Adams County, Ohio, from Colonel Benjamin F. Coates. The two had agreed on the transaction in April 1864, but apparently the deal did not occur. Perhaps the two put their agreement on hold because of the fierce fighting they both experienced in the summer and fall of 1864. In February, Coates wrote to his wife on the matter, saying: "Dr. Newton talks a little about buying the place he thinks it would suit him to live with his boys and farm and practice medicine."[3] The next month they finalized the deal. The letters that followed were devoted to preparing to move to the farm. There was a clear sense that Newton believed that farming represented an idyllic lifestyle and way to teach his children the value of hard work and patience. He wrote letters to Ned during this period, and it appears that the teenager was again having behavior problems but took an interest in joining the church. Newton wanted both of his boys to be men of business instead of "town loafers."[4] Newton's instructions for growing crops, cleaning fencerows, and tending to a new home were aimed at teaching Ned important life lessons in a more wholesome setting with fewer temptations.

In his 1865 letters, Newton made no direct references to the important concluding moments of the Civil War, such as the fall of Richmond on April 2, Confederate surrender at Appomattox on April 9, and Lincoln's assassination on April 15. His only letter from that important month, dated April 24, was instead focused on plans for his farm, including the care of cows and chickens. In a May 4 letter he mentioned that the president, Andrew Johnson, encouraged military resignations to speed up the process of reconciliation. During this period he also talked about quitting chewing tobacco, which was one of his few vices. Newton alluded to the difficult reunification of North and South. In June he mentioned that there were "plenty of Secesh women within the picket line, and they are just as rebellious as ever, and spit out their venom on every occasion."[5] He also commented on the lively festivities of the first Fourth of July of the postwar. Newton's July 20 letter, the final letter selected for this book, was focused on returning home, which he expected to do in August.

152

Hosp 1st Inf Div A. W.V.
Cumberland Jany 26/65

My Dear Wife

Had intended to send this by Mrs. Q. M. Turner, but she started at 7 this morning about one hour before I was out of bed.

Warwick goes home today for twenty days, and Coates is expected here today as President of a Court Martial. Presume they will be down on the same train. Genl Crook gives a grand party tonight where I suppose the Cumberland ladies will do their best to entrap some of the Military, and as the Genl is an old bachelor, will be the big fish to be caught. He is not, however, very susceptible to the smiles of ladies. Yet a *certain kind* are said to employ his attention.

Genl Duval is suffering with neuralgia of the ear, which threatens his usefulness as a soldier. His wife & sister-in-law are here.

Brig Genl Hay[e]s[6] & Surg Webb[7] are both at home, but theirs expires on the 2nd of February. So you see, go & come, is the order, while we are in winter quarters. Am pleased to see it, for they have had a hard summer of it, and deserve some respite. But oh, when will my turn come again, perhaps not till my term of service is over. Hope you and the children keep well. My love to all.

Your Husband
Wm S Newton

153

Camp near Cumberland Md
Feb 9th 1865

My Dear Wife

Almost a month has now passed since I left you at Harmar, and I feel that only a few days more and winter will be over. How fast time flies. I succeeded yesterday in getting four months pay including all of 1864. My pay for four months after the tax deducted amounts to $441.60. I will try to send you, by Lt. Turner 400.$ He now expects to start on Monday next, if his leave is approved. You had better deposit with Stephen or John, or get them to invest it for you in Gov Bonds, which can be converted into money at any time, and the interest be accruing. The Comp Int[erest] bearing notes, if they think best, should also be included in the investment. You had better save 100.$ from this I now send, and the amount that is due from Will, and the little balance in Bank, will probably serve you till another payment is due. However, make *your own calculations, lest I do not calculate right.*

Have not yet got any answer from any letter from John about Coates farm, nor have you said a word about it, in fact I have just got two letters from you since I left, two per month is rather slow.

Got one from Em this morning, by Col Cadot. She says the boys have been very good during our absence, that Father H. is much better with his stomach, that your mother is suffering with rheumatism, etc.

Says too the Church were about to give a donation party to Mr. Van Dusen.[8] It was to be held at Capt. Merideth's.[9] I understand the oil fever is now raging at Gallipolis, and is likely to assume an epidemic form. Perhaps if I should get Coates farm, the fever would reach that locality, and if it raged high, and nothing but greenbacks would cure it, we would of course, resort to the pleasant remedy. Things here remain the same, Cols Ewart[10] of 8th Ohio Cav, & Furney[11] of 34th Inf are both dismissed [from] the service, for their *questionable defence* of the town of Beverly.[12] Write soon, my love to all.

Your Husband
Wm. S. Newton

154

Cumberland Md
Feb 21st 1865

My Dear Boy,

Yours written on the 12th and posted on 16th reached me this morning, just at the time we were much exercised with the daring boldness of the Rebels in dashing into Cumberland and capturing Genls Crook & Kelley also Adj Genl Melvin. They came in at 3 or 4 this morning on the principal street, halted, and sent two separate squads to the Revere & Barnum Houses, took the Genls from their beds, at the same time another party destroyed the telegraph office. It was all done in a very few minutes, before any alarm could be given.[13]

They started off, leaving Colonels, Captains and any amount of staff officers sleeping in the town, but I suppose they were in too much haste to stop for any, below the rank of Maj Genl. They passed up the towpath only three hundred yards from where the ambulance train is parked, where they might have taken loo good horses. This event has caused deep feeling, for Genl Crook is a *favorite* with officers & men, and all the good news from Sherman & Charleston fails to bring one cheer, so melancholy do we feel.

In reference to the interest manifested by you, in the prayer meetings, I hope it is sincere, and you may continue to feel the importance of the subject. Don't mistake your desire to do right for a change of heart, nor trust in *your own strength* to keep good resolutions, for you will meet many temptations, and find you have a hard warfare with your own wicked heart. *God alone can help you* to overcome the many difficulties which will constantly beset your path. Therefore pray for strength to overcome your *violent temper*. This certainly will be a great gain, also remember that *strict veracity* is one of the *virtues consistent* with a Christian. Without it, no one can long sustain the

Christian character, and you little realize now, how often it would be necessary to implore forgiveness of him, who only can forgive. That he will have
mercy, and help you to hold your temper in check, and enable you not only
to speak, but act the truth.

You should not be discouraged at the first failure, but go to the right
place for help. Your conscience will tell you when you have done wrong,
at such time don't try to reconcile the wrong but confess it, if necessary *to
men*, but *by all means to him who knows your heart, there* is the only refuge
for a sin sick soul, and if these confessions are sincere and humble, you will
always find comfort, and if you persevere, will also find peace of mind. He
will not turn a deaf ear to those who importune, with sincerity and sorrow
for sin.

Don't start in this thing unless you have fully made up your mind, it is
for life for it is very hard to attempt to live the life of a Christian, if your
heart is not in it, for your heart will constantly lead you astray. But when the
heart is right, it will be a happy and easy life and the consciousness that you
are a child of god will afford more pleasure, than this world can give.

I will pray that you may succeed in finding that pearl of great price, and
hope you may have abundant evidence, that your heart is changed, that your
actions may show to others the value of religion.

Hope you will write me again. Tell me all your trials & joys. Would also
like to hear from Mott. My love to all,

Your Father
Wm.S.N.

155

Cumberland Md Feb 28th/65

Dear Wife

Brother Will forwarded to me a letter from John X. Davidson in which
Davidson says he wishes the two notes forwarded to my Act at Ironton, as
he wants to take them up. I wrote him that you were the custodian, etc.

But that you would be at Gallipolis on the 15th of March, and as Dr.
Neal was absent he had better entrust the money to someone who could
take them up by calling on you.

The interest at 6 per cent will be calculated to the time they are paid.
You had probably best ask Geo Jackson to attend to the business for you,
& if he does, give you a credit, or certificate of deposit for the amount.
Davidson also claims to have paid the last half years tax, which he very mod-
estly asks me to instruct my Act to pay back. Now I think the tax was paid

up to June 31st, and if it is the tax from July 1st to Dec 31st which has accrued since the conveyance was made to him. Do not think it right or just. You will ask Stephen about it. He will know what the custom in such cases is.

Perhaps John will be going to Ironton, if so let him take the notes and transact the business for you, and if I do not buy Col Coates farm, would like to have him invest them in bonds, or what ever he thinks best. I wish he had told me what to do in this matter. Coates is waiting, and it seems as if this payment of notes comes just in time to invest in real estate, if I only knew what is best to be done.

I suppose I must give him an answer in a very short time. Brother Will writes that the boys are doing very well, that the meetings have had a very serious effect upon Ned, that he seems really in earnest, will join church. Also that himself & Rene will also join with a doz more. Do you not think it is time you were there to advise Ned in this step.

Give my love to all,

Your Husband
Wm. S. Newton

156

Cumberland Md March 4th 1865

My Dear Boy

Yesterday I entered into an arrangement which will give you an opportunity to exhibit whatever of the man there is in you, and I hope you will show mother and all others that you are able to cope with difficulties, endure hardships, and make yourself useful as opportunity offers. You are, with the help of Mott, my main dependence, in this undertaking, and I was induced to go into it, for the benefit of you & Mott, that you might learn how to do, and carry on business.

I have no objection to you telling our own folks, but do not talk of our plans to everyone about town, these are matters which interest us alone. I have purchased a farm of 100 acres close to the town of West Union, Adams Co, where Dr. Coleman[14] lives. House, barn, apple trees, already upon it, and as the fencing is not very good, it will require much of your time & attention to look after it, particularly the outside fence will have to be looked after, so that the stock from town will not run over the fields. You will have to go around the outside fence often, and put up the rails which fell off, and where some are lacking, take from some of the inside fences, to supply the deficiency. Don't have the rails burned for fire wood, for timber is very scarce with which to make more. You will have to buy wood of some of the farmers, delivered in the yard. You will also get someone to plow the garden, and raise vegetables, perhaps Grandpa can furnish you with some garden seed, with which to plant the garden. Put at least one half of the garden in potatoes, some good early corn also.

The potato seed you can get at West Union. Get Mr. Baldridge, the former owner of the farm, to tell you which kind of potatoes grow the best, also have him tell you of some good man whom you can hire to help you put in your crop.

If you make things go well, you will have to be industrious, energetic & watchful.

And along in May or June, the pasture will be grown, so that you can make something, at pasturing the town cows. I presume they pay 50 or 60 cts a week, perhaps more. Would have them pay a month in advance, in this way will make no bad debts. There will be wood to chop and many other things which will employ your whole time and attention. Mother will have to depend on you boys for almost everything, so you must show yourselves equal to the task, and when I get home, we will have some stock of our own to look after, and will try to make things look up. You have no idea how much you can do till you are tried. You will have to help Mother get ready to move, as I would like to have you ready on the farm by the 1st of April, at which time I get possession.

Now this has long been, a favorite project of mine, and I hope you boys will enter into it with spirit, determined to accomplish something. You are now getting old enough to be of some importance, and I desire to give you an opportunity to do something.

Remember always to be patient if things do not go right the first time, don't give up but try again. After we have been there a year or two, it will be very pleasant to have a visit from your cousins or relatives. Think perhaps you will have something to show them, for the year or two spent in getting things in order.

Hope you will have everything picked up, and not have it in Grampa's way. There are many things which we will need on the farm, so keep together everything on hand. I presume Mother will be with you soon, as I wrote her last evening. Write me what you think about matters. My love to all. Your Father

Wm. S. Newton

Benjamin F. Coates was a doctor and politician from West Union, Adams County, Ohio. In 1862, he was commissioned lieutenant colonel of the 91st Ohio Volunteer Infantry and rose to the rank of brigadier general. William S. Newton made numerous references to Coates and admired his leadership. In March 1865, Newton purchased the farm that Coates owned in West Union. Col. Benjamin F. Coates, Eugene B. Willard Photograph Album, Special Collections, Marietta College, Marietta, Ohio.

157

Cumberland Md
March 12th 1865

My Dear Wife

Have not yet got an answer from my 3rd of March letter.

Am very anxious to have your letters now, as I wish to make payment on the farm, and receive the deed while Coates & I are here. The papers can be executed, for perhaps we will not be here long, as I received an order today, to turn over Gov Property, to Med Purveyor, and then rejoin my Reg. I presume they will give me some ten days to make out the papers, take invoices, etc.

This will keep me here till about 22nd. So lose no time after you have got the money in sending forward the 1200. If you send by express, mail a letter at the same time, letting me know. Should Jackson think best to send by letter, get him to dispatch the certificate for you. But have it done immediately, as Coates is daily expecting the deed from West Union.

I still feel that you have a big job on hand to move, but hope you will accomplish all on time. Should Warwick's resignation be accepted, they are very anxious to have me with the Reg.

Will write you again in a day or two. Tell the boys I want them to show themselves men in this matter, there is a chance to exhibit, whether there is anything in them, for they will have enough to do & attend to.

Much love to all, write often
Your Husband
Wm. S. Newton

158

Cumberland Md March 17th 1865

My Dear Wife

Yours of 12th came by Lt. Turner, was really pleased to have you take things philosophically, for I have really worried a good deal over the matter, thinking I had imposed a great task upon you.

But I really feel encouraged today for reasons I will state. I saw Mr. Battelle[15] from Marietta today, and learn from him that he is one of a company, who are already operating in lands in Adams Co. This will of itself, enhance the value of land in the Co, and may enable us, if you do not like the location, to sell at an advanced price, but this we must not talk about now except between ourselves. If I were only at home, could operate there successfully.

But I learn today also, that I am appointed Surgeon of the 193rd Ohio. The Reg is now here on its way to Martinsburg or Winchester. The Asst Surg called on me, telling me of my appointment, and asking instructions etc. I presume I shall get my commission in a day or two, thus you see the end is not yet.

Will hope all to turn out for the best. Give my love to all friends, and hasten on this certificate for 1200., as the Col has just received the deed, and holds it ready to turn over to me. I very much desire to have this business done up before I leave here.

Your Husband
Wm. S Newton

159

Cumberland Md March 18th/65

My Dear Boys,

As I wrote to Mother Last eve, will address this to you, and hope thereby, to interest you somewhat in the duties & work before you, at the same time I must confess that I have some pride in the matter, and hope to see you, acquit yourselves like men, as you now are getting old enough to lay aside many of your childish ways & plays. Mother too, at this time, very much needs your help. And instead of being a care & anxiety to her, could in many ways very much lighten the trials she will be called on to exercise.

There will be wood to cut, and it should be all carried into the house, for you must not allow Mother to do anything of this kind. I know very well, that I never allowed my mother to do so, and I was raised on a farm, and now too you are really doing it for yourselves, and much depends on the start you make.

You must remember that the people of W. Union will judge of you boys, very much in the light you treat & respect your mother. Should they see you careless of her comfort, and wishes, will at once make an unfavorable opinion of you, and this certainly would be a bad start to make among strangers. And the business men, in seeking for boys to fill *positions* of *trust* and *honor*, would hardly select those who were not respectful to their parents. On the other hand, if they see you careful of her interests & wishes, this of itself would be the best guarantee that you would be attentive & trustworthy in any place you might be needed. I do not write this, for the sake of writing, but as your father, one who holds a deeper interest in you, than any one else can, one who very much desires that you make a good beginning. And if you could only realize the importance of this step, the great influence it will exert on your manhood in after life I think you would make every exertion, to establish a good record.

The 193 Reg passed here last evening. They were here some hours, Asst Surg called on me, asking advice etc, saying also that I had been promoted to Surg of the same, very much desiring any immediate presence with them. His name is J. P. Waste, the other Asst Ambrose Brown, was not along. Waste is a fine looking man, 28 years old. Both are young in med experience, and I shall for a time have a big burden upon me, till they get broke in a little. I feel many misgivings in leaving the 91st, for they have made a record in which I shall always take a great pride.

Should I get my commission within a day or two, will not be here but a few days longer, only till I can get my papers fixed up. You can still direct letters to Cumberland, and if I leave will have them forwarded on to me.

Have written to Dr. Coleman, to have him obtain teams of transportation from Manchester. Have also had the wharf master there, apprised of the part he is to act, think mother will be able to get a man after she gets down, to assist her until she gets straightened up. This would save much expense, for his passage both ways would be to pay, and the board too all the time. Some delay might occur there, but if she had no one under wages, it would not matter so much.

Besides I have written to Br Doug, and if he can possibly leave, will go down with her. Mrs Coates or Mrs Coleman will tell her, who to employ after she gets there, and if he does not suit, she can dispose of him, and get some one else.

I have not heard from Coleman, but have no doubt he will take pleasure in giving her the necessary assistance. So that if you get all things ready to ship, in order to reach Manchester on Friday morning, the last day of March, this will give two days to get the goods out. Br Will or Doug can make all the necessary arrangements for shipping etc. Every box and every piece of furniture should have a mark like this, Wm S Newton West Union Ohio. So that if anything should be left aboard of the boat, it could be left on the upward trip.

Now boys, don't read this letter and then think no more of it, for then I should have lost the time in writing it. But consider, I as your father have endeavored to give that counsel which will be for your own good & happiness. In this way we all may be made happy. Give my love to all the friends, and write to me often, especially when you get to your new home. I shall wish to know all about it, not having seen it at all. Your Father.

Wm. S. Newton

160

Cumberland Md March 19th/65

My Dear Wife

This is Sabbath, but although I am pressed with business, and lots of company, the 91st having arrived at this place last evening, hungry & without rations, so I took in Major Neal, Adjutant Findley, Wellons & Pixley, and on this account have not so good an opportunity to write etc.

But Col Turley expects to start home and will take this and leave it at wharf. He is very gay and just returned from Washington, and seems very much gratified at my promotion. My commission came yesterday and I was mustered in to the 193rd Reg as its Surgeon for the term of one year. Have not yet received my order for transfer of Gov Property, and now, am not so particular, as I have not yet received the remittance to pay for farm.

But I did receive an answer from Dr. Coleman, very satisfactory, in reference to moving you out to W. Union, and I shall have cause to remember his kindness. He told me he had written to you, that teams would be in reins on 31st of March, and that you were to stop at his house. Now be ready to make the connections, so that you will not give unnecessary delay or trouble, nor make too long a stay at the Drs.

I may leave here in three or four days to join the 193rd, which was ordered to report at Harpers Ferry. Shall try to get my business all done up, and when I get my deed will forward it to you at W. Union, and you must take it to the Recorder of the County and leave it with him for record, paying for the recording in advance. I wrote a day or two ago, to the boys, but presume you will get this first, will notify you by letter as soon as I leave here, and how to direct your letters, My love to all

Your Husband
Wm. S Newton

161

Cumberland Md
March 24th 1865

My Dear Wife

Yours of 15th came to hand yesterday and I was glad to know you were at work, making ready for your new home, hope all will be arranged satisfactory.

I am getting almost out of patience waiting for the order relieving me from my present duty. I wish very much now to join my new Reg and feel that they need me very much as their Asst is very young in practice & experience. I have applied three times now for a relief of duty, and cannot help their action on the matter.

The Ajut Genl of the Dept promised to attend to it immediately, but I have all day waited for the necessary paper, but it has not come.

Have also anxiously waited for the 1200. to pay Col Coates, this too has not come, perhaps "all things work together for good," and I will not complain.

Have now no uneasiness on the score of paying for the farm, as the present increased pay will help me out very much.

Dr. Dickinson[16] took my Muster Out Roll, with his own, and went to Wheeling, was paid on it for two months & 17 days. So I begin in the new Reg on Maj's pay, as they will not give us transportation to our commands, and I have a new coat to purchase, which will cost 60$, another horse to buy to supply the place of Old Tom, will not have too much to start in my new command, as they will not probably pay a new Reg for 6 or 8 months. I shall need all I have. Hope you will make out, however, if you do not, let me know. In this case you might dispose of your bonds. If you keep them by you, you had better take the number of each, in case they were lost or stolen, that you could advertise them, and prevent their doing anyone any good, and in this case could have them duplicated.

Will direct this to West Union, in care of Dr. Coleman. Write often. Your Husband

Wm. S. Newton
Surg 193.

162

Camp Stevenson near
Winchester Va. April 24th 1865

My Dear Wife

Have not received a letter from you since the 9th, yet can imagine how many are the cares & anxieties which beset you in the fixing up to stay even.

After you have been there awhile, hope you will like things better. If I could only be there, if only for a few days, think I would make arrangements which would make the place tolerable, and if you can make out to stay, just let things be till I come. The fences should be kept up, especially the outside one, and if the boys cannot do it, get some man for a day, or week, as long as it takes to go around it. Let the boys go with him, & learn what is to be done, in this way the[y] will soon learn how, and what, is necessary to be done, in order to keep things in order.

I do hope they will take some pride in this work, and as the grass gets well up, they will be able to keep more stock. Would prefer to keep cows, as the horses crop the grass so closely, will injure the crop more than cows. Would not especially like to pasture work horses, for they go in hungry at night, and do all their feeding while the dew is on, & the grass wet. Tell Ned I want to see what good potatoes he can raise, how much of everything can be grown in the garden, to get some early tomatoe plants, if a good kind is not coming up spontaneously. Have manure put in each hole, then good soft earth over it, in this way he will have fine large ones.

I can hardly wait for the time, as the war to us all seems over, for the muster out of the reg. They may conclude to keep the new, & let the old Regs go out, various are the opinions about it, and were it not for the expectation of better pay, than formerly, I should even now try to get home.

Col. Powell came to us today, he is just from Shermans Army, is a splendid looking man, and talks right, for the present occupies my tent, am glad to have him. Lt. Col. & Maj occupy another. Drs Waste & Brown another, Q Master[17] & Adjt[18] the other. This makes up the Head Qts, and I have the honor to be with the ranking officer. Col. P. lives in the town of Delaware, is well acquainted with Brother O, has just left them & says they are all well. I have made fifty dollars speculating in horses, but am obliged to credit one of my Assts & another Surg to the amount of 100$, This will be all right. Can now get an advance of 50$ more on one of the horses I now own, but have not decided to sell, as I desire very much to have them both for the farm, and am keeping this in view all the while.

Have not had one word from Harmar or Gallipolis, since joining this Reg. In fact, yours of 9th is the only one, beside Official letters.

Tell the boys to write, if you do not get the time. In fact, I am very hungry for letters, and will try to open a correspondence with some other parties if my old ones do not do better.

Tell Miss Kate I think she will be very fine when she gets to be a country girl.

Tell Mott I think he had better go into the chicken business. Buy a doz young hens, last springs chickens, one cock, two years old, then see they have a good place to roost, a secure place to lay their eggs, to keep count how many they produce, and I will pay him the market price for all that are consumed at home. After the laying season is pretty well over to set some five or six of them on good eggs, which have not been handled too much, and if he selects good places, they will hatch well & if he takes good care of them, and raises them, they will bring him a good round sum.

If I can only get home for a few days, will take the first opportunity. Much love to all, and my regards Dr. & Mrs. Coleman.

> Your Husband
> Wm. S. Newton

163

> Camp Stevenson Near
> Winchester Va May 4th 1865

My Dear Wife

Your last was dated April 15th and then you were not very well. I had written twice before receiving it and on the 24th when it came. I had put in an application for leave of absence, and have been waiting for a letter from you, and my leave till I am tired, neither has come to hand. So will write again, am very anxious to get sight of the farm, and have been very anxious, lest you were really sick, did not like the symptoms of your case, was afraid fever would be the result.

The old command to which I was attached started up the Valley this morning, report says they are going to Staunton. The war by all is now considered over, and the President gives opportunity for resignations, but few officers are willing to offer while the prospect for being mustered out, with the three months extra pay to those who hold out to the end, is in prospect of being lost. I feel for one, if the three months extra pay is given to anyone, I am entitled to it, having served faithfully and done the work of Surgeon all the while, now that surgeons pay is in prospect, think I will try to obtain it at least for a time.

My Leave is only for twenty days, but if they will grant it, can see how you are fixed, and make any changes necessary to be made. From Sister Mary & letter, would infer that Br John is attracted, as in days gone by, and only waits for the troubling of the waters, to step in.

We had yesterday, another grand review of our Div by Genl Torbert.[19] This is the order of things now, that the fighting is over, and I do not care, for if they have no fighting, it is well enough to put on style.

I do not know what I should do, were it not I had fixed up, with new coat, etc, for they call on me to appear on each occasion, and as I have the outfit, must comply. Many of the Surgeons, Asst. Surgs are yet without horses, and they do not look well on inspection, or review, dismounted.

Will probably let Col. Powell have one of my horses. Lt. Col. Jewett left a day or two since for New York. Report says he is to be married to some southern girl whom he rescued from negroes on a Mississippi Plantation, while with Sherman's army in the Southwest, about a year ago.

All the Field & Staff of my Reg are young men, at least unmarried, so you see I am all alone in this respect.

Should think the boys might write often, Mott has not written at all.

Think they would have something interesting to write about now that they are on the farm. Not a word from Gallipolis.

My love to all

> Your Husband
> Wm. S. Newton

164

> Gallipolis May 22nd/65
> Monday Morning

Dear Wife

I landed here last eve, just at supper time found all the folks as well as usual

Br. Will proposes to go to the city on the 4th of June & on the morning of the 6th. Will leave you two bedstands on the upward trip of Bostonia, which will be Wednesday morning of the week after next. I think Mr. Prather[20] can take them out on the top of his bus, better than any other way. So by speaking to him on Wednesday, he bring them out on Thursday.

Will tell Will to send you a check for 50$ about the 10th of June, that you may be able to meet any expense that may occur. Report says that Em will eventually marry Mr. Jeffreys [Jeffers]. I don't know what to think about it, not having seen him, and he is so very aged.[21] Will take the Golden Era for Marietta in the morning. I told the Editor of the Scion[22] to send you the paper for one year, so I suppose you will get the next number.

Ask Kate if I shall bring the pantaloons when I come, or is she going to stay in the house more, and wear her bonnet when she goes out. Be sure to show Jennie the chickens.

Much love to all.

> Your Husband
> Wm. S. Newton

165

Camp Stevenson
June 4th 1865

My Dear Wife

Yours of 28th and postmarked 30th came last eve only 4 days, now that would do pretty well. Yet I don't see why you had not received my letter from Gallipolis, in which I told you of the anticipated wedding of Em & a Mr. Jeffreys. I saw the man, and did not think he was so very old.

Yet I could not really give her the advice she craved, for my acquaintance was none, and was unable to learn anything concerning this man from others.

Will opposes the thing, whether from selfish motives I cannot tell, but if he was confident Em would leave home for good, I think would be reconciled to the match, as affording him a better opportunity to appropriate the remainder of the homestead property to his own private use.

I may judge wrong, but think I can see the matter in its true light.

The 91st started for Cumberland on the 2nd. All suppose that this is only a preliminary to a final muster out. Our boys are very much exercised in relation to going home. I do believe we have some who would forfeit all bounty & pay to be discharged. They are really homesick. We used to think men were cowardly when they were so anxious to get home, but now think the fighting is supposed to be over, we must assign some other reason.

Have been attending a very sick babe, just outside our camp. I think the symptoms are now favorable, and the mother last evening in the gratitude of her heart presented me with a basket of cherries, and we are anticipating quite a dessert for dinner. Should you not think I would like your experience in the preparation of this repast, how different are our dishes from home. The cake you gave me was equally divided between the two Cols & two Majors. All praised it, whether from a compliment to you or me, is not yet solved in my mind.

Two Brigadiers were here & took dinner with us yesterday. They stayed all afternoon and we had a very gay time.

We are all invited to visit them this week at Summit Point and if we go, there will be *some noise.*

I wrote you in reference to the mowing the briars in the two fields, and not having it plowed as we had first intended, Mr. Ricker saying the former the best plan. We will find out, if he mows one field in June, & the other in August. Tell him to keep mowing them as often as they show themselves. Am also anxious to have him secure the wood and have it placed in a good rank in the back yard. He can drive up close to the fence, and have it ranked close to the fence, in this way it will be near the wood house, and easy of sawing. Tell the boys to keep up a reputation for work. Mr. Ricker says, "his Ned does a man's work on the farm every day." My love [to] all.

Your Husband

Wm. S. Newton

166

Camp Stevenson near
Winchester Va June 8th 1865

My Dear Wife

Yours of the 1st came last eve, pretty soon, as it was posted on the 2nd and arrived on the 7th. Perhaps they are learning the way, I think it is time.

Were it not for the loaves & fishes, I would be very discontented here, but I am willing to stay that I may be the better able to improve my farm when I get home.

The business here is dull, no excitement in the way of battles, & very little in the way of movements.

There is more interest in whom shall be mustered out or who will command this or that Brigade, than in any other way. There is plenty of Secesh women within the picket line, and they are just as rebellious as ever, and spit out their venom on every occasion.

Our officers visit them almost every night & day, play Seven up, Euchre,[23] etc, and many are the sparring & thrusts given about the North & South.

Although they fight, there seems to be a generous good feeling with all the quarreling. I am not sure, but too great an intimacy exists in some cases, from the frequent absences at unreasonable hours. I received another basket of cherries and another invitation to visit the wife & mother of the sick child spoken of in my last letter. The child is now getting better, and every prospect of recovery.

It seems almost certain if people are sick, they will call on me for help, whether Rebel or Union, all right.

Tell the boys I hope they have more gallantry than to allow Sophy to do their work in the garden.

Have they no pride about them, while Mr. Ricker is able to boast of his Neddie doing a mans work? What would I be able to say of them now, if I should meet with him again? I was quite proud to tell him, of their work while I was at home, but from your letter, would not like to report upon the subject now.

If they ever expect to be anything, they must begin to manifest it pretty soon, they are getting to be young men, and if they have any pride, they will certainly take some responsibility, and do something while I am gone. I hope you will present this matter to them, & let them see how it will look to the neighbors, and others, who know what is expected of them, now that I am away.

Should think they would be afraid the girls in town would find out how worthless they are at home, when they can go to town & spend so much time.

They are certainly forming habits for life and must consider whether they will be something or nothing, whether they will be men of business, or town loafers.

Whether students striving to store their minds with knowledge, or will they be street walkers, the terror of all good people.

Will they be an honor to their parents, or a constant solicitude lest something will go wrong. Hope they will ponder these things, and so acquit themselves that I may be able to get them situations of trust & confidence. Your Husband.

Wm. S. Newton

Have chewed no tobacco for the last ten days

167

Camp near the Opequan
July 2nd 1865

My Dear Wife

Your letter of 26th came this morning, the only one since June 11th, and I suppose ere this Em has passed off the stage, and become a staid old matron some 8 or 10 years, your senior.

Am glad to learn that the little ones show some symptoms of convalescence with their whooping cough, before this month has passed, they will have recovered.

Col. Powell received notice of his appointment as Brig Genl and you may suppose there was some rejoicing, while with me it was very different, for this takes him permanently from our Reg, and for this I am very sorry.

Am truly pleased that you are now enjoying the fruits of my toil while at home, and I would like very much to be there, to help you. Tell the boys they must plant a hill of sweet corn, for every one of potatoes they now dig, in this way, if they will give it their attention, they can have nice new corn until frost comes. Please have them attend to it. In that case I may get home to enjoy some of it with you.

We have plenty of Daw Berries[24] here. Our cook gathered more than a gallon yesterday for our mess. We will have a chicken, peas, berries, etc for dinner today. We had the promise of new potatoes, but the rain prevented the digging. Brig. Genl. Powell takes dinner with us, & says he likes the old mess best.

You did not tell me how the potatoes yielded, I am anxious to know how the boys have cared for them. If you need money, send to Will for it, for no knowing when we will be paid, our muster rolls have been forwarded, and we hope it will not be long, ere the Paymaster will return with them.

How do the melon vines look, do they promise any fruit? Should think the boys & Sophy could secure berries enough for you, if they do not you had best purchase.

I have now three young mocking birds shut up in a box, at the rear of my tent, and it is really amusing to watch the old ones feed them. We have now had them about a week and they have given us no trouble as the old birds keep them well supplied with grasshoppers, crickets & worms. They will feed them while we sit not ten feet off. In one company, they have a whole nest of young hawks petted, they are quite tame, go out & come in at will. Thus you see we have some amusements, very different from last summer. The *Jonny Rebs* were all the pets we then had time to attend, no time for bird taming then. Lt. Col. Jewett says he is going to have a fine 4th, but I am yet at a loss to know how, for we are all shut up in the picket line, and cannot get out without a pass, a thing, I feel, is too degrading to ask often.

Hope you will all enjoy it, as it still marks the anniversary of our independence as a nation. How many poor fellows now sleep underground, who four years since were willing to offer up their lives to maintain this noted day. This is a sad thought, yet how dearly we must treasure the gift they have left us.

Counsel the boys to good deeds & actions, tell them to emulate virtues not vices, then their father will be proud of them. Give my love to all.

> Your Husband
> Wm. S. Newton

Direct to Stevenson Depot near Winchester, and then there can be no mistake. Also send me a few postage stamps, cannot get them here.

168

> Camp on the Opequan near
> Stevenson Depot July 9th 1865

My Dear Wife

The prospect for getting home is not now so flattering as when I last wrote, as I see from the papers that many of the veteran Regs have been ordered out of the service, every one of these makes our stay more certain. Maj. Murrin[25] came back yesterday, he met Cadot, Coates & Warwick in

Cincinnati, and from the account he gave, you I am certain, would not be proud, if your husband would do, as they done, while in the city, & so soon to meet their families at home.

The 4th was rather lively, among the soldiers in the Shenandoah Valley. 1/4 of a pint of whiskey was ordered for each enlisted man, this with the little they were able to procure of the sutlers, made them quite merry, and they had a few Irish weddings[26] in the Indiana Brigades, one or two in our own Reg, as a matter of course these were put in the guardhouse, and were not released until next day. Some of our Staff Surgeons were demoralized, lost their position in the regiments, when marched out to hear the Declaration of Inde[pendence] read, Old Warfield[27] our Brig Surgeon, captured Dr. Gentry the Brig. Surg of the Indiana Brigade.[28] The latter did not know his position until an orderly was sent after him by his Brig Commander, all this for Independence Day.

Some three or 4 men were sun struck during the day, two died, the weather was very warm. If you would hear all the stories, Lt. Col. Jewett tells on me, you would not be flattered, but as he tells it, to those who know me, am not much disturbed about it. I told him the other day, would not like to have you hear it. But he affirmed, he would write to *Frances Ann* and tell her all about it, would make a dog laugh to hear his talk sometimes.

Brig Genl Powell is back again. Col Kimberly[29] has returned, this relieved Powell from the command of Brig, so he reports to the Reg to await orders. I am very glad of this, for we like to have him around.

I received yours of 2nd on the 7th, also one from Brother S. He wrote a very long letter, gave me the full history of things, among the rest Capt Woodruff[30] had been there, and is to return soon I suppose to claim Mollie, hope she may have better health than Almira did, and enjoy life more.

Br S. does not get along very well with his new teeth, the old snags on the lower jaw don't fit the new, but knock out of place while eating. He advises me to have a set, while the under teeth are good. How would you like to have a set? It seems a very small job when you can have it done in a day, and for 25$. If I thought I could learn to use them, I would try, for my upper teeth are very bad, and trouble me very much about eating.

Have not chewed any tobacco since the 1st of June, have not smoked since the 4th. I do not say I have quit, but left it off for a while. Think Mr. Eagle[31] might have saved the little hay there. I am not pleased with that kind of help, and hope ere long to be able to get better. I think some of the returned soldiers would be glad to work a day now & then. Am sorry your frail crop is not promising. Hope you will try to preserve all you can for winter use.

Tell Ned I really feel indignant that he should shirk the little work he has on to Mott, a younger brother. He should be more manly and show a better feeling. I hope I shall not hear of it again. Why don't the boys write?

Your Husband
Wm. S. Newton

169

Hed Qts 193rd O.V.I. near
Stevenson Depot July 20th 1865

My Dear Wife

Yours of 13th came last eve and I was truly grateful, to learn my instruments were found. I did not get your letter of 16th and of course know nothing of the circumstances. I was under the impression you will recollect, that they had been put away somewhere, for more security, and when you did not find them, I felt almost sure they were lost.

I don't know, but almost venture to say, that in the interruption in Em's case, is for the best, at least I hope so, although I feel that I have no right to advise, the thing will I trust work out for good. As a matter of course you will send to Will for money, when you need it. I feel as if my expenses were pretty heavy here, more than ever before, do the best I can. My mess mates are all in my debt, and not able to pay. I am most out, and will be wholly if the Paymaster does not soon come. If they will only pay me the amount due, and my mess mates ditto, I will be all right, and send you enough to supply all the wants of the farm. You can get enough to advance money on the wool as fast as it is delivered, be sure to have done, lest the price still advances. If Mr. Eagle had done as I advised, he would have secured it at 90 cts. I do not see how he would have done, to put in the wheat, contemplated if he cannot secure one acre of grass.

I think the boys might have hauled it before this, they do not seem to feel any responsibility. I don't know how they expect to get on in the world. I think if Ned Ricker had been there, he would have had it in the barn long ago. It would seem to one, there had been rain enough, to make the hay almost worthless, perhaps not. I want the briars cut during the month of August, in all the fields. Mott & Ned can do this very well, at least work at it, they will find some in almost every lot.

Mr Eagle get hands enough he can make short work of it, if they have begun to grow where they were cut before, let them be cut again.

Urge the matter upon him if necessary, for I do not want to come there, after August, and find a living briar. *No Postage Stamps.*

My love to the little ones.

Your Husband
Wm. S. Newton

Epilogue

On August 9, 1865, William S. Newton mustered out as surgeon of the 193rd Ohio Volunteer Infantry, after three years and four months of service in the Union army. His previous correspondence indicated that he was going to move to West Union, Ohio, to become a farmer, but all postwar information about Newton and his family revolves around Gallipolis. Newton's 1865 letters indicated that Ned and Mott were working on the farm, and that his wife and other children had moved to West Union. Their residence in West Union, however, was short lived. The clearest evidence that the Newton family abandoned the idyllic farm life in West Union came in October 1865, when he placed an advertisement in the *Gallipolis Journal*. The announcement stated that Dr. Newton offered his medical services to the people of Gallia County and listed his residence and office in downtown Gallipolis near Third Street and the Baptist Church.[1]

Like many Civil War veterans, William S. Newton reconnected with members of his former regiment. In early 1867 a Grand Army of the Republic post formed in Gallipolis. Lemuel Z. Cadot was the post commander, Samuel F. Neal was the senior vice commander, and Newton was listed as the post surgeon. The next year, Newton was part of the first known gathering of members of the 91st Ohio Volunteer Infantry. The reunion took place in Portsmouth, Ohio, on April 8, 1868. Benjamin Coates, who had opened a medical practice in Portsmouth, invited Rutherford B. Hayes, then a second-term US congressman, to attend the festivities. Hayes declined the invitation due to a prior engagement, but in his letter to Coates he applauded the work of the 91st in turning the tide of battle for the Union army in the Shenandoah Valley during the summer of 1864. Hayes closed the letter saying: "If toasts should be in order, permit me to give, 'The Old Kanawha Division.'" The April reunion featured toasts, songs, and speeches from surviving members of the 91st. John Turley presided over the event, and Newton was listed as an attendee. E. E. Ewing, a lieutenant from Company A and K, read an epic poem titled "The Story of the Ninety-First." The poem was published the following year to mark the event. The reunion closed with all in attendance singing "John Brown's Body" and the announcement that the 1869 reunion would be held in Ironton the following April.[2]

Newton put down roots in Gallipolis after the war. He was an active member and trustee of the First Presbyterian Church, treasurer of the Gallia Medical Society, and later a city councilman. An 1871 directory of Ohio River towns listed Newton as a physician and insurance agent with an office on the corner of Third and State streets in Gallipolis.[3] His most significant role was as postmaster of Gallipolis. He was appointed postmaster on March 28, 1867. Newspaper articles confirm that Newton employed his sons Ned and Mott as postal assistants. In fact, Newton advertised that he was available to see patients in his office at the post office.[4]

Newton's position as postmaster for Gallipolis was marked with some controversy. In early December 1868, Ned was arrested and charged with abstracting a $100 bill from a package. A trial took place in Cincinnati before Judge Franklin Halliday, a United States commissioner for the US Circuit Court, on December 7–8. Many witnesses testified to recount the history of the letter and its missing contents. By noon on December 8, the government moved to dismiss the case, and the inquiry seemed to be quashed. Just after the trial ended, Thomas P. Shallcross, superintendent of mails and a postal investigator, filed a new affidavit charging that Ned Newton, Mott Newton, and William S. Newton had conspired to steal valuables from the mail in the Gallipolis post office during a lengthy period of May 1–November 17, 1868. As a result of the new inquiry, Judge Halliday scheduled a hearing for January 12, 1869, and set bond for each of the Newtons at $1,500.[5]

The new trial investigating embezzlement charges against the Newtons occurred in March 1869 and featured a variety of witnesses who claimed to have lost money, jewelry, and other valuables through the mail. Several witnesses from Gallipolis claimed that Ned Newton bragged about being able to detect money inside letters and that he often bought expensive presents for girls. After three days of testimony, the trial was held over until the April term of the US Court. On April 28, US district attorney Warren M. Bateman filed an indictment with nine counts of embezzlement against Ned Newton and his father William S. Newton (Mott Newton was not included, most likely because he was seventeen years old). Each charge related to a specific letter, item, or amount of money that had allegedly gone missing from the mail going through the Gallia post office. The defendants were arrested on May 6 and appeared before a judge. They plead not guilty and were released on a bond of $3,000 each.[6]

The charges were serious, and newspaper accounts of the legal proceedings indicated that there was substantial evidence against the Newtons, but government attorneys were slow to pursue the matter. In July the court re-scheduled the trial until October. Then, on October 5, the court issued the notice of *nolle prosequi* for William S. Newton, which removed him from the case entirely. The court scheduled the case against Ned Newton for the February 1870 term. In late January 1870, however, government attorneys abandoned the case against Ned Newton with the notice of *nolle prosequi*.[7]

There was no further mention of the charges against either Newton. The reappointment of William S. Newton as postmaster of Gallipolis on March 30, 1871, indicated that he was fully exonerated and had regained his stature in the community. Newton kept that position until March 10, 1875. Thereafter, he focused on his medical practice in Gallipolis, which was located next to the post office. In the years that followed, Newton served as a member of the board of examiners for the Pension Bureau and was an examining surgeon for the government.[8]

In late May 1880, Newton applied for an invalid pension. He cited that his capture and brief imprisonment after the Battle of Cloyd's Mountain in 1864 led to his poor health. The documentation explained that, while at Libby Prison, the "malarious atmosphere," the "insufficient covering," and the "insufficient and unwholesome food" resulted in dysentery, piles, and a torpid liver. After release, Dr. N. F. Graham of the 12th Ohio Volunteer Infantry, who was also captured at Cloyd's Mountain, performed the amputation surgery on General Albert G. Jenkins, and was detained at Libby Prison alongside Newton, tended to his fellow prisoner of war. Newton explained that he had never recovered from the illness, which had impaired his health, limited his ability to practice medicine, and rendered his life miserable. The Pension Bureau approved the claim. In February 1882 Newton renewed his invalid pension claim, which was quickly approved by the Pension Bureau.[9]

In mid-November 1882 Newton fell ill from stomach pains. In addition to liver damage, he suffered from ulcers and other internal ailments caused by his wartime service. Newton died on Saturday, November 18, 1882, just a few months shy of his sixtieth birthday. An autopsy revealed that he died from an intestinal hemorrhage caused by liver disease and stomach ulcers. He was buried in the Pine Street Cemetery in Gallipolis. Frances Ann Hayward Newton, his wife and Civil War correspondent, received a widow's pension beginning in March 1883. She died on February 9, 1896, and was buried beside her husband in Pine Street Cemetery.[10]

Newton's sometimes troubled son Ned followed in his father's footsteps and became a doctor. Newton graduated from the Medical College of Ohio in 1873 and practiced medicine in Madison, Indiana, also a river town. He married Melissa G. Wilson in October 1874. In 1878 he moved to Lincoln,

Kansas, and continued his medical practice. An advertisement in the *Lincoln Sentinel* announced: "E. S. Newton, M.D. (Physician & Surgeon.) Cancer, Piles and Catarrh cured. Special attention to Surgery of diseases of women." Newton found success as a rural doctor, and there were several newspaper articles praising his medical service to the community. He was married two more times: in 1887 to Annie Robertson and then in 1894 to Lettie Richardson.[11]

As in his young adulthood, legal trouble continued for Ned. According to the *Lincoln Beacon*, in March 1886 the sheriff in Lincoln, Kansas, captured "a nest of gamblers in Dr. E. S. Newton's office in the Bryant Block. Dr. Newton among the rest." Newton and the others were fined and quickly released. Then, in November 1888, Ned Newton was arrested for stealing an express package of money sent through the Pacific Express Company. He was charged with grand larceny and briefly put in jail. On February 14, 1889, Valentine's Day, a grand jury issued an indictment of grand larceny against Newton. The trial occurred two weeks later. Newton pled guilty, and the court sentenced him to one year at the Kansas State Penitentiary in Lansing. After serving his prison time, Newton returned to his medical practice in Lincoln and earned back the trust of the community. An 1899 article in the *Lincoln Republican* described Newton as a "prominent and popular figure" who contributed to the "progress and well doing of our city." Following a brief illness, Edward S. Newton died in July 1901 at age fifty-one.[12]

William S. Newton's Civil War letters to his wife remained in the family or in private hands for decades. The letters were microfilmed and accessible at the Ohio Historical Society, but only a handful of scholars made use of them. The acquisition of the original letters at auction by Virginia Tech Special Collections and University Archives in 2017 made Newton's words much more discoverable and accessible. This book is designed to bring his words to even larger audiences who do not often visit archives or conduct online research using unedited primary sources. Dr. William S. Newton deserves the final words of this book. A wish from his November 22, 1864, letter to his wife, written just two days before a Thanksgiving dinner that he could not spend with her, is the most appropriate concluding remark: "Now I wish we were all to go home to remain there, no more war, but peace, happiness & plenty."[13]

Appendix
Frequently Appearing People and Places

Family

Wife and Children

Frances Ann Hayward Newton (January 14, 1827–February 9, 1896), originally from Gallipolis the daughter of Solomon Hayward and Catharine Tillaye Hayward. Her father was from Connecticut or Vermont and moved to Gallipolis in 1807. He served as a volunteer in the War of 1812. Newton's letters refer to her parents as "Father H." and "Mother H." Frances married William S. Newton on October 28, 1934, and had seven children. Nearly all of letters in the William S. Newton Civil War collection are written to Frances. During his absence, she was charged with managing a range of activities—a newborn child, an unruly teenager, visiting family, settling medical accounts, buying and selling property, and organizing a move to a new home and farm in West Union, Adams County, Ohio. She lived most of her life in Gallipolis. Her husband died in November 1882, and in March 1883 she received a widow's pension. In the early 1890s, she moved in with her daughter Kate, who lived in Columbus. Frances Ann died on February 9, 1896, at the age of sixty-nine and was buried beside her husband in Pine Street Cemetery in Gallipolis.[1]

Oren Hayward (1846–1858), first child of Frances and William S. Newton. On June 26, 1858, twelve-year-old Oren Newton drowned in the Ohio River. In a February 1, 1863[4], letter to Francis, William S. Newton referred to Oren and spoke highly of his character.[2]

Lewis Garland (May–October 1848), second child of Frances and William S. Newton. He is not mentioned directly in the Newton Civil War correspondence.[3]

Edward (Ned) Seymore (April 28, 1850–July 21, 1901), third child of Frances and William S. Newton. Ned is a central character in the Newton correspondence and is the recipient of several letters from his father. Like many teenagers, Ned showed signs of rebellion, disrespect for his parents, and a lack of focus for his life. His father made numerous direct pleas for Ned to advance his life through hard work, respect for elders, getting practical education and skills, and most importantly demonstrating good penmanship. Newton believed that proper penmanship was a way to advance in business or in the military. During the Civil War period, Ned was too young to serve, but it is clear that, had he been only two to three years older, the military would have been an obvious choice for the unfocused youth. Ned was encouraged to visit his father in camp, perhaps as a way to talk through their differences. In early May 1863, Ned arrived in camp and spent most of his time fishing and exploring the woods. He returned to Ironton in August. His father continued to emphasize the importance of respectful behavior and preparing for farm life in West Union, Ohio. Ned's postwar life was perhaps the most colorful of all of the Newton children. The epilogue provides more details about Ned's adventures life after his father returned from the military. In short, he faced embezzlement charges twice (the second time he was convicted), became a doctor, and eventually settled in Lincoln, Kansas. He died on July 21, 1901, at the age of fifty-one.[4]

Valentine Mott (September 26, 1852–November 18, 1870), fourth child of Frances and William S. Newton. Mott is featured often in the Newton correspondence. Early in the war, his father attempted to collect Confederate "souvenirs" for him and brother Ned. After a successful visit from older brother Ned to the front lines, William S. Newton encouraged Mott to visit him in camp, which he did from late November through late December 1863. Later correspondence from his father encourages Mott to be industrious, learn to conduct business, be a good role model for younger sister Kate, and finally to prepare to help with a family farm in West Union, Ohio. After the Civil War, Mott joined his older brother Ned to assist with the mail at the Gallipolis Post Office under the guidance of their father who was postmaster. He was included in the original charges from 1868 that the Newton family had embezzled valuable letters from the Gallipolis Post Office. He was dropped from later inquiries, most likely because he was still a minor. In the fall of 1870, he matriculated as a freshman at Marietta College. That semester, he contracted pneumonia, and on November 18, 1870, he died at the home of his uncle Stephen Newton in Marietta.[5]

Fanny Lillian (1857–1858), fifth child of Frances and William S. Newton. She is not mentioned in the Newton Civil War correspondence.[6]

Kate May (May 29, 1860–December 4, 1957), sixth child of Frances and William S. Newton. The Newton Civil War correspondence makes numerous references to Kate. Her father was greatly concerned with her upbringing and the potential influences from her brothers Mott and especially Ned. On December 23, 1880, she married John William Dages, whose family owned a successful boot and shoe store in Gallipolis. They moved to Columbus, where he was the head of the Dages, Andrews & Company, a shoe manufacturer. She died on December 4, 1957, at the age of ninety-seven.[7]

John Beverly or John William (November 9, 1863–May 14, 1940), seventh child of Frances and William S. Newton. He was born while William S. Newton was serving in the 91st Ohio Volunteer Infantry. The Newton letters discuss picking his name, and his parents decided upon John Beverly in honor of William's brother John Newton and the middle name Beverly in honor of his medical colleague Dr. John Beverly Warwick. John B. Newton appeared in the 1870 census as a six-year-old student "at school," but in the 1880 census the sixteen-year-old student is listed as John W. Newton. It is unclear why his middle name changed from Beverly to William during this period. In 1886 he married Maggie Jacobs from Maytown, Pennsylvania, and they had four children. He first worked as a druggist in Gallipolis and by the late 1890s had settled in Philadelphia and was working as a chemical and dye salesman. He retired in the 1930s and moved to Maytown, Pennsylvania. He died of a coronary thrombosis on May 14, 1940, at the age of seventy-six.[8]

Extended Family Mentioned in Correspondence

William Greenleaf Fuller (1827–1903) was born in Massachusetts. In 1846 he served as a fireman on the US steamer USS *Mississippi* and became responsible for the ship's stores. Fuller participated in several battles during the Mexican War. Upon his return in 1847, he focused on telegraphy. As an employee of the New Orleans and Ohio Telegraph Company, Fuller worked on expanding telegraph lines from Pittsburgh to New Orleans. In 1850 he married Lucy Lucretia Newton, the younger sister of William S. Newton. They had three children and lived in Marietta. In 1854 he was appointed the superintendent of the telegraph line between Marietta and Cincinnati. In May 1861 he was appointed to manage the government telegraphs on the branch of the Baltimore and Ohio Railroad in West Virginia. He was appointed assistant quartermaster at the rank of captain on October 27, 1863. Fuller played a vital role in keeping the Union telegraph lines open. His service extended to Kentucky, Tennessee, Mississippi, Alabama, and Texas. Fuller was

Newton's brother-in-law and a few of the references to Will or even Brother Will may refer to him. The majority of Newton's references to Will or Brother Will, however, would refer to another brother-in-law, William C. Hayward. This assumption is based on the reality that William C. Hayward did not serve in the military and was in Gallipolis throughout the war, while William Greenleaf Fuller managed telegraph lines for the Union across the South and would have been less likely to be in Gallipolis on a regular basis. Fuller mustered out of service on August 25, 1865, and was breveted as a lieutenant colonel. He returned to Gallipolis and helped found Gatewood, Fuller & Company, which built the first furniture factory in Gallipolis. Fuller died in 1903 at the age of seventy-six.[9]

Emily Hayward (1832–1879) was a younger sister of Frances Hayward Newton. She lived in Gallipolis with her parents and was quite close with her sister Frances. She was a regular topic in William S. Newton's letters. He referred to "Em" in over twenty letters and also maintained an active correspondence with her. But, as with other family members who corresponded with William S. Newton, letters to or from Emily have not been located. Early in the war, he invited Em to visit the camp. In May 1865 William S. Newton discussed with his wife the upcoming marriage of Em to Mr. Jeffers, who was thirty years her senior. Em married Mr. Jeffers and they lived in Gallipolis. She died of heart disease in 1879 at the age of forty-seven.[10]

William C. Hayward (1835–1912) was a younger brother of Frances Hayward Newton. He grew up in Gallipolis and in 1853 he went into the undertaking and coffin making business with his father under the name of Hayward & Son. He married Irene Neal in 1860, and they had one son. Hayward did not serve in the military and remained in Gallipolis throughout the war. He was Newton's brother-in-law, and many of the references in the correspondence to Will or Brother Will would likely be him. Newton also had another brother-in-law named William, William Greenleaf Fuller, but Fuller managed telegraph lines for the Union across the South and would have been less likely to be in Gallipolis on a regular basis. Hayward was a member of the First Presbyterian Church and a charter member of the Odd Fellows. In 1867 he served as the treasurer of the Gallia County Agricultural Society. He died in 1912 at the age of seventy-seven.[11]

Charles Humphreys Newton (1842–1926) was the son of Stephen Newton and the half-nephew of William S. Newton. Charles graduated from Marietta College in 1863. After graduating, he served as a first lieutenant in Company D of the 2nd Ohio Heavy Artillery. In a July 5, 1863, letter, William S. Newton refers to Charley and his graduation from Marietta College, but none of the other letters refer to Charles or his military service. After the Civil War, he returned to Washington County, Ohio, and joined his father in the real estate and insurance business. In November 1865 he married Mary Elizabeth Dana, and they had two children. After a brief period living in Iowa City, Iowa, Charles returned to Marietta, Ohio, and worked as a banker. He was treasurer of the Dime Savings Society of Marietta. Charles died in 1926 at the age of eighty-four.[12]

Douglas E. Newton (1838–1917) was William S. Newton's younger brother. In the early 1860s, he and his half-brother John were early investors in the oil industry in Ohio and also part owners of the Marietta Bucket Factory. In 1863 he registered for military service, but there is no indication that he served. The Newton correspondence mentioned brother John in sixteen different letters, including discussion of John's involvement in the oil business, working to deliver supplies on river barges, and his October 1864 marriage Jennie Moredock from Hartford City, West Virginia. They lived in Hartford City and had two children. He was a banker and, according to his obituary "one of the wealthiest coal and salt operators of Pomeroy Bend." He died on February 8, 1917 at the age of seventy-nine.[13]

Elizabeth Fuller Newton (1802–1892) was William S. Newton's mother. She was originally from Massachusetts or Vermont. Her older sister Almira Fuller married Oren Newton (1786–1852) in 1810. They settled in Marietta and had four children (Stephen, John, Elizabeth, and Oren H.). Almira died in 1821. The next year, in 1822, Elizabeth Fuller married Oren Newton. They lived in Marietta and had seven children: William S., Almira, Lucy L., Emily H., Mary Frances, Douglas E., and Alice U. The Newton correspondence made several references to his mother, and throughout the war William corresponded with her. Their letters have not been located. William's father, Oren Newton, died in 1852, so throughout his adulthood he maintained a strong line of communication with his mother. She died in 1892 at the age of ninety.[14]

John Newton (1817–1886) was born in Warren, Washington County, Ohio, an older half-brother of William S. Newton. He held various occupations, including the cutting stone, working on the Muskingum and Ohio Rivers, and working as an agent for the Marietta Bucket Factory. John married four times and had five children. His fourth wife, Jane Means, died from complications due to childbirth in December 1862. In September 1861 he helped organize a company of soldiers in Washington County that served as Company L of the 1st Ohio Volunteer Cavalry. He continued to assist with the recruitment of soldiers, and on September 8, 1862, Company H of the newly organized 7th Ohio Volunteer Cavalry was named the "Newton Guards" in his honor. William S. Newton's correspondence mentioned his brother John over a dozen times. The letters indicate that John managed some of William's business affairs, including the selling of real estate and other potential investments. William and Frances named their newborn son John Beverly after John Newton. A businessman at heart, he and his half-brother Douglas were early investors in the oil industry in Ohio and also part owners of the Marietta Bucket Factory. In 1863 John was one of the incorporators of the First National Bank in Marietta. He served as president of the Agricultural and Manufacturing Society of Washington and Wood Counties multiple terms for the years 1868, 1872–1873, and 1880. He died in 1886 at the age of sixty-nine.[15]

Lucy L. Newton (1828–1910) was a younger sister of William S. Newton. In 1850 she married William Greenleaf Fuller, and they had three children. William S. Newton referred to her in two letters in late 1862. Lucy was a member of the First Presbyterian Church and other organizations in Gallipolis. She died in March 1910 at the age of eighty-one.[16]

Mary Frances Newton (1835–1906) was born in Warren, Washington County, Ohio, a younger sister of William S. Newton. As with other members of his family, William S. Newton corresponded with Mary Frances, but none of those letters have been located. In his letters, Newton referred to her Mary Frank or Sister Mary. In December 1864 she married George H. Lord. He worked for the Baltimore and Ohio Railroad and was the brother of John Newton's fourth wife, Helen Maria Lord. Mary and George lived in Washington County and had one daughter. In April 1904 her husband died, and in August of that year she moved to Welland, Ontario, Canada. She died in July 1906 at the age of seventy-one.[17]

Oren H. Newton (1820–1878) was born in Warren, Washington County, Ohio, an older half-brother of William S. Newton. He graduated from Marietta College in 1845 and entered the ministry. In 1848 he graduated from Lane Theological Seminary and led congregations in New Richmond, Ohio, and later Delaware, Ohio. He was married to Catherine Walter, and they had eight children. In an April 24, 1865, letter, Newton referred to him as Brother O. In 1870 he became chaplain of the state penitentiary in Columbus. He died in 1878 at the age of fifty-eight.[18]

Stephen Newton (1813–1903) was born in Warren, Washington County, Ohio, an older half-brother of William S. Newton. He married twice and had six children. Stephen was a businessman in the Marietta area. William S. Newton mentioned Brother Steve or Brother S. in several letters. He died on September 17, 1903 at the age of ninety.[19]

Friends, Associates, and Military Acquaintances

E. B. Andrews was an 1842 graduate of Marietta College. He enrolled at Princeton Theological Seminary two years later. In 1846 he was ordained by the Berkshire County Congregational Association in Massachusetts. In 1851 Andrews delivered a commencement address at Marietta College, which led to an offer to serve as a professor of geology at Marietta College. He stayed in that position until the outbreak of the Civil War. On July 28, 1861, he was commissioned as major in the 36th Ohio Volunteer Infantry. In September 1862 he was promoted to the rank of colonel. Andrews resigned April 9, 1863. He returned to teach at Marietta College and then, in 1869, accepted a position as an assistant geologist for a statewide geological survey. He died in 1880 at the age of sixty.[20]

Lewis A. Atkinson was commissioned as a first lieutenant in Company K of the 91st Ohio Volunteer Infantry on July 8, 1862. He was promoted to captain of Company G on April 13, 1863. Atkinson was wounded at the Battle of Opequan (Third Battle of Winchester) on September 19, 1864. He resigned on January 31, 1865.[21]

William W. Averell was a West Point graduate from Cameron, New York. In 1861 he served as acting assistant adjutant to General Andrew Porter. He was involved in the First Battle of Bull Run and then received a commission as colonel of the 3rd Pennsylvania Cavalry. In September 1863 he rose to the rank of brigadier general, and the next year he was part of operations in western Virginia. Just after the Battle of Cloyd's Mountain, Averell led an unsuccessful raid in Wytheville known as the Battle of Cove Mountain. He was brevetted brigadier and major general at the end of the war. Averell invented steel castings, asphalt pavement, and electric cable. He died in 1900. His memoirs, *Ten Years in the Saddle*, were published posthumously.[22]

Stephen Cooper Ayres was from Troy, Ohio. He studied medicine at Miami University and, after graduation in April 1861, enlisted as a private in the 20th Ohio Volunteer Infantry for a three-month term of service. He next attended the Medical College of Ohio and in 1863 was appointed as an acting medical cadet in the US Army. Ayres served as assistant surgeon for the US Volunteer Surgeons. He was the brigade surgeon for William S. Newton beginning in late 1863.[23]

Levi Barber was a railroad agent from Harmar. He was commissioned quartermaster of the 36th Ohio Volunteer Infantry on August 31, 1861. He resigned November 29, 1862. Newton referred to a Miss Barber his November 24, 1863 letter, which is most likely Elizabeth F. Barber, the teenage daughter of Levi and Abagail Barber.[24]

James Van Zant Blaney was a doctor from Chicago with a strong background in chemistry. In August 1861 he was appointed medical director in the US Volunteer Surgeons. At the Battle of Opequan (Third Battle of Winchester) he was on General Sheridan's staff and was in charge of all of the hospitals. He mustered out as a brevetted lieutenant colonel.[25]

John R. Blessing was a farmer from Green in Gallia County. He was commissioned as a major of the 91st Ohio Volunteer Infantry on August 11, 1862. He was held in high regard by the officers and soldiers of the 91st. In an April 12, 1863, letter Newton referred to him as one of the best men in the regiment. In March 1863 he became very ill and had to return to his home. He died on April 10, 1863. In the April 23, 1863, issue of the *Gallipolis Journal*, the officers of the 91st published a resolution expressing their condolences for the loss of such "kind and gallant officer, a true patriot, and an honest and confiding friend."[26]

Sydney Brammer was from Gallipolis. He enlisted as a private in Company B of the 2nd Virginia Cavalry on October 10, 1862. Brammer transferred to the 66th Company, 2nd Battalion, Veteran Reserve Corps. The 66th Company organized at Gallipolis on September 30, 1863, and disbanded August 30, 1865. The National Park Service's Civil War Soldiers and Sailors System Database misidentified him as Samuel S. Brammer with the 66th Veteran Reserve Corps and Silas I. Brammer with the 2nd Virginia Cavalry.[27]

Ambrose Brown was appointed assistant surgeon of the 193rd Ohio Volunteer Infantry on March 10, 1865. He mustered out with the regiment on August 4, 1865.[28]

Lemuel Z. Cadot was born in Scioto County. He moved to Gallipolis in the late 1850s and in 1861 began working for his brother J. J. Cadot, who owned a grocery store. He was commissioned as captain of Company A, 91st Ohio Volunteer Regiment on April 10, 1863. Cadot was promoted to major in April 1863. At the Battle of Opequan (Third Battle of Winchester) on September 19, 1864, his horse was shot out from under him. Cadot was unconscious for several hours but recovered. On December 9, 1864, he was promoted to lieutenant colonel and mustered out with the regiment on June 24, 1865. After the Civil War, he opened a cigar business in Gallipolis. Cadot died of asthma on October 29, 1885.[29]

Jacob Caldwell was from Scioto County. He was commissioned as captain of Company C of the 91st Ohio Volunteer Infantry on July 16, 1862. He was wounded in action near Lynchburg on June 17, 1864. Caldwell fell ill a month later and died on August 9, 1864, at a Union hospital in Frederick, Maryland.[30]

Albert Campbell was from Lawrence County, Ohio. He was commissioned as a corporal in Company H of the 91st Ohio Volunteer Infantry on August 22, 1862. Campbell rose to the rank of sergeant and mustered out with the regiment on June 24, 1865.[31]

George H. Carpenter was a doctor from Athens, Ohio. He was commissioned as surgeon of the 91st Ohio Volunteer Infantry on August 19, 1862. Carpenter resigned on May 23, 1863.[32]

Benjamin F. Coates was raised in Wilmington, Clinton County, Ohio. Similar to Newton, he studied medicine at the Medical College of Ohio in Cincinnati. He practiced medicine in Highland County and then in 1853 moved to West Union, in Adams County, Ohio. Coates finished his training at the Jefferson Medical College in Philadelphia in 1860. In 1861 Coates put his medical career on hold and won a seat in the Ohio Senate as a Democrat. His politics put him at odds with the Republican politicians in Columbus. On August 10, 1862, he was commissioned lieutenant colonel of the 91st Ohio Volunteer Infantry. From January until April 1863, Coates took a leave of absence to attend the adjourned session of the 55th Ohio General Assembly. He was wounded on August 24, 1864, at the Battle of Hallstown in Jefferson County, West Virginia. On December 9, 1864, Coates was promoted to the rank of colonel and was brevetted brigadier general on March 13, 1865. He mustered out of service on June 24, 1865, and relocated to Portsmouth, Ohio, to resume his medical practice. Coates was also an insurance and real estate agent. He took a role in national politics as a Republican. Coates was an active participant in reunion activities for the 91st Ohio Volunteer Regiment. He died in 1899 at the age of seventy-one.[33]

Thomas K. Coles was from Scioto County. He was commissioned as sergeant in Company H of the 91st Ohio Volunteer Infantry on August 22, 1862. After service in many battles, including Cloyd's Mountain and Lynchburg, Coles rose to the rank of first lieutenant. In October 1864 he volunteered to serve on a mission led by Captain Richard Blazer to pursue

Confederate guerillas led by Colonel John Mosby. On November 18, 1864, Coles was killed during the Battle of Myerstown, near Kabletown, West Virginia.[34]

Wilson V. Cowan was a doctor and postmaster from Turtle Creek in Shelby County, Ohio. In 1856 he was elected to the Lower House of the Ohio General Assembly. In 1861 he joined the Fremont Body Guards as an assistant surgeon. The group disbanded in November 1861. Cowan was commissioned as an assistant surgeon of the 34th Ohio Volunteer Infantry on July 4, 1862. He received a promotion to surgeon of the 1st Ohio Volunteer Cavalry on December 16, 1863. Cowan resigned on October 4, 1864, and returned to Shelby County to resume his medical practice.[35]

Benjamin R. Cowen was born in Moorefield, Ohio. He studied medicine and was a newspaper editor. In the 1850s he operated a mercantile business in Bellair, Ohio. In 1860 Cowen served as chief clerk of the Ohio House of Representatives. He was elected Ohio secretary of state in 1861 but resigned the following year. Cowen held several appointments during the Civil War. In May 1861, he enlisted as a private in the 15th Ohio Volunteer Infantry. He was quickly commissioned as first lieutenant and assigned duty as the assistant commissary of subsistence. In the summer of 1861, he was appointed as paymaster and pay agent for Ohio. Cowen received numerous appointments, including adjutant general of Ohio, and by the end of the war he rose to the rank of brevet brigadier general. After the war he was a candidate for governor of Ohio but lost to fellow Republican Rutherford B. Hayes. During the Grant administration, Cowen served as secretary of the interior and helped establish Yellowstone as a national park.[36]

James Crawford was a farmer from Tiffin, Adams County, Ohio. He was commissioned as a lieutenant in Company D of the 91st Ohio Volunteer Regiment on July 25, 1862. Crawford was promoted to captain of Company E of the 91st on August 15, 1863. He resigned October 11, 1864.[37]

George Crook was born on a farm in Montgomery County near Dayton, Ohio. He graduated from West Point in 1852 and was assigned to the 4th United States Infantry, then serving in California. In spring 1861 he rose to the rank of captain. In August 1861 he returned to Ohio and was commissioned colonel of the 36th Ohio Volunteer Infantry. In spring 1862 he was placed in command of the 3rd Brigade of the Army of West Virginia. He served in various capacities for the Army of the Potomac and the Army of the Cumberland. In February 1864 he was assigned the command of the Third Division of the Department of West Virginia. He led Union forces at the Battle of Cloyd's Mountain on May 9, 1864. During the campaign, Crook's forces marched nearly nine hundred miles. On July 20, 1864, he was brevetted major general. That summer he led the Army of the Kanawha during several important battles, including Opequan (Third Battle of Winchester), Fisher's Hill, and Cedar Creek. As Newton described in a February 21, 1865, letter, Crook and other Union leaders were captured during a surprise Confederate raid in Cumberland, Maryland. Upon release a month later, Crook returned to his command and led Union forces at the Battles of Dinwiddie Court House, Amelia Springs, and finally Appomattox Court House. Newton wrote frequently about Crook and held him in high regard. After the Civil War, Crook commanded military forces in the West against several Indigenous peoples nations.[38]

Allen D. Crossland was born in Connellsville, Pennsylvania. At age eighteen, he moved to Ironton and secured a teaching position in the county. Crossland was commissioned as a second lieutenant in Company F of the 91st Ohio Volunteer Infantry on July 22, 1862. He was promoted to first lieutenant and regimental quartermaster on February 8, 1863. After the war he moved to Jackson, Ohio.[39]

Simeon Crossley was born in Clermont County, Ohio, near Cincinnati. Prior to the Civil War he lived in Hamilton in Lawrence County. On September 7, 1862, he was commissioned as captain of Company H, 91st Ohio Volunteer Infantry. Crossley was wounded in the right arm on July 20, 1864, at the Battle of Stephenson's Depot in Frederick County, Virginia. Newton was the surgeon who removed the minié ball from his wound, but in August Newton learned that Crossley's injured arm had been amputated. In early December, Crossley received a promotion to major but did not accept the post because of his wounds. He was discharged on December 28, 1864. Crossley returned to Hamilton and worked as a machinist.[40]

William Crull was a doctor from Harrison, Scioto County, Ohio. His son Ira was a drummer in the 91st Ohio Volunteer Infantry. Newton knew Dr. Crull before the Civil War. In his letters, Newton mentioned treating Ira Crull for typhoid fever and a visit from Dr. Crull.[41]

Kennedy R. Culbertson was from Scioto County, Ohio. He was commissioned as captain of Company F in the 91st Ohio Volunteer Infantry on July 28, 1862. Culbertson resigned and was discharged on September 19, 1864.[42]

David Dove was from Jackson County, Ohio. On April 30, 1861, he was commissioned as a first lieutenant in Company I of the 18th Ohio Volunteer

Infantry for three months of service. On November 22, 1861, Dove was commissioned as captain of Company H, 2nd Virginia Cavalry. On May 2, 1863, Dove led his company on an expedition to Lewisburg. They were ambushed, and Dove received a severe wound in his foot. While still recovering from the wound, he was promoted to lieutenant colonel on May 18, 1863. Dove returned to his command in October. Beginning in November 1863, Newton mentioned several times in his letters that he was tending to Col. Dove's lame foot, dressing it twice a day. Dove continued, but the wound did not heal as expected. Dove resigned on July 5, 1864, and returned to Jackson County. He died on January 12, 1868.[43]

Alfred N. Duffié was from Paris and fought in the French Army during the Crimean War. He immigrated to New York in 1859. In August 1861 he was commissioned as a captain in the 2nd New York Volunteer Cavalry. In July 1862 Duffié received a commission as colonel of the 1st Rhode Island Volunteer Cavalry. In June 1863 he was promoted to the rank of brigadier general and by the fall was assigned to raise cavalry units in West Virginia. Newton was fond of Duffié, but others were more critical of his leadership. In fall 1864 he was captured by Confederate forces and remained imprisoned until February 1865. After the war, Duffié was appointed as US consul in Cadiz, Spain.[44]

Isaac H. Duval was from the river town of Wellsburg, West Virginia. After working as a hunter and trapper in the West and in South America, he became a merchant in Wellsburg. On June 1, 1861, he was appointed major of the 1st Virginia Infantry. Duval was promoted to colonel of the 9th Virginia Infantry on September 1862. He spent most of his military career fighting in West Virginia. Duval was engaged in more than thirty battles and skirmishes, was wounded three times, and had eleven horses shot from under him. At the Battle of Cloyd's Mountain in May 1864, Duval led his regiment in an uphill charge against the Confederate breastworks. The risky maneuver broke the Confederate line and changed the course of the battle, but his regiment suffered 30 percent casualties. On September 24, 1864, Duval was promoted to brigadier general and was assigned to General Crook's Army of West Virginia. Two months later, he was given command of the 1st Virginia Veteran Infantry. After the war, he served in the state legislature as a representative and senator, was adjutant general of West Virginia from 1867–1869, and served one term as US representative, 1869–1871.[45]

Elmore E. Ewing was born in 1840 in Ewington, Gallia County, Ohio. In 1860 he was a schoolteacher in Lawrence County, Ohio. That fall, at the age of twenty, he enrolled as a freshman at Ohio University. After finishing his sophomore year, Ewing joined the military. He was commissioned as a sergeant in Company A of the 91st Ohio Volunteer Infantry on July 31, 1862. He was promoted to second lieutenant in June 1863 and then was transferred to Company K as first lieutenant on July 13, 1864. In a July 1864 letter to his wife, Newton mentioned sending a photograph of Lt. Ewing. Later in the month, he reported that Ewing had been badly wounded during the Second Battle of Kernstown. A later account explained that Ewing was shot through the left lung and left for dead on the field. Ewing recovered, but due to ill health he resigned on December 4, 1864. He settled in Portsmouth, Ohio, and after the war became very active in GAR reunion activities. As noted in the Epilogue, he attended the first reunion of the 91st Ohio Volunteer Infantry in April 1868. Ewing was a well-known poet and at the reunion read a lengthy poem chronicling the history of the regiment. It was published as a book later that year and in 1899, he published *Bugles and Bells*, a lengthy volume of Civil War reunion poems. Ewing operated a business in Portsmouth until a major flood forced him in bankruptcy. He relocated to San Francisco in 1895 and worked for the Welsbach Commercial Company. Ewing was in poor health from his Civil War service and in 1898 suffered a stroke. In the fall of 1900, Ewing made some bookkeeping errors that resulted in panic and fear that he would lose his job. On the night of October 21, 1900, Ewing committed suicide by gas asphyxiation, and his body was discovered the next morning.[46]

William T. Falwell was a farmer from Lawrence County, Ohio. He was appointed corporal of Company H of the 91st Ohio Volunteer Infantry on August 20, 1862. Newton mentioned that Falwell was cooking for him, and in May 1863 Falwell served as his orderly. Falwell was promoted to sergeant major of the regiment on November 1, 1864. He mustered out with the regiment on June 24, 1865.[47]

James G. D. Findley was a farmer from Delaware County, Ohio. He made numerous advancements in the 91st Ohio Volunteer Infantry. He enlisted as a private in Company F of the 91st on August 11, 1862. He was then appointed sergeant major on August 22, 1862 and then promoted to first lieutenant in Company K on January 3, 1864. In a January 29, 1864, letter to his wife, Newton mentioned that Findley was a lieutenant and that his good penmanship helped secure the promotion. On March 20, 1864, he was appointed adjutant for the regiment. Findley was wounded on September 19, 1864, at the Battle of Opequan (Third Battle of Winchester). He recovered and mustered out with the regiment on June 24, 1865.[48]

Elijah Fisher Gillen was married to Caroline Gillen and lived in Ironton. His older brother Martin Gillen was a furniture dealer in Ironton. In the 1860 census, Elijah was listed as a clerk, most likely for his brother's furniture business, Gillen & Brother. Elijah was commissioned as a lieutenant in the 2nd Virginia Cavalry on November 5, 1862. He also served as adjutant for the 2nd. During his military service, Elijah was quite ill and under Newton's care at several points. Newton makes several references to Mrs. Gillen, sometimes Mrs. G., in his correspondence.[49]

Daniel W. Glassie was born in Kentucky. On April 20, 1861, he was appointed sergeant in the 23rd Independent Battery of the Ohio Volunteer Light Artillery, also known as Simmond's Kentucky Battery. In October 1861 Glassie was promoted to second lieutenant. He was with General Crook in the Shenandoah Valley Campaign and saw action at the Battles of Cloyd's Mountain, Antietam, Cedar Creek, and Fredericksburg. He rose to the rank of captain on March 18, 1864, and mustered out with the battery on July 10, 1865. After the war he became a lawyer.[50]

Neil F. Graham was born in February 1840 in Canada near the city of London. At age nineteen, he moved to Cleveland, and enrolled in the Cleveland Medical College. Graham graduated in early 1861 and began a residency program at the US Marine Hospital in Cleveland. He was commissioned assistant surgeon in the 12th Ohio Volunteer Infantry on May 30, 1861. In October 1862 he was ordered to establish a general hospital at Clarksburg, West Virginia. Graham was promoted to surgeon of the 12th on December 28, 1862. Graham was alongside Newton at the Battle of Cloyd's Mountain in May 1864. They were both captured after the battle, operated on Confederate general Albert G. Jenkins, and then were briefly detained at Libby Prison. He mustered out with the regiment on July 11, 1865. In August he returned as an acting staff surgeon for the Union and was in charge of the general field hospital at Sandy Hook, Maryland. Later, he operated a medical practice in Xenia, Ohio, taught at the Cleveland Medical College, and served as an assistant medical referee for the Pension Bureau.[51]

Charles E. Hambleton was born in Alliance County, Ohio. He was commissioned lieutenant in Company B of the 2nd West Virginia Cavalry on November 22, 1861. Hambleton was promoted to the rank of major on October 9, 1862. He was at the Battles of Opequan (Third Battle of Winchester), Fisher's Hill, and Cedar Creek. After the war he was involved in steamboat navigation on the Mississippi River and a life insurance business in Chicago.[52]

Joel Hull was born in Meigs County, Ohio. He attended Ohio Wesleyan, worked in law offices, and just before the Civil War he was a leather dealer. Hull was commissioned second lieutenant of Company B of the 91st Ohio Volunteer Infantry on July 23, 1862. He was promoted to first lieutenant on April 13, 1863, and then was appointed adjutant for the 91st on September 22, 1863. After the war he settled in Toledo and then later moved to Kearney County, Nebraska, where he worked as a lawyer.[53]

David Hunter was born in Princeton, New Jersey, in 1802. His maternal grandfather, Richard Stockton, was a signer of the Declaration of Independence. Hunter graduated from West Point and was commissioned as lieutenant in the 5th US Infantry Regiment. In 1860 his anti-slavery views attracted attention from Abraham Lincoln. At the beginning of the Civil War, Hunter was appointed brigadier general, commanding a brigade in the Department of Washington. He was wounded in the neck at the First Battle of Bull Run in July 1861. Hunter had various assignments and promotions, but his enlistment of freed slaves to fight for the Union drew the most attention and controversy. By late summer 1864, Hunter was in command of the Department of West Virginia and issued orders to dismiss Newton and twenty-two other officers for allegedly deserting after the Second Battle of Kernstown. Hunter was promoted to brevet major general in March 1865.[54]

John E. Jewett was born in Belmont County, Ohio. He was a student at Ohio Wesleyan when the Civil War began. Jewett was appointed quartermaster and sergeant in Company E of the 3rd Ohio Volunteer Infantry on June 13, 1861. In July he was discharged to accept a promotion to first lieutenant in Company A of the 23rd Ohio Volunteer Infantry. On October 29, 1861, he was mustered out of the regiment and transferred to the 78th Ohio Volunteer Infantry to serve as adjutant. Jewett was promoted to captain and aide-de-camp on June 13, 1862. In that role he reported to Brigadier General Irvin McDowell. In March 1865 he was promoted to the rank of lieutenant colonel of the 193rd Ohio Volunteer Infantry. Jewett mustered out with the regiment on August 4, 1865. After the war, he studied law and operated a legal practice in Lawrence, Kansas.[55]

Benjamin F. Kelley (Kelly) was born in New Hampton, New Hampshire, in 1807. In the 1820s he moved to Wheeling, Virginia, and was a merchant. In the 1850s he worked for the Baltimore and Ohio Railroad as a freight agent. In May 1861 Kelley organized the 1st Virginia Volunteer Infantry, a ninety-day regiment. He was appointed colonel of the regiment and led them at the Battle of Philippi on June 3, 1861. Kelley was severely wounded in the battle and was reported as the first Union officer wounded in the Civil War. He received a promotion to the rank of brigadier general for his bravery. Kelley recovered and resumed command of the 1st Virginia. By 1863 he was in command of the West Virginia department and pursued Lee after Gettysburg. In early 1865, he and General Crook were captured in Cumberland, Maryland, and briefly imprisoned at Libby Prison. He resigned from military service in June 1865.[56]

George M. Kellogg graduated from Oberlin College in 1848 and then received a medical degree from the Medical College of Ohio in 1852. In 1860 he was a physician living in Keokuk, Iowa. He was appointed brigade surgeon in the US Volunteer Surgeons on April 28, 1862. In August 1862 he became medical director of the Kanawha district. In August 1865 he mustered out with the rank of brevet lieutenant colonel. After the war Kellogg lectured at the Keokuk Medical College.[57]

Richard A. Kirker was from Lawrence County, Ohio. His father was Thomas A. Kirker, the brother of William W. Kirker. Richard was William's nephew and Robert's first cousin. He began as a sergeant in Company B of the 2nd Virginia Cavalry on November 8, 1861, and rose to the rank of corporal. Newton referred to him several times as Dick Kirker. In June 1864 he was sent into enemy lines with false dispatches to create a diversion so Union troops could withdraw from Lynchburg. The gamble was successful, but Kirker was captured. He was sent to Confederate prison camps at Belle Isle near Richmond, Danville, and then finally to Andersonville in Georgia. In early April 1865, he was exchanged at Fortress Monroe. He suffered from malnutrition and died in Annapolis on April 19, 1865. In 1875, Company D of 6th Regiment of the Ohio National Guard chose to honor Richard Kirker's Civil War sacrifice by naming themselves the "Kirker Rifles."[58]

Robert A. Kirker was from Ironton and was the son of William W. Kirker. He enlisted as a private in Company B of the 2nd Virginia Cavalry on November 24, 1862. Newton, who referred to him as Bob several times, treated Kirker for a bout of pneumonia in March 1863.[59]

William W. Kirker was a butcher from Ironton. He was commissioned as first lieutenant in Company H of the 91st Ohio Volunteer Infantry on August 5, 1862. His son Robert was a private in the 2nd Virginia Cavalry. Kirker resigned his position on February 8, 1863, but thereafter made frequent trips from Ironton to the location of the 91st to deliver supplies and messages. Newton mentioned Mr. Kirker frequently.[60]

Joseph Andrew Jackson Lightburn was born at Webster, Pennsylvania, in 1824. In the late 1830s, his family moved to Lewis County, West Virginia. Lightburn became good friends with Thomas J. "Stonewall" Jackson, whose family lived nearby. He served in the Mexican War, rising to the rank of sergeant. In 1859 Lightburn became a Baptist minister. Two years later, he was elected to the loyalist convention in Wheeling to consider establishing a separate state of West Virginia. A staunch Unionist, Lightburn was commissioned as colonel of the 4th Virginia Infantry in August 1861. After defeats at Charleston and Gauley Bridge, he was transferred to operations in the Vicksburg area. On March 16, 1863, he was promoted to brigadier general. Lightburn led troops at the Battle of Missionary Ridge and was part of the Atlanta Campaign under the command of General William T. Sherman. In August 1864 he was shot in the head during a skirmish. He recovered and returned to command troops in West Virginia and Maryland. After his discharge from the military in June 1865, Lightburn returned to preaching.[61]

Matthew H. McEwen was born in Northumberland County, Pennsylvania. He was a doctor and in the early 1860s he had a medical practice in Charleston, West Virginia. McEwen was commissioned as surgeon of the 2nd Virginia Cavalry on January 17, 1863. As Newton's letters indicated, McEwen was temporarily removed from the position in October 1863, and Newton took his place in an interim role. In late January 1864, McEwen was cleared of all charges and restored to his position. He served on the staff of several notable Union commanders, including Sheridan, Custer, Crook, and Averell. McEwen was promoted to brevet brigadier general in March 1865. After the war, he moved to Washington, DC, and became an agent for the US Pension Bureau. McEwen also testified about the desertion of soldiers and their reinstatement during the 1867 impeachment trial of President Andrew Johnson.[62]

James R. McMullen was from Mansfield, in Richland County, Ohio. In July 1861 he organized the 1st Ohio Volunteer Independent Light Artillery Battery and served as its captain. Under his command the battery served in western Virginia and was at the Battle of Cloyd's Mountain in May 1864. The battery saw action at battles throughout Virginia, including Lexington, Lynchburg, Parkersburg, and Winchester. Newton mentioned serving as surgeon and hospital manager for the battery. McMullen mustered out of service in July 1864. A later newspaper account mentioned that James McMullen had lost both hands during the war and lived in the Central Branch of the National Home for Disabled Volunteer Soldiers in Dayton.[63]

Thayer Melvin was a lieutenant in Company F of the 1st Virginia Infan-
try. He later became the adjutant general on the staff of Brigadier General
Benjamin Franklin Kelley of the Department of West Virginia. Melvin
was a lawyer and after the Civil War was elected attorney general of West
Virginia. He was later elected judge of the First Judicial District of West
Virginia.[64]

George Millard (Miller) was appointed as a first sergeant in Company B of
the 2nd Virginia Cavalry on September 1, 1861. He was promoted to second
lieutenant of Company F in July 1862. Millard rose to the rank of captain
and led a detachment to destroy the tracks of the Virginia and Tennessee
Railroad during the July 1863 raid at Wytheville. Newton incorrectly referred to him as Captain Miller, but there was no soldier named Miller in
the 2nd Virginia Cavalry who held the rank of captain. Millard mustered
out on November 28, 1864, at the end of his term of service.[65]

Charles A. Miller was born in Ireland and in 1860 was listed as a doctor in
Bellefontaine, Logan County, Ohio. He was commissioned assistant surgeon in the 34th Ohio Volunteer Infantry on August 27, 1862. Miller mustered out on expiration of term of service on September 13, 1864. After the
war he settled in Louisville, Ohio.[66]

Jonathan Morris was born in Morgan County, Ohio. In 1838 he moved to
Washington County to clerk at a store. Two years later, Morris moved to
Gallipolis and took an interest in medicine. He graduated from the Cleve-
land Medical College in 1847 and began a medical practice in Burlington,
Ohio. By 1860 Morris had a medical practice in Ironton. He was commis-
sioned surgeon of the 9th Virginia Infantry in early November 1861. On
November 10, just a few days after his service began, he was captured when
Confederate forces took control of the town of Guyandotte, West Virginia.
Morris spent four months at Libby Prison and was released in March 1862.
He was discharged in November 1864, when the 9th consolidated with the
5th Virginia Volunteers to form the 1st Virginia Veteran Regiment. After
his discharge, Morris resumed his medical practice in Ironton.[67]

William H. Mussey was from New Hampshire. His father was well-known
physician Reuben D. Mussey, who taught a number of medical schools, including Dartmouth College, Middlebury College, and the Medical College
of Ohio in Cincinnati. William Mussey followed in his father's medical
footsteps. He graduated from the Medical College of Ohio in 1848 and
thereafter opened a medical practice in Cincinnati. Mussey was appointed
to the US Volunteer Surgeons at the rank of major in October 1861. He was

promoted to the rank of lieutenant colonel with the role of medical inspector in June 1862. Mussey managed a small board of medical inspectors and coordinated the delivery of necessary medical supplies to Ohio regiments, especially those in Virginia. He resigned in January 1864 and returned to his medical practice in Cincinnati.[68]

Henry Safford Neal was from Gallipolis. He graduated from Marietta College in 1847 and then studied law. He was admitted to the bar in 1851, opened a practice in Ironton, and was the prosecuting attorney for Lawrence County. Neal did not serve in the military during the Civil War but was a state senator for the eighth district from 1862–1866. Newton made several references to Neal related to selling his Ironton home. Neal continued in politics and served as US representative for Ohio from 1877–1883.[69]

Samuel Finley Neal was from Gallipolis. His family operated a dry goods store in the town. His sister was Eliza Neal, to whom Newton referred in an October 23, 1862, letter. Neal was commissioned as a first lieutenant in Company A of the 91st Ohio Volunteer Infantry on July 19, 1862. He was promoted to captain in June 1863 and finally to the rank of major on January 4, 1865. Newton refers to him as Finn or Captain Neal or Lieutenant Neal. Neal mustered out with the regiment on June 24, 1865. After the war, he returned to Gallipolis, serving as postmaster beginning in 1879, only a few years after Newton had resigned from that position. Neal was active member and officer in the GAR post in Gallipolis. He died in 1930 at the age of eighty-nine.[70]

Ozias Nellis was born in New York. In the 1840s Nellis was a doctor with a medical practice serving Washington County, Ohio. By 1850 he lived in Williamstown, Virginia, just across the Ohio River from Marietta, Ohio. He was appointed postmaster for Williamstown in 1861. Nellis was commissioned assistant surgeon of the 2nd Virginia Cavalry on March 6, 1863. He was wounded at the raid on Wytheville in July 1863 and was briefly imprisoned at Libby Prison. He returned to his regiment and mustered out with his term of service in November 1864. In January 1865 he was commissioned assistant surgeon of the 10th Virginia Infantry. He received a promotion to the rank of surgeon for the 10th in July 1865 and then mustered out with the regiment the next month. After the war he relocated to Indiana and then to Johnstown, New York.[71]

James E. Niday was from Gallipolis. In the fall of 1862, he began recruiting a company for three years of service. Niday was commissioned captain of Company B of the 91st Ohio Volunteer Infantry on July 16, 1862. Three of his brothers, John, Stephen, and Harvey, also served in Company B. Niday died at Fayetteville, West Virginia, on April 21, 1864.[72]

John C. Paxton was born in Gettysburg, Pennsylvania, and spent his youth in Noble County, Ohio. In 1853 his family moved to Marietta, and by 1860 he owned a mercantile business. On June 1, 1861, Paxton joined the 18th Ohio Volunteer Infantry for a three-month term as quartermaster. He mustered out with the regiment on August 28, 1861 and began organizing a regiment of cavalry from the Marietta area. On September 1, 1861, Paxton was appointed lieutenant colonel of the 2nd Virginia Cavalry. Following the resignation of Colonel William M. Boles, Paxton was promoted to the rank of colonel on July 18, 1862. In that role, Paxton commanded troops to scout in the Virginia counties of Raleigh, Fayette, and Wyoming. This region featured difficult terrain, and the 2nd encountered many bushwhackers and skirmishes. Under his command, the 2nd captured an entire Confederate cavalry camp during a raid near Sinking Creek in late November 1862. In early May 1863, Paxton led an expedition to Lewisburg that resulted in the regiment's first defeat. The regiment suffered heavy losses, with fifteen killed or severely wounded and many taken prisoner. A later account explained that Paxton's poor leadership resulted in "Some of the best officers and men in the command had been needlessly sacrificed." Paxton was dismissed from service on May 7, 1863, and returned to Marietta.[73]

William G. Pinckard was from Alton, Madison County, Illinois. He learned the printing trade and by 1860 was editor of the *Madison County Advertiser*. Pinckard was commissioned as quartermaster of the 9th Illinois Infantry on August 26, 1861. On April 30, 1862, he was promoted to the rank of captain and assistant quartermaster. In May 1863 he was ordered to Charleston, West Virginia, to serve on the staff of General E. P. Scammon. On February 3, 1864, Scammon and several members of his staff, including Pinckard, were on a steamboat traveling from Point Pleasant to Charleston. After the boat's captain docked for the night, a group of Confederate guerrillas from the 16th Virginia Cavalry boarded the vessel and surprised all aboard. Scammon, Pinckard, and other officers were detained and ordered to march to Libby Prison. On February 15, near Round Hill, Virginia, Pinckard was killed while trying to escape.[74]

Milton S. Pixley was born near Wheelersburg in Scioto County, Ohio. In 1859 he attended Ohio Wesleyan University and took an interest in medicine. The 1860 census listed Pixley as a student living in the town of Porter, Ohio. In 1861 Pixley enrolled at the Medical College of Ohio and was a student for the following two years. On August 18, 1863, he enlisted as a private in Company F of the 91st Ohio Volunteer Infantry. Eleven days later, Pixley was promoted to hospital steward. Pixley mustered out with the regiment on June 24, 1865. After the war he resumed his medical studies at Miami Medical College. Pixley graduated in 1866 and briefly practiced medicine in Catlettsburg, Kentucky. In 1867 he settled in Portsmouth and opened a medical practice. Dr. Pixley was an active member of the Portsmouth community. He died in 1909.[75]

Eugene Powell* was from Delaware County, Ohio. He worked as a machinist. At the outbreak of the Civil War, Powell helped organize Company C of the 4th Ohio Volunteer Infantry. On June 4, 1861, he was commissioned captain of Company I of the 4th. Four months later, in October 1861, Powell was promoted to the rank of major for the 66th Ohio Volunteer Infantry. Powell was present at many significant battles, including Rich Mountain, Antietam, Chancellorsville, Gettysburg, Lookout Mountain, and Sherman's march to the sea. In March 1865 Powell rose to the rank of colonel of the 193rd Ohio Volunteer Infantry, which included William S. Newton as surgeon. He was breveted brigadier general on March 13, 1865, and mustered out with the regiment on August 4, 1865. Powell returned to Delaware County and opened a successful fence company.[76]

William Henry Powell* was born in Wales and emigrated to the United States when he was five years old. His father was an iron worker, and he learned the same trade. In 1843, at age eighteen, he moved to Wheeling, Virginia, and opened a nail factory. Ten years later, in 1853, he moved to Ironton and opened the Bellfonte Nail Works. In August 1861 Powell organized a company of soldiers from southern Ohio counties that resulted in Company B of the 2nd Virginia Cavalry. He was commissioned captain of Company B on November 22, 1861. Powell was promoted to major on June 25, 1862, to lieutenant colonel four months later, and then to colonel in May 1863. During the raid on Wytheville in July 1863, he was wounded and unable to be transported. He stayed behind and was captured by Confederate troops, who later sent him to Libby Prison. Powell was released through a prisoner exchange in January 1864 and in March returned to his command

---

*William S. Newton referred to "Powell" several times in his correspondence but it is sometime unclear if he is referring to Eugene Powell or William Henry Powell because both held similar ranks. In most cases he refers to William Henry Powell because of the Ironton connection, with Eugene Powell appearing near the end of the wartime correspondence, when Newton was part of the 193rd Ohio Volunteer Infantry.

of the 2nd Virginia Cavalry. Powell led the 2nd at the Battles of Lynchburg, Stephenson's Depot, Opequan (Third Battle of Winchester), and Fisher's Hill. In October 1864 he rose to the rank of brigadier general and was breveted major general of volunteers at the end of the war. After the war, Powell returned to Ironton and later settled in Mason County, West Virginia.[77]

Alexander H. Ricker was from New Hampshire. In 1860 he lived in Ironton with his wife Adaline and their four children Helen, Arthur, Edward (Ned), and Adeline. Ricker was a machine shop manager in Ironton. Throughout the Civil War, Newton makes frequent references to Ricker and his family. Several times Newton refers to him as "Mr. R." Ricker was commissioned quartermaster of the 91st Ohio Volunteer Infantry on July 24, 1862. In March 1863 he was transferred to Company H of the 91st with the rank of first lieutenant. Two months later, in May 1863, he was promoted to the rank of captain for Company D of the 2nd Virginia Cavalry. He mustered out with the expiration of his term of service and returned to Ironton.[78]

James D. Robinson was a doctor from Cincinnati. He was appointed assistant medical director of the Department of the Cumberland on August 5, 1861.[79]

Eliakim P. Scammon was born in Whitefield, Lincoln County, Maine, in 1816. At age sixteen, he obtained a cadetship at West Point. Scammon graduated in 1837 and was assigned to duty as assistant professor of mathematics at West Point. In 1838 he took part in the Seminole War in Florida and later saw military service in the Mexican War. In 1850 Scammon resigned from the military and became professor of mathematics at Mount Saint Mary's College near Cincinnati. When the war began, he was principal of the Polytechnic College of Cincinnati. Scammon was appointed colonel of the 23rd Ohio Volunteer Infantry in June 1861. He led the 23rd, which included future presidents Rutherford B. Hayes and William McKinley, during operations in western Virginia. Scammon was appointed brigadier general in October 1862. He was then placed in charge of the District of Kanawha. On February 3, 1864, Scammon and several members of his staff were on a steamboat traveling from Point Pleasant to Charleston. After the boat's captain docked for the night, a group of Confederate guerrillas from the 16th Virginia Cavalry boarded the vessel and surprised all aboard. Scammon and other officers were detained and sent to Libby Prison. He was held as a prisoner in several locations including: Libby Prison; Danville, Virginia; Macon, Georgia; and Charleston, South Carolina until August 1864. Scammon returned to service and led troops in Florida before mustering out of service in August 1865.

Scammon later returned to the classroom as a professor of mathematics at Seton Hall University in New Jersey.[80]

Samuel M. Smith was a doctor from Columbus, Ohio. He studied medicine in Paris and by the early 1860s was professor of theory and practice of medicine at the Starling Medical College, part of Ohio State University. He served as Surgeon General of Ohio from 1862–1864. Newton referred to Smith as "Surg. Genl." in May and July 1863. After the war, Smith served as president of the Ohio State Medical Society, 1869–1870.[81]

John T. Toland was born in Ireland and immigrated to the United States with his family. He settled in Ohio and pursued dentistry. In the late 1850s, Toland was a dentist who sold dental supplies in Cincinnati at his store, Toland's Dental Depot. In 1858 he edited and published a journal focused on dental instruments and materials called *The Dental Reporter* and later *The Dental Register of the West*. In mid-1861 Toland and Abraham Piatt began organizing troops for the 34th Ohio Volunteer Infantry. Toland was appointed lieutenant colonel on August 2, 1861, and promoted to colonel of the 34th on May 14, 1862. In late summer 1862, he led the 34th into a series of raids in western Virginia. As Newton recalled, in September 1862, Toland engaged Confederates near Fayetteville. While on the skirmish line, Toland had three horses shot out from under him but was uninjured. The incident resulted in Toland saying that "he bore a charmed life which Rebel bullets could not reach." During the raid on Wytheville in July 1863, which Newton referred to in several letters, Toland was killed by enemy fire.[82]

John A. Turley was born in Hardy County, Virginia. He came to Ohio in the 1830s, settling in Scioto County. Turley was elected to the Ohio House of Representatives as a Whig for the 1846–1847 term. He was a farmer, and the 1860 census listed his occupation as a gentleman. On April 27, 1861, he enlisted for service in the 22nd Ohio Volunteer Infantry, a three-month regiment. Turley was made captain of Company G. He mustered out with the regiment in August 1861 and was appointed lieutenant colonel of the 81st Ohio Volunteer Infantry. Turley resigned from the post in December 1861. In August 1862 he was appointed colonel of the 91st Ohio Volunteer Infantry. Newton made frequent references to Turley in his correspondence and expressed great respect for him. Turley received high praise for his leadership at the Battle of Cloyd's Mountain in May 1864. After that victory, he led the 91st in an effort to capture Lynchburg. He was wounded in the leg on June 17, 1864, and his command was given to Benjamin F. Coates. Surgeon Joseph T. Webb of the 23rd Ohio Volunteer Infantry removed the bullet five days later. Turley returned to Ohio to recover but was unable to return to service and resigned on November 4, 1864. In March 1865 he was brevetted brigadier general for his bravery at the Battle of Cloyd's Mountain. He returned to Portsmouth and served as mayor of the city for two terms. He died in March 1900.[83]

James M. Turner was born in Pennsylvania. He worked as a grocer in Washington, Licking County, Ohio. By 1863 he lived in Wellsville, Columbiana County, Ohio, and worked as a butcher. In July 1863 Turner enlisted for one year of service. He was mustered in as a private in Company H of the 91st Ohio Volunteer Infantry on August 3, 1864. By September he had been assigned to help Newton as a hospital orderly. Newton made several references to Orderly Turner. The regimental history of the 91st indicated that Turner deserted on December 16, 1864.[84]

Thomas McMillan Turner was from Barlow, Washington County, Ohio. He enlisted on August 31, 1861, at the rank of quartermaster sergeant in the 36th Ohio Volunteer Infantry. In early December 1862 he was offered a promotion to the rank of captain, but he declined and was given the rank of lieutenant and quartermaster. Turner saw action at the Battles of Second Bull Run, Antietam, and Chickamauga. He mustered out with the regiment in July 1865 and in 1866 was brevetted the rank of major. After the war he returned to Washington County and became a dry goods merchant in Harmar. In the late 1890s, he moved to Evanston, Illinois, to work for the Standard Oil Company's Chicago office.[85]

James L. Waller (Wallar) was born near Burlington, Vermont, in 1817. In 1836 he moved to Zanesville, Ohio, and studied law. On April 25, 1861, Waller (identified as Wallace) was commissioned captain of the 18th Ohio Volunteer Infantry. After the three months of service concluded, he helped organize a company for the 2nd Virginia Cavalry. On October 19, 1861, he was appointed captain of Company A of the 2nd. Waller was discharged on April 25, 1864, and after the war he moved to Centralia, Illinois. In 1866 he joined the ministry and spent the rest of his life working in Methodist Episcopal churches in Illinois. [86]

John B. Warwick was from Augusta County, Virginia, and was the older brother of Newton R. Warwick. Their father, Dr. Beverly Green Warwick, was opposed to slavery and moved the family to Scotio County, Ohio, in the mid-1850s. Warwick also pursued a medical career. He graduated from the Medical College of Ohio in 1858 and moved to Portsmouth, Ohio. In 1859 he settled in Lucasville, Scotio County, Ohio, and opened a medical practice.

He was appointed assistant surgeon of the 91st Ohio Volunteer Infantry on August 19, 1862. In May 1863 George H. Carpenter resigned as surgeon of the 91st and both Newton and Warwick applied for the position. Warwick was promoted to the rank of surgeon for the 91st on May 23, 1863. Newton made frequent references to Warwick in his correspondence. Warwick mustered out with the regiment in June 1865. He returned to Lucasville to practice medicine. Warwick served as a pension examining surgeon in the 1890s.[87]

Newton R. Warwick was from Augusta County, Virginia, and was the younger brother of John B. Warwick. Their father, Dr. Beverly Green Warwick, was opposed to slavery and moved the family to Scotio County, Ohio, in the mid-1850s. Warwick enlisted as a private in Company C of the 91st Ohio Volunteer Infantry on July 20, 1862. Warwick was promoted to commissary sergeant to work with the quartermaster's department three months later, on October 22, 1862. On January 4, 1864, he was promoted to second lieutenant in Company D of the 91st. Warwick transferred to Company A of the 91st on January 1, 1865 and mustered out with the regiment in June 1865. Newton referred to him as Newt in several letters. After the war, Warwick operated a mercantile business in Portsmouth and also served as postmaster. He later became a railroad agent.[88]

John P. Waste was born in Greenwich, New York. He was listed as a medical student at the University of Michigan in 1860 and 1863. By 1864 he was living in Mulberry Corners, Ohio, near Cleveland, and attending medical school at Western Reserve University in Cleveland through the Charity Hospital Medical College. Waste graduated from the program in early 1865. He was commissioned assistant surgeon of the 193rd Ohio Volunteer Infantry, the same regiment with William S. Newton, on March 10, 1865. Waste mustered out with the regiment on August 4, 1865. He moved to Plainview, Minnesota, and opened a medical practice. He served in the state senate from 1871–1872 and was also appointed postmaster in 1902. Waste was an active member of the GAR. He died in December 1906.[89]

Granville S. Wellons was from Somerton, in Belmont County, Ohio. He took an interest in medicine and enrolled at the Medical College of Ohio in the early 1860s. Wellons graduated in 1863, and that August he was commissioned as assistant surgeon of the 91st Ohio Volunteer Infantry. Newton discussed that many of the officers and medical staff did not like Wellons. In an April 19, 1864, letter Newton explained that Coates had charges against Wellons that could result in dismissal. Wellons held his position throughout the war and mustered out with the regiment in June 1865. He returned to

Belmont County and operated a medical practice and drug store in Barnesville. Wellons also served as a medical examiner for the government and was
a surgeon for the Baltimore and Ohio Railroad.[90]

Carr B. White was born in Mason County, Kentucky, in 1824. His family moved to Georgetown, Brown County, Ohio, the childhood home of
Ulysses S. Grant, when White was ten years old. White's father was a
schoolteacher and taught Grant in the public school in Georgetown. White
took an interest in medicine and in the early 1840s enrolled at Jefferson Medical College in Philadelphia. In 1846 he enlisted as a private in the 1st Ohio
Infantry and fought in the Mexican War. He rose to the rank of captain.
Around 1848 White graduated with his medical degree and began practicing
medicine in Brown County. In May 1861 he was commissioned as major in
the 12th Ohio Volunteer Infantry for three months of service. On June, 28,
1861, White was appointed lieutenant colonel of the 12th. During the Battle
of Carnifex Ferry in September 1861, Colonel John W. Lowe was killed, and
White was promoted to the rank of colonel. He led the 12th through battles
in Virginia, including Second Bull Run, Lynchburg, and Cloyd's Mountain.
He mustered out on July 11, 1864, and in March 1865 was brevetted for his
service at the Battle of Cloyd's Mountain. After the war, White returned to
his medical practice in Georgetown, Ohio. He died in 1871.[91]

Robert Wilson was from Canada and moved to Ohio. The 1860 census
listed him as a twenty-six-year-old papermaker living in Middletown, Butler County. He was commissioned as first lieutenant in Company G of the
12th Ohio Volunteer Infantry on June 11, 1861. Wilson was appointed adjutant on January 1, 1862. Two months later, in March 1862, he was promoted
to captain of Company A of the 12th. Wilson mustered out with the company on July 11, 1864. After the war, he returned to Butler County, Ohio. In
1877 Wilson and his brother-in-law Daniel McCallay founded the Wilson
& McCallay Tobacco Company, which specialized in plug tobacco.[92]

William F. Wilson (Willson) was a doctor from Ironton who, like Newton,
advertised his medical services in the local newspaper. Newton made several
references to Dr. Wilson in his correspondence.[93]

Geographic Locations

Kentucky
Catlettsburg

Maryland
Cumberland
Frederick
Hagerstown
Middletown
Monocacy River
Sandy Hook
Sharpsburg
Williamsport
Wolfsville

Ohio
Albany
Athens
Barnesville
Buckeye Furnace
Burlington
Cincinnati
Coal Grove
Delaware
Harmar
Ironton
Gallipolis
Manchester
Marietta
Moscow
New Richmond
Portland
Portsmouth
Proctorville
West Union

Virginia
Berryville
Dublin
Front Royal
Kernstown
Richmond
Strasburg
Winchester
Woodstock
Wytheville

West Virginia
Beverly
Bolton
Buffalo
Bull Town
Bunker Hill
Charleston
Charles Town
Clarksburg
Coalsmouth
Cotton Mountain
Fayetteville
Gauley Bridge
Gormley
Guyan
Guyandotte
Harpers Ferry
Hartford City
Kanawha Falls
Lewisburg
Little Birch
Loup Creek
Lowell Mountains
Malden

Parkersburg
Pocatalico
Point Pleasant
Powell Mountain
Princeton
Raleigh
Raleigh Road (Rolla
    Road)
Red House
Shepherdstown
Sinking Creek
Summersville
Summit Point
Sutton
20 Mile Creek
Wheeling

Notes

Preface

1. William S. Newton to Benjamin R. Cowen, October 8, 1867, William S. Newton Papers, 1862–1879, Ms.2021.024, Special Collections and University Archives, Virginia Tech, Blacksburg, Virginia (hereafter cited as Newton Papers, SCUA VT).
2. Ibid.
3. Ibid.
4. "Death of W. S. Newton," *Gallipolis Bulletin*, November 21, 1882; Pension File of William S. Newton, 91st Ohio Volunteer Infantry, Civil War Pension Index: General Index to Pension Files, 1861–1934, Record Group 15, Records of the Veterans Administration (RG 15), National Archives and Records Administration (NARA).
5. Recent scholarship on this area of research includes: Lisa Tendrich Frank and LeeAnn Whites, eds., *Household War: How Americans Lived and Fought the Civil War* (Athens: Univ. of Georgia Press, 2020); Lorien Foote, "Rethinking the Confederate Homefront" *Journal of the Civil War Era* 7 (September 2017): 446–65; John Hammond Moore, *Southern Homefront, 1861–1865* (Columbia, SC: Summerhouse Press, 1998); Judith Giesberg, *Army at Home: Women and the Civil War on the Northern Home Front* (Chapel Hill: Univ. of North Carolina Press, 2009); LeeAnn Whites and Alecia P. Long, eds., *Occupied Women: Gender, Military Occupation, and the American Civil War* (Baton Rouge: Louisiana State Univ. Press, 2009).
6. Recent scholarship on Civil War medical history includes: Glenna R. Schroeder-Lein, *The Encyclopedia of Civil War Medicine* (2008; New York: Routledge, 2015); Margaret Humphreys, *Marrow of Tragedy: The Health Crisis of the American Civil War* (Baltimore: Johns Hopkins Univ. Press, 2013); Shauna Devine, *Learning from the Wounded: The Civil War and the Rise of American Medical Science* (Chapel Hill: Univ. of North Carolina Press, 2014); Ira Rutkow, *Bleeding Blue and Gray: Civil War Surgery and the Evolution of*

American Medicine (2005; Mechanicsburg, PA: Stackpole Books, 2015); James M. Schmidt and Guy R. Hasegawa, *Years of Change and Suffering: Modern Perspectives on Civil War Medicine* (Roseville, MN: Edinborough Press, 2009); Brian Craig Miller, *Empty Sleeves: Amputation in the Civil War South* (Athens: Univ. of Georgia Press, 2015).

7. Donald B. Koonce, ed., *Doctor to the Front: The Recollections of Confederate Surgeon Thomas Fanning Wood, 1861–1865* (Knoxville: Univ. of Tennessee Press, 2000); Michael B. Chesson, ed., *J. Franklin Dyer: The Journal of a Civil War Surgeon* (Lincoln: Univ. of Nebraska Press, 2003); James M. Greiner, Janet L. Coryell, and James R. Smither, eds., *A Surgeon's Civil War: The Letters and Diary of Daniel M. Holt, M.D.* (Kent, OH: Kent State Univ. Press, 1994); and Robert D. Hicks, ed., *Civil War Medicine: A Surgeon's Diary* (Bloomington: Indiana Univ. Press, 2019).

8. A. H. Windsor, *History of the Ninety-First Regiment, O.V.I.* (Cincinnati: Gazette Steam Printing House, 1865); E. E. Ewing, *The Story of the Ninety-First* (Portsmouth, OH: Republican Printing Company, 1868); Lois J. Lambert, *Ninety-First Ohio Volunteer Infantry with the Civil War Letters of Lieutenant Colonel Benjamin Franklin Coates and an Annotated Roster of the Men of Company C* (Milford, OH: Little Miami Publishing Co., 2005); Howard Rollins McManus, *The Battle of Cloyds Mountain: The Virginia and Tennessee Railroad Raid, April 29-May 19, 1864* (Lynchburg: H. E. Howard, 1989); Patricia Givens Johnson, *The United States Army Invades the New River Valley, May 1864* (Christiansburg, VA: Walpa Publishing, 1986).

9. Dale Emerson Floyd, "The Life of a Civil War Surgeon from the Letters of William S. Newton" (Master's thesis, University of Dayton, 1968); Richard R. Duncan, *Beleaguered Winchester: A Virginia Community at War, 1861–1865* (Baton Rouge: Louisiana State Univ. Press, 2007); Richard S. Duncan, *Lee's Endangered Left: The Civil War in Western Virginia, Spring of 1864* (Baton Rouge: Louisiana State Univ. Press, 1998); Joan E. Cashin, ed., *The War Was You and Me: Civilians in the American Civil War* (Princeton: Princeton Univ. Press, 2002).

10. "Auction of Legendary Dealer Norm Flayderman Brings $1.1M and Achieves Record Prices," ARTFIXdaily, February 24, 2017, http://www.artfixdaily .com/artwire/release/6796-auction-of-legendary-dealer-norm-flayderman -brings-11m-and-achiev.

11. See, "Collections of Special Collections and University Archives," University Libraries, Virginia Tech, https://spec.lib.vt.edu/collections/index .html#areas.

12. Newton Papers, SCUA VT, finding aid, http://ead.lib.virginia.edu/vivaxtf /view?docId=oai/lib.vt.edu/repositories/2/resources/3546.oai_ead.xml.

Editorial Policy and Practice

1. Mary-Jo Kline, *A Guide to Documentary Editing*, 3rd ed. (Charlottesville: Univ. of Virginia Press, 2008); Steven Burg, *Editing Historical Documents: A Handbook of Practice* (Walnut Creek, CA: AltaMira Press, 1997); Jedediah Mannis and Galen R. Wilson, eds., *Bound to Be a Soldier: The Letters of Private James T. Miller, 111th Pennsylvania Infantry, 1861–1864* (Knoxville: Univ. of Tennessee Press, 2001); William Lee White and Charles Denny Runion, eds., *Great Things Are Expected of Us: The Letters of Colonel C. Irvine Walker, 10th South Carolina Infantry, C.S.A.* (Knoxville: Univ. of Tennessee Press, 2009).

Introduction

1. "Death of W. S. Newton," *Gallipolis Bulletin*, November 21, 1882; *Newton Genealogy of the Newton Families* (n.p.: n.p., n.d.), 5–7, 12–13, Special Collections, Marietta College, Marietta, Ohio; Martin R. Andrews, *History of Marietta and Washington County, Ohio, and Representative Citizens* (Chicago: Biographical Publishing Company, 1902), 1009; David McCullough, *The Pioneers: The Heroic Story of the Settlers Who Brought the American Ideal West* (New York: Simon and Schuster, 2019), 178; Julia Perkins Cutler, *The Life and Times of Ephraim Cutler* (Cincinnati: Robert Clarke and Company, 1890), 85–87.

2. *Catalogue of the Officers and Students of Marietta College, 1839–40* (Marietta, OH: G. W. Tyler and Company Printers, 1840), 10, 11 (quotations).

3. *Catalogue of the Officers and Students of Marietta College, 1840–41* (Marietta, OH: G. W. Tyler and Company Printers, 1841), 9.

4. *Catalogue of the Officers and Students of Marietta College, 1841–42* (Marietta, OH: G. W. Tyler and Company Printers, 1841), 11.

5. *Catalogue of the Officers and Students of Marietta College, 1842–43* (Marietta, OH: G. W. Tyler and Company Printers, 1842), 8, 12.

6. "Robert Safford Newton," in *Dictionary of American Biography*, ed. Dumas Malone (New York: Charles Scribner's Sons, 1934), 13:475–76; "Robert Safford Newton" in Howard A. Kelly and Walter L. Burrage, *American Medical Biographies* (Baltimore: Norman, Remington Company, 1920), 849; Robert L. Numbers, "The Making of an Eclectic Physician: Joseph M. McElhinney and the Eclectic Medical Institute of Cincinnati," *Bulletin of the History of Medicine* 47 (March–April 1973): 159; John S. Haller Jr., *A Profile in Alternative Medicine: The Eclectic Medical College of Cincinnati* (Kent, OH: Kent State Univ. Press, 1999), 3.

7. "What is the American Eclectic System of Medicine?" *Eclectic Medical Journal* 13 (August 1854): 360–62; Numbers, "The Making of an Eclectic Physician," 155–57, 162, 163; Haller, *A Profile in Alternative Medicine*, 31–32; G. W. L. Bickley, "Newton's Clinical Institute," *Eclectic Medical Journal* 13 (March 1854):

118–19; Robert S. Newton, "Calomel and Bleeding," _Eclectic Medical Journal_ 11 (November 1852): 528.

8. See, William Frederick Norwood, _Medical Education in the United States before the Civil War_ (New York: Arno Press, 1971), 304–10.

9. _Annual Announcement of the Medical College of Ohio. For the Years 1846–7_ (Cincinnati: n.p., [ca. 1847]), 15; F. C. Waite, "Medical Education in Ohio," _Ohio State Medical Journal_ 49 (July 1953): 623–26; Robert G. Slawson, "Medical Training in the United States Prior to the Civil War," _Journal of Evidence-Based Complementary and Alternative Medicine_ 17 (January 2012): 16–17; F. C. Waite, "The Professional Education of Pioneer Ohio Physicians," _Ohio State Archaeological and Historical Quarterly_ 48 (1939): 192–95.

10. _Annual Catalogue of the Officers and Students of the Medical College of Ohio, Session 1843–4_ (Cincinnati: R. P. Brooks, 1844), 7, 8.

11. M. B. Wright, _A Lecture Delivered to the Students of the Medical College of Ohio, at the Opening of the Session, 1843–4_ (Cincinnati: R. P. Donogh, 1844), 5 (quotation), 4, 14.

12. _University of Cincinnati, Directory of Graduates_ (Cincinnati: University of Cincinnati, 1926); _Medical College of Ohio, Cincinnati, Sixtieth Annual Catalogue and Announcement, Session of 1880–81_ (Cincinnati: n.p., [ca. 1881]), 21.

13. "Excerpts from Dr. Seth Hart's Day Book Dated August 19, 1844 to April 4, 1846," _Tallow Light: Bulletin of the Washington County, Ohio, Historical Society_ 14 (April–June 1983): 27.

14. W. S. Newton, "An Extensive Injury, with Recovery," _Western Lancet_ 11 (August 1850): 501.

15. _Newton Genealogy of the Newton Families_, 7.

16. _Ironton Register_, July 27, 1854.

17. US Census 1860, Ironton, Lawrence County, Ohio, 181.

18. _Spirit of the Times_ (Ironton), January 29, 1856, https://chroniclingamerica.loc .gov/lccn/sn84028880/1856-01-29/ed-1/seq-3/.

19. _Ironton Register_, January 2, 1862, September 11, 1862, October 2, 1862, October 9, 1862; Floyd, "The Life of a Civil War Surgeon," 2.

20. _Newton Genealogy of the Newton Families_, 8; Whitelaw Reid, _Ohio in the War: Her Statesmen, Her Generals and Soldiers_ (Cincinnati: Moore, Wilstach, and Baldwin, 1868), 2:909.

21. See, Brian D. McKnight, _Contested Borderland: The Civil War in Appalachian Kentucky and Virginia_ (Lexington: Univ. Press of Kentucky, 2006); Noel C. Fisher, _War at Every Door: Partisan Politics and Guerrilla Violence in East Tennessee_ (Chapel Hill: Univ. of North Carolina Press, 1997).

22. Recent scholarship in this area of research includes the following: Megan Kate Nelson, _Ruin Nation: Destruction and the Civil War_ (Athens: Univ. of Georgia Press, 2012); Joan E. Cashin, _War Stuff: The Struggle for Human_

and Environmental Resources in the American Civil War (Cambridge, UK: Cambridge Univ. Press, 2018); Brian Allen Drake, ed., *The Blue, the Gray, and the Green: Toward an Environmental History of the Civil War* (Athens: Univ. of Georgia Press, 2015); Lisa Brady, *War Upon the Land: Military Strategy and the Transformation of Southern Landscapes During the American Civil War* (Athens: Univ. of Georgia Press, 2012); Jonathan Engel, "'It Hasn't Been Squashmolished': Environment, Sense of Place, and the Army of the Tennessee," *The Journal of East Tennessee History* 92 (2020): 28–49; Mark E. Neely Jr., *The Civil War and the Limits of Destruction* (Cambridge, MA: Harvard Univ. Press, 2007); Erin Steward Mauldin, *Unredeemed Land: An Environmental History of Civil War and Emancipation in the Cotton South* (New York: Oxford Univ. Press, 2018); Judkin Browning, *An Environmental History of the Civil War* (Chapel Hill: Univ. of North Carolina Press, 2020).

23. Recent scholarship in this area of research includes the following: Chandra Manning, *What This Cruel War Was Over: Soldiers, Slavery, and the Civil War* (New York: Vintage Books, 2007); David W. Blight, *Race and Reunion: The Civil War in American Memory* (Cambridge, MA: Belknap Press of Harvard Univ. Press, 2001); Susannah J. Ural, *Civil War Citizens: Race, Ethnicity, and Identity in America's Bloodiest Conflict* (New York: New York Univ. Press, 2010); John C. Inscoe, *Race, War, and Remembrance in the Appalachian South* (Lexington: Univ. Press of Kentucky, 2010); Amy Murrell Taylor, *Embattled Freedom: Journeys through the Civil War's Slave Refugee Camps* (Chapel Hill: Univ. of North Carolina Press, 2020).

1. In the Cause of Humanity

1. Abraham Lincoln, "A Proclamation by the President of the United States, April 15, 1861," Record Group 46, Records of the US Senate (RG 46), NARA, https://www.visitthecapitol.gov/exhibitions/artifact/proclamation-president -united-states-april-15–1861; Reid, *Ohio in the War*, 1:21 (quotation), 25, 27.

2. Reid, *Ohio in the War*, 1:245–46, 248.

3. Floyd, "The Life of a Civil War Surgeon," 2–3; Windsor, *History of the Ninety-First Regiment*, 40; Jack L. Dickinson, *Jenkins of Greenbottom: A Civil War Saga* (Charleston, WV: Pictorial Histories Publishing Company, 1988), 38–39; Jack L. Dickinson and Kay Stamper Dickinson, *Gentleman Soldier of Greenbottom: The Life of Brigadier General Albert Gallatin Jenkins, CSA* (Huntington, WV: self-pub., 2011), 74–75.

4. *Official Roster of the Soldiers of the State of Ohio in the War of the Rebellion, 1861–1866* (Cincinnati: Ohio Valley Press, 1888), 7:127; Floyd, "The Life of a Civil War Surgeon," 3; Windsor, *History of the Ninety-First Regiment*, 6.

5. See, James A. Ramage, *Rebel Raider: The Life of General John Hunt Morgan* (Lexington: Univ. Press of Kentucky, 1986); Edison H. Thomas, *John Hunt*

Morgan and His Raiders (Lexington: Univ. Press of Kentucky, 1985); Cecil Fletcher Holland, *Morgan and His Raiders: A Biography of the Confederate General* (New York: Macmillan Co., 1942); Basil Duke, *Morgan's Cavalry* (New York: Neale Publishing Co., 1909).

6. There is no record of W. R. Earheart serving as surgeon or assistant surgeon in the Union army. He did not appear in N. A. Strait's *Roster of Regimental Surgeons and Assistant Surgeons during the War of the Rebellion* (Washington, DC: N. A. Strait, 1882), which is the standard source for service verification. An Ancestry.com search yielded that William R. Earheart married Sophia D. Scott on December 9, 1856, in Lawrence County, Ohio. Additional searches of federal tax lists during the war years (1862, 1864, and 1865) include a W. R. Earheart as a physician living in Champaign, Illinois. If these two Earhearts are the same, it is likely that he relocated to Illinois in the summer or fall of 1862 (a tax assessor created the listing for Earheart in November) and did not serve.

7. The *Victor* was a Union transport steam boat.

8. This is most likely Elizabeth Sisson, wife of Francis W. Sisson. Francis served in the 13th Virginia Infantry, rising to the rank of first lieutenant and quartermaster. He mustered out in June 1865. The 1870 census lists him as recorder of deeds for Mason County and Elizabeth as keeping house. As another possibility, there was also a Mrs. Mariah T. Sisson, the spouse of Wilson C. Sisson, living in Point Pleasant at that time. Theodore F. Lang, *Loyal West Virginia from 1861 to 1865* (Baltimore: Deutsch Publishing Company, 1895), 287, 289; US Census, 1870, Point Pleasant, Mason County, West Virginia, 14.

9. J. S. Roddarmour lived with his wife Margaret B. and sixteen-year-old son Franklin in Ironton. US Census, 1860, Ironton, Lawrence County, Ohio, 192.

10. David Nixon operated a variety store in Ironton on Second Street, above the Iron Bank. US Census, 1860, Ironton, Lawrence County, Ohio, 17; *Spirit of the Times* (Ironton), January 29, 1856, https://chroniclingamerica.loc.gov/lccn /sn84028880/1856–01–29/ed-1/seq-4/

11. Flux is also known as dysentery.

12. Edwin S. Morgan was a second lieutenant for the 2nd Virginia Cavalry. He was later promoted to major. J. J. Sutton, *History of the Second Regiment, West Virginia Cavalry Volunteers, during the War of the Rebellion* (Portsmouth, OH: n.p., 1892), 6, 49, 262.

13. Diaphoretics were designed to induce perspiration in patients and were commonly used to treat a variety of illnesses in the nineteenth century. Gross, *A Manual of Military Surgery*, 17; Mark J. Schaadt, *Civil War Medicine: An Illustrated History* (Quincy, IL: Cedarwood Publishing, 1998), 87.

14. This is most likely James Vanden, a carriage maker from Gallipolis who was married to Esther Vanden. Their son Charles was an assistant carriage maker. US Census, 1860, Gallipolis, Gallia County, Ohio, 188.

15. Quincy Adams Gillmore was a native Ohioan who began his military career in the Corps of Engineers. He rose to the rank of brigadier general during the siege of Fort Pulaski in Georgia. In the fall of 1862, he was ordered to Point Pleasant to reorganize troops for service in the Kanawha Valley. Gillmore then led forces in Kentucky and in 1863, as a major general, became commander of the Department of the South. Reid, *Ohio in the War*, 1:617–55.

16. Eliza Neal was the sister of Samuel Finley Neal, a major in the 91st Ohio Volunteer Infantry. The Neal family were longtime residents of Gallipolis.

17. A Sibley was a portable, conical tent that could accommodate up to a dozen soldiers. H. H. Sibley, a West Point graduate, invented the tent and also a portable stove known as a Sibley stove. John D. Billings, *Hardtack and Coffee: Or, The Unwritten Story of Army Life* (Boston: George M. Smith and Company, 1887), 46–48.

18. An Enfield was a rifle-musket used by both the North and South during the Civil War. Ian V. Hogg, *Weapons of the Civil War* (New York: Military Press, 1987), 17, 34–35, 39; "Enfield Rifle," Smithsonian Institution, http://www.civilwar.si.edu/weapons_enfield.html.

19. Joseph Warren Keifer began his military service in the 3rd Ohio Volunteer Infantry and saw action in western Virginia. He rose to the rank of lieutenant colonel, and, when his term expired in 1862, he became colonel for the 110th Ohio Volunteer Infantry. In April 1865 he was breveted as a major general. He later served in the House of Representatives and was a major general in the Spanish American War. *Official Roster of the Soldiers of the State of Ohio*, 8:3; Thomas E. Pope, *The Weary Boys: Col. J. Warren Keifer and the 110th Ohio Volunteer Infantry* (Kent, OH: Kent State Univ. Press, 2002), 112; John H. Eicher and David J. Eicher, *Civil War High Commands* (Stanford: Stanford Univ. Press, 2001), 749.

20. Edwin S. Morgan was a second lieutenant for the 2nd Virginia Cavalry. He was later promoted to major. Sutton, *History of the Second Regiment, West Virginia*, 6, 49, 262

21. Dr. O. E. Davis was from Lancaster, Ohio. In fall 1862 he was the surgeon in charge of the Gallipolis General Hospital. US Census, 1860, Lancaster, Fairfield County, Ohio, 26; *Gallipolis Journal*, October 9, 1862, October 30, 1862.

22. A Sibley stove was a portable stove invented by H. H. Sibley, a West Point graduate. He also invented the Sibley, a portable, conical tent that could accommodate up to a dozen soldiers. Billings, *Hardtack and Coffee*, 46–48.

23. John Stinson was born in Virginia in 1841 as a slave. At the beginning of the Civil War, he was married and worked as a blacksmith in Malden. Most likely his owner rented him out to work in the Dickinson and Shrewsbury salt works in Malden. When he met William S. Newton in October 1862, Stinson was most likely a runaway slave seeking protection by the Union

army in exchange for his cooking skills. On June 18, 1863, Ohio Governor David Tod authorized the beginning of a regiment of colored soldiers, originally known as the 127th Ohio Volunteer Infantry and later re-designated the 5th United States Colored Infantry. In October 1863 Stinson registered for military service in the Union army and listed Pomeroy, Ohio, as his residence. On August 3 the twenty-six-year-old Stinson enlisted for one year of service. On September 2, 1864, he was mustered into service at Camp Delaware, Ohio. Stinson's military record indicates that he was transferred to the 15th United States Colored Infantry, which was assigned to Springfield, Tennessee, just north of Nashville. On November 18, 1864, he was appointed sergeant in Company B of the 9th United States Colored Heavy Artillery. At the end of the war, Stinson was listed as sick in hospital in Nashville, in June 1865. He was mustered out in Nashville on August 5, 1865. In 1882 his widow Eliza Huffman applied for a military pension. Consolidated Lists of Civil War Draft Registration Records, West Virginia, 3rd District, 1:198, Record Group 110, Records of the Provost Marshal General's Bureau (Civil War) (RG 110); Compiled Military Service Records of Volunteer Union Soldiers Who Served with the United States Colored Troops: Artillery Organizations, Microfilm Serial, M1818, Microfilm Roll 158; John Stinson, Pension Card, Civil War Pension Index: General Index to Pension Files, 1861–1934, RG 15, all in NARA; *Official Roster of the Soldiers of the State of Ohio*, 1:672; Reid, *Ohio in the War*, 2:916–17; Charles H. Wesley, *Ohio Negroes in the Civil War* (Columbus: Ohio State Univ. Press, 1962), 26–27, 33–34, 37.

24. Completed in the early 1850s, the Tennessee and Virginia Railroad connected Lynchburg with Bristol. The railroad served as a critical transportation route during the Civil War. See, Kenneth W. Noe, *Southwest Virginia's Railroad: Modernization and the Sectional Crisis* (Urbana: Univ. of Illinois Press, 1994); *Charter and By-Laws of the Virginia and Tennessee Rail Road Company* (Lynchburg: R. K. Irving and Company, 1840).

25. *Cincinnati Daily Commercial.*

26. George P. Rodgers was a second lieutenant in the 91st Ohio Volunteer Infantry. He enlisted on August 15, 1862, and resigned on February 19, 1863. *Official Roster of the Soldiers of the State of Ohio*, 7:148.

27. On November 10, 1861, Confederate forces took control of the town of Guyandotte, West Virginia. During the process of clearing the town of Union soldiers, Confederate colonel John Clarkson accidently shot and killed Confederate captain Tom Huddleston of the 8th Virginia Cavalry. Joe Geiger Jr., "The Tragic Fate of Guyandotte," *West Virginia History* 54 (1995): 32–34; Jack L. Dickinson, *8th Virginia Cavalry* (Lynchburg: H. E. Howard, Inc., 1986), 12; J. H. Rouse, *Horrible Massacre at Guyandotte, VA, and a Journey to the Rebel*

Capital, with a Description of Prison Life in a Tobacco Warehouse in Richmond (n.p.: n.p., 1862), 6–7.

28. When the Civil War began, Jacob D. Cox was a Republican state senator. In 1862 he was appointed major general and later governor. Reid, *Ohio in the War*, 1:770–77; "Jacob Dolson Cox," in Rossiter Johnson, ed., *The Twentieth Century Biographical Dictionary of Notable Americans* (Boston: Biographical Society, 1904), 3:4–5.

29. John T. Irwin (Erwin) was a first lieutenant in Company D of the 91st Ohio Volunteer Infantry. *Official Roster of the Soldiers of the State of Ohio*, 7:136.

30. A batten refers to wooden planks used to build wagons and train cars. See, "Railway Carriage and Wagon Construction (VII)," *Locomotive Magazine* 6 (November 1901): 192.

31. Casper H. Sterneman was a private in Company B of the 91st Ohio Volunteer Infantry. His father was Dr. C. R. Sterneman, a surgeon and dentist in Gallipolis. *Official Roster of the Soldiers of the State of Ohio*, 7:132; US Census, 1860, Gallipolis, Gallia County, Ohio, 117; *Gallipolis Journal*, December 11, 1862, 4.

32. Alexander Ricker and his wife Adeline had a child in 1862 named Alexander. US Census, 1870, Ironton, Lawrence County, Ohio, 129.

33. John Reeves was a twenty-six-year-old stove molder who lived with his wife Sarah and infant son Edward in Ironton. Reeves joined Company G of the 140th Ohio Volunteer Infantry for one hundred days of service on May 2, 1864. US Census, 1860, Ironton, Lawrence County, 38–39; *Official Roster of the Soldiers of the State of Ohio*, 8:702.

34. William H. G. Adney began service as a captain in the 36th Ohio Volunteer Infantry on August 14, 1861. He rose to the rank of major on September 17, 1862. Reid, *Ohio in the War*, 2:231.

35. Albin or Albion B. Stimson served in Company B of the 2nd Virginia Cavalry. He mustered in on November 8, 1861, as a corporal and was mustered out on November 28, 1864, as a private. Sutton, *History of the Second Regiment, West Virginia*, 14.

36. Mr. English's brother was James English, a private who enlisted in the 91st Ohio Volunteer Infantry on August 2, 1861, for three years of service. James English was discharged on May 3, 1863, on surgeon's certificate of disability. *Official Roster of the Soldiers of the State of Ohio*, 7:134.

37. Nancy Harvey Huddleston was the widow of George Paddy Huddleston, who had died in 1859. Celia Flora Huddleston, July 12, 2019, Geni.com, https://www.geni.com/people/Celia-Huddleston/6000000001563044982; "George Paddy Huddleston," Find A Grave, https://www.findagrave.com/memorial/50546880.

2. The More Strange Faces You See the More Lonely You Are

1. Martin B. Gilbert was a thirteen-year-old "side drummer" who joined the 91st Ohio Volunteer Infantry on July 29, 1862. He mustered out with the company on June 24, 1865. *Official Roster of the Soldiers of the State of Ohio*, 7:134; Windsor, *History of the Ninety-First Regiment*, 39.

2. F. S. Wright, was a druggist in Ironton. He was married to Mary E. Wright. US Census, 1860, Ironton, Lawrence County, Ohio, 24.

3. Jacob Wycoff enlisted in Company D of the 116th Ohio Volunteer Infantry on August 18, 1862. He began as a sergeant and rose to the rank of second lieutenant. *Official Roster of the Soldiers of the State of Ohio*, 8:192; Thomas E. Wildes, *Record of the One Hundred and Sixteenth Regiment, Ohio Infantry Volunteers in the War of the Rebellion* (Sandusky, OH: I. F. Mack and Brothers Printers, 1884), 231, 271, 336.

4. Canton flannel is a heavy cotton fabric first produced in Canton, China. The fabric has fleece on one side and twill on the other, which makes it warm and absorbent. It is still used in sleepwear and undergarments. "Canton Flannel," Conservation and Art Materials Encyclopedia Online, http://cameo.mfa .org/wiki/Canton_flannel; Rosalie Rosso King, *Textile Identification, Conservation, and Preservation* (Park Ridge, NJ: Noyes Publications, 1985), 297.

5. A puncheon is a type of wooden flooring.

6. Latin phrase translated to English as "Woe is me."

7. Puerperal convulsions refer to seizures occurring during childbirth or shortly after giving birth. W. S. Oke, "Puerperal Convulsions," *Association Medical Journal* 2 (May 5, 1854): 386.

8. John W. Campbell enlisted on August 22, 1862, as a private in Company H of the 91st Ohio Volunteer Infantry. He was only sixteen years old. *Official Roster of the Soldiers of the State of Ohio*, 7:148; Windsor, *History of the Ninety-First Regiment*, 30.

9. John R. Philson was a doctor from Racine, Ohio. He was commissioned assistant surgeon for the 4th Virginia Infantry on November 19, 1861. He received a promotion to surgeon of the 4th on May 9, 1863. He was discharged from service on October 3, 1864, and died later that month. Strait, *Roster of All Regimental Surgeons and Assistant Surgeons*, 273; T. H. Barton, *Autobiography of Dr. Thomas H. Barton, The Self-Made Physician of Syracuse, Ohio, Including a History of the Fourth Regiment West Virginia Volunteer Infantry* (Charleston: West Virginia Printing Company, 1890), 144, 205; *Official Army Register of the Volunteer Force of the United States Army for the Years 1861, '62, '63, '64, '65* (Washington, DC: Government Printing Office, 1865), 4:1126; Stillman Carter Larkin, *Pioneer History of Meigs County* (Columbus: Berlin Publishing Company, 1908), 200; Lang, *Loyal West Virginia*, 244.

10. James H. Dayton was from New Creek, Virginia. He was commissioned as a captain for the 4th Virginia Infantry on July 15, 1861. He received a promotion to lieutenant colonel on March 19, 1863, and then to colonel on May 9, 1863. He mustered out with the expiration of his term of service on July 4, 1864. Reid, *Ohio in the War*, 2:918; Barton, *Autobiography of Dr. Thomas H. Barton*, 202; *Official Army Register*, 4:1126; Lang, *Loyal West Virginia*, 244.

11. Lorenzo A. Phelps was commissioned as a captain on September 23, 1861, for the 5th Virginia Infantry. He rose to the rank of colonel on April 19, 1862. In April 1863 he was court martialed for inappropriate behavior including drinking on duty, contracting gonorrhea from a prostitute, and deserting. Witnesses testified that Phelps also beat his wife when she visited. He was dismissed August 15, 1863. Lang, *Loyal West Virginia*, 251, 252; Judith Giesberg, *Sex and the Civil War: Soldiers, Pornography, and the Making of American Morality* (Chapel Hill: Univ. of North Carolina Press, 2017), 53.

12. Tompkins farm was another name for Gauley Mountain, where the 47th Ohio Volunteer Infantry established a camp and maintained a Union presence. The farm was owned by Christopher and Ellen Tompkins. She is referred to as Mrs. Tompkins in several of Newton's letters. He served as a Confederate colonel in the 22nd Virginia Infantry but resigned after being ask to open fire on his own home. "Christopher Q. Tompkins" and "Gauley Mount," West Virginia's Sesquicentennial Highway Historical Markers, West Virginia Archives and History, West Virginia Department of Arts, Culture and History, http://www.wvculture.org/history/markers/sesqui /christopherqtompkins.html; Reid, *Ohio in the War*, 2:292; Bruce S. Allardice, *Confederate Colonels: A Biographical Register* (Columbia: Univ. of Missouri Press, 2008), 374; Joseph A. Saunier, ed., *Forth-Seventh Regiment Ohio Veteran Volunteer Infantry, Second Brigade, Second Division, Fifteenth Army Corps, Army of the Tennessee* (Hillsboro, OH: Lyle Printing Company, [1903]), 33.

13. Josiah D. Cotton was a doctor from Marietta, Ohio. He was surgeon for the 92nd Ohio Volunteer Infantry. He served from August 19, 1862, until his mustering out with the regiment on June 10, 1865. *Official Roster of the Soldiers of the State of Ohio*, 7:157; Strait, *Roster of Regimental Surgeons and Assistant Surgeons*, 207.

14. Thomas D. Howell was a doctor from Pine Grove, Ohio. He was assistant surgeon for the 92nd Ohio Volunteer Infantry. He resigned on April 29, 1863. *Official Roster of the Soldiers of the State of Ohio*, 7:157; Strait, *Roster of Regimental Surgeons and Assistant Surgeons*, 207.

15. W. Clark's letter to the editor of the *Ironton Register* applauded the high quality of the public schools in Ironton, which he believed rivaled schools in Cleveland and Columbus. W. Clark, "The Union Schools," *Ironton Register*, December 18, 1862.

16. A coverlid is a bedspread or quilt.

17. In late December 1863, Union major general William Rosecrans's troops fought Confederate forces led by General Braxton Bragg at the Battle of Stones River near Murfreesboro in Middle Tennessee. Rosecrans was victorious and pushed the Confederates toward Tullahoma. William M. Lamers, *The Edge of Glory: A Biography of General William S. Rosecrans* (New York: Harcourt, Brace and World, Inc., 1961), 217–43; Peter Cozzens, *No Better Place to Die: The Battle of Stones River* (Urbana: Univ. of Illinois Press, 1990).

18. Drill is a durable twill weave textile made of cotton, linen, or hemp.

19. Warren G. Hibbard was listed in the 1860 census as living in Ironton with Alexander Ricker's family. His occupation was listed as a clerk. Hibbard served as a second lieutenant in the 18th Ohio Volunteer Infantry for a three-month term from April to August 1861. US Census, 1860, Ironton, Lawrence County, 43; *Official Roster of the Soldiers of the State of Ohio*, 1:378.

20. In 1864 Warren G. Hibbard married Celia F. Huddleston, the daughter of Nancy Harvey Huddleston. They moved to Iowa and then later California. When he died in 1906, she applied for a widow's pension. US Census, 1870 Brooklyn, Poweshiek County, Iowa, 1; US Census, 1900, Los Angeles, Los Angeles Ward 1, District 0001, 2; Augustine George Hibbard, *Genealogy of the Hibbard Family, Who Are Descendants of Robert Hibbard of Salem, Massachusetts* (Hartford, CT: Case, Lockwood and Brainard Company, 1901), 263; Warren G. Hibbard, Pension Card, Civil War Pension Index: General Index to Pension Files, 1861–1934, RG 15, NARA.

21. A "grass widow" refers to a married woman whose husband has been away for a lengthy period of time.

22. The roster of the 91st Ohio Volunteer Infantry does not list a William Jones as hospital steward. There are three soldiers with the name William Jones: William G. Jones, a sergeant in Company A; William N. Jones, a private in Company E; and William P. Jones, a private in Company E. It is uncertain which William Jones served Newton as a hospital steward. *Official Roster of the Soldiers of the State of Ohio*, 7:128, 140.

23. Cimicifuga is a genus of flowering plant native to the northern hemisphere. Translated from Latin, cimicifuga means bedbug repellent. During the nineteenth century it was commonly used as an expectorant. Michael A. Flannery, *Civil War Pharmacy: A History* (New York: Pharmaceutical Products Press, 2004), 34; J. U. Lloyd and C. G. Lloyd, *Drugs and Medicines of North America: A Publication Devoted to the Historical and Scientific Discussions of the Botany, Pharmacy, Chemistry and Therapeutics of the Medicinal Plants of North America* (Cincinnati: Robert Clarke and Co., 1884), 1:244–88.

24. The *Victor No. 2* was a Union transport steam boat. On March 29, 1863, just a month after Newton's ride on the steamboat, Confederate general Albert G.

Jenkins attempted to capture the *Victor No. 2* and its $100,000 worth of military supplies. Frederick Ford, captain of the *Victor No. 2*, escaped the blockade near Point Pleasant and delivered the supplies to the Union quartermaster in Gallipolis. *History of Gallia County*, xxx, 42–43; Lenette S. Taylor, *"The Supply for Tomorrow Must Not Fail": The Civil War of Captain Simon Perkins Jr., a Union Quartermaster* (Kent, OH: Kent State Univ. Press, 2004), 180.

25. The southbound *Bostonia* was a Union transport steamboat. In April 1862 the *Bostonia No. 1* and *Bostonia No. 2* were part of the Union support fleet of steamers on the Tennessee River during the Battle of Shiloh. In April 1865 the *Bostonia No. 2* was the first rescue craft to assist after the *Sultana* riverboat disaster on the Mississippi. T. M. Hurst, "The Battle of Shiloh," *American Historical Magazine* 7 (January 1902): 31; Allen R. Coggins, *Tennessee Tragedies: Natural, Technological, and Societal Disasters in the Volunteer State* (Knoxville: Univ. of Tennessee Press, 2011), 178.

26. This is most likely Tom Lewis, a private in Company H of the 91st Ohio Volunteer Infantry. *Official Roster of the Soldiers of the State of Ohio*, 7:149.

27. Thomas Graham enlisted as a private in Company C of the 91st Ohio Volunteer Infantry on August 11, 1862. He was transferred to the Veteran Reserve Corps on March 29, 1863. *Official Roster of the Soldiers of the State of Ohio*, 7:134.

28. Mary E. Wright was married to F. S. Wright, a druggist in Ironton. US Census, 1860, Ironton, Lawrence County, Ohio, 24.

29. Captain Malbridge was most likely the captain of one of the steamboats that transported soldiers and supplies on the Ohio and Kanawha Rivers, and not a captain in the military.

30. Henry Rider enlisted as a private in Company K of the 91st Ohio Volunteer Infantry on August 15, 1862. He died on April 1, 1863, at Fayetteville, West Virginia. *Official Roster of the Soldiers of the State of Ohio*, 7:154.

31. Joseph Dumble was a printer who worked for the *Ironton Register*. US Census 1860, Ohio, Lawrence County, Ironton, 42.

3. The Booming of Cannon at Every Moment Strikes the Ear

1. Dickinson and Dickinson, *Gentleman Soldier of Greenbottom*, 85–87.

2. See, Richard Orr Curry, *A House Divided: A Study of Statehood Politics and the Copperhead Movement in West Virginia* (Pittsburgh: Univ. of Pittsburgh Press, 1964).

3. William S. Newton to Frances Ann Hayward Newton, April 5, 1863, Newton Papers, SCUA VT.

4. *Official Roster of the Soldiers of the State of Ohio*, 7:127

5. John H. Dempsey was a clerk from Ironton when the Civil War began. In November 1861 he enlisted as a corporal in Company B of the 2nd Virginia

Cavalry. He reenlisted in January 1864. US Census 1860, Ohio, Lawrence County, Ironton, 41; Sutton, *History of the Second Regiment, West Virginia*, 15.

6. Asafoetida is the dried latex from several species of perennial herbs, from the celery family. It is used as a spice in cooking and is considered a digestive aid. Ivan A. Ross, *Medicinal Plants of the World: Chemical Constituents, Traditional and Modern Medical Uses* (Totowa, NJ: Humana Press, 2005), 3:223–34.

7. Harrison Holcomb enlisted as a private in Company K of the 91st Ohio Volunteer Infantry on August 13, 1862. He died on March 24, 1863, at Fayetteville, West Virginia. *Official Roster of the Soldiers of the State of Ohio*, 7:154.

8. Henry Rider enlisted as a private in Company K of the 91st Ohio Volunteer Infantry on August 15, 1862. He died on April 1, 1863, at Fayetteville, West Virginia. *Official Roster of the Soldiers of the State of Ohio*, 7:154.

9. Joseph R. Safford enlisted as a private in Company B of the 91st Ohio Volunteer Infantry on August 8, 1862. He mustered out with the company on June 24, 1865. *Official Roster of the Soldiers of the State of Ohio*, 7:132.

10. A razor strop is a thin flexible piece of leather, canvas, or other soft material used to straighten and polish the blade of a razor or knife.

11. James Riley Ramsey was a farmer who lived in Nicholas County, Virginia. He was fifty-one years old when the Civil War began. He became a scout for the 36th and 47th Ohio regiments. To help combat Confederate raids, he organized a small home guard known as Ramsey's Scouts. In August 1862 the group officially became Company A of the 126th West Virginia State Militia, with Ramsey serving as its captain. US Census, 1860, Virginia, Nicholas County, District of Nicholas, 29; Richard T. Childress, *A Historical Lottery: Europe to Appalachia and Beyond—A Ramsey Family Through 1500 Years of Social and Cultural Change* (Pittsburg: Dorrance Publishing Company, 2016), 311–12, 375–79; Karissa A. Marken, "'They Cannot Catch Guerrillas in the Mountains Any More Than Cows Can Catch Fleas': Guerrilla Warfare in Western Virginia, 1861–1865" (Master's thesis, Liberty University, 2014), 79.

12. Erastus B. Tyler was colonel of the 7th Ohio Volunteer Infantry. In August 1861 the 7th began operations in western Virginia. Later that month, Confederate forces led by General John B. Floyd surprised and routed the 7th in Nicholas County at what would be called the Battle of Cross Lanes. "Battle of Keslers Cross Lanes," *The West Virginia Encyclopedia*, https://www.wvencyclopedia.org/articles/1192; Reid, *Ohio in the War*, 1:317–318, 2:57–58; Mark A. Snell, *West Virginia and the Civil War: Mountaineers are Always Free* (Charleston, SC: History Press, 2011), 48–49.

13. This is most likely Nancy Eagle, the wife of David Eagle, both of whom lived in Nicholas County, Virginia, in 1860. US Census, 1860, Nicholas County, Virginia, Summersville District, Virginia, 4.

14. "The Southern Wagon" was an adapted version of the 1850s folk song "Wait for the Wagon." "The Southern Wagon" was a popular Confederate song that promoted secession and called for the defeat of the "Lincoln cut-throats." In response, songwriter Jerry Blossom released a pro-Union version of the song called "That Southern Wagon," which ridiculed the Confederacy and celebrated Union military victories. Irwin Silber, *Songs of the Civil War* (New York: Dover Publications, Inc., 1995), 171; "The Southern Wagon," David M. Rubenstein Rare Book and Manuscript Library, Duke University, https://library.duke.edu/digitalcollections/hasm_conf0383/; "The Southern Wagon," Library of Congress, https://www.loc.gov/resource/amss.cw201840/?st=text; Jerry Blossom, "That Southern Wagon," Library of Congress, https://www.loc.gov/item/ihas.200001360/.

15. John R. Blessing, who served as major in the 91st Ohio Volunteer Infantry, died April 10, 1863, at his home in Gallia County, Ohio. *Official Roster of the Soldiers of the State of Ohio*, 7:127.

16. Jonathon Pool was a musician who enlisted in the 91st Ohio Volunteer Infantry on August 8, 1862. He died on April 18, 1863, in Summersville, West Virginia. *Official Roster of the Soldiers of the State of Ohio*, 7:142.

17. Ira M. Crull enlisted as a musician in Company F of the 91st Ohio Volunteer Infantry on August 11, 1862. He was the son of Dr. Crull of Scioto County. Crull mustered out with his company on June 24, 1865. *Official Roster of the Soldiers of the State of Ohio*, 7:142; Windsor, *History of the Ninety-First Regiment*, 23.

18. Macadam is a type of road construction invented by John Loudon McAdam. The road is constructed by layering tightly packed gravel to bind the roadway. See, Roy Devereux, *John Loudon McAdam: Chapters in the History of Highways* (London: Oxford Univ. Press, 1936).

19. James E. Thomas was commissioned as captain of Company D of the 91st Ohio Volunteer Infantry on July 24, 1862. He was dismissed through a general court martial on August 15, 1863. *Official Roster of the Soldiers of the State of Ohio*, 7:136; Windsor, *History of the Ninety-First Regiment*, 16.

20. Owen Duffy was born in Ireland in 1800 and in 1860 was a farmer in Nicholas County, Virginia. He and his wife Ann had a large family. US Census, 1860, Nicholas County, Virginia, District of Nicholas, 76; US Census, 1850, Nicholas County, Virginia, District of Nicholas, 383.

21. The *Levi* was a Union transport steam boat. In February 1864 Confederate forces captured the *Levi* commanded by Brigadier General Eliakim P. Scammon of the 23rd Ohio Volunteer Infantry. The Confederates forced the Union soldiers off the vessel, docked the *Levi* down river, stole the cargo, and set it ablaze. *Point Pleasant Register*, February 11, 1864; Taylor, *The Supply for Tomorrow*, 180.

22. The blue pill, also known as blue mass, was a mercury-based medicine used in the nineteenth century to treat a variety of diseases and ailments. This purgative was a highly toxic remedy and caused mercury poisoning. President Abraham Lincoln took the pills regularly to combat his melancholia but ceased taking the medicine a few months after becoming president because he found the blue pills made him cross. S. D. Gross, *A Manual of Military Surgery: Or, Hints on the Emergencies of the Field, Camp and Hospital Practice* (Augusta, GA: Chronicle and Sentinel, 1861), 17; Norbert Hirschhorn, Robert G. Feldman, and Ian A. Greaves, "Abraham Lincoln's Blue Pills: Did Our 16th President Suffer from Mercury Poisoning?" *Perspectives in Biology and Medicine* 44 (Summer 2001): 315–32; Alka Agrawal, "All the President's Pills," June 20, 2001, ScienceMag, https://www.sciencemag.org /news/2001/07/all-presidents-pills.

23. Oliver C. Ong was commissioned as a first sergeant in Company E of the 2nd Virginia Calvary on November 8, 1861. He was promoted to second lieutenant in Company F on April 7, 1863. Confederate troops captured Ong on May 12, 1863, at Summersville, West Virginia. He was confined in Confederate prisons in Macon, Georgia, and Columbia, South Carolina. He was discharged from service in March 1865. Sutton, *History of the Second Regiment, West Virginia*, 8, 26; *Official Roster of the Soldiers of the State of Ohio*, 12:343.

24. John J. Medlicott was commissioned as a lieutenant in Company G, 2nd Virginia Cavalry on November 8, 1861. He was honorably discharged from service on September 27, 1864. Sutton, *History of the Second Regiment, West Virginia*, 7, 29.

25. W. R. Looker served as aide-de-camp for Governor David Tod. Richard F. Miller, *States at War: A Reference Guide for Ohio in the Civil War* (Hanover, NH: Univ. Press of New England, 2015), 5:404; *Eighth Annual Report of the Trustees and Superintendent of the Ohio State Asylum for the Education of Idiotic and Imbecile Youth to the Governor of the State of Ohio for the Year 1864* (Columbus: n.p., 1864), 464, 465.

26. This is most likely Dolly Blazer, who lived in Gallipolis. Her husband, Richard Blazer, was first lieutenant and later captain in Company B of the 91st Ohio Volunteer Regiment. US Census, 1860, Gallia County, Gallipolis, 208; *Official Roster of the Soldiers of the State of Ohio*, 7:130.

4. Still Rumors of a Fight

1. Windsor, *History of the Ninety-First Regiment*, 41.

2. Clement Laird Vallandigham was an Ohio politician who led the Copperheads, an anti-war faction of the Democratic Party. After a term as a US representative, he returned to Ohio and offered scathing criticisms of the

war. Union general Ambrose Burnside, the commander of the Department
of the Ohio, believed that Vallandigham's rhetoric was damaging to the
Union and sympathetic to southerners. Vallandigham was arrested in early
1863 and tried before a military court martial. That body found him guilty of
opposing the war, and in May 1863 President Lincoln ordered Vallandigham
to be expelled from the Union. Vallandigham met with Confederate leaders
in North Carolina and Virginia before fleeing to Canada. While in exile, he
ran for governor of Ohio as a Democrat but lost to pro-Union War Democrat John Brough. "Clement Laird Vallandigham," *Appleton's Cyclopaedia of
American Biography*, ed. James Grant Wilson and John Fiske (New York:
D. Appleton and Company, 1889), 6:227–28; Frank L. Klement, *The Limits
of Dissent: Clement L. Vallandigham and the Civil War* (Lexington: Univ.
Press of Kentucky, 1970); Thomas C. Mackey, *Opposing Lincoln: Clement L.
Vallandigham, Presidential Power, and the Legal Battle over Dissent in Wartime*
(Lawrence: Univ. Press of Kansas, 2020).

3. William S. Newton to Frances Ann Hayward Newton, August 14, 1863,
    Newton Papers, SCUA VT (quotation).
4. William S. Newton to Frances Ann Hayward Newton, August 23, 1863,
    Newton Papers, SCUA VT (quotations).
5. Charles Humphreys Newton was the son of Stephen Newton and the half-
    nephew of William S. Newton. Charles graduated from Marietta College in
    1863. After graduating, he served as a first lieutenant in Company D of the
    2nd Ohio Heavy Artillery. *Marietta College in the War of Secession, 1861–1865*
    (Cincinnati: Peter G. Thomson, 1878), 84; *Official Roster of the Soldiers of the
    State of Ohio*, 10:324; Reid, *Ohio in the War*, 2:909.
6. This is most likely the home of James B. Munsey or Muncy. In the 1830s he
    settled near Gauley Bridge with his wife. He contracted with the James and
    Kanawha Company to operate a toll house for travelers to cross the bridge.
    Munsey was sheriff of Fayette County from 1855 to 1859. He was referred to
    as Colonel Munsey, which was likely an honorary title and not an indication
    of military service. Thomas C. Miller and Hu Maxwell, *West Virginia and
    Its People* (New York: Lewis Historical Publishing Company, 1913), 2:456;
    William Alexander MacCorkle, *The White Sulphur Springs: The Traditions,
    History, and Social Life of the Greenbrier White Sulphur Springs* (New York:
    Neale Publishing Company, 1916), 34; US Census, 1860, Gauley Bridge, Fay-
    ette County, West Virginia, 299; *Fayette Journal* (Fayetteville, WV), Novem-
    ber 2, 1911; *Collection of all Acts of the General Assembly, Relating to the James
    River and Kanawha Company; Together with the By-Laws and Resolutions of the
    Stockholders of the Company, and Rules and Regulations of the Presidents and
    Directors, and Other Documents* (Richmond: Samuel Shepherd, 1835), 180; "A
    Statement of the Names, and Amount and Manner of Compensation of All

the Officers, Agents and Servants in the Employment of the James River and Kanawha Company, Together with a Statement of the Amount Paid Upon Their Respective Subscriptions by the Corporations which Have Subscribed to the Company's Capital Stock," February 14, 1837, 4, document 46, *Journal of the House of Delegates of the Commonwealth of Virginia, Begun and Held at the Capitol, In the City of Richmond, On Monday, The Fifth Day of December, One Thousand Eight Hundred and Thirty-Six* (Richmond: Thomas Ritchie, 1836).

7. A bracken is a type of fern.

8. A summersweet is a type of flowering shrub that attracts butterflies and songbirds.

9. This is most likely Mary Caroline Tyree, born in 1840. She died in Gauley Bridge in 1863. "Mary Carolina Tyree," Find A Grave, https://www.findagrave.com/memorial/137366146.

10. Charles N. Hall was from Adams County, Ohio. He was commissioned as a sergeant in Company I of the 91st Ohio Volunteer Infantry on August 9, 1862. By the fall of 1863, Hall served as a hospital orderly for Newton. Hall rose to the rank of first lieutenant and was discharged in March 21, 1865. US Census, 1860, Green, Adams County, Ohio, 13; *Official Roster of the Soldiers of the State of Ohio*, 7:150.

11. This refers to taking French leave, which means a leisurely absence from a military unit without seeking approval.

12. Name searches for Mary Ann McDonald in the US Census and other sources that include details on slaves did not yield any clear results. Newton's letters indicated that she was a slave in the Wytheville area who was emancipated by the 34th Ohio Regiment during Colonel John T. Toland's raid of Wytheville in July 1863.

13. Joseph L. Hilt was commissioned captain of Company G of the 12th Ohio Volunteer Infantry on June 11, 1861. He was wounded at the Battle of Scary Creek, West Virginia, in July 1861 and at the Battle of South Mountain in September 1862. Hilt mustered out with the company on July 11, 1864. *Official Roster of the Soldiers of the State of Ohio*, 2:371.

14. Henry C. Duncan was from Lawrence County, Ohio, and was listed in the 1860 Census as a day laborer. He was commissioned as a second lieutenant in Company D of the 9th Virginia Infantry on February 17, 1863. On December 12, 1864, Duncan was promoted to captain of Company K in the 1st Virginia Veteran Infantry. He mustered out with the regiment on July 21, 1865. US Census, 1860, Upper, Lawrence County, Ohio, 122; Lang, *Loyal West Virginia*, 270, 304.

15. This was either Samuel or Joseph Kriebel (Cribble), brothers who were both privates in Company K of the 91st Ohio Volunteer Infantry. They were

born in Pennsylvania and moved to Ohio. Samuel lived in Huntington near Gallipolis, and Joseph lived in Milton near Jackson. US Census, 1860, Huntington, Gallia County, Ohio, 48; US Census, 1860, Milton, Jackson County, Ohio, 40; *Official Roster of the Soldiers of the State of Ohio*, 7:154; Windsor, *History of the Ninety-First Regiment*, 37.

16. This was either Andrew or Calvin Beller (Bellar or Belles). Both were privates in Company C of the 91st Ohio Volunteer Infantry. They were likely brothers and were both from Scioto, Pike County, Ohio. US Census, 1870, Scioto, Pike County, Ohio, 12, 17; *Official Roster of the Soldiers of the State of Ohio*, 7:134.

17. The Kingsbury family was from Ironton. Charles Kingsbury was a schoolteacher. His wife was Harriet. Martha, referred to as Mattie, was one of their daughters. US Census, 1860, Ironton, Lawrence County, Ohio, 39.

18. Matthew Stafford enlisted as a private in Company K of the 2nd Virginia Cavalry on November 8, 1861. He mustered out with the regiment on June 30, 1865. Sutton, *History of the Second Regiment, West Virginia*, 39.

19. Benjamin F. Coates, who had been a doctor before the Civil War, wanted to resume his medical practice upon return to civilian life. This desire explains why he was so interested in purchasing Newton's house in Ironton, which featured a once-thriving medical practice and living quarters in the same structure. In an August 23, 1863, letter written just after Newton mentioned the offer from Coates to buy his home, Coates told his wife that he wanted to "purchase us a comfortable home in some respectable place . . . and practice my profession." Benjamin F. Coates to Elizabeth Coates, August 23, 1863, folder 2, Benjamin F. Coates Collection, Rutherford B. Hayes Presidential Library and Museums, Fremont, Ohio.

20. This was either Andrew or Calvin Beller (Bellar or Belles), who were both privates in Company C of the 91st Ohio Volunteer Infantry and on furlough as Newton mentioned in his August 12, 1863, letter. *Official Roster of the Soldiers of the State of Ohio*, 7:134.

21. George Theobald enlisted as a corporal in Company G of the 91st Ohio Volunteer Infantry on August 8, 1862. He died of typhoid fever at Fayetteville, West Virginia, on August 22, 1863. *Official Roster of the Soldiers of the State of Ohio*, 7:145.

22. In late August the general court martial proceedings moved from Fayetteville to Gauley Bridge. Colonel Benjamin F. Coates and Captain Allen T. Wikoff or Wykoff of the 91st Ohio Volunteer Regiment were part of the tribunal. *Knapsack* (Gauley Bridge, WV), September 3, 1863, 3.

23. This was a reference to Granville S. Wellons a doctor from Barnesville, Ohio, who was commissioned as assistant surgeon for the 91st Ohio Volunteer

Infantry on August 29, 1863. *Official Roster of the Soldiers of the State of Ohio*, 7:127; Windsor, *History of the Ninety-First Regiment*, 5.

24. This is most likely John Corson, a doctor from Butler County, Ohio. US Census, 1860, Jacksburg, *Butler County, Ohio*, 40.

25. The 91st Ohio Volunteer Infantry roster indicated that Barnabus Canter, a private in Company K, died on August 29, 1863, and that George Christman, a sergeant in Company G, died on September 9, 1863. These were likely the two soldiers that Newton referred to as succumbing to typhoid fever. *Official Roster of the Soldiers of the State of Ohio*, 7:145, 153; Windsor, *History of the Ninety-First Regiment*, 26, 36.

26. This is most likely Jonathan Dunn, who was listed in the 1870s census as a journeyman carpenter living in Monroe County, Ohio. US Census, 1870, Beallsville, Monroe County, Ohio, 5.

27. Richard J. Preston Jr., *North American Trees (Exclusive of Mexico and Tropical United States)* (Ames, IA: Iowa State College Press, 1948), 169, 190–91; Steve Nix, "The Essential Chinkapin: A Small Tree with a Large Potential," July 3, 2019, ThoughtCo, https://www.thoughtco.com/the-essential-chinkapin-1343342.

28. Henry Bowman enlisted as a private in Company A of the 91st Ohio Volunteer Regiment on August 12, 1862. He mustered out with the company on June 24, 1865. *Official Roster of the Soldiers of the State of Ohio*, 7:128.

29. George W. Kirker was a wagoner from Adams County, Ohio. He enlisted as a private in Company E of the 91st Ohio Volunteer Infantry on August 11, 1862. He mustered out with the company on June 24, 1865. US Census, 1860, Manchester, Adams County, Ohio, 48; *Official Roster of the Soldiers of the State of Ohio*, 7:141.

30. John Stewart enlisted as a private in Company C of the 91st Ohio Volunteer Regiment on July 28, 1862. He mustered out with the company on June 24, 1865. *Official Roster of the Soldiers of the State of Ohio*, 7:135.

31. John Stevens enlisted as a private in Company H of the 91st Ohio Volunteer Regiment on August 22, 1862. He mustered out with the company on June 24, 1865. *Official Roster of the Soldiers of the State of Ohio*, 7:150.

32. Nancy Harvey Huddleston was the widow of George Paddy Huddleston, who died in 1859. "George Paddy Huddleston," Find A Grave, https://www.findagrave.com/memorial/50546880.

33. John Brough was a newspaper publisher, railroad owner, and Democrat from Athens County. A former state legislator and master orator, he emerged as a candidate for governor following a pro-Union speech in Marietta, Ohio, on June 10, 1863. He declared that the act of rebellion had destroyed slavery and urged all patriots of any political affiliation to unite against the southern

rebels. The publicity bolstered his campaign, and he won the election that November against anti-war Democrat Clement Laird Vallandigham. "John Brough," *Appleton's Cyclopaedia of American Biography*, 1:391.

34. A butternut referred to a Confederate soldier or supporter because the fabric of the uniform was usually homemade and dyed with butternut extract. "Butternut," Glossary of Civil War Terms, American Battlefield Trust, https://www.battlefields.org/glossary-civil-war-terms#B.

35. In mid-September Union major general William Rosecrans fought Confederate troops led by General Braxton Bragg at the Battle of Chickamauga in Northwest Georgia. The Confederate defeat of Rosecrans became the most significant Union loss in the Western Theatre of the Civil War. Lamers, *The Edge of Glory*, 325–61; Peter Cozzens, *This Terrible Sound: The Battle of Chickamauga* (Urbana: Univ. of Illinois Press, 1992).

36. Virgil Gates was a blacksmith from Gallipolis. US Census, 1860, Gallia County, Gallipolis, 209.

37. Silas T. Buck was assistant surgeon in 12th Ohio Volunteer Infantry. Strait, *Roster of Regimental Surgeons and Assistant Surgeons*, 192.

38. Airish is an Appalachian adjective either meaning cool, breezy weather or fancy (*e.g.*, "They were putting on airs."). In this context it referred to cooler temperatures.

39. The Iron Bank in Ironton opened in 1851. It was the predecessor of the First National Bank, which took over the Iron Bank in 1863. Eugene B. Willard, ed., *A Standard History of the Hanging Rock Iron Region of Ohio: An Authentic Narrative of the Past, with an Extended Survey of the Industrial and Commercial Development* ([Chicago]: Lewis Publishing Company, 1916), 1:305; "Iron Bank of Ironton," The Lawrence Register, https://lawrencecountyohio.wordpress.com/history/businesses/iron-bank/.

40. Charles Vanden, the son of Esther and James Vanden. James was a carriage maker from Gallipolis, and his son Charles was an assistant carriage maker. James (listed in the regimental roster as Henry J.) was a sergeant in Company A of the 91st Ohio Volunteer Infantry. US Census, 1860, Gallipolis, Gallia County, Ohio, 188; *Official Roster of the Soldiers of the State of Ohio*, 7:128.

41. Issac De La Mater was born in Sand Lake, New York, on November 20, 1818. He graduated from Williams College in Williamstown, Massachusetts, in 1844 and then studied theology at Lane Seminary in Cincinnati. De La Mater was ordained by the Dayton Presbytery in 1847. He served Presbyterian churches in southwestern Ohio for over thirty years and then in Indiana during the early 1860s. In October 1863 he joined the 72nd Indiana Volunteer Infantry as chaplain. "'44 Isaac De La Mater," *Delta Upsilon Quarterly* 11 (September 1893): 182; B. F. McGee, *History of the 72nd Indiana Volunteer*

Infantry of the Mounted Lightning Brigade (Lafayette, IN: S. Vater and Co., Printers, 1882), 221, 223, 676–78; John W. Brinsfield et al., eds., *Faith in the Fight: Civil War Chaplains* (Mechanicsburg, PA: Stackpole Books, 2003), 148.

42. The Union meeting was held on September 29 and featured dozens of speeches and events. The article in the *Ironton Register* called it the "Largest Crowd of People Ever Assembled in Ironton." "Great Union Meeting!" *Ironton Register*, October 1, 1863, 2; *Ironton Register*, September 24, 1863.

5. The Formation of Character, Is Perhaps the Most Important

1. Terry D. Lowry, *22nd Virginia Infantry* (Lynchburg: H. E. Howard, 1988), 190.

2. William S. Newton to Frances Ann Hayward Newton, November 13, 1863, Newton Papers, SCUA VT (quotations); Sutton, *History of the Second Regiment, West Virginia*, 109–11.

3. Windsor, *History of the Ninety-First Regiment*, 41 (quotation).

4. William S. Newton to Frances Ann Hayward Newton, November 13, 1863, Newton Papers, SCUA (quotation).

5. This is likely Ann Reppert, the twenty-year-old daughter of Lewis and Susan Reppert from Harmar, Ohio. US Census 1860, Harmar, Washington County, Ohio, 131.

6. John C. Ruby was born in Gallia County, Ohio, which may explain why Newton knew him and his family. Lowry, *22nd Virginia Infantry*, 190.

7. A pannier consists of a basket or container carried by a pack animal such as a horse or a mule.

8. John J. Hoffman was commissioned as a major in the 2nd Virginia Cavalry on October 2, 1861. He was promoted to lieutenant colonel on July 14, 1864, and mustered out when his term of service expired that October. Sutton, *History of the Second Regiment, West Virginia*, 5.

9. James H. Tagg was forty-two years old when he enlisted as a private in Company D of the 91st Ohio Volunteer Infantry. Tagg was born in England, but prior to the Civil War he lived with his family in Mason, which is a township in Lawrence County, not far from Ironton. The 1850 census listed him as a painter. US Census, 1850, Mason, Lawrence County, Ohio, 722; *Official Roster of the Soldiers of the State of Ohio*, 7:138.

10. The Ruffner family had deep roots in the Kanawha Valley. There were several families with the name Ruffner in the Charleston area at this time, so it is unclear which Ruffner family members Newton was referring to in his correspondence. See, Gerald S. Ratliff, "Ruffner Family," October 29, 2010, e-WV: The West Virginia Encyclopedia, https://www.wvencyclopedia.org/articles/138.

11. The *Bostonia* was a Union transport steamboat. In April 1862 the *Bostonia No. 1* and *Bostonia No. 2* were part of the Union support fleet of steamers on

the Tennessee River during the Battle of Shiloh. Hurst, "The Battle of Shiloh," 31.

12. Ann Reppert was the daughter of Lewis and Susan Reppert from Harmar, Ohio. US Census 1860, Harmar, Washington County, Ohio, 131.

13. Ms. Capt. Brown referred to the wife of Captain John Brown of the 92nd Ohio Volunteer Infantry. Reid, *Ohio in the War*, 2:511.

14. This refers to the last stanza of Thomas Moore's poem "Song." *Poetical Works of Thomas Moore, Including his Melodies, Ballads, Etc.* (Philadelphia: J. Crissy, 1845), 277.

15. There were two Mr. Andersons in the 2nd West Virginia Cavalry: Samuel J. Anderson, a private in Company E; and Boyd Anderson, a private in Company G. *Official Roster of the Soldiers of the State of Ohio*, 12:340, 347.

16. Ezra W. Clark was adjutant for the 34th Ohio Volunteer Infantry. He was from Tiffin, Seneca County, Ohio. *Official Roster of the Soldiers of the State of Ohio*, 3:555; US Census 1860, Tiffin, Seneca County, Ohio, 10.

17. Hiram G. Lasley was a farmer who lived in Wellston, Jackson County, Ohio, near the Buckeye Furnace. US Census 1880, District 78, Wellston, Jackson County, Ohio, 1.

18. Edward Lanton was a blacksmith who lived in Ironton. US Census 1860, Ironton, Lawrence County, Ohio, 60.

19. John McNally was a lieutenant in Company K of the 2nd Virginia Cavalry. He rose to the rank of captain and mustered out at the close of the war. *Official Roster of the Soldiers of the State of Ohio*, 12:336, 351; Sutton, *History of the Second Regiment, West Virginia*, 6, 7, 8, 20, 39, 49.

20. Seth J. Simmonds was captain of the 23rd Independent Battery Ohio Volunteer Light Artillery. The battery was formerly Company E of the 1st Kentucky Infantry. *Official Roster of the Soldiers of the State of Ohio*, 10:623; *Official Army Register*, 4:1243.

21. Lowell is in Summers County, West Virginia, near the Greenbrier River.

22. Daniel W. Higgins was a hospital steward for the 2nd Virginia Cavalry. Sutton, *History of the Second Regiment, West Virginia*, 9.

23. Stephen Girard was a banker and philanthropist who is often credited with saving the US government from financial collapse during the War of 1812. When he died in 1831, his estimated wealth was $7.5 million. See, John Bach McMaster, *The Life and Times of Stephen Girard, Mariner and Merchant*, 2 vols. (Philadelphia: J. B. Lippincott Company, 1918); "Stephen Girard," *Appleton's Cyclopaedia of American Biography*, 3:660–61; Robert E. Wright and David J. Cowen, *Financial Founding Fathers: The Men Who Made America Rich* (Chicago: Univ. of Chicago Press, 2006).

24. The 22nd Virginia Volunteer Infantry (CSA) was organized in April 1861 as the Kanawha Regiment. Its service for the Confederacy began on July 1,

1861. Lee A. Wallace, *A Guide to Virginia Military Organizations, 1861–1865*, rev. 2nd ed. (Lynchburg: H. E. Howard, 1986), 104–5; Lowry, *22nd Virginia Infantry*.

25. John Beverly William Newton was born November 9, 1863, but did not have a name at this point.

26. This is likely Abby E. McClain, a schoolteacher in Ironton. US Census 1860, Ironton, Lawrence County, Ohio, 64.

27. Clara C. Davidson was the wife of Jeremiah Davidson, a merchant from Ironton, who rose to the rank of captain in Company E of the 2nd Virginia Cavalry. Sutton, *History of the Second Regiment, West Virginia*, 6, 23, 49; "Jeremiah 'Jere' Davidson," Find a Grave, https://www.findagrave.com/memorial/118524272.

28. James Craig was a carpenter who lived in Ironton. US Census 1860, Ironton, Lawrence County, Ohio, 4.

29. Edward Lanton was a blacksmith who lived in Ironton. US Census 1860, Ironton, Lawrence County, Ohio, 60.

6. Shipwreck of Your Own Hopes

1. Windsor, *History of the Ninety-First Regiment*, 41–42.

2. William S. Newton to Frances Ann Hayward Newton, January 22, 1864, Newton Papers, SCUA VT.

3. John A. Turley was colonel of the 91st Ohio Volunteer Infantry. In Newton's letter to his wife on December 1, 1863, he mentioned that Turley was facing arrest for charges of gambling. By early January the charges had apparently been dropped. *Official Roster of the Soldiers of the State of Ohio*, 7:127; William S. Newton to Frances Ann Hayward Newton, December 1, 1863, Newton Papers, SCUA VT.

4. Viz is a synonym for "namely."

5. William F. Curtis was a state senator from Marietta, Ohio, who began his term in early 1864. *History of Washington County, Ohio with Illustrations and Biographical Sketches* (Cleveland: H. Z. Williams and Brothers Publishers, 1881), 111.

6. Dr. Edward L. Gilliam was assistant surgeon for the 2nd Virginia Cavalry. He began the war as a private in Company I, served as hospital steward, and rose to the rank of assistant surgeon in May 1863. Sutton, *History of the Second Regiment, West Virginia*, 5, 38, 49; Strait, *Roster of All Regimental Surgeons and Assistant Surgeons*, 271.

7. In January 1864 Unionist John Brough began as Ohio's governor. He appointed Dr. R. N. Barr, a personal friend and professor of anatomy at the Cleveland Medical College, as surgeon general to replace Dr. Samuel M. Smith. Reid, *Ohio in the War*, 1:64, 247.

8. The Amanda Furnace was one of the many iron furnaces in the Ironton region. It was located on the Kentucky side of the Ohio River in Boyd County. The *Ironton Register* for January 21, 1864, announced that the Amanda Furnace was to be sold at public auction in February, but the auction and sale did not take place until July. *Ironton Register*, January 21, 1864, July 14, 1864; Willard, *History of the Hanging Rock Iron Region of Ohio*, 1:56; Lori Shafer, *Iron Furnaces of Lawrence County, Ohio*, 2nd ed. (self-pub., CreateSpace, 2019), 197.

9. A. Paul and George P. Walker were two of the investors from Greenup County, Kentucky, who purchased the Amanda Furnace in 1857. The Greenup County Circuit Court ordered the public auction of the property. *Ironton Register*, January 21, 1864.

10. George W. Willard was a banker from Ironton. US Census, 1860, Ironton, Lawrence County, Ohio, 45; US Census, 1870, Ironton, Lawrence County, Ohio, 136; Willard, *History of the Hanging Rock Iron Region of Ohio*, 1:311; "George W. Willard," Find A Grave, https://www.findagrave.com/memorial/138729341.

11. On June 26, 1858, twelve-year-old Oren Newton drowned in the Ohio River. *Ironton Register*, July 1, 1858.

12. William Johnson was a physician from Moscow, Ohio. His son John W. Johnson was a private who also served as a hospital steward for the 1st Ohio Volunteer Independent Light Artillery Battery. US Census 1860, Moscow, Clermont County, Ohio, 86; *Official Roster of the Soldiers of the State of Ohio*, 10:448.

13. Diaphoretics were designed to induce perspiration in patients and were commonly used to treat a variety of illnesses in the nineteenth century. Gross, *A Manual of Military Surgery*, 17; Schaadt, *Civil War Medicine*, 87.

14. Camphor is the oil taken from trees and was used as a stimulant, often by injection. Gross, *A Manual of Military Surgery*, 78; "Camphor-Zhang Nao," Civil War Rx: The Source Guide to Civil War Medicine, http://civilwarrx .blogspot.com/2016/03/camphor-zhang-nao.html.

15. For a full account of the capture of Scammond and Pinckard, see, *Gallipolis Journal*, February 11, 1864, 2; "The Civil War Memoir of Russell Hastings, Chapter 4: March 1st, 1863 to April 8th, 1864," [transcript], Hayes Library and Museum, https://www.rbhayes.org/research/chapters -4-through-6/.

16. Jeremiah Davidson was a merchant from Ironton. He rose to the rank of captain in Company E of the 2nd Virginia Cavalry. Sutton, *History of the Second Regiment, West Virginia*, 6, 23, 49; "Jeremiah 'Jere' Davidson," Find a Grave, https://www.findagrave.com/memorial/118524272.

17. The Sons of Temperance was a secret fraternal organization that supported the temperance movement and provided support for other members. Membership grew in the nineteenth century with hundreds of chapters across the United States. See, Samuel F. Cary, *Historical Sketch of the Order of the Sons of Temperance* (Halifax, Nova Scotia: W. Theakston, Printer, 1884); *Constitution, Revised Rules, Rules of Order, and Funeral Ceremony of the Sons of Temperance* (Halifax, Nova Scotia: R. M. Barratt, 1852).

18. John Mills was a lifelong Marietta resident who was a merchant, banker, and an original trustee of Marietta College. He was president of the Marietta Chair Company, which manufactured buckets, tubs, and chairs. Newton's letter suggested that Mills had been an investor in the Marietta Bucket Factory. Israel Ward Andrews, *Washington County and the Early Settlement of Ohio: Being the Centennial Historical Address, Before the Citizens of Washington County* (Cincinnati: Peter G. Thomson, Publisher, 1877), 64; Andrews, *History of Marietta and Washington County*, 903–4, 938–39.

19. George W. Johnson was elected probate judge in 1864. Prior to the election he served as a second lieutenant in Company E of 87th Ohio Volunteer Infantry for a three-month term. Willard, *History of the Hanging Rock Iron Region of Ohio*, 1:469, 507, 558; *Official Roster of the Soldiers of the State of Ohio*, 7:11.

7. To Be Realized, It Must Be Experienced

1. John Holliday Diary, 1864, MS 2012–028, SCUA VT; *Official Roster of the Soldiers of the State of Ohio*, 7:133; Lambert, *Ninety-First Ohio Volunteer Infantry*, 128.

2. See, Paul Magid, *George Crook: From the Redwoods to Appomattox* (Norman: Univ. of Oklahoma Press, 2011); Kenneth P. Werrell, *Crook's Regulars: The 36th Ohio Volunteer Infantry Regiment in the War of the Rebellion* (Christiansburg, VA: self-pub., 2012); McManus, *The Battle of Cloyds Mountain*; Johnson, *The United States Army Invades the New River Valley*; Scott C. Patchan, *Shenandoah Summer: The 1864 Valley Campaign* (Lincoln: Univ. of Nebraska Press, 2007); Scott C. Patchan, *The Last Battle of Winchester: Phil Sheridan, Jubal Early, and the Shenandoah Valley Campaign, August 7–September 19, 1864* (El Dorado Hill, CA: Savas Beatie, 2013); Robert C. Whisonant, *Arming the Confederacy: How Virginia's Minerals Forged the Rebel War Machine* (New York: Springer, 2015).

3. George W. Jackson, was a bookkeeper from Alabama who lived in Ironton. US Census, 1860, Ironton, Lawrence County, Ohio, 92.

4. The 1860 census for Adams County includes several farmers with the name Baldridge, so it is uncertain who was the former owner and caretaker of the farm that Coates sold to Newton. Most likely it was James W. Baldridge

Sr. Samuel P. Baldridge was a schoolteacher from Adams County who rose to the rank of captain in the 91st Ohio Volunteer Regiment, but there is no indication that he was related to the owner of the farm. Nelson W. Evans and Emmons B. Stivers, *A History of Adams County, Ohio From its Earliest Settlement to the Present Time* (West Union, OH: E. B. Stivers, 1900), 697–98; Reid, *Ohio in the War*, 2:504.

5. Sherman (S. G.) Johnson was a clerk from Ironton. His wife was Rose (Roseann). US Census, 1860, Ironton, Lawrence County, Ohio, 27.

6. Turpentine and whiskey were used as a stimulant and diuretic. Quinine was more a general tonic used for fever or malaria. Gross, *A Manual of Military Surgery*, 17, 77, 78; Schaadt, *Civil War Medicine*, 89–91.

7. Amorphous sulphur is produced by pouring melted sulphur into water. See, Alexander Smith and Willis B. Holmes, "On Amorphous Sulphur: III. The Nature of Amorphous Sulphur and Contributions to the Study of the Influence of Foreign Bodies on the Behavior of Supercooled Melted Sulphur," *Journal of the American Chemical Society* 27, no. 8 (1905): 979–1013.

8. B. F Oviate was a clerk in Ironton. US Census, 1860, Ironton, Lawrence County, Ohio, 77.

9. The Charleston shooting story appeared in several regional newspapers about a week after the incident. "The Charleston Va. Seduction Case—The Antecedents of One of the Parties," *Daily Register* (Wheeling, WV), April 25, 1864, 2; "The Late Charleston (West Virginia) Tragedy," *Daily Intelligencer* (Wheeling, WV), April 30, 1864, 2; "The Charleston Tragedy, A Wife's Infidelity and a Husband's Vengeance," *Weekly Pioneer and Democrat* (St. Paul, MN), May 6, 1864, 8.

10. John H. Dingess, a former showman, retired to Charleston to become a druggist and confectioner. In April 1864 Dingess shot hospital steward William Nelson after discovering him in bed with his wife, Jane Dingess. Their marriage survived the affair. The 1870 census lists a circus agent named John "Dinges" living in Cincinnati with wife Jane and nine-year-old daughter. Advertisement in *Journal* (Charleston, WV), December 28, 1864, February 1, 1865; US Census 1870, Cincinnati Ward 05, Hamilton County, Ohio, 67; "John A. Dingess," Find A Grave, https://www.findagrave.com/memorial/78919363/john-a-dingess.

11. Anna Nowlin was married to Burrell Nowlin. They were a farming family who in 1860 lived near Gallipolis. Two of their sons, Charles and Levi, served as privates in the 36th Ohio Volunteer Infantry, which was part of Kanawha Division. US Census 1860, Clay, Gallia County, Ohio, 59; *Official Roster of the Soldiers of the State of Ohio*, 3:688.

12. Robert R. Hedden was a lieutenant in Company D of the 6th Ohio Volunteer

Cavalry. In official reports about the Battle of Cloyd's Mountain, General
Duffié referred to Captain Robert E. Hedden, division commissary of sub-
sistence. *Official Roster of the Soldiers of the State of Ohio*, 11:328; *Official Army
Register*, 5:11; *OR*, ser. 1, vol. 37, pt. 1, 144, 325.

13. Dr. Horace P. Kay was assistant surgeon of the 12th Ohio Volunteer Infantry. Strait, *Roster of Regimental Surgeons and Assistant Surgeons*, 192; *Official
Roster of the Soldiers of the State of Ohio*, 2:353.

14. John X. Davidson was the editor of the *Ironton Register*. Willard, *History of
the Hanging Rock Iron Region of Ohio*, 1:322–23; *Ironton Register*, March 3,
1864, 1.

15. Henry (H. S.) Neal was a lawyer in Ironton. US Census 1860, Ironton,
Lawrence County, 24.

16. The Cloyd family owned a significant amount of property and slaves in Pulaski County, Virginia, not far from the county seat of Dublin. James Cloyd
(1828–1892) owned thirty-three slaves and just over 1,800 acres in a part of the
county known as Back Creek. The property included a mountain known as
Cloyd's Mountain, where much of the battle unfolded on May 9, 1864. James
was referred to as a major and assisted General Albert G. Jenkins prior to the
battle. His brother Joseph Cloyd (1813–1884) lived nearby and owned fifty-one
slaves. During the Battle of Cloyd's Mountain, the Cloyds' home on Back
Creek became a Union hospital and headquarters for General George Crook.
Virginia Historic Landmarks Commission Staff, "National Register of Historic Places Inventory/Nomination: Back Creek Farm," February 1975, http://
www.dhr.virginia.gov/registers/Counties/Pulaski/077–0002_Back_Creek
_Farm_1975_Final_Nomination.pdf; US Census 1860, Western District,
Pulaski County, Virginia, 24, 96; US Census, Slave Schedules, 1860, Western
District, Pulaski County, 7, 20; McManus, *The Battle of Cloyds Mountain*, 19,
46–47; Johnson, *The United States Army Invades the New River Valley*, 20.

17. Dr. Joseph F. Watkins was surgeon for the 36th Virginia Infantry. J. L. Scott,
36th Virginia Infantry (Lynchburg: H. E. Howard, 1987), 104.

18. Union forces used the home of John Guthrie as a hospital for wounded
Confederate officers. Johnson, *The United States Army Invades the New River
Valley*, 37; Dickinson and Dickinson, *Gentleman Soldier of Greenbottom*, 107.

19. In 1900 a small connection in William S. Newton's Civil War story came full
circle. That year, Lucy C. Beardsley purchased Greenbottom, the former es-
tate of Albert G. Jenkins in Cabell County, West Virginia. Her husband was
Andrew J. Beardsley, Civil War veteran, Gallipolis native, and first cousin to
William S. Newton. Beardsley was born in 1844 and grew up in Gallipolis.
He served as a private in Company D of the 141st Ohio Volunteer Infantry
and as a first sergeant in Company G of the 195th Ohio Volunteer Infantry.
After the Civil War, he became a doctor practicing in Cabell County. The

Beardsley family lived in the house owned by Albert G. Jenkins beginning in
1900 and stayed there for the next ten years. There is no mention of Beardsley in the Newton correspondence, but Newton was close to his family,
including his first cousins. Dickinson and Dickinson, *Gentleman Soldier of
Greenbottom*, 124; *Official Roster of the Soldiers of the State of Ohio*, 9:7, 10:197;
Patrick W. O'Bannon, "Archival Research on the History of the Albert
Gallatin Jenkins House Green Bottom, Cabell County, West Virginia," September 28, 2005, https://www.lrh.usace.army.mil/Portals/38/docs/2005%20
History%20of%20Jenkins%20House2.pdf.

20. In 1862, Confederate leaders entered into a contract with Emory and Henry
    College in Emory, Virginia, to use their main campus building as a hospital.
    McManus, *The Battle of Cloyds Mountain*, 48; "History," Emory and Henry
    College, https://www.ehc.edu/about/history/.

21. Constructed in the 1850s, the Virginia and Tennessee Railroad connected
    Southwest Virginia with the Tidewater. At the time of the Civil War, the
    railroad stretched from Lynchburg to Bristol and served as a significant
    supply line for the Confederates. McManus, *The Battle of Cloyds Mountain*, 2.

22. John S. Pride was an assistant surgeon from Tennessee. Arthur Wyllie, *Con-
    federate Officers* (n.p.: Art's Books and Images, 2007), 414; "Dr. John Sharp
    Pride," Find A Grave, https://www.findagrave.com/memorial/11143046.

23. John T. McFarland was an assistant surgeon from Georgia. He served in the
    1st Georgia Sharpshooters, the 5th Georgia Cavalry, and later on the surgical
    staff of Brigadier General Robert H. Anderson. *List of Staff Officers of the
    Confederate States Army, 1861–1865* (Washington, DC: Government Printing
    Office, 1891), 109; Wyllie, *Confederate Officers*, 341.

24. Walter S. Welch was a surgeon for the 15th Virginia Infantry. Prior to that
    position, he had been an assistant surgeon with the 14th Virginia Infantry.
    Strait, *Roster of Regimental Surgeons and Assistant Surgeons*, 274, 275; Lang,
    Loyal West Virginia, 291, 296.

25. James J. Johnson was assistant surgeon for the 15th Virginia Infantry. Strait,
    Roster of Regimental Surgeons and Assistant Surgeons, 275; Lang, *Loyal West
    Virginia*, 296.

26. Charles A. Thatcher (Thacker) was a doctor and assistant surgeon for the
    14th Virginia Infantry. Strait, *Roster of Regimental Surgeons and Assistant
    Surgeons*, 274; Lang, *Loyal West Virginia*, 291.

27. Whisonant, *Arming the Confederacy*, 176; US War Department, *The War of
    the Rebellion: A Compilation of the Official Records of the Union and Con-
    federate Armies* (Washington, DC, 1880–1901), ser. 1, vol. 37, pt. 1, 8–68;
    Michael Egan, *The Flying, Grey-Haired Yank: Or the Adventures of a Volunteer*
    (Philadelphia: Hubbard Brothers, 1888); R. B. Wilson, "The Dublin Raid,"
    in *Grand Army of the Republic War Papers: Papers Read before Fred C. Jones*

Post, No. 401, Department of Ohio, G.A.R. (Cincinnati: Fred C. Jones Post, No. 401, 1891), 1:92–120; Milton W. Humphreys, *A History of the Lynchburg Campaign* (Charlottesville: Michie Company, 1924).

28. Rutherford B. Hayes noted in his diary the heavy Union casualties in the 23rd Ohio Volunteer Infantry regiment at the Battle of Cloyd's Mountain. Charles Richard Williams, ed., *Diary and Letters of Rutherford Birchard Hayes: Nineteenth President of the United States* (Columbus: Ohio State Archaeological and Historical Society, 1922), 2:456–57.

29. *Official Roster of the Soldiers of the State of Ohio*, 3:71, 73, 109; McManus, *The Battle of Cloyds Mountain*, 94; E. C. Arthur, "The Dublin Raid, Campaigning with Gen. Geo. Crook in 1864," *Ohio Soldier*, January 5, January 19, February 2, February 16, March 2, March 16, March 30, April 13, 1889.

30. Arthur, "The Dublin Raid," *Ohio Soldier*, February 16, 1889, 371.

31. See, *Famous Adventures and Prison Escapes of the Civil War* (New York: Century Company, 1917), 184–242; Joseph Wheelan, *Libby Prison Breakout: The Daring Escape from the Notorious Civil War Prison* (New York: Public Affairs, 2010).

32. Frank L. Byrne, "Libby Prison: A Study in Emotions," *Journal of Southern History* 24 (November 1958): 430–34, 440–42; Sandra V. Parker, "A History of Libby Prison, 1862–1865" (Master's thesis, Virginia Tech, 1981), 3–4, 125; *Examiner* (Richmond, VA), May 28, 1864.

33. "Register of Captured Federal Officers Confined in Libby Prison, Richmond, Virginia, 1862-65," entry 132, pp. 159-60, Records of the Office of the Commissary General of Prisoners, Record Group 249, National Archives and Records Administration, Washington, DC.

34. *Examiner* (Richmond, VA), May 23, 1864.

35. Pension File of William S. Newton, 91st Ohio Volunteer Infantry, RG 15, NARA.

36. Nelson D. Furguson (sometimes Ferguson) was a doctor from Carthage, New York. He was commissioned as surgeon of the 8th New York Cavalry in March 1862. The 8th New York Cavalry was near Spotsylvania Court House in early May 1864. On May 12, Confederate forces captured Furguson in Mechanicsville, which is in Hanover County not far from Richmond. That same day he was admitted to Libby Prison and released on May 28. He mustered out of service when his term of service expired in December 1864. Henry Norton, *Deeds of Daring, or History of the Eight N.Y. Volunteer Cavalry* (Norwich, NY: Chenango Telegraph Printing House, 1889), 159, 166; *Annual Report of the Adjutant-General of the State of New York for the Year 1894* (Albany: James B. Lyon, 1895), 2:886; Strait, *Roster of Regimental Surgeons and Assistant Surgeons*, 146; Frederick H. Dyer, *A Compendium of the War of the*

Rebellion (New York: Sagamore Press, 1959), 3:1376; "Register of Captured Federal Officers Confined in Libby Prison, Richmond, Virginia, 1862–65," entry 132, pp. 77-78, RG 249, NARA.

37. Daniel W. Richards was a doctor from Easton, Pennsylvania. He was commissioned as assistant surgeon of the 145th Pennsylvania Volunteer Infantry on June 20, 1863. The 145th Pennsylvania Volunteer Infantry was near Spotsylvania Court House in early May 1864. On May 10, Confederates captured Richards, who at that time was suffering from a case of scabies. On May 20, he was admitted to Libby Prison and paroled at Aiken's Landing on May 28. He was discharged from service on a special order on November 11, 1864. Samuel P. Bates, *History of the Pennsylvania Volunteers, 1861–5* (Harrisburg: B. Singerly, 1870) 4:524; Dyer, *A Compendium of the War of the Rebellion*, 3:1617; Strait, *Roster of Regimental Surgeons and Assistant Surgeons*, 252; Verel R. Salmon, *Common Men in the War for the Common Man: The Civil War of the United States of America History of the 145th Pennsylvania Volunteer from Organization through Gettysburg* (self-pub., Xlibris, 2013), 672, 680; Verel R. Salmon, *Common Men in the War for the Common Man, Book 2: The Civil War of the United States of America History of the 145th Pennsylvania Volunteer after Gettysburg through War's End* (self-pub., Xlibris, 2019), 402; Kathleen E. Harris and Paul L. Harris, *A Soldier's Story: The 145th Pennsylvania Volunteer Infantry Regiment in the Civil War* (Chicora, PA: Mechling, 2011), 146–47; "Register of Captured Federal Officers Confined in Libby Prison, Richmond, Virginia, 1862-65," entry 132, pp. 209-10, RG 249, NARA.

38. John L. Irwin was a Methodist minister. He was commissioned chaplain of the 14th Virginia Infantry on November 1, 1862. The 14th Virginia was part of the Battle of Cloyd's Mountain. Irwin was taken prisoner at the same time as the surgeons and was also briefly a prisoner at Libby Prison. Strait, *Roster of Regimental Surgeons and Assistant Surgeons*, 274; Lang, *Loyal West Virginia*, 291; Brinsfield, *Faith in the Fight*, 166.

39. *Cincinnati Lancet and Observer* 7 (July 1864): 446.

8. In Line of Battle All Day, and I Am Very Tired

1. See, Magid, *George Crook*; Werrell, *Crook's Regulars*; Patchan, *Shenandoah Summer*; Patchan, *The Last Battle of Winchester*.

2. Patchan, *Shenandoah Summer*, 139–51; Jack H. Lepa, *The Shenandoah Valley Campaign of 1864* (Jefferson, NC: McFarland and Company, 2003), 123–25; William S. Newton to Frances Ann Hayward Newton, July 23, 1864, Newton Papers, SCUA VT; George E. Pond, *The Shenandoah Valley in 1864* (New York: Charles Scribner's Sons, 1892), 96–99.

3. William S. Newton to Frances Ann Hayward Newton, August 2, 1864, Newton Papers, SCUA VT.

4. Richard R. Duncan, ed., *Alexander Neil and the Last Shenandoah Campaign: Letters of an Army Surgeon to His Family, 1864* (Shippensburg, PA: White Mane, 1996), 55 (quotation); Magid, *George Crook*, 229; Strait, *Roster of All Regimental Surgeons and Assistant Surgeons*, 274.

5. William S. Newton to Frances Ann Hayward Newton, August 3, 1864; William S. Newton to Frances Ann Hayward Newton, August 4, 1864; and William S. Newton to Frances Ann Hayward Newton, August 8, 1864, all in Newton Papers, SCUA VT.

6. William S. Newton to Frances Ann Hayward Newton, July 17, 1864; William S. Newton to Frances Ann Hayward Newton, July 23, 1864; and William S. Newton to Frances Ann Hayward Newton, August 8, 1864, all in Newton Papers, SCUA VT.

7. James M. White was a schoolteacher from Jackson, Pike County, Ohio. He was commissioned first lieutenant in Company G of the 91st Ohio Volunteer Infantry on July 29, 1862. White was promoted to captain of Company F of the 91st on November 3, 1864. He mustered out with the regiment on June 24, 1865. After the war he returned to teaching school and began farming in Darke County. In 1880 White moved to Northwest Missouri, near Burlington Junction. US Census, 1860, Jackson, Pike County, Ohio, 165; *Official Roster of the Soldiers of the State of Ohio*, 7:142, 145; *The History of Darke County, Ohio* (Chicago: W. H. Beers and Company, 1880), 757–58; *St. Joseph (MO) Herald*, January 20, 1892, 5.

8. Alva F. Kendall was from Portsmouth, Scioto County, Ohio. He was commissioned first sergeant in Company F of the 91st Ohio Volunteer Infantry on August 6, 1862. He received several promotions, and in May 1864 he rose to the rank of first lieutenant in Company B. On March 29, 1865, he was promoted to the rank of captain in Company G of the 91st. He assisted with the mustering out of the regiment on June 24, 1865. US Census, 1860, Portsmouth, Scioto County, Ohio, 131; *Official Roster of the Soldiers of the State of Ohio*, 7:130, 142, 153; Nelson W. Evans, *A History of Scioto County, Ohio, Together with a Pioneer Record of Southern Ohio* (Portsmouth, OH: Nelson W. Evans, 1903), 1021–22.

9. Israel Robinson was a prominent lawyer and Democrat from Martinsburg, Virginia. He served as circuit court clerk for Berkeley County in the 1850s. In 1855 he took ownership of the *Virginia Republican*, published in Martinsburg. Robinson represented Berkeley County in the state legislature beginning in the late 1850s and continued in that role after Virginia seceded in 1861. He was also a member of the Confederate Congress when it met in Richmond. A handful of sources suggest that he served in Confederate military, including as a sergeant in Company D of the 2nd Virginia Infantry (known as the Berkeley

Border Guards) and the 67th Virginia Military Regiment, but there is no official record of his military service. He died on October 25, 1863, in Richmond at age forty-four. F. Vernon Aler, *Aler's History of Martinsburg and Berkeley County, West Virginia* (Hagerstown, MD: Mail Publishing Company, 1888), 227, 268, 389; James Morton Callahan, *History of West Virginia, Old and New* (Chicago: American Historical Society, 1923), 1:300; Ainsworth P. Spofford, *Eminent and Representative Men of Virginia and the District of Columbia, of the Nineteenth Century* (Madison, WI: Brant and Fuller, 1893), 227; Dennis D. Frye, *2nd Virginia Infantry* (Lynchburg: H. E. Howard, 1984), 127; "Miscellaneous Items," *Daily Intelligencer* (Wheeling, WV), November 4, 1863, 1.

10. Edward S. Wilson was appointed a sergeant in Company H of the 91st Ohio Volunteer Infantry on August 15, 1862. Wilson was wounded on July 20, 1864, at the Battle of Stephenson's Depot. He rose to the rank of first lieutenant and mustered out with the company on June 24, 1865. *Official Roster of the Soldiers of the State of Ohio*, 7:147.

11. Eugene B. Willard (Williard) was appointed a sergeant in Company H of the 91st Ohio Volunteer Infantry on August 15, 1862. Willard was wounded on July 20, 1864, at the Battle of Stephenson's Depot. He rose to the rank of second lieutenant in Company E and mustered out with the company on June 24, 1865. *Official Roster of the Soldiers of the State of Ohio*, 7:139, 148.

12. Samuel Brady Steece (Stuce) was appointed a sergeant in Company H of the 91st Ohio Volunteer Infantry on August 15, 1862. Stuce was wounded on July 20, 1864, at the Battle of Stephenson's Depot. He mustered out with the company on June 24, 1865. *Official Roster of the Soldiers of the State of Ohio*, 7:148.

13. Daniel D. Johnson was born in Tyler County, West Virginia. He attended Marietta College and later transferred to Columbian University (now George Washington University) in Washington, DC, where he graduated in June 1860. In August 1862 he was commissioned as major of the 14th Virginia Infantry and then promoted to colonel on July 29, 1863. He was wounded at the Battle of Opequan (Third Battle of Winchester) but recovered and mustered out on July 3, 1865. Lang, *Loyal West Virginia*, 291; George W. Atkinson and Alvaro F. Gibbens, *Prominent Men of West Virginia* (Wheeling: W. L. Callin, 1890), 467.

14. John W. Shaw was a lieutenant colonel in the 34th Ohio Volunteer Infantry. He was killed on July 24, 1864, at the Second Battle of Kernstown, near Winchester. Reid, *Ohio in the War*, 2:221, 225; *Official Roster of the Soldiers of the State of Ohio*, 3:555.

15. Colonel Coates wrote his wife on August 4, 1864, explaining that "a great injustice had been done" by dismissing Dr. W. S. Newton. Benjamin F. Coates to Elizabeth Coates, August 4, 1864, folder 3, Coates Collection, Hayes Library and Museum.

9. We Are Now in Face of the Enemy

1. William S. Newton to Frances Ann Hayward Newton, September 9, 1864, Newton Papers, SCUA VT.

2. William S. Newton to Frances Ann Hayward Newton, September 18, 1864, Newton Papers, SCUA VT.

3. See, Gary W. Gallagher, ed., *The Shenandoah Valley Campaign of 1864* (Chapel Hill: Univ. of North Carolina Press, 2006); Lepa, *The Shenandoah Valley Campaign of 1864*; Duncan, *Beleaguered Winchester*; Edward J. Stackpole, *Sheridan in the Shenandoah: Jubal Early's Nemesis* (Harrisburg: Stackpole Company, 1961); *The Shenandoah Campaigns of 1862 and 1864 and the Appomattox Campaign, 1865*, vol. 6 (Boston: Military Historical Society of Massachusetts, 1907); Jeffry D. Wert, *From Winchester to Cedar Creek: The Shenandoah Campaign of 1864* (Carlisle, PA: South Mountain Press, Inc., 1987).

4. William S. Newton to Frances Ann Hayward Newton, September 18, 1864, Newton Papers, SCUA VT.

5. William S. Newton to Frances Ann Hayward Newton, September 24, 1864, Newton Papers, SCUA VT.

6. William S. Newton to Frances Ann Hayward Newton, October 23, 1864, Newton Papers, SCUA VT.

7. See, Theodore C. Mahr, *The Battle of Cedar Creek: Showdown in the Shenandoah, October 1–30, 1864* (Lynchburg: H. E. Howard, 1992); Thomas A. Lewis, *The Guns of Cedar Creek* (New York: Harper & Row, 1988); Patchen, *Shenandoah Summer*; Lepa, *Shenandoah Valley Campaign*.

8. See, James A. Ramage, *Gray Ghost: The Life of Col. John Singleton Mosby* (Lexington: Univ. Press of Kentucky, 1999); Kevin H. Siepel, *Rebel: The Life and Times of John Singleton Mosby* (New York: St. Martin's Press, 1983); Jeffry D. Wert, *Mosby's Rangers* (New York: Simon and Schuster, 1990); Charles Wells Russell, ed., *The Memoirs of Colonel John S. Mosby* (Bloomington: Indiana Univ. Press, 1959); J. Marshall Crawford, *Mosby and His Men* (New York: G. W. Carleton and Co., 1867).

9. William S. Newton to Frances Ann Hayward Newton, September 24, 1864, Newton Papers, SCUA VT.

10. William S. Newton to Frances Ann Hayward Newton, August 16, 1864, Newton Papers, SCUA VT.

11. William S. Newton to Frances Ann Hayward Newton, August 27, 1864, Newton Papers, SCUA VT.

12. Charles A. Thatcher (Thacker) was a doctor and assistant surgeon for the 14th Virginia Infantry. Strait, *Roster of Regimental Surgeons and Assistant Surgeons*, 274; Lang, *Loyal West Virginia*, 291.

13. James W. Vance enlisted in Company A of the 91st Ohio Volunteer Infantry

on August 11, 1862. He rose to the rank of corporal and also served in Company E of the 91st. Vance mustered out on June 13, 1865. *Official Roster of the Soldiers of the State of Ohio*, 7:130, 141.

14. Henry (Charley) Dennison Kingsbury was commissioned first lieutenant in the 14th Ohio Volunteer Infantry on April 27, 1861. He rose to the rank of colonel for the 189th Ohio Volunteer Infantry. Reid, *Ohio in the War*, 1:970–71; Eicher and Eicher, *Civil War High Commands*, 334.

15. Jennie Moredock married Douglas Newton on October 18, 1864. *Newton Genealogy of the Newton Families*, 13.

16. *Qui vive* is a French phrase for on alert or always ready.

17. A fly is an extra piece of canvas attached to a tent, usually used as extra protection from the elements. Within this context, however, Newton was using the tent flies as their own stand-alone tents, supported by a rope stretched between at least two poles. Billings, *Hardtack and Coffee*, 51.

18. David L. Morton was a sergeant in Company B of the 91st Ohio Volunteer Infantry. He had been working as a hospital steward for Newton. He was killed on September 19, 1864, at the Battle of Opequan (Third Battle of Winchester). *Official Roster of the Soldiers of the State of Ohio*, 7:130; Windsor, *History of the Ninety-First Regiment*, 62.

19. John A. Hamilton was from Gallipolis. Prior to the war, he taught school, worked in a book store, and was a bookkeeper at a grocery store. He was commissioned as a sergeant in Company B of the 91st Ohio Volunteer Infantry on August 4, 1862. Hamilton was promoted to second lieutenant in April 1863 and then to first lieutenant on August 10, 1864. As Newton noted in a letter to his wife, Hamilton was wounded in September 1864 near Winchester, but the official regimental history did not include him in the list of wounded soldiers. In January 18, 1865, he received the promotion to captain and mustered out with the company on June 24, 1865. Hamilton returned to Gallipolis, later serving as town treasurer. *Official Roster of the Soldiers of the State of Ohio*, 7:130; *History of Gallia County*, v; *Gallipolis Bulletin*, September 9, 1884.

20. Dr. James H. Hysell was an assistant surgeon for the 9th Virginia Infantry. He was later promoted to surgeon in the 1st Virginia Veteran Infantry. Lang, *Loyal West Virginia*, 269, 305; Strait, *Roster of All Regimental Surgeons and Assistant Surgeons*, 273, 274.

21. Because this was an assignment parallel to Newton and his regiment was near Winchester at this time, this was most likely Dr. Joseph T. Smith from Collinwood, Ohio. He served as surgeon for the 2nd Ohio Volunteer Cavalry. Strait, *Roster of All Regimental Surgeons and Assistant Surgeons*, 187; Reid, *Ohio in the War*, 2:754.

22. Dr. John H. Brinton was from Pennsylvania. He was commissioned as brigade surgeon in the US Volunteer Surgeons in 1861. He first served as medical

director for General Ulysses S. Grant and in September 1864 was ordered to Winchester to coordinate the medical team tending to the wounded from the Battle of Opequan (Third Battle of Winchester). He arrived in Winchester on September 21 or 22 and moved all of the wounded from scattered temporary hospitals into a giant tent hospital just south of Winchester. John H. Brinton, *Personal Memoirs of John H. Brinton, Major and Surgeon U.S.V., 1861–1865* (New York: Neale Publishing Company, 1914), 10, 18, 291; William Grace, *The Army Surgeon's Manual, For the Use of Medical Officers, Cadets, Chaplains, and Hospital Stewards* (New York: Bailliere Brothers, 1864), 10, 31; Delauter, *The Third Battle of Winchester*, 74.

23. James M. Leete was a doctor from New York. He was commissioned as a brigade surgeon in the US Volunteer Surgeons in 1862. He was in ten battles in the Shenandoah Valley and, upon recommendation from General Crook, was brevetted lieutenant colonel "for gallant and meritorious services." He later served as medical director of the 20th Army Corps under General William T. Sherman. Edward L. Leete, comp., *The Family of William Leete, One of the First Settlers of Guilford, Connecticut, and Governor of New Haven and Connecticut Colonies* (New Haven: Tuttle, Morehouse, and Taylor Printers, 1884), 107 (quotation); Francis Bernard Heitman, *Historical Register and Dictionary of the United States Army* (Washington, DC: Government Printing Office, 1903), 1:626; Grace, *The Army Surgeon's Manual*, 12.

24. It is unclear to which Dr. Kemp Newton was referring. It may have been John A. Kemp, a doctor from Belmont County, Ohio, or his son George H. Kemp, also a doctor from Belmont County, Ohio. However, neither doctor appears in any military rosters. The only regimental listing for an Ohio doctor with the surname Kemp was George W. Kemp. He was assistant surgeon of the 113th Ohio Volunteer Infantry; however, he resigned in October 1863 and the 113th did not see action in Virginia. Further, there were no regimental surgeons listed with the surname Kemp in any of the West Virginia regiments. US Census, 1860, Washington, Belmont County, Ohio, 4; US Census, 1870, Barnesville, Belmont County, Ohio, 14; Strait, *Roster of All Regimental Surgeons and Assistant Surgeons*, 210.

25. Daniel D. Johnson was born in Tyler County, West Virginia. He attended Marietta College and later transferred to Columbian University (now George Washington University) in Washington, DC, where he graduated in June 1860. In August 1862 he was commissioned as major of the 14th Virginia Infantry and then promoted to colonel on July 29, 1863. He was wounded at the Battle of Opequan (Third Battle of Winchester) but recovered and mustered out on July 3, 1865. Lang, *Loyal West Virginia*, 291; Atkinson and Gibbens, *Prominent Men of West Virginia*, 467.

26. The main Confederate hospital near Winchester was referred to as York Hospital. It was named for Confederate brigadier general Zebulon York, who commanded two Louisiana brigades at the Battle of Opequan (Third Battle of Winchester). He was severely wounded during the battle and later lost his left arm. Delauter, *The Third Battle of Winchester*, 9; Eicher and Eicher, *Civil War High Commands*, 585.

27. William S. Love was a doctor and Confederate surgeon. After the war he stayed in Winchester. "Dr. William S. Love," *Virginia Medical Semi-Monthly* 17 (December 27, 1912): 468; Wyllie, *Confederate Officers*, 313.

28. Dr. Arthur B. Monahan was a doctor from Jackson County, Ohio. He was surgeon for the 63rd Ohio Volunteer Infantry. *Official Roster of the Soldiers of the State of Ohio*, 5:383. Strait, *Roster of All Regimental Surgeons and Assistant Surgeons*, 202; Willard, *History of the Hanging Rock Iron Region of Ohio*, 1:503.

29. Dorothea Dix was an advocate for the mentally ill and during the Civil War served as superintendent of army nurses. She arranged for nineteen carloads of supplies to aid the wounded Union soldiers following the Battle of Opequan (Third Battle of Winchester). Daniel A. Master, ed., *Army Life According to Arbaw: Civil War Letters of William A. Brand, 66th Ohio Volunteer Infantry* (Perrysburg, OH: Columbian Arsenal Press, 2019), 46; Duncan, *Beleaguered Winchester*, 78; "Dorothea Lynde Dix," *Appleton's Cyclopaedia of American Biography*, 2:183.

30. Joseph Thoburn was a doctor in Wheeling just before the Civil War. In May 1861 he was commissioned as a surgeon of the 1st Virginia Infantry, a three-month regiment commanded by Colonel Benjamin F. Kelley. In August the 1st Virginia Infantry reorganized, and Thoburn was commissioned colonel. Thoburn led the 1st Virginia Infantry during the Shenandoah Valley Campaign of 1864, but was killed at the Battle of Cedar Creek on October 19, 1864. J. H. Newton, *History of the Pan-Handle: Being Historical Collections of the Counties of Ohio, Brooke, Marshall, and Hancock, West Virginia* (Wheeling, WV: J. A. Caldwell, 1879), 178, 253; Lang, *Loyal West Virginia*, 233, 236, 238–40; *History of the Upper Ohio Valley, with Family History and Biographical Sketches, a Statement of Its Resources, Industrial Growth and Commercial Advantages* (Madison, WI: Brant and Fuller, 1891), 1:580–81, 586.

31. Thomas J. Shannon was a doctor from Youngstown who was commissioned as an assistant surgeon for the 2nd Ohio Volunteer Infantry in February 1862. In July 1863 he transferred to the 116th Ohio Volunteer Infantry and served as a surgeon. In early June, following the Battle of Opequan (Third Battle of Winchester), Shannon was appointed surgeon of the 116th Ohio Volunteer Infantry, chief of the First Division of the Army of West Virginia. He was killed on October 19, 1864, at the Battle of Cedar Creek. Reid, *Ohio*

in the War, 1:250, 2:21, 2:604; Wildes, *Record of the One Hundred and Sixteenth Regiment Ohio Infantry Volunteers*, 51, 312–13; "Youngstown Physicians
in the Civil War," *Bulletin of the Mahoning County Medical Society* 33 (August
1963): 245–46; Strait, *Roster of Regimental Surgeons and Assistant Surgeons*,
190; *Official Roster of the Soldiers of the State of Ohio*, 8:181.

32. Andrew Ward was listed as a private in Company E of the 54th Pennsylvania
Volunteer Infantry. The regimental history lists his death date as unknown,
with a burial location at the National Cemetery in Winchester, Virginia.
Bates, *History of the Pennsylvania Volunteers*, 2:160.

10. The War by All Is Now Considered Over

1. William S. Newton to Frances Ann Hayward Newton, April 24, 1865,
Newton Papers, SCUA VT.

2. Reid, *Ohio in the War*, 2:738.

3. Benjamin F. Coates to Elizabeth Coates, February 15, 1865, folder 4, Coates
Collection, Hayes Library and Museum.

4. William S. Newton to Frances Ann Hayward Newton, June 8, 1865, Newton
Papers, SCUA VT.

5. William S. Newton to Frances Ann Hayward Newton, June 8, 1865, Newton
Papers, SCUA VT.

6. Rutherford B. Hayes was a lawyer in Cincinnati before the Civil War. On
June 7, 1861, he was appointed major of the 23rd Ohio Volunteer Infantry.
He served under General William Rosecrans in West Virginia during 1861.
He rose steadily to the rank of colonel. In December 1862 he took command
of the First Brigade of the Kanawha Division. Hayes was at the Battle of
Cloyd's Mountain, but his leadership at the Battles of Opequan (Third
Battle of Winchester), Fisher's Hill, and Cedar Creek earned him the rank
of brigadier general. In early 1865, as Newton mentioned in his January 26
letter, Hayes was on home leave for a few weeks. After the Civil War, Hayes
served as governor of Ohio, US representative, and president of the United
States, 1877–1881. Reid, *Ohio in the War*, 1:848–49, 2:158, 160–68; Williams,
ed., *Diary and Letters of Rutherford Birchard Hayes*, 2:456–57, 555–59.

7. Joseph T. Webb was a doctor from Fremont, Ohio. He was appointed surgeon of the 23rd Ohio Volunteer Infantry on July 2, 1861, and mustered out
with the regiment on July 26, 1865. He was the brother-in-law of Rutherford
B. Hayes. Reid, *Ohio in the War*, 2:158; Strait, *Roster of All Regimental Surgeons and Assistant Surgeons*, 194.

8. Russell D. Van Dusen was a Presbyterian minister in Gallipolis. He served
as chaplain of the 12th Ohio Volunteer Infantry. *History of Gallia County*, xiv;
Reid, *Ohio in the War*, 2:87.

9. Thomas Meredith (Merideth) was a Cincinnati steamboat owner and captain. He was listed as a forty-year-old clerk in the Civil War registration list for Gallia County, but there is no indication that he served in the military. Taylor, *The Supply for Tomorrow Must Not Fail*, 180; Thomas Merideth, Ohio, 11th, 3:39, Consolidated Lists of Civil War Draft Registration Records, RG 110, NARA.

10. Robert Youart, misspelled Ewart by Newton, was commissioned as a captain in the 44th Ohio Volunteer Infantry in December 1861. He transferred to the 8th Ohio Volunteer Cavalry in January 1864 at the rank of lieutenant colonel. Reid, *Ohio and the War*, 2:277, 804.

11. Luther Furney was commissioned as a major in the 34th Ohio Volunteer Infantry in March 1864. He rose to the rank of lieutenant colonel. Reid, *Ohio and the War*, 2:221; *Official Roster of the Soldiers of the State of Ohio*, 3:555.

12. On January 11, 1865, Confederate forces led by General Thomas L. Rosser attacked the town of Beverly, West Virginia, which was protected by a small force from the 8th Ohio Volunteer Cavalry and the 34th Ohio Volunteer Infantry. The attack happened so suddenly that a majority of the Union soldiers were captured. Colonels Youart and Furney, who were initially captured and then escaped, were later dismissed because of the incident. Reid, *Ohio and the War*, 2:227; *Wheeling (WV) Daily Intelligencer*, January 16, 19, 20, 1865.

13. Accounts of the capture of Crook and Kelley were detailed in several sources, including the following: Will H. Loudermilk, *History of Cumberland, Maryland* (Washington, DC: James Anglim, 1878), 420–22; Samuel Clarke Farrar, *The Twenty-Second Pennsylvania Cavalry and the Ringgold Battalion, 1861–1865* (Pittsburgh: S. C. Farrar, 1911), 451–52; *Wheeling (WV) Daily Intelligencer*, February 22, 23, 24, 25, 1865; *Richmond Daily Dispatch*, February 25, 28, 1865.

14. David Coleman was a doctor from Tiffin township, near West Union, Ohio. His wife was Elizabeth Coleman. In the 1850s he advertised his medical services in Ironton. US Census 1860, Tiffin, Adams County, Ohio, 90; *Spirit of the Times*, January 29, 1856, 4.

15. The Battelle family had deep roots in Marietta. In 1788 Ebenezer Battelle, a Revolutionary War veteran and member of the Ohio Company, was one of the first settlers of Marietta. The 1860 census for Washington County, Ohio, where Marietta is located, listed several people who could have been Mr. Battelle. Emilius O. Randall and Daniel J. Ryan, *History of Ohio: The Rise and Progress of an American State* (New York: Century History Company, 1915), 6:126–37.

16. John Dickinson was a doctor from Cleveland. He was appointed assistant surgeon of the 36th Ohio Volunteer Infantry on July 4, 1862. Dickinson received a promotion to surgeon of the 195th Ohio Volunteer Infantry on

March 16, 1865. Reid, *Ohio and the War*, 2:231, 740; Strait, *Roster of All Regimental Surgeons and Assistant Surgeons*, 197, 222.

17. Nelson Sinnet was the quartermaster for the 193rd Ohio Volunteer Infantry. *Official Roster of the Soldiers of the State of Ohio*, 10:147.

18. John T. Matthews was the adjutant for the 193rd Ohio Volunteer Infantry. *Official Roster of the Soldiers of the State of Ohio*, 10:147.

19. August Alfred Thomas Archimedes Torbert was from Delaware and graduated from West Point in 1855. In March 1861 he was appointed as a first lieutenant in the Confederate Army but declined the position. In April he recruited Union troops in New Jersey, and in September he became colonel of the 1st New Jersey Infantry. In November 1862 he rose to the rank of brigadier general and led troops during the Battles of Fredericksburg, Chancellorsville, and Gettysburg. In spring 1864 Torbert led the cavalry for the Army of the Shenandoah at the Battles of Opequan (Third Battle of Winchester) and Cedar Creek. He remained near Winchester during early 1865, and after the war he served in several diplomatic roles. Ezra J. Warner, *Generals in Blue: Lives of the Union Commanders* (Baton Rouge: Louisiana State Univ. Press, 1964), 508–9; Eicher and Eicher, *Civil War High Commands*, 533.

20. William W. Prather enlisted as a private in the 91st Ohio Volunteer Infantry on October 24, 1863. He rose to the rank of quartermaster on June 1, 1865, and mustered out with the regiment on June 24, 1865. After the Civil War, Prater operated a steamboat in Gallipolis. *Official Roster of the Soldiers of the State of Ohio*, 7:127; US Steamboat Inspection Service, *List of Masters, Mates, Pilots, and Engineers of Merchant Steam and other Motor Vessels Licenses During the Year Ended December 31, 1897* (Washington, DC: Government Printing Office, 1898), 201.

21. Mathias Jeffers was born about 1802 and would have been sixty years old during the Civil War period. Emily Hayward, born in 1834, would have been thirty years old during the Civil War period, about half of the age of Jeffers. Matthias Jeffers and Emily Hayward, October 3, 1865, 107, Gallia County, Ohio, County Marriage Records, 1860–1865.

22. The *Scion* was a newspaper published in West Union, Ohio. After the Civil War the newspaper changed its name to the *West Union Scion*, and its banner declared, "Devoted to the Republican Party and the Adams County." "About the Scion," Chronicling America, Library of Congress, https://chronicling america.loc.gov/lccn/sn83035191/; "About the West Union Scion," Chronicling America, Library of Congress, https://chroniclingamerica.loc.gov/lccn /sn83035192/.

23. Euchre is a popular card game, usually featuring four players in two teams with a deck of twenty-five cards that includes a joker. There are many variations, including Seven Up, which adds the seven and eight cards, bringing

the deck up to thirty-three cards total. David Parlett, *A Dictionary of Card Games* (New York: Oxford Univ. Press, 1992), 1–3, 104–6, 254; Charles Henry Wharton Meehan, *The Law and Practice of the Game of Euchre, By a Professor* (Philadelphia: T. B. Peterson and Brothers, 1862); "Rules for 7's up Euchre," Silver Creek Entertainment Discussion Forum, https://forums.silvercrk.com /phpBB3/viewtopic.php?t=15139.

24. Daw berries or dewberries are a purple- or black-colored berry native to North America, similar to blackberries. Fred W. Card, *Bush-Fruits: A Horticultural Monograph of Raspberries, Blackberries, Dewberries, Currants, Gooseberries, and Other Shrub-Like Fruits* (New York: Macmillan Company, 1901), 132–45.

25. Luke Murrin enlisted as a private in Company A of the 10th Ohio Volunteer Infantry on June 3, 1861. He was quickly appointed as quartermaster sergeant. Murrin was appointed quartermaster on May 2, 1863, and he mustered out with the regiment on June 17, 1864. In March 1865 he was commissioned major in the 193rd Ohio Volunteer Infantry. Murrin mustered out with the regiment on August 4, 1865. *Official Roster of the Soldiers of the State of Ohio*, 2:293, 10:147.

26. There is a modern-day drinking challenge referred to as an Irish wedding, but most likely this was a more general slang phrase indicating rowdy drinking.

27. James W. Warfield, a doctor from Belmont, Ohio, was appointed surgeon of the 77th Ohio Volunteer Infantry on February 3, 1862. He was honorably discharged on May 15, 1864, but returned as surgeon of the 191st Ohio Volunteer Infantry in March 1865. Reid, *Ohio in the War*, 2:444, 734; Strait, *Roster of Regimental Surgeons and Assistant Surgeons*, 204, 221.

28. Zachariah B. Gentry was a doctor from Frankfort, Kentucky. He was appointed surgeon of the 154th Indiana Volunteer Infantry in April 1865. Strait, *Roster of Regimental Surgeons and Assistant Surgeons*, 61.

29. Robert L. Kimberly was a newspaper reporter in Cleveland prior to the start of the Civil War. He was appointed second lieutenant in the 41st Ohio Volunteer Infantry on March 17, 1862. He advanced quickly, and in January 1863, he became a lieutenant colonel for the 41st. On February 28, 1865, he took command of the 191st Ohio Volunteer Infantry as a colonel. In March he received the rank of brevet colonel for meritorious service. After the Civil War, Kimberly returned to newspaper publishing and became active in reunion events. In 1897 he co-authored the regimental history of the 41st Ohio. Reid, *Ohio in the War*, 2:259, 260; *Official Roster of the Soldiers of the State of Ohio*, 4:169, 182, 10:109; Eicher and Eicher, *Civil War High Commands*, 333; "Robert Lewis Kimberly," Find A Grave, https://www.findagrave.com /memorial/10468843/robert-lewis-kimberly; Robert L. Kimberly and Ephraim S. Holloway, *The Forty-First Ohio Veteran Volunteer Infantry in the War of the Rebellion, 1861–1865* (Cleveland: W. R. Smellie, 1897).

30. Charles Grundy Woodruff married Amelia C. Eno in 1835. Newton misidentified her as Almira. Woodruff was related to the Newton family and had connections in Marietta, but he lived in Buchanan County, Iowa. Amelia died in 1858, and Charles remarried. There is no indication that Woodruff was a captain in the military. There is also no information about the identification of Mollie, whom Woodruff was going to claim while visiting Marietta. Sarah Hall Johnston, comp., *Lineage Book, National Society of the Daughters of the American Revolution* (Harrisburg, PA: Telegraph Printing Company, 1902), 41:7; "Charles Grundy Woodruff," Find A Grave, https://www.finda grave.com/memorial/75776880.

31. This is most likely John Eagle, a farmer from West Union, Ohio. US Census, 1870, Tiffin, Adams County, Ohio, 17; "John Eagle," Find A Grave, https:// www.findagrave.com/memorial/81653736.

Epilogue

1. *Gallipolis Journal*, October 26, 1865, 1.

2. *Portsmouth Daily Times*, July 22, 1865, 3; Lambert, *Ninety-First Ohio Volunteer Infantry*, 85–86; *Gallipolis Journal*, February 21, 1867, 3, April 26, 1868, April 30, 1868, 1; *Official Roster of the Soldiers of the State of Ohio*, 7:128; Ewing, *The Story of the Ninety-First*, 1868.

3. *History of Gallia County*, xv; *Newton Genealogy of the Newton Families*, 12; *Gallipolis Journal*, July 13, 1876, 3; *Wiggins and Weaver's Ohio River Directory For 1871–72* (Cleveland: Fairbanks, Benedict and Co., 1871), 226.

4. *List of Post Office and Postmasters of the United States, Revised and Corrected by the Post Office Department to October 20, 1867* (Washington, DC: Government Printing Office, 1868), 55; W. S. Newton, Gallia County, Ohio, 25A:149, U.S. Appointments of U.S. Postmasters, 1832–1971, Record Group 28, Records of the Post Office Department (RG 28), NARA; *Cincinnati Enquirer*, March 29, 1867, 3; *Gallipolis Journal*, December 17, 1868, 2, March 18, 1869, 1; Andrew Johnson, W.S. Newton Appointment as Deputy Postmaster of Gallipolis, Ohio, March 28, 1867, Newton Papers, VT SCUA.

5. *Cincinnati Enquirer*, December 10, 1868, 3; *Gallipolis Journal*, December 17, 1868, 2; *Evansville (IN) Daily Journal*, December 9, 1868, 1; Norris F. Schneider, "Banker's Money Stolen By Stagecoach Manager," *Times Recorder* (Zanesville, OH), June 24, 1973, 23.

6. *Cincinnati Enquirer*, March 18, 1869, 8; *Gallipolis Journal*, March 25, 1869, 2, May 13, 1869, 3, December 2, 1869, 2; Warren M. Bateman, "Indictment for embezzling letters et al, *The United States v William S. Newton and Edward S. Newton*, Filed April 18, 1869," United States Circuit Court, Cincinnati, Criminal Case 567; United States Circuit Court, Cincinnati, Criminal Docket, Case 567, vol.

A, p. 301, all in Records of the U.S. Circuit Court for the Southern District of Ohio, Record Group 21, Records of District Courts of the United States, National Archives and Records Administration, Chicago, Illinois (RG 21 NARA).

7. United States Circuit Court, Cincinnati, Criminal Docket, Case 567, vol. A, p. 301, RG 21 NARA; *Gallipolis Journal*, December 2, 1869.

8. William S. Newton, Gallia County, Ohio, 38:164, U.S. Appointments of U.S. Postmasters, 1832–1971, RG 28, NARA; *Gallipolis Journal*, December 30, 1875, 1, November 23, 1882; *Gallipolis Bulletin*, November 21, 1882; J.W. Marshall, W.S. Newton Appointment as Deputy Postmaster of Gallipolis, Ohio, April 11, 1871, Newton Papers, VT SCUA.

9. Pension File of William S. Newton, 91st Ohio Volunteer Infantry, RG 15, NARA.

10. *Gallipolis Bulletin*, November 21, 1882; *Gallipolis Journal*, November 23, 1882; "Dr. William S. Newton," Find a Grave, https://www.findagrave.com /memorial/14263972/william-s_-newton; "Frances Ann Hayward Newton," Find A Grave, https://www.findagrave.com/memorial/14263973/frances -ann-newton; Pension File of William S. Newton, 91st Ohio Volunteer Infantry, RG 15, NARA.

11. *Newton Genealogy of the Newton Families*, 12; *Medical College of Ohio, Sixtieth Annual Catalogue, 1880–81*, 21; US Census, 1880, Madison, Jefferson County, Indiana, 15; "Edward Seymour Newton," Find A Grave, https://www.finda grave.com/memorial/101812996/edward-seymour-newton; *Lincoln (KS) Republican*, July 25, 1901, 1, 6; *Lincoln (KS) Sentinel*, October 13, 1898, 3; *Lincoln (KS) County Democrat*, December 8, 1887, 5.

12. *Newton Genealogy of the Newton Families*, 12; "Edward Seymour Newton," Find A Grave, https://www.findagrave.com/memorial/101812996/edward -seymour-newton; *Lincoln (KS) Beacon*, March 25, 1886, 5 (first quotation), February 28, 1889, 5; *Lincoln (KS) Republican*, July 25, 1901, 1, 6, March 16, 1899, 1 (second quotation), November 15, 1888, 4; *Lincoln (KS) County Democrat*, January 26, 1888, 4, November 15, 1888, 1, February 14, 1889, 1; *Sylvan Grove (KS) Sentinel*, February 15, 1889, 1.

13. William S. Newton to Frances Ann Hayward Newton, November 22, 1864, Newton Papers, SCUA VT.

Appendix

1. *Newton Genealogy of the Newton Families*, 12; *Gallipolis Journal*, January 1, 1880; "Death of Mrs. Dr. Newton," *Lincoln (KS) Sentinel*, February 20, 1896, 1; *Lincoln (KS) Sentinel*, February 13, 1896, 1; *Gallipolis Bulletin*, February 15, 1896; "Frances Ann Hayward Newton," Find a Grave, https://www.finda grave.com/memorial/14263973/frances-ann-newton.

2. *Newton Genealogy of the Newton Families,* 13; *Ironton Register,* July 1, 1858; William S. Newton to Frances Ann Hayward Newton, February 1, 1863[4], Newton Papers, SCUA VT.

3. *Newton Genealogy of the Newton Families,* 13.

4. *Newton Genealogy of the Newton Families,* 13; *Lincoln (KS) Republican,* July 25, 1901, 1.

5. *Newton Genealogy of the Newton Families,* 13; "Lawrence County, Ohio, Abstracted Obituaries, 1850–1900," 407, The Lawrence Register, https:// lawrencecountyohio.com/wp-content/uploads/2020/06/Obit-Index-1850 -1900.pdf.

6. *Newton Genealogy of the Newton Families,* 13.

7. *Newton Genealogy of the Newton Families,* 13; *Gallipolis Journal,* December 30, 1880, 1; *Lincoln (KS) Sentinel,* February 12, 1896, 1; "Kate May Newton Dages," Find A Grave, https://www.findagrave.com/memorial/23694100 /kate-may-dages;

8. *Newton Genealogy of the Newton Families,* 13; US Census, 1870, Gallipolis, Gallia County, Ohio, 16; US Census, 1880, Gallipolis, Gallia County, Ohio, 12; US Census, 1900, District 0973, Philadelphia Ward 38, Philadelphia, Pennsylvania, B3; *Lincoln (KS) Sentinel,* February 13, 1896, 1; *Intelligencer Journal* (Lancaster, PA), May 16, 1940, 2; John W. Newton, Certificate of Death, 5/14/1940, #50523, Pennsylvania Death Certificates, 1906–1968, Record Group 11, Pennsylvania Historical and Museum Commission, Harrisburg, Pennsylvania.

9. *Newton Genealogy of the Newton Families,* 13; *History of Gallia County,* 43; "William Greenleaf Fuller," Find A Grave, https://www.findagrave.com /memorial/17129230/william-greenleaf-fuller; "Grim Reaper: Colonel William G. Fuller," *Cincinnati Enquirer,* July 18, 1903, 2; Reid, *Ohio in the War,* 1:1015. See also, William R. Plum, *The Military Telegraph during the Civil War in the United States,* 2 vols. (Chicago: Jansen, McClurg & Company, 1882).

10. Matthias Jeffers and Emily Hayward, October 3, 1865, 107, Gallia County, Ohio, County Marriage Records, 1860–1865; Emily Jeffers, US Census, Mortality Schedules, 1850–1885, 1880, Gallia, Ohio, p. 1, enumeration district 24.

11. *Gallipolis Journal,* May 7, 1863, 2; "Death Comes to Many Homes the Past Week," *Gallipolis Journal,* April 11, 1912; *Report of the Commissioner of Agriculture for the Year 1867* (Washington, DC: Government Printing Office, 1868): 394.

12. *Newton Genealogy of the Newton Families,* 8; Reid, *Ohio in the War,* 2:909; "Charles Humphrey Newton," Find A Grave, https://www.findagrave.com /memorial/32618887/charles-humphrey-newton; Andrews, *History of Marietta and Washington County,* 412, 632, 1009–10.

13. *Newton Genealogy of the Newton Families*, 13; "Douglas E. Newton," Find A Grave, https://www.findagrave.com/memorial/84187218/douglas-e-newton; John Adams Bownocker, "The Occurrence and Exploitation of Petroleum and Natural Gas in Ohio," in *Geological Survey of Ohio*, Fourth Series, Bulletin No. 1 (Springfield, OH: Springfield Publishing Company, 1903), 151–52; Douglas E. Newton, Ohio, 15th, 1:5, Consolidated Lists of Civil War Draft Registration Records, RG 110, NARA; "Colonel Douglas E. Newton," *Pittsburgh Daily Post*, February 13, 1917, 4.

14. *Newton Genealogy of the Newton Families*, 6–7; "Elizabeth Newton," Find A Grave, https://www.findagrave.com/memorial/20277901/elizabeth-newton.

15. *Newton Genealogy of the Newton Families*, 10; Andrews, *History of Marietta and Washington County*, 410, 633, 1033, 1160, 1296; *History of Washington County, Ohio*, 153, 161, 190, 349, 663; Bownocker, "The Occurrence and Exploitation of Petroleum and Natural Gas in Ohio," 151–52; "Families, John Newton," Marietta Castle, https://mariettacastle.org/about/families/; "John Newton," Find A Grave, https://www.findagrave.com/memorial/20277865/john-newton.

16. *Newton Genealogy of the Newton Families*, 13; "Lucy L. Fuller," Find A Grave, https://www.findagrave.com/memorial/17129242/lucy-l-fuller; "Mrs. Fuller," *Gallipolis Bulletin*, April 1, 1910.

17. *Newton Genealogy of the Newton Families*, 10; "Families, John Newton," Marietta Castle, https://mariettacastle.org/about/families/; "Mary Francis Newton Lord," Find A Grave, https://www.findagrave.com/memorial/50595562/mary-frances-lord; "George H. Lord," Find A Grave, https://www.findagrave.com/memorial/9114036/george-h-lord; "Mary Frances Lord," Ontario, Canada, Deaths and Deaths Overseas, 1869–1948, Welland, 1906, 625, Archives of Ontario, Toronto, Ontario, Canada.

18. *Newton Genealogy of the Newton Families*, 10–11; "Rev. Orin H. Newton," Find A Grave, https://www.findagrave.com/memorial/86349283/orin-h-newton.

19. *Newton Genealogy of the Newton Families*, 7–8; "Stephen Newton," Find A Grave, https://www.findagrave.com/memorial/32618809/stephen-newton.

20. Andrews, *History of Marietta and Washington County*, 206, 581, 650, 655, 709–14, 806; *Necrological Report Presented to the Alumni Association of Princeton Theological Seminary at Its Annual Meeting, April 26th, 1881, By a Committee of the Association* (Philadelphia: Grant, Faires, and Rodgers, 1881), 65–67; *Marietta College in the War of Secession*, 79; Reid, *Ohio in the War*, 2:231; John McClintock and James Strong, "Ebenezer B. Andrews," *Cyclopaedia of Biblical, Theological, and Ecclesiastical Literature* (New York: Harper and Brothers, 1885), suppl. 1:163–64; J. S. Newberry, *Geologic Survey of Ohio, Report of Progress in 1870* (Columbus: Nevins and Myers State Printers, 1871), 9, 55–142.

21. *Official Roster of the Soldiers of the State of Ohio*, 7:145, 153.

22. Warner, *Generals in Blue*, 12–13; Eicher and Eicher, *Civil War High Commands*, 110–11; Lang, *Loyal West Virginia*, 353–81; Edward K. Eckert and Nicholas J. Amato, eds., *Ten Years in the Saddle: The Memoir of William Woods Averell* (San Rafael, CA: Presidio Press, 1978).

23. Heitman, *Historical Register and Dictionary of the United States Army*, 1:177; *Official Roster of the Soldiers of the State of Ohio*, 1:411; "Dr. S. C. Ayres Expires," *Cincinnati Enquirer*, September 3, 1921, 5; "Stephen Cooper Ayres," Abraham Lincoln Library and Museum, Lincoln Memorial University, Harrogate, Tennessee, at https://lmuweb02.lmunet.edu/uploads/OnlineResources /virtual_exhibit1/vex20/ACF4DBEF-12C4–49DA-ADFC-000625106152. htm; Stephen Cooper Ayres, "Miami in the Civil War: Alumni Address Delivered June 13, 1906," *Miami Bulletin* 5 (October 1906): 1–14.

24. *Official Roster of the Soldiers of the State of Ohio*, 3:637; US Census, 1860, Harmar, Washington County, Ohio, 122.

25. "Death of Dr. J. V. Z. Blaney," *Chicago Tribune*, December 12, 1874, 5; Heitman, *Historical Register and Dictionary of the United States Army*, 1:224; F. M. Sperry, comp., *A Group of Distinguished Physicians and Surgeons of Chicago* (Chicago: J. H. Beers and Company, 1904), 77–78.

26. *Official Roster of the Soldiers of the State of Ohio*, 7:127; US Census, 1860, Green, Gallia County, Ohio, 337; William S. Newton to Frances Ann Hayward Newton, April 12, 1863, Newton Papers, SCUA VT; *Gallipolis Journal*, April 23, 1863; "Letters from the 91st Ohio Volunteer Infantry," Gallia Genealogy, http://www.galliagenealogy.org/civil%20war/MainCWletters /miles91st.html.

27. Sutton, *History of the Second Regiment, West Virginia*, 16, 255; "Samuel S. Brammer," "Silas I. Brammer," Civil War Soldiers and Sailors System Database, National Park Service.

28. *Official Roster of the Soldiers of the State of Ohio*, 10:147; Strait, *Roster of Regimental Surgeons and Assistant Surgeons*, 221.

29. Windsor, *History of the Ninety-First Regiment*, 5, 6, 61; Evans, *A History of Scioto County, Ohio*, 925; *Official Roster of the Soldiers of the State of Ohio*, 7:128; Reid, *Ohio in the War*, 2:507; *Gallipolis Journal*, July 1, 1885; "Col. Lemuel Zenus Cadot," Find A Grave, https://www.findagrave.com/memorial/52036594; *History of Gallia County*, 42; Lambert, *Ninety-First Ohio Volunteer Infantry*, 93.

30. Evans, *A History of Scioto County, Ohio*, 233; Lambert, *Ninety-First Ohio Volunteer Infantry*, 94; Reid, *Ohio in the War*, 2:504; Windsor, *History of the Ninety-First Regiment*, 13, 61.

31. *Official Roster of the Soldiers of the State of Ohio*, 7:148; Windsor, *History of the Ninety-First Regiment*, 30.

32. *Official Roster of the Soldiers of the State of Ohio*, 7:127; Windsor, *History of the*

Ninety-First Regiment, 6; Strait, Roster of All Regimental Surgeons and Assistant Surgeons, 207; US Census, 1860, Athens, Athens County, Ohio, 62.

33. Official Roster of the Soldiers of the State of Ohio, 7:127; Windsor, History of the Ninety-First Regiment, 5–6; Evans, A History of Scioto County, Ohio, 116–17; Lambert, Ninety-First Ohio Volunteer Infantry, 91–92; Reid, Ohio in the War, 2:504; Evans and Stivers, A History of Adams County, Ohio, 270–71; Eicher and Eicher, Civil War High Commands, 177.

34. Official Roster of the Soldiers of the State of Ohio, 7:133, 145, 148; Windsor, History of the Ninety-First Regiment, 30, 61; US Census, 1860, Hamilton, Lawrence County, Ohio, 129.

35. Strait, Roster of Regimental Surgeons and Assistant Surgeons, 187, 196; Reid, Ohio in the War, 2:221, 745; History of Shelby County, Ohio, with Illustrations and Biographical Sketches of Some of Its Prominent Men and Pioneers (Philadelphia: R. Sutton and Company, 1883), 123, 168, 302; Mike Mangus, "Fremont Body Guards (1861)," July 19, 2011, Ohio Civil War Central, https://www.ohio civilwarcentral.com/entry.php?rec=712.

36. Reid, Ohio in War, 1:963–65; W. H. MacKoy, "General Benjamin Rush Cowen," Ohio Archaeological and Historical Society Publications 18 (April 1909): 149–56; Eicher and Eicher, Civil War High Commands, 187; A. T. McKelvey, Centennial History of Belmont County, Ohio, and Representative Citizens (Chicago: Biographical Publishing Company, 1903), 91–93.

37. Official Roster of the Soldiers of the State of Ohio, 7:139; Windsor, History of the Ninety-First Regiment, 19; Evans and Stivers, A History of Adams County, Ohio, 353; US Census 1860, Tiffin, Adams County, Ohio, 106.

38. Reid, Ohio in the War, 2:799–804; Eicher and Eicher, Civil War High Commands, 191–92; William S. Newton to Frances Ann Hayward Newton, February 21, 1865, Newton Papers, SCUA VT; Warner, Generals in Blue, 102–3; Martin F. Schmitt, General George Crook, His Autobiography (Norman: Univ. of Oklahoma Press, 1946); Magid, George Crook; Werrell, Crook's Regulars.

39. Evans, A History of Scioto County, Ohio, 943; Official Roster of the Soldiers of the State of Ohio, 7:127, 142; Windsor, History of the Ninety-First Regiment, 23.

40. Windsor, History of the Ninety-First Regiment, 29, 61; Official Roster of the Soldiers of the State of Ohio, 7:147; US Census, 1870, Hamilton, Lawrence County, Ohio, 15; Capt. Simeon Crossley, Find A Grave, https://www.finda grave.com/memorial/17825006.

41. Evans, A History of Scioto County, Ohio, 69, 374; US Census, 1860, Harrison, Scioto County, Ohio, 176.

42. Windsor, History of the Ninety-First Regiment, 23; Official Roster of the Soldiers of the State of Ohio, 7:142; Evans, A History of Scioto County, Ohio, 233.

43. Official Roster of the Soldiers of the State of Ohio, 1:384; Sutton, History of the Second Regiment, West Virginia, 5, 6, 32, 77, 81.

44. Frederic Denison, *Sabres and Spurs: The First Regiment Rhode Island Cavalry in the Civil War, 1861–1865* ([Central Fall, RI]: First Rhode Island Cavalry Veteran Association, 1876), 103–6; Warner, *Generals in Blue*, 131–32; Eicher and Eicher, *Civil War High Commands*, 216–17; Lang, *Loyal West Virginia*, 312, 375.

45. Warner, *Generals in Blue*, 134; Lang, *Loyal West Virginia*, 233, 236, 240, 242, 254, 269, 271–72, 305–6, 351–52; Eicher and Eicher, *Civil War High Commands*, 220.

46. Evans, *A History of Scioto County, Ohio*, 973; *Annual Catalogue of the Officers and Students of the Ohio University, Athens, Ohio for 1860–61* (Athens: T. F. Wildes, 1861), 9; *Official Roster of the Soldiers of the State of Ohio*, 7:128, 153; US Census, 1860, Elizabeth, Lawrence County, Ohio, 176; Windsor, *History of the Ninety-First Regiment*, 6, 61; "Veteran Ends His Life," *San Francisco Examiner*, October 21, 1900, 4; "Captain Elmore E. Ewing Ends His Life with Gas," *San Francisco Chronicle*, October 21, 1900, 20; Ewing, *The Story of the Ninety-First*; Thomas William Herringshaw, ed. and comp., *Local and National Poets of America with Interesting Biographical Sketches and Choice Selections from Over One Thousand Living Poets* (Chicago: American Publishers' Association, 1892), 475; E. E. Ewing, *Bugles and Bells: Or, Stories Told Again* (Cincinnati: Press of Curts and Jennings, 1899).

47. US Census, 1860, Upper, Lawrence County, Ohio, 114; *Official Roster of the Soldiers of the State of Ohio*, 7:127, 148.

48. US Census, 1860, Delaware, Delaware County, Ohio, 3; *Official Roster of the Soldiers of the State of Ohio*, 7:127, 143, 153; Windsor, *History of the Ninety-First Regiment*, 5, 24, 61; William S. Newton to Frances Ann Hayward Newton, January 29, 1864, Newton Papers, SCUA VT.

49. US Census, 1860, Ironton, Lawrence County, Ohio, 39; *Ironton Register*, April 21, 1864, 4; Diana Gould Hall, "Ancestors in the News—Gillen & Brother Furniture Business, 1850s–1860s Ohio," November 16, 2018, Michigan Family Trails, http://www.michiganfamilytrails.com/2018/11/ancestors-in-news-gillen-brother.html; Sutton, *History of the Second Regiment, West Virginia*, 5.

50. *Official Roster of the Soldiers of the State of Ohio*, 10:622–23; Dyer, *A Compendium of the War of the Rebellion*, 3:1197; "Col. D. W. Glassie Dies of Pneumonia," *Washington Times*, January 14, 1905, 5.

51. *Official Roster of the Soldiers of the State of Ohio*, 2:354; Strait, *Roster of All Regimental Surgeons and Assistant Surgeons*, 192; William H. Powell, ed., *Officers of the Army and Navy (Volunteer) Who Served in the Civil War* (Philadelphia: L. R. Hamersly and Company, 1893), 342; McManus, *The Battle of Cloyds Mountain*, 46, 47, 48; Johnson, *The United States Army Invades the New River Valley*, 36, 52.

52. Sutton, *History of the Second Regiment, West Virginia*, 5, 6, 14; Lang, *Loyal*

West Virginia, 177, 178; "Major Hambleton, Noted Civil War Veteran, Dies," *Inter Ocean* (Chicago, IL), January 11, 1914), 7.

53. *Official Roster of the Soldiers of the State of Ohio*, 7:127, 130; "The Death of Joel Hull," *Nebraska State Journal* (Lincoln), March 1, 1914, 8.

54. Warner, *Generals in Blue*, 243–44; Eicher and Eicher, *Civil War High Commands*, 310; David Hunter, *Report of the Military Services of Gen. David Hunter, U.S.A. During the War of the Rebellion Made to the U.S. War Department, 1873* (New York: D. Van Nostrand Publisher, 1873).

55. *Official Roster of the Soldiers of the State of Ohio*, 2:62, 72, 3:73, 103; 6:351, 10:147; Reid, *Ohio in the War*, 1:1013, 2:738; Thomas M. Stevenson, *History of the 78th Regiment O.V.V.I. from Its "Muster-In" to Its "Muster-Out"* (Zanesville, OH: Hugh Dunne, 1865), 100–101; "Col. Jewett Dead," *Lawrence (KS) Daily Journal*, October 14, 1895, 4.

56. Benson J. Lossing, *Pictorial History of the Civil War* (Philadelphia: George W. Childs, 1866), 1:496–97, 2:102; Warner, *Generals in Blue*, 260–61; Eicher and Eicher, *Civil War High Commands*, 328–29; Lang, *Loyal West Virginia*, 233–35.

57. *Triennial Catalogue of the Officers and Students of Oberlin College for the College Year, 1854–55* (Oberlin, OH: James M. Fitch, 1854), 36; *General Catalogue of Oberlin College, 1833–1908* (Oberlin, OH: Oberlin College, 1909), 542; Grace, *The Army Surgeon's Manual*, 47; OR, ser. 1, vol. 51, pt. 1, 742; "Deaths," *Journal of the American Medical Association* 43 (September 25, 1904): 904; US Census, 1860, Keokuk Ward 1, Lee County, Iowa, 36; Heitman, *Historical Register and Dictionary of the United States Army*, 1:589.

58. Sutton, *History of the Second Regiment, West Virginia*, 14; *Ironton Register*, June 10, 1869; *Portsmouth Daily Times*, August 16, 1879, 2; "Lawrence County, Ohio, Abstracted Obituaries, 1850–1900," 290; " A Youthful Martyr," *Richmond (IN) Weekly Palladium*, July 13, 1865, 1.

59. Sutton, *History of the Second Regiment, West Virginia*, 14; *Portsmouth (OH) Daily Times*, August 16, 1879, 2.

60. US Census, 1850, Upper, Lawrence County, Ohio, 909; *Official Roster of the Soldiers of the State of Ohio*, 7:147.

61. Warner, *Generals in Blue*, 279–80; Lang, *Loyal West Virginia*, 244, 246–49; Reid, *Ohio in the War*, 2:918–20; Eicher and Eicher, *Civil War High Commands*, 348.

62. Sutton, *History of the Second Regiment, West Virginia*, 5; Lang, *Loyal West Virginia*,178; Eicher and Eicher, *Civil War High Commands*, 378; *Evening Star* (Washington, DC), November 12, 1883, 1; *Impeachment Investigation, Testimony Taken Before the Judiciary Committee of the House of Representatives in the Investigation of the Charges Against Andrew Johnson, Second Session Thirty-Ninth Congress, and First Session, Fortieth Congress, 1867* (Washington, DC: Government Printing Office, 1867), 56–65.

63. Reid, *Ohio in the War*, 2:828–29; *Official Roster of the Soldiers of the State of Ohio*, 10:443–45; "Why He Left, The Reason Captain Joseph Ensign Can Not Be Found," *Dayton Herald*, August 8, 1885, 2.

64. *History of the Upper Ohio Valley*, 1:546–47; Lang, *Loyal West Virginia*, 237, 323; *Annual Report of the Adjutant General of the State of West Virginia for the Year Ending, December 31, 1864* (Wheeling: John F. M'Dermot, 1865), 59.

65. *Official Roster of the Soldiers of the State of Ohio*, 12:329, 343; Sutton, *History of the Second Regiment, West Virginia*, 6, 7, 8, 16, 26, 55; Gary C. Walker, *The War in Southwest Virginia, 1861–65* (Roanoke: Gurtner Graphics and Print Company, 1985), 45, 52–55.

66. US Census, 1860, Bellefontaine, Logan County, Ohio, 63; Strait, *Roster of All Regimental Surgeons and Assistant Surgeons*, 196; *Official Roster of the Soldiers of the State of Ohio*, 3:555.

67. US Census, 1860, Ironton, Lawrence County, Ohio, 91; *The Biographical Encyclopedia of Ohio of the Nineteenth Century* (Cincinnati: Galaxy Publishing Company, 1876), 640; Strait, *Roster of All Regimental Surgeons and Assistant Surgeons*, 274; Lang, *Loyal West Virginia*, 269; *Official Army Register*, 4:1132; *Ironton Register*, January 2, 1896; "Dr. Jonatha[n] Morris," The Lawrence Register, https://lawrencecountyohio.com/pioneers/dr-jona-morris-obituary/.

68. Edward Mussey Hartwell, *A Memorial Sketch of William Heberden Mussey, M.D.* (n.p.: n.p., 1883), 3–7, 10–11; US Census, 1860, Cincinnati Ward 5, Hamilton County, Ohio, 92; J. Fletcher Brennan, ed., *The Biographical Cyclopaedia and Portrait Gallery of Distinguished Men, with an Historical Sketch of the State of Ohio* (Cincinnati: John C. Yorston and Company, 1880), 1:110–11; "The Mussey Family," The Henry R. Winkler Center for the History of the Health Professions, University of Cincinnati, https://digital.libraries.uc.edu/exhibits/winkler/mussey/family.html; Reid, *Ohio in War*, 1:248; *Medical College of Ohio, Cincinnati, Sixtieth Annual Catalogue*, 210; Heitman, *Historical Register and Dictionary of the United States Army*, 1:739; Reid, *Ohio in the War*, 1:248, 252.

69. "Henry Safford Neal," in Johnson, ed., *The Twentieth Century Biographical Dictionary of Notable Americans*, 8:35–36; Charles B. Galbreath, *History of Ohio* (Chicago: American Historical Society, Inc., 1925), 2:83; *Catalogue of the Officers and Alumni of Marietta College, 1835–1901* (Marietta, OH: Marietta College, 1901), 40.

70. "Another Proclamation! New Goods Just Received at S. F. Neal's," *Gallipolis Journal*, December 4, 1862, 4; *Official Roster of the Soldiers of the State of Ohio*, 7:127, 128; Windsor, *History of the Ninety-First Regiment*, 5, 6; *History of Gallia County*, 44; "Last Rites for Major S. F. Neal to be Sunday," *Gallipolis Daily Tribune*, December 20, 1930, 1.

71. US Census, 1860, Williamstown, Wood County, Virginia, 240; Sutton,

History of the Second Regiment, West Virginia, 5; Strait, *Roster of All Regimental Surgeons and Assistant Surgeons*, 271, 274; Lang, *Loyal West Virginia*, 178, 188, 273.

72. US Census, 1860, Gallipolis, Gallia County, Ohio, 165; *Gallipolis Journal*, April 28, 1864, 2; *Official Roster of the Soldiers of the State of Ohio*, 7:130; Windsor, *History of the Ninety-First Regiment*, 9; "James E. Niday," Find A Grave, https://www.findagrave.com/memorial/44501800; *History of Gallia County*, 21.

73. *History of Washington County, Ohio*, 243–45; US Census, 1860, Marietta, Washington County, Ohio, 69; *Official Roster of the Soldiers of the State of Ohio*, 1:371; Sutton, *History of the Second Regiment, West Virginia*, 81 (quotation), 5, 55, 76–81; Lang, *Loyal West Virginia*, 177, 187.

74. Heitman, *Historical Register and Dictionary of the United States Army*, 1:792–93; Marion Morrison, *A History of the Ninth Regiment Illinois Volunteer Infantry* (Monmouth, IL: John S. Clark, Printer, 1864), 13, 15, 37; *Gallipolis Journal*, February 11, 1864, 2; Reid, *Ohio in the War*, 1:916; Jack L. Dickinson, *16th Virginia Cavalry* (Lynchburg: H. E. Howard, 1989), 39–41; *Point Pleasant Register*, February 11, 1864; Taylor, *The Supply for Tomorrow*, 180.

75. US Census, 1860, Porter, Scioto County, Ohio, 23; *Official Roster of the Soldiers of the State of Ohio*, 7:127; Windsor, *History of the Ninety-First Regiment*, 6; Evans, *A History of Scioto County, Ohio*, 233, 544, 545, 572; *Alumni Catalogue of Miami Medical College of Cincinnati: Including Members of the Faculty, 1852–1900* (Cincinnati: Miami Medical College, 1901), 27; "Dr. Pixley Is Laid to Rest," *Portsmouth Daily Times*, December 1, 1909, 8.

76. US Census, 1860, Delaware, Delaware County, Ohio, 257; Reid, *Ohio in the War*, 1:981, 2:34, 2:385, 2:738; *Official Roster of the Soldiers of the State of Ohio*, 1:78, 5:519, 10:147; *History of Delaware County and Ohio* (Chicago: O. L. Basking and Company, 1880), 639–40.

77. Warner, *Generals in Blue*, 384–85; Sutton, *History of the Second Regiment, West Virginia*, 5, 6, 14, 60, 82, 92, 102–8, 110–12; Jeriah Bonham, *Fifty Years' Recollections with Observations and Reflections on Historical Events Giving Sketches of Eminent Citizens, Their Lives and Public Services* (Peoria, IL: J. W. Franks and Sons, Printers and Publishers, 1883), 330–34; Eicher and Eicher, *Civil War High Commands*, 438; Reid, *Ohio in the War*, 1:909–10.

78. US Census, 1860, Ironton, Lawrence County, Ohio, 42–43; *Official Roster of the Soldiers of the State of Ohio*, 7:127, 147; Sutton, *History of the Second Regiment, West Virginia*, 6, 20, 32; Lang, *Loyal West Virginia*, 178; Windsor, *History of the Ninety-First Regiment*, 6.

79. Reid, *Ohio in the War*, 1:248; Grace, *The Army Surgeon's Manual*, 31.

80. Reid, *Ohio in the War*, 1:915–16, 2:158; Warner, *Generals in Blue*, 421–22; Eicher and Eicher, *Civil War High Commands*, 471; *Gallipolis Journal*, February 11, 1864, 2; Dickinson, *16th Virginia Cavalry*, 39–41; *Point Pleasant Register*, February 11, 1864; Taylor, *The Supply for Tomorrow*, 180.

81. Reid, *Ohio in the War*, 1:64, 247; Emil R. Pinta, "Samuel Smith, M.D.: First American Professor of Psychiatry," *Psychiatric Services* 45 (April 1994): 369–71.

82. John T. Toland, "Introduction," *Dental Reporter* 1 (April 1858): 1–5; *A History of Dental and Oral Science in America* (Philadelphia: S. S. White, 1876), 232, 234; US Census, 1860, Cincinnati Ward 14, Hamilton County, Ohio, 96; Reid, *Ohio in the War*, 1:1002, 2:221, 224; "Col. John T. Toland," Find A Grave, https://www.findagrave.com/memorial/64995074/john-t-toland; Sutton, *History of the Second Regiment, West Virginia*, 92.

83. Evans, *A History of Scioto County, Ohio*, 142–43; Lambert, *Ninety-First Ohio Volunteer Infantry*, 90–91; US Census, 1860, Portsmouth, Scioto County, Ohio, 57; Reid, *Ohio in the War*, 1:984; *Official Roster of the Soldiers of the State of Ohio*, 7:127 "Dead in Old Scioto," *Los Angeles Times*, April 7, 1900, 9; "John Alexander Turley," Find A Grave, https://www.findagrave.com/memorial/8150834/john-alexander-turley; Windsor, *History of the Ninety-First Regiment*, 6; "Death of Col. Turley," *Dayton Herald*, March 21, 1900.

84. US Census, 1860, Washington, Licking County, Ohio, 28; James Turner, Ohio, 17th, 1:267, Consolidated Lists of Civil War Draft Registration Records, RG 110, NARA; *Official Roster of the Soldiers of the State of Ohio*, 7:150; Windsor, *History of the Ninety-First Regiment*, 32.

85. US Census, 1850, Barlow, Washington County, Ohio, 690; *Official Roster of the Soldiers of the State of Ohio*, 3:638; Reid, *Ohio in the War*, 2:231; Andrews, *History of Marietta and Washington County*, 650, 794; US Census, 1870, Harmar, Washington, Ohio, 23; *Memorial of Deceased Companions of the Commandery of the State of Illinois Military Order of the Loyal Legion of the United States From January 1, 1912 to December 31, 1922* (Chicago: n.p., 1923), 165–66.

86. "Rev. Dr. Wallar," *Mount Carmel (IL) Register*, December 27, 1900, 1; Sutton, *History of the Second Regiment, West Virginia*, 6, 49, 254; Lang, *Loyal West Virginia*, 178; Reid, *Ohio in the War*, 2:126.

87. Evans, *A History of Scioto County, Ohio*, 233, 1175–76; *Medical College of Ohio, Cincinnati, Sixtieth Annual Catalogue*, 23; *Official Roster of the Soldiers of the State of Ohio*, 7:127; Strait, *Roster of Regimental Surgeons and Assistant Surgeons*, 207; Lambert, *Ninety-First Ohio Volunteer Infantry*, 93–94; Windsor, *History of the Ninety-First Regiment*, 5, 6.

88. Evans, *A History of Scioto County, Ohio*, 233, 1176; *Official Roster of the Soldiers of the State of Ohio*, 7:127, 135, 136; Lambert, *Ninety-First Ohio Volunteer Infantry*, 154–55.

89. "Dr. John Pratt Waste," Find A Grave, https://www.findagrave.com/memorial/33701238; *Catalogue of the Officers and Students of the University of Michigan for 1861* (Ann Arbor: University of Michigan, 1861), 25; *University of Michigan Catalogue of the Officers and Students for 1861* (Ann Arbor: University of Michigan, 1864), 28; Frederick C. Waite, *Alumni Catalogue of the*

School of Medicine of Western Reserve University (Cleveland: Western Reserve University, 1930), 102; *Official Roster of the Soldiers of the State of Ohio*, 10:147; Reid, *Ohio in the War*, 2:738; *Minneapolis Journal*, April 18, 1906, 19; "Deaths," *Journal of the American Medical Association* 46 (April 28, 1906): 1306.

90. James Willis Wellons, *A Historical Sketch of the Wellons Family* (Richmond: Central Publishing Company, 1910), 56, 57; McKelvey, *Centennial History of Belmont County, Ohio*, 531–32; *Medical College of Ohio, Cincinnati, Sixtieth Annual Catalogue*, 23; *Official Roster of the Soldiers of the State of Ohio*, 7:127; Strait, *Roster of Regimental Surgeons and Assistant Surgeons*, 207; Windsor, *History of the Ninety-First Regiment*, 5.

91. *The History of Brown County, Ohio* (Chicago: W. H. Beers and Company, 1883), 47; Heitman, *Historical Register and Dictionary of the United States Army*, 1:1027; William Hugh Robarts, *Mexican War Veterans: A Complete Roster of the Regular and Volunteer Troops in the War Between the United States and Mexico, From 1846 to 1848* (Washington, DC: Brentano's, 1887), 66; US Census, 1860, Georgetown, Brown County, Ohio, 5; Reid, *Ohio in the War*, 1:987; 2:87, 90; Eicher and Eicher, *Civil War High Commands*, 565; James E. Ward, *Twelfth Ohio Volunteer Infantry* (Ripley, OH: n.p., 1864), 16, 20, 43; *Official Roster of the Soldiers of the State of Ohio*, 2:24; "The Late Col. Carr B. White, 12th O.V.I.," *Highland Weekly News* (Hillsboro, OH), January 4, 1872.

92. US Census, 1860, Middletown, Butler County, Ohio, 104; *Official Roster of the Soldiers of the State of Ohio*, 2:353, 371; Reid, *Ohio in the War*, 2:88; "Cutler County in the Civil War," *Butler County Democrat*, December 2, 1915, 4; Bert S. Bartlow, *Centennial History of Butler County, Ohio* (n.p.: B. F. Bowen and Company Publishers, 1905), 334; *Biographical Cyclopaedia of Butler County, Ohio* (Cincinnati: Western Biographical Publishing Company, 1882), 655.

93. *Ironton Register*, January 2, 1862; US Census, 1870, Ironton, Lawrence County, Ohio, 62.

Bibliography

Archives, Manuscripts, and Government Records

Coates, Benjamin F. Collection. Rutherford B. Hayes Presidential Library and Museums, Fremont, Ohio.

Compiled Military Service Records of Volunteer Union Soldiers Who Served with the United States Colored Troops: Artillery Organizations, Microfilm Serial, M1818, Microfilm Roll, 158, National Archives and Records Administration, Washington, DC.

Consolidated Lists of Civil War Draft Registration Records, Ohio and West Virginia, Record Group 110, Records of the Provost Marshal General's Bureau (Civil War), National Archives and Records Administration, Washington DC.

Gallia County, Ohio, County Marriage Records, 1860–1865, Gallipolis, Ohio.

Holliday, John, Diary, 1864. MS 2012–028, Special Collections and University Archives, Virginia Tech, Blacksburg, Virginia.

Lincoln, Abraham. "A Proclamation by the President of the United States, April 15, 1861." Record Group 46, Records of the U.S. Senate, National Archives and Records Administration, Washington, DC.

Newton, John W. Certificate of Death, 5/14/1940, #50523, Pennsylvania Death Certificates, 1906–1968, Record Group 11, Pennsylvania Historical and Museum Commission, Harrisburg, Pennsylvania.

Newton, William S. Papers, 1862-1879. Ms.2021.024. Special Collections and University Archives, Virginia Tech, Blacksburg, Virginia.

———. W. S. Newton, Gallia County, Ohio, U.S. Appointments of U.S. Postmasters, 1832–1971, Record Group 28, Records of the Post Office Department, National Archives and Records Administration, Washington, DC.

Newton Genealogy of the Newton Families. N.p.: n.p., n.d. Special Collections, Marietta College, Marietta, Ohio.

Ontario, Canada, Deaths and Deaths Overseas, 1869–1948, Archives of Ontario, Toronto, Ontario, Canada.

Pension Cards and Files, Civil War Pension Index: General Index to Pension Files,
    1861–1934, Record Group 15, Records of the Veterans Administration,
    National Archives and Records Administration, Washington, DC.

"Register of Captured Federal Officers Confined in Libby Prison, Richmond,
    Virginia, 1862-65," Entry 132, Records of the Office of the Commissary
    General of Prisoners, Record Group 249, National Archives and Records
    Administration, Washington, DC.

US Census, 1850, 1860, 1870, 1880, 1900.

US Census, Mortality Schedules, 1850–1885.

US Census, Slave Schedules, 1860.

US War Department. *The War of the Rebellion: A Compilation of the Official
    Records of the Union and Confederate Armies.* 127 vols. Washington,
    DC, 1880–1901.

The United States v William S. Newton and Edward S. Newton, Filed April 18, 1869,
    United States Circuit Court, Cincinnati, Criminal Case 567, Records of
    the U.S. Circuit Court for the Southern District of Ohio, Record Group
    21, Records of District Courts of the United States, National Archives
    and Records Administration, Chicago, Illinois.

Books, Articles, Theses, Dissertations, and Other Published Sources

Aler, F. Vernon. *Aler's History of Martinsburg and Berkeley County, West Virginia.*
    Hagerstown, MD: Mail Publishing Company, 1888.

Allardice, Bruce S. *Confederate Colonels: A Biographical Register.* Columbia: University of Missouri Press, 2008.

*Alumni Catalogue of Miami Medical College of Cincinnati: Including Members of the
    Faculty, 1852–1900.* Cincinnati: Miami Medical College, 1901.

Anderson, Robert H. *List of Staff Officers of the Confederate States Army, 1861–1865.*
    Washington, DC: Government Printing Office, 1891.

Andrews, Israel Ward. *Washington County and the Early Settlement of Ohio: Being
    the Centennial Historical Address, Before the Citizens of Washington County.*
    Cincinnati: Peter G. Thomson, Publisher, 1877.

Andrews, Martin R. *History of Marietta and Washington County, Ohio, and Representative Citizens.* Chicago: Biographical Publishing Company, 1902.

Annual Announcement of the Medical College of Ohio. For the Years 1846–7. Cincinnati: n.p., [ca. 1847].

*Annual Catalogue of the Officers and Students of the Medical College of Ohio, Session
    1843–4.* Cincinnati: R. P. Brooks, 1844.

*Annual Catalogue of the Officers and Students of the Ohio University, Athens, Ohio
    for 1860–61.* Athens: T. F. Wildes, 1861.

Annual Report of the Adjutant-General of the State of New York for the Year 1894.
4 vols. Albany: James B. Lyon, 1895.

Annual Report of the Adjutant General of the State of West Virginia for the Year Ending, December 31, 1864. Wheeling: John F. M'Dermot, 1865.

Appleton's Cyclopaedia of American Biography, eds. James Grant Wilson and John Fiske. 7 vols. New York: D. Appleton and Company, 1887–1901.

Arthur, E. C. "The Dublin Raid, Campaigning with Gen. Geo. Crook in 1864." *Ohio Soldier,* January 5, January 19, February 2, February 16, March 2, March 16, March 30, April 13, 1889.

Atkinson, George W., and Alvaro F. Gibbens. *Prominent Men of West Virginia.* Wheeling: W. L. Callin, 1890.

Ayres, Stephen Cooper. "Miami in the Civil War: Alumni Address Delivered June 13, 1906." *Miami Bulletin* 5 (October 1906): 1–14.

Bartlow, Bert S. *Centennial History of Butler County, Ohio.* N.p.: B. F. Bowen and Company Publishers, 1905.

Barton, T. H. *Autobiography of Dr. Thomas H. Barton, The Self-Made Physician of Syracuse, Ohio, Including a History of the Fourth Regiment West Virginia Volunteer Infantry.* Charleston: West Virginia Printing Company, 1890.

Bates, Samuel P. *History of the Pennsylvania Volunteers, 1861–5.* 5 vols. Harrisburg: B. Singerly, 1869–1871.

Bickley, G. W. L. "Newton's Clinical Institute." *Eclectic Medical Journal* 13 (March 1854): 118–19.

Billings, John D. *Hardtack and Coffee: Or, The Unwritten Story of Army Life.* Boston: George M. Smith and Company, 1887.

Biographical Cyclopaedia of Butler County, Ohio. Cincinnati: Western Biographical Publishing Company, 1882.

The Biographical Encyclopedia of Ohio of the Nineteenth Century. Cincinnati: Galaxy Publishing Company, 1876.

Blight, David W. *Race and Reunion: The Civil War in American Memory.* Cambridge, MA: Belknap Press of Harvard University Press, 2001.

Bonham, Jeriah. *Fifty Years' Recollections with Observations and Reflections on Historical Events Giving Sketches of Eminent Citizens, Their Lives and Public Services.* Peoria, IL: J. W. Franks and Sons, Printers and Publishers, 1883.

Bownocker, John Adams. "The Occurrence and Exploitation of Petroleum and Natural Gas in Ohio," in *Geological Survey of Ohio,* Fourth Series, Bulletin No. 1. Springfield, OH: Springfield Publishing Company, 1903.

Brady, Lisa. *War upon the Land: Military Strategy and the Transformation of Southern Landscapes during the American Civil War.* Athens: University of Georgia Press, 2012.

Brennan, J. Fletcher, ed. *The Biographical Cyclopaedia and Portrait Gallery of*

Distinguished Men, with an Historical Sketch of the State of Ohio. 2 vols. Cincinnati: John C. Yorston and Company, 1880.

Brinsfield, John W., et al., eds. *Faith in the Fight: Civil War Chaplains.* Mechanicsburg, PA: Stackpole Books, 2003.

Brinton, John H. *Personal Memoirs of John H. Brinton, Major and Surgeon U.S.V., 1861–1865.* New York: Neale Publishing Company, 1914.

Browning, Judkin. *An Environmental History of the Civil War.* Chapel Hill: University of North Carolina Press, 2020.

Burg, Steven. *Editing Historical Documents: A Handbook of Practice.* Walnut Creek, CA: AltaMira Press, 1997.

Byrne, Frank L. "Libby Prison: A Study in Emotions." *Journal of Southern History* 24 (November 1958): 430–44.

Callahan, James Morton. *History of West Virginia, Old and New.* 3 vols. Chicago: American Historical Society, 1923.

Card, Fred W. *Bush-Fruits: A Horticultural Monograph of Raspberries, Blackberries, Dewberries, Currants, Gooseberries, and Other Shrub-Like Fruits.* New York: Macmillan Company, 1901.

Cary, Samuel F. *Historical Sketch of the Order of the Sons of Temperance.* Halifax, Nova Scotia: W. Theakston, Printer, 1884.

Cashin, Joan E., ed. *The War Was You and Me: Civilians in the American Civil War.* Princeton: Princeton University Press, 2002.

———. *War Stuff: The Struggle for Human and Environmental Resources in the American Civil War.* Cambridge, UK: Cambridge University Press, 2018.

Catalogue of the Officers and Alumni of Marietta College, 1835–1901. Marietta, OH: Marietta College, 1901.

Catalogue of the Officers and Students of Marietta College, 1839–40. Marietta, OH: G. W. Tyler and Company Printers, 1840.

Catalogue of the Officers and Students of Marietta College, 1840–41. Marietta, OH: G. W. Tyler and Company Printers, 1841.

Catalogue of the Officers and Students of Marietta College, 1841–42. Marietta, OH: G. W. Tyler and Company Printers, 1841.

Catalogue of the Officers and Students of Marietta College, 1842–43. Marietta, OH: G. W. Tyler and Company Printers, 1842.

Catalogue of the Officers and Students of the University of Michigan for 1861. Ann Arbor: University of Michigan, 1861.

Charter and By-Laws of the Virginia and Tennessee Rail Road Company. Lynchburg: R. K. Irving and Company, 1840.

Chesson, Michael B., ed. *J. Franklin Dyer: The Journal of a Civil War Surgeon.* Lincoln: University of Nebraska Press, 2003.

Childress, Richard T. *A Historical Lottery: Europe to Appalachia and Beyond—A*

Ramsey Family through 1500 Years of Social and Cultural Change. Pittsburg: Dorrance Publishing Company, 2016.

Cincinnati Lancet and Observer 7 (July 1864): 446.

Coggins, Allen R. *Tennessee Tragedies: Natural, Technological, and Societal Disasters in the Volunteer State.* Knoxville: University of Tennessee Press, 2011.

Collection of all Acts of the General Assembly, Relating to the James River and Kanawha Company; Together with the By-Laws and Resolutions of the Stockholders of the Company, and Rules and Regulations of the Presidents and Directors, and Other Documents. Richmond: Samuel Shepherd, 1835.

Constitution, Revised Rules, Rules of Order, and Funeral Ceremony of the Sons of Temperance. Halifax, Nova Scotia: R. M. Barratt, 1852.

Cozzens, Peter. *No Better Place to Die: The Battle of Stones River.* Urbana: University of Illinois Press, 1990.

———. *This Terrible Sound: The Battle of Chickamauga.* Urbana: University of Illinois Press, 1992.

Crawford, J. Marshall. *Mosby and His Men.* New York: G. W. Carleton and Co., 1867.

Curry, Richard Orr. *A House Divided: A Study of Statehood Politics and the Copperhead Movement in West Virginia.* Pittsburgh: University of Pittsburgh Press, 1964.

Cutler, Julia Perkins. *The Life and Times of Ephraim Cutler.* Cincinnati: Robert Clarke and Company, 1890.

"Deaths." *Journal of the American Medical Association* 43 (September 25, 1904): 904.

"Deaths." *Journal of the American Medical Association* 46 (April 28, 1906): 1306.

Denison, Frederic. *Sabres and Spurs: The First Regiment Rhode Island Cavalry in the Civil War, 1861–1865.* [Central Fall, RI]: First Rhode Island Cavalry Veteran Association, 1876.

Devereux, Roy. *John Loudon McAdam: Chapters in the History of Highways.* London: Oxford University Press, 1936.

Devine, Shauna. *Learning from the Wounded: The Civil War and the Rise of American Medical Science.* Chapel Hill: University of North Carolina Press, 2014.

Dickinson, Jack L. *8th Virginia Cavalry.* Lynchburg: H. E. Howard, Inc., 1986.

———. *Jenkins of Greenbottom: A Civil War Saga.* Charleston, WV: Pictorial Histories Publishing Company, 1988.

———. *16th Virginia Cavalry.* Lynchburg: H. E. Howard, 1989.

Dickinson, Jack L., and Kay Stamper Dickinson. *Gentleman Soldier of Greenbottom: The Life of Brigadier General Albert Gallatin Jenkins, CSA.* Huntington, WV: Self-published, 2011.

Dictionary of American Biography. Edited by Dumas Malone. Vol. 13. New York: Charles Scribner's Sons, 1934.

"Dr. William S. Love." *Virginia Medical Semi-Monthly* 17 (December 27, 1912): 468.

Drake, Brian Allen, ed. *The Blue, the Gray, and the Green: Toward an Environmental History of the Civil War*. Athens: University of Georgia Press, 2015.

Duke, Basil. *Morgan's Cavalry*. New York: Neale Publishing Co., 1909.

Duncan, Richard R., ed. *Alexander Neil and the Last Shenandoah Campaign: Letters of an Army Surgeon to His Family, 1864*. Shippensburg, PA: White Mane, 1996.

———. Beleaguered Winchester: A Virginia Community at War, 1861–1865. Baton Rouge: Louisiana State University Press, 2007.

———. *Lee's Endangered Left: The Civil War in Western Virginia, Spring of 1864*. Baton Rouge: Louisiana State University Press, 1998.

Dyer, Frederick H. *A Compendium of the War of the Rebellion*. 3 vols. New York: Sagamore Press, 1959.

Eckert, Edward K., and Nicholas J. Amato, eds. *Ten Years in the Saddle: The Memoir of William Woods Averell*. San Rafael, CA: Presidio Press, 1978.

Egan, Michael. *The Flying, Grey-Haired Yank: Or, the Adventures of a Volunteer*. Philadelphia: Hubbard Brothers, 1888.

Eicher, John H., and David J. Eicher. *Civil War High Commands*. Stanford: Stanford University Press, 2001.

Eighth Annual Report of the Trustees and Superintendent of the Ohio State Asylum for the Education of Idiotic and Imbecile Youth to the Governor of the State of Ohio for the Year 1864. Columbus: n.p., 1864.

Engel, Jonathan. "'It Hasn't Been Squashmolished': Environment, Sense of Place, and the Army of the Tennessee," *The Journal of East Tennessee History* 92 (2020): 28–49.

Evans, Nelson W. *A History of Scioto County, Ohio, Together with a Pioneer Record of Southern Ohio*. Portsmouth, OH: Nelson W. Evans, 1903.

Evans, Nelson W., and Emmons B. Stivers. *A History of Adams County, Ohio from its Earliest Settlement to the Present Time*. West Union, OH: E. B. Stivers, 1900.

Ewing, E. E. *Bugles and Bells: Or, Stories Told Again*. Cincinnati: Press of Curts and Jennings, 1899.

———. *The Story of the Ninety-First*. Portsmouth, OH: Republican Printing Company, 1868.

"Excerpts from Dr. Seth Hart's Day Book Dated August 19, 1844 to April 4, 1846," *Tallow Light: Bulletin of the Washington County, Ohio, Historical Society* 14 (April–June 1983): 17–27.

Famous Adventures and Prison Escapes of the Civil War. New York: Century Company, 1917.

Farrar, Samuel Clarke. *The Twenty-Second Pennsylvania Cavalry and the Ringgold Battalion, 1861–1865*. Pittsburgh: S. C. Farrar, 1911.

Fisher, Noel C. *War at Every Door: Partisan Politics and Guerrilla Violence in East Tennessee.* Chapel Hill: University of North Carolina Press, 1997.

Flannery, Michael A. *Civil War Pharmacy: A History.* New York: Pharmaceutical Products Press, 2004.

Floyd, Dale Emerson. "The Life of a Civil War Surgeon from the Letters of William S. Newton." Master's thesis, University of Dayton, 1968.

Foote, Lorien. "Rethinking the Confederate Homefront" *Journal of the Civil War Era* 7 (September 2017): 446–65.

"'44 Isaac De La Mater." *Delta Upsilon Quarterly* 11 (September 1893): 182.

Frank, Lisa Tendrich, and LeeAnn Whites, eds. *Household War: How Americans Lived and the Fought the Civil War.* Athens: University of Georgia Press, 2020.

Frye, Dennis D. *2nd Virginia Infantry.* Lynchburg: H. E. Howard, 1984.

Galbreath, Charles B. *History of Ohio.* Chicago: American Historical Society, Inc., 1925.

Gallagher, Gary W., ed. *The Shenandoah Valley Campaign of 1864.* Chapel Hill: University of North Carolina Press, 2006.

Geiger, Joe, Jr. "The Tragic Fate of Guyandotte." *West Virginia History* 54 (1995): 28–41.

General Catalogue of Oberlin College, 1833–1908. Oberlin, OH: Oberlin College, 1909.

Giesberg, Judith. *Army at Home: Women and the Civil War on the Northern Home Front.* Chapel Hill: University of North Carolina Press, 2009.

———. *Sex and the Civil War: Soldiers, Pornography, and the Making of American Morality.* Chapel Hill: University of North Carolina Press, 2017.

Grace, William. *The Army Surgeon's Manual, For the Use of Medical Officers, Cadets, Chaplains, and Hospital Stewards.* New York: Bailliere Brothers, 1864.

Greiner, James M., Janet L. Coryell, and James R. Smither. *A Surgeon's Civil War: The Letters and Diary of Daniel M. Holt, M.D.* Kent, OH: Kent State University Press, 1994.

Gross, S. D. *A Manual of Military Surgery: Or, Hints on the Emergencies of the Field, Camp and Hospital Practice.* Augusta, GA: Chronicle and Sentinel, 1861.

Haller, John S., Jr. *A Profile in Alternative Medicine: The Eclectic Medical College of Cincinnati.* Kent, OH: Kent State University Press, 1999.

Harris, Kathleen E., and Paul L. Harris. *A Soldier's Story: The 145th Pennsylvania Volunteer Infantry Regiment in the Civil War.* Chicora, PA: Mechling, 2011.

Hartwell, Edward Mussey. *A Memorial Sketch of William Heberden Mussey, M.D.* N.p.: n.p., 1883.

Heitman, Francis Bernard. *Historical Register and Dictionary of the United States Army.* 2 vols. Washington, DC: Government Printing Office, 1903.

Herringshaw, Thomas William, ed. and comp. *Local and National Poets of America with Interesting Biographical Sketches and Choice Selections from Over One Thousand Living Poets*. Chicago: American Publishers' Association, 1892.

Hibbard, Augustine George. *Genealogy of the Hibbard Family, Who Are Descendants of Robert Hibbard of Salem, Massachusetts*. Hartford, CT: Case, Lockwood and Brainard Company, 1901.

Hicks, Robert D., ed. *Civil War Medicine: A Surgeon's Diary*. Bloomington: Indiana University Press, 2019.

Hirschhorn, Norbert, Robert G. Feldman, and Ian A. Greaves. "Abraham Lincoln's Blue Pills: Did Our 16th President Suffer from Mercury Poisoning?" *Perspectives in Biology and Medicine* 44 (Summer 2001): 315–32.

The History of Brown County, Ohio. Chicago: W. H. Beers and Company, 1883.

The History of Darke County, Ohio. Chicago: W. H. Beers and Company, 1880.

History of Delaware County and Ohio. Chicago: O. L. Basking and Company, 1880.

A History of Dental and Oral Science in America. Philadelphia: S. S. White, 1876.

History of Gallia County: Containing a Condensed History of the County; Biographical Sketches; General Statistics; Miscellaneous Matter, &c. Chicago: H. H. Hardesty and Company, 1882.

History of Shelby County, Ohio, with Illustrations and Biographical Sketches of Some of Its Prominent Men and Pioneers. Philadelphia: R. Sutton and Company, 1883.

History of the Upper Ohio Valley, with Family History and Biographical Sketches, a Statement of Its Resources, Industrial Growth and Commercial Advantages. 2 vols. Madison, WI: Brant and Fuller, 1890.

History of Washington County, Ohio with Illustrations and Biographical Sketches. Cleveland: H. Z. Williams and Brothers Publishers, 1881.

Hogg, Ian V. *Weapons of the Civil War*. New York: Military Press, 1987.

Holland, Cecil Fletcher. *Morgan and His Raiders: A Biography of the Confederate General*. New York: Macmillan Co., 1942.

Humphreys, Margaret. *Marrow of Tragedy: The Health Crisis of the American Civil War*. Baltimore: Johns Hopkins University Press, 2013.

Humphreys, Milton W. *A History of the Lynchburg Campaign*. Charlottesville: Michie Company, 1924.

Hunter, David. *Report of the Military Services of Gen. David Hunter, U.S.A. During the War of the Rebellion Made to the U.S. War Department, 1873*. New York: D. Van Nostrand Publisher, 1873.

Hurst, T. M. "The Battle of Shiloh," *American Historical Magazine* 7 (January 1902): 22–37.

Impeachment Investigation, Testimony Taken Before the Judiciary Committee of the House of Representatives in the Investigation of the Charges Against Andrew Johnson, Second Session Thirty-Ninth Congress, and First Session, Fortieth Congress, 1867. Washington, DC: Government Printing Office, 1867.

Inscoe, John C. *Race, War, and Remembrance in the Appalachian South.* Lexington: University Press of Kentucky, 2010.

Johnson, Patricia Givens. *The United States Army Invades the New River Valley, May 1864.* Christiansburg, VA: Walpa Publishing, 1986.

Johnson, Rossiter, ed. *The Twentieth Century Biographical Dictionary of Notable Americans.* 10 vols. Boston: Biographical Society, 1904.

Johnston, Sarah Hall, comp. *Lineage Book, National Society of the Daughters of the American Revolution.* Vol. 41. Harrisburg, PA: Telegraph Printing Company, 1902.

Journal of the House of Delegates of the Commonwealth of Virginia, Begun and Held at the Capitol, In the City of Richmond, On Monday, The Fifth Day of December, One Thousand Eight Hundred and Thirty-Six. Richmond: Thomas Ritchie, 1836.

Kelly, Howard A., and Walter L. Burrage. *American Medical Biographies.* Baltimore: Norman, Remington Company, 1920.

Kimberly, Robert L., and Ephraim S. Holloway. *The Forty-First Ohio Veteran Volunteer Infantry in the War of the Rebellion, 1861–1865.* Cleveland: W. R. Smellie, 1897.

King, Rosalie Rosso. *Textile Identification, Conservation, and Preservation.* Park Ridge, NJ: Noyes Publications, 1985.

Klement, Frank L. *The Limits of Dissent: Clement L. Vallandigham and the Civil War.* Lexington: University Press of Kentucky, 1970.

Kline, Mary-Jo. *A Guide to Documentary Editing.* 3rd ed. Charlottesville: University of Virginia Press, 2008.

Koonce, Donald B., ed. *Doctor to the Front: The Recollections of Confederate Surgeon Thomas Fanning Wood, 1861–1865.* Knoxville: University of Tennessee Press, 2000.

Lambert, Lois J. *Ninety-First Ohio Volunteer Infantry with the Civil War Letters of Lieutenant Colonel Benjamin Franklin Coates and an Annotated Roster of the Men of Company C.* Milford, OH: Little Miami Publishing, Co., 2005.

Lamers, William M. *The Edge of Glory: A Biography of General William S. Rosecrans.* New York: Harcourt, Brace and World, Inc., 1961.

Lang, Theodore F. *Loyal West Virginia from 1861 to 1865.* Baltimore: Deutsch Publishing Company, 1895.

Larkin, Stillman Carter. *Pioneer History of Meigs County.* Columbus: Berlin Publishing Company, 1908.

Leete, Edward L., comp. *The Family of William Leete, One of the First Settlers of Guilford, Connecticut, and Governor of New Haven and Connecticut Colonies.* New Haven: Tuttle, Morehouse, and Taylor Printers, 1884.

Lepa, Jack H. *The Shenandoah Valley Campaign of 1864.* Jefferson, NC: McFarland and Company, 2003.

Lewis, Thomas A. *The Guns of Cedar Creek*. New York: Harper & Row, 1988.

List of Post Office and Postmasters of the United States, Revised and Corrected by the Post Office Department to October 20, 1867. Washington, DC: Government Printing Office, 1868.

Lloyd, J. U., and C. G. Lloyd. *Drugs and Medicines of North America: A Publication Devoted to the Historical and Scientific Discussions of the Botany, Pharmacy, Chemistry and Therapeutics of the Medicinal Plants of North America*. 2 vols. Cincinnati: Robert Clarke and Co., 1884–1887.

Lossing, Benson J. *Pictorial History of the Civil War*. 3 vols. Philadelphia: George W. Childs, 1866–1870.

Loudermilk, Will H. *History of Cumberland, Maryland*. Washington, DC: James Anglim, 1878.

Lowry, Terry D. *22nd Virginia Infantry*. Lynchburg: H. E. Howard, 1988.

MacCorkle, William Alexander. *The White Sulphur Springs: The Traditions, History, and Social Life of the Greenbrier White Sulphur Springs*. New York: Neale Publishing Company, 1916.

Mackey, Thomas C. *Opposing Lincoln: Clement L. Vallandigham, Presidential Power, and the Legal Battle over Dissent in Wartime*. Lawrence: University Press of Kansas, 2020.

MacKoy, W. H. "General Benjamin Rush Cowen." *Ohio Archaeological and Historical Society Publications* 18 (April 1909): 149–56.

Magid, Paul. *George Crook: From the Redwoods to Appomattox*. Norman: University of Oklahoma Press, 2011.

Mahr, Theodore C. *The Battle of Cedar Creek: Showdown in the Shenandoah, October 1–30, 1864*. Lynchburg: H. E. Howard, 1992.

Manning, Chandra. *What This Cruel War Was Over: Soldiers, Slavery, and the Civil War*. New York: Vintage Books, 2007.

Mannis, Jedediah, and Galen R. Wilson, eds. *Bound to Be a Soldier: The Letters of Private James T. Miller, 111th Pennsylvania Infantry, 1861–1864*. Knoxville: University of Tennessee Press, 2001.

Marietta College in the War of Secession, 1861–1865. Cincinnati: Peter G. Thomson, 1878.

Marken, Karissa A. "'They Cannot Catch Guerrillas in the Mountains Any More Than Cows Can Catch Fleas': Guerrilla Warfare in Western Virginia, 1861–1865." Master's thesis, Liberty University, 2014.

Master, Daniel A., ed. *Army Life According to Arbaw: Civil War Letters of William A. Brand, 66th Ohio Volunteer Infantry*. Perrysburg, OH: Columbian Arsenal Press, 2019.

Mauldin, Erin Steward. *Unredeemed Land: An Environmental History of Civil War and Emancipation in the Cotton South*. New York: Oxford University Press, 2018.

McClintock, John, and James Strong. *Cyclopaedia of Biblical, Theological, and Ecclesiastical Literature.* 10 vols. 2 suppl. New York: Harper and Brothers, 1867–1887.

McCullough, David. *The Pioneers: The Heroic Story of the Settlers Who Brought the American Ideal West.* New York: Simon and Schuster, 2019.

McGee, B. F. *History of the 72nd Indiana Volunteer Infantry of the Mounted Lightning Brigade.* Lafayette, IN: S. Vater and Co., Printers, 1882.

McKelvey, A. T. *Centennial History of Belmont County, Ohio, and Representative Citizens.* Chicago: Biographical Publishing Company, 1903.

McKnight, Brian D. *Contested Borderland: The Civil War in Appalachian Kentucky and Virginia.* Lexington: University Press of Kentucky, 2006.

McManus, Howard Rollins. *The Battle of Cloyds Mountain: The Virginia and Tennessee Railroad Raid, April 29–May 19, 1864.* Lynchburg: H. E. Howard, 1989.

McMaster, John Bach. *The Life and Times of Stephen Girard, Mariner and Merchant.* 2 vols. Philadelphia: J. B. Lippincott Company, 1918.

Medical College of Ohio, Cincinnati, Sixtieth Annual Catalogue and Announcement, Session of 1880–81. Cincinnati: n.p., [ca. 1881].

Meehan, Charles Henry Wharton. *The Law and Practice of the Game of Euchre, By a Professor.* Philadelphia: T. B. Peterson and Brothers, 1862.

Memorial of Deceased Companions of the Commandery of the State of Illinois Military Order of the Loyal Legion of the United States From January 1, 1912 to December 31, 1922. Chicago: n.p., 1923.

Miller, Brian Craig. *Empty Sleeves: Amputation in the Civil War South.* Athens: University of Georgia Press, 2015.

Miller, Richard F. *States at War: A Reference Guide for Ohio in the Civil War.* 6 vols. Hanover, NH: University Press of New England, 2013–2018.

Miller, Thomas C., and Hu Maxwell. *West Virginia and Its People.* 3 vols. New York: Lewis Historical Publishing Company, 1913.

Moore, John Hammond *Southern Homefront, 1861–1865.* Columbia, SC: Summerhouse Press, 1998.

Morrison, Marion. *A History of the Ninth Regiment Illinois Volunteer Infantry.* Monmouth, IL: John S. Clark, Printer, 1864.

Necrological Report Presented to the Alumni Association of Princeton Theological Seminary at Its Annual Meeting, April 26th, 1881, By a Committee of the Association. Philadelphia: Grant, Faires, and Rodgers, 1881.

Neely, Mark E., Jr. *The Civil War and the Limits of Destruction.* Cambridge, MA: Harvard University Press, 2007.

Nelson, Megan Kate. *Ruin Nation: Destruction and the Civil War.* Athens: University of Georgia Press, 2012.

Newberry, J. S. *Geologic Survey of Ohio, Report of Progress in 1870.* 3 parts. Columbus: Nevins and Myers State Printers, 1871.

Newton, J. H. *History of the Pan-Handle: Being Historical Collections of the Counties of Ohio, Brooke, Marshall, and Hancock, West Virginia*. Wheeling, WV: J. A. Caldwell, 1879.

Newton, Robert S. "Calomel and Bleeding." *Eclectic Medical Journal* 11 (November 1852): 528.

Newton, William S. "An Extensive Injury, with Recovery." *Western Lancet* 11 (August 1850): 501.

Noe, Kenneth W. *Southwest Virginia's Railroad: Modernization and the Sectional Crisis*. Urbana: University of Illinois Press, 1994.

Norton, Henry. *Deeds of Daring, or History of the Eight N.Y. Volunteer Cavalry*. Norwich, NY: Chenango Telegraph Printing House, 1889.

Norwood, William Frederick. *Medical Education in the United States before the Civil War*. New York: Arno Press, 1971.

Numbers, Robert L. "The Making of an Eclectic Physician: Joseph M. McElhinney and the Eclectic Medical Institute of Cincinnati." *Bulletin of the History of Medicine* 47 (March–April 1973): 155–66.

Official Army Register of the Volunteer Force of the United States Army for the Years 1861, '62,'63, '64, '65. 8 vols. Washington, DC: Government Printing Office, 1865.

Official Roster of the Soldiers of the State of Ohio in the War of the Rebellion, 1861–1866. 12 vols. Akron, Cincinnati, and Norwalk: various publishers, 1886–1895.

Oke, W. S. "Puerperal Convulsions." *Association Medical Journal* 2 (May 5, 1854): 386–89.

Parker, Sandra V. "A History of Libby Prison, 1862–1865." Master's thesis, Virginia Tech, 1981.

Parlett, David. *A Dictionary of Card Games*. New York: Oxford University Press, 1992.

Patchan, Scott C. *The Last Battle of Winchester: Phil Sheridan, Jubal Early, and the Shenandoah Valley Campaign, August 7–September 19, 1864*. El Dorado Hill, CA: Savas Beatie, 2013.

———. *Shenandoah Summer: The 1864 Valley Campaign*. Lincoln: University of Nebraska Press, 2007.

Pinta, Emil R. "Samuel Smith, M.D.: First American Professor of Psychiatry." *Psychiatric Services* 45 (April 1994): 369–71.

Plum, William R. *The Military Telegraph during the Civil War in the United States*. 2 vols. Chicago: Jansen, McClurg & Company, 1882.

Poetical Works of Thomas Moore, Including his Melodies, Ballads, Etc. Philadelphia: J. Crissy, 1845.

Pond, George E. *The Shenandoah Valley in 1864*. New York: Charles Scribner's Sons, 1892.

Pope, Thomas E. *The Weary Boys: Col. J. Warren Keiffer and the 110th Ohio Volunteer Infantry.* Kent, OH: Kent State University Press, 2002.

Powell, William H., ed. *Officers of the Army and Navy (Volunteer) Who Served in the Civil War.* Philadelphia: L. R. Hamersly and Company, 1893.

Preston, Richard J., Jr. *North American Trees (Exclusive of Mexico and Tropical United States).* Ames, IA: Iowa State College Press, 1948.

"Railway Carriage and Wagon Construction (VII)." *Locomotive Magazine* 6 (November 1901): 192.

Ramage, James A. *Gray Ghost: The Life of Col. John Singleton Mosby.* Lexington: University Press of Kentucky, 1999.

———. *Rebel Raider: The Life of General John Hunt Morgan.* Lexington: University Press of Kentucky, 1986.

Randall, Emilius O., and Daniel J. Ryan. *History of Ohio: The Rise and Progress of an American State.* 6 vols. New York: Century History Company, 1912–1915.

Reid, Whitelaw. *Ohio in the War: Her Statesmen, Her Generals and Soldiers.* 2 vols. Cincinnati: Moore, Wilstach, and Baldwin, 1868.

Report of the Commissioner of Agriculture for the Year 1867. Washington, DC: Government Printing Office, 1868.

Robarts, William Hugh. *Mexican War Veterans: A Complete Roster of the Regular and Volunteer Troops in the War Between the United States and Mexico, From 1846 to 1848.* Washington, DC: Brentano's, 1887.

Ross, Ivan A. *Medicinal Plants of the World: Chemical Constituents, Traditional and Modern Medical Uses.* 3 vols. Totowa, NJ: Humana Press, 2001–2005.

Rouse, J. H. *Horrible Massacre at Guyandotte, VA, and a Journey to the Rebel Capital, with a Description of Prison Life in a Tobacco Warehouse in Richmond.* N.p.: n.p., 1862.

Russell, Charles Wells, ed. *The Memoirs of Colonel John S. Mosby.* Bloomington: Indiana University Press, 1959.

Rutkow, Ira. *Bleeding Blue and Gray: Civil War Surgery and the Evolution of American Medicine.* 2005; Mechanicsburg, PA: Stackpole Books, 2015.

Salmon, Verel R. *Common Men in the War for the Common Man: The Civil War of the United States of America History of the 145th Pennsylvania Volunteer from Organization through Gettysburg.* Self-published, Xlibris, 2013.

———. *Common Men in the War for the Common Man, Book 2: The Civil War of the United States of America History of the 145th Pennsylvania Volunteer after Gettysburg through War's End.* Self-published, Xlibris, 2019.

Saunier, Joseph A., ed. *Forth-Seventh Regiment Ohio Veteran Volunteer Infantry, Second Brigade, Second Division, Fifteenth Army Corps, Army of the Tennessee.* Hillsboro, OH: Lyle Printing Company, [1903].

Schaadt, Mark J. *Civil War Medicine: An Illustrated History.* Quincy, IL: Cedarwood Publishing, 1998.

Schmidt, James M., and Guy R. Hasegawa. *Years of Change and Suffering: Modern Perspectives on Civil War Medicine.* Roseville, MN: Edinborough Press, 2009.

Schmitt, Martin F. *General George Crook, His Autobiography.* Norman: University of Oklahoma Press, 1946.

Schroeder-Lein, Glenna R. *The Encyclopedia of Civil War Medicine.* 2008; New York: Routledge, 2015.

Scott, J. L. *36th Virginia Infantry.* Lynchburg: H. E. Howard, 1987.

Shafer, Lori. *Iron Furnaces of Lawrence County, Ohio.* 2nd ed. Self-published, CreateSpace, 2019.

The Shenandoah Campaigns of 1862 and 1864 and the Appomattox Campaign, 1865. Vol. 6. Boston: Military Historical Society of Massachusetts, 1907.

Siepel, Kevin H. *Rebel: The Life and Times of John Singleton Mosby.* New York: St. Martin's Press, 1983.

Silber, Irwin. *Songs of the Civil War.* New York: Dover Publications, Inc., 1995.

Slawson, Robert G. "Medical Training in the United States Prior to the Civil War." *Journal of Evidence-Based Complementary and Alternative Medicine* 17 (January 2012): 11–27.

Smith, Alexander, and Willis B. Holmes. "On Amorphous Sulphur: III. The Nature of Amorphous Sulphur and Contributions to the Study of the Influence of Foreign Bodies on the Behavior of Supercooled Melted Sulphur." *Journal of the American Chemical Society* 27, no. 8 (1905): 979–1013.

Snell, Mark A. *West Virginia and the Civil War: Mountaineers are Always Free.* Charleston, SC: History Press, 2011.

Sperry, F. M., comp. *A Group of Distinguished Physicians and Surgeons of Chicago.* Chicago: J. H. Beers and Company, 1904.

Spofford, Ainsworth P. *Eminent and Representative Men of Virginia and the District of Columbia, of the Nineteenth Century.* Madison, WI: Brant and Fuller, 1893.

Stackpole, Edward J. *Sheridan in the Shenandoah: Jubal Early's Nemesis.* Harrisburg: Stackpole Company, 1961.

Stevenson, Thomas M. *History of the 78th Regiment O.V.V.I. from Its "Muster-In" to Its "Muster-Out."* Zanesville, OH: Hugh Dunne, 1865.

Strait, N. A. *Roster of Regimental Surgeons and Assistant Surgeons during the War of the Rebellion.* Washington, DC: N. A. Strait, 1882.

Sutton, J. J. *History of the Second Regiment, West Virginia Cavalry Volunteers, during the War of the Rebellion.* Portsmouth, OH: n.p., 1892.

Taylor, Amy Murrell. *Embattled Freedom: Journeys through the Civil War's Slave Refugee Camps.* Chapel Hill: University of North Carolina Press, 2020.

Taylor, Lenette S. "The Supply for Tomorrow Must Not Fail": The Civil War of Captain Simon Perkins Jr., a Union Quartermaster.* Kent, OH: Kent State University Press, 2004.

Thomas, Edison H. *John Hunt Morgan and His Raiders*. Lexington: University Press of Kentucky, 1985.

Toland, John T. "Introduction." *Dental Reporter* 1 (April 1858): 1–5.

Triennial Catalogue of the Officers and Students of Oberlin College for the College Year, 1854–55. Oberlin, OH: James M. Fitch, 1854.

University of Cincinnati, Directory of Graduates. Cincinnati: University of Cincinnati, 1926.

University of Michigan Catalogue of the Officers and Students for 1861. Ann Arbor: University of Michigan, 1864.

Ural, Susannah J. *Civil War Citizens: Race, Ethnicity, and Identity in America's Bloodiest Conflict*. New York: New York University Press, 2010.

US Steamboat Inspection Service, *List of Masters, Mates, Pilots, and Engineers of Merchant Steam and other Motor Vessels Licenses During the Year Ended December 31, 1897*. Washington, DC: Government Printing Office, 1898.

Waite, Frederick C. *Alumni Catalogue of the School of Medicine of Western Reserve University*. Cleveland: Western Reserve University, 1930.

———. "Medical Education in Ohio." *Ohio State Medical Journal* 49 (July 1953): 623–26.

———. "The Professional Education of Pioneer Ohio Physicians." *Ohio State Archaeological and Historical Quarterly* 48 (1939): 189–97.

Walker, Gary C. *The War in Southwest Virginia, 1861–65*. Roanoke: Gurtner Graphics and Print Company, 1985.

Wallace, Lee A. *A Guide to Virginia Military Organizations, 1861–1865*. Rev. 2nd ed. Lynchburg: H. E. Howard, 1986.

Ward, James E. *Twelfth Ohio Volunteer Infantry*. Ripley, OH: n.p., 1864.

Warner, Ezra J. *Generals in Blue: Lives of the Union Commanders*. Baton Rouge: Louisiana State University Press, 1964.

Wellons, James Willis. *A Historical Sketch of the Wellons Family*. Richmond: Central Publishing Company, 1910.

Werrell, Kenneth P. *Crook's Regulars: The 36th Ohio Volunteer Infantry Regiment in the War of the Rebellion*. Christiansburg, VA: self-published, 2012.

Wert, Jeffry D. *Mosby's Rangers*. New York: Simon and Schuster, 1990.

———. *From Winchester to Cedar Creek: The Shenandoah Campaign of 1864*. Carlisle, PA: South Mountain Press, Inc., 1987.

Wesley, Charles H. *Ohio Negroes in the Civil War*. Columbus: Ohio State University Press, 1962.

"What is the American Eclectic System of Medicine?" *Eclectic Medical Journal* 13 (August 1854): 359–63.

Wheelan, Joseph. *Libby Prison Breakout: The Daring Escape from the Notorious Civil War Prison*. New York: PublicAffairs, 2010.

Whisonant, Robert C. *Arming the Confederacy: How Virginia's Minerals Forged the Rebel War Machine.* New York: Springer, 2015.

White, William Lee, and Charles Denny Runion, eds. *Great Things Are Expected of Us: The Letters of Colonel C. Irvine Walker, 10th South Carolina Infantry, C.S.A.* Knoxville: University of Tennessee Press, 2009.

Whites, LeeAnn, and Alecia P. Long, eds. *Occupied Women: Gender, Military Occupation, and the American Civil War.* Baton Rouge: Louisiana State University Press, 2009.

Wiggins and Weaver's Ohio River Directory For 1871–72. Cleveland: Fairbanks, Benedict and Co., 1871.

Wildes, Thomas E. *Record of the One Hundred and Sixteenth Regiment, Ohio Infantry Volunteers in the War of the Rebellion.* Sandusky, OH: I. F. Mack and Brothers Printers, 1884.

Willard, Eugene B., ed. *A Standard History of the Hanging Rock Iron Region of Ohio: An Authentic Narrative of the Past, with an Extended Survey of the Industrial and Commercial Development.* 2 vols. [Chicago]: Lewis Publishing Company, 1916.

Williams, Charles Richard., ed. *Diary and Letters of Rutherford Birchard Hayes: Nineteenth President of the United States.* 5 vols. Columbus: Ohio State Archaeological and Historical Society, 1922–1926.

Wilson, R. B. "The Dublin Raid," in *Grand Army of the Republic War Papers: Papers Read before Fred C. Jones Post, No. 401, Department of Ohio, G.A.R.* Cincinnati: Fred C. Jones Post, No. 401, 1891.

Windsor, A. H. *History of the Ninety-First Regiment, O.V.I.* Cincinnati: Gazette Steam Printing House, 1865.

Wright, M. B. *A Lecture Delivered to the Students of the Medical College of Ohio, at the Opening of the Session, 1843–4.* Cincinnati: R. P. Donogh, 1844.

Wright, Robert E., and David J. Cowen. *Financial Founding Fathers: The Men Who Made America Rich.* Chicago: University of Chicago Press, 2006.

Wyllie, Arthur. *Confederate Officers.* N.p.: Art's Books and Images, 2007.

"Youngstown Physicians in the Civil War." *Bulletin of the Mahoning County Medical Society* 33 (August 1963): 245–47.

Newspapers

Butler County Democrat, 1915.

Chicago Tribune, 1874.

Cincinnati Daily Commercial, 1862–1863.

Cincinnati Enquirer, 1867, 1868, 1869, 1903, 1921

Daily Intelligencer (Wheeling, WV), 1863–1865.

Daily Register (Wheeling, WV), 1864.

Dayton Herald, 1885, 1900.

Evansville (IN) Daily Journal, 1868.

Evening Star (Washington, DC), 1883.

Examiner (Richmond, VA), 1864.

Fayette Journal (Fayetteville, WV), 1911.

Gallipolis Bulletin, 1882, 1896, 1910.

Gallipolis Daily Tribune, 1930.

Gallipolis Journal, 1862–1865, 1867–1869, 1875–1876,
    1880, 1882, 1885, 1912.

Highland Weekly News (Hillsboro, OH), 1872.

Intelligencer Journal (Lancaster, PA), 1940.

Inter Ocean (Chicago, IL), 1914.

Ironton Register, 1854, 1858, 1862–1864, 1869, 1896.

Knapsack (Gauley Bridge, WV), 1863.

Lawrence (KS) Daily Journal, 1895.

Lincoln (KS) Beacon, 1886, 1889.

Lincoln (KS) County Democrat, 1887–1889.

Lincoln (KS) Republican, 1889, 1901.

Lincoln (KS) Sentinel, 1896, 1898.

Los Angeles Times, 1900.

Minneapolis Journal, 1906.

Mount Carmel (IL) Register, 1900.

Nebraska State Journal (Lincoln), 1914.

Pittsburgh Daily Post, 1917.

Point Pleasant Register, 1864.

Portsmouth Daily Times, 1865, 1879, 1909.

Richmond (IN) Weekly Palladium, 1865.

Richmond Daily Dispatch, 1865.

San Francisco Chronicle, 1900.

San Francisco Examiner, 1900.

Scion (Adams County, OH), 1865.

Spirit of the Times (Ironton), 1856.

St. Joseph (MO) Herald, 1892.

Sylvan Grove (KS) Sentinel, 1889.

Times Recorder (Zanesville, OH), 1973.

Washington Times, 1905.

Weekly Pioneer and Democrat (St. Paul, MN), 1864.

West Union Scion (Adams County, OH), 1865.

Wheeling (WV) Daily Intelligencer, 1865.

Online Collections, Databases, and Websites

"About the Scion." Chronicling America, Library of Congress. https://chronicling america.loc.gov/lccn/sn83035191/.

"About the West Union Scion." Chronicling America, Library of Congress. https://chroniclingamerica.loc.gov/lccn/sn83035192/.

Agrawal, Alka. "All the President's Pills." ScienceMag, June 20, 2001. https://www.sciencemag.org/news/2001/07/all-presidents-pills.

Ancestry.com. https://www.ancestry.com.

"Auction of Legendary Dealer Norm Flayderman Brings $1.1M and Achieves Record Prices." ARTFIXdaily, February 24, 2017. http://www.artfix daily.com/artwire/release/6796-auction-of-legendary-dealer-norm -flayderman-brings-11m-and-achiev.

"Battle of Keslers Cross Lanes." West Virginia Encyclopedia. https://www .wvencyclopedia.org/articles/1192

Blossom, Jerry. "That Southern Wagon." Library of Congress. https://www.loc .gov/item/ihas.200001360/.

"Butternut." Glossary of Civil War Terms, American Battlefield Trust. https:// www.battlefields.org/glossary-civil-war-terms#B.

"Camphor-Zhang Nao." Civil War Rx: The Source Guide to Civil War Medicine. http://civilwarrx.blogspot.com/2016/03/camphor-zhang-nao.html.

"Canton Flannel." Conservation and Art Materials Encyclopedia Online. http:// cameo.mfa.org/wiki/Canton_flannel.

Chronicling America, Historic American Newspapers, Library of Congress. https://chroniclingamerica.loc.gov/.

"The Civil War Memoir of Russell Hastings, Chapter 4: March 1st, 1863 to April 8th, 1864" [transcript]. Hayes Library and Museum. https://www.rb hayes.org/research/chapters-4-through-6/.

Civil War Soldiers and Sailors System Database, National Park Service. https:// www.nps.gov/civilwar/soldiers-and-sailors-database.htm.

"Collections of Special Collections and University Archives." University Libraries, Virginia Tech. https://spec.lib.vt.edu/collections/index.html #areas.

"Dr. Jonatha[n] Morris." The Lawrence Register. https://lawrencecountyohio .com/pioneers/dr-jona-morris-obituary/.

"Enfield Rifle." Smithsonian Institution. http://www.civilwar.si.edu/weapons _enfield.html.

"Families, John Newton." Marietta Castle. https://mariettacastle.org/about /families/.

Find A Grave. https://www.findagrave.com/.

Geni.com. https://www.geni.com/.

Google Books. https://books.google.com/.

Hall, Diana Gould. "Ancestors in the News—Gillen & Brother Furniture Business, 1850s-1860s Ohio." Michigan Family Trails, November 16, 2018. http://www.michiganfamilytrails.com/2018/11/ancestors-in-news-gillen -brother.html.

HathiTrust Digital Library. https://www.hathitrust.org/.

"History." Emory and Henry College. https://www.ehc.edu/about/history/.

Internet Archive. https://archive.org/.

"Iron Bank of Ironton." The Lawrence Register. https://lawrencecountyohio .wordpress.com/history/businesses/iron-bank/.

"Lawrence County, Ohio, Abstracted Obituaries, 1850–1900." The Lawrence Register. https://lawrencecountyohio.com/vital/. [the direct web address which goes to the PDF version is: https://lawrencecountyohio.com/wp -content/uploads/2020/06/Obit-Index-1850-1900.pdf]

"Letters from the 91st Ohio Volunteer Infantry." Gallia Genealogy. http://www .galliagenealogy.org/civil%20war/MainCWletters/miles91st.html.

Mangus, Mike. "Fremont Body Guards (1861)." Ohio Civil War Central, July 19, 2011. https://www.ohiocivilwarcentral.com/entry.php?rec=712.

"The Mussey Family." The Henry R. Winkler Center for the History of the Health Professions, University of Cincinnati. https://digital.libraries .uc.edu/exhibits/winkler/mussey/family.html.

Newspapers.com. https://www.newspapers.com/.

Nix, Steve. "The Essential Chinkapin: A Small Tree with a Large Potential." ThoughtCo, July 03, 2019. https://www.thoughtco.com/the-essential -chinkapin-1343342.

O'Bannon, Patrick W. "Archival Research on the History of the Albert Gallatin Jenkins House Green Bottom, Cabell County, West Virginia." US Army Corps of Engineers, Huntington District. September 28, 2005. https:// www.lrh.usace.army.mil/Portals/38/docs/2005%20History%20of%20 Jenkins%20House2.pdf.

Ratliff, Gerald S. "Ruffner Family." e-WV: The West Virginia Encyclopedia, October 29, 2010. https://www.wvencyclopedia.org/articles/138.

"Rules for 7's up Euchre." Silver Creek Entertainment Discussion Forum. https:// forums.silvercrk.com/phpBB3/viewtopic.php?t=15139.

"The Southern Wagon." David M. Rubenstein Rare Book and Manuscript Library, Duke University. https://library.duke.edu/digitalcollections /hasm_conf0383/.

"The Southern Wagon." Library of Congress. https://www.loc.gov/resource/amss .cw201840/?st=text.

"Stephen Cooper Ayres." Abraham Lincoln Library and Museum, Lincoln Memorial University, Harrogate, Tennessee. https://lmuweb02.lmunet

.edu/uploads/OnlineResources/virtual_exhibit1/vex20/ACF4DBEF
-12C4–49DA-ADFC-000625106152.htm.

Virginia Historic Landmarks Commission Staff. "National Register of Historic
Places Inventory/Nomination: Back Creek Farm." February 1975.
http://www.dhr.virginia.gov/registers/Counties/Pulaski/077–0002
_Back_Creek_Farm_1975_Final_Nomination.pdf.

West Virginia's Sesquicentennial Highway Historical Markers. West Virginia
Archives and History, West Virginia Department of Arts, Culture and
History. http://www.wvculture.org/history/markers/sesqui/christopher
qtompkins.html.

Index

Page numbers in **boldface** refer to illustrations.